Also available at all good book stores

9781785313264

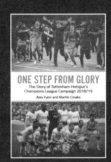

9781785315985

9781785314902

9781908051776

9781785310126

9781848182004

9781785311802

9781785314391

9781785314995

9781785315220

9781785315442

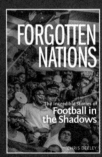

9781785314568

The King of
WHITE HART LANE

The King of
DENS
PARK

The Authorised Biography of
ALAN GILZEAN

Foreword by Ian Gilzean

MIKE DONOVAN

The King of
WHITE
HART
LANE

The Authorised Biography of
ALAN GILZEAN

Foreword by Ian Gilzean

MIKE DONOVAN

First published by Pitch Publishing, 2019

Pitch Publishing
A2 Yeoman Gate
Yeoman Way
Worthing
Sussex
BN13 3QZ

www.pitchpublishing.co.uk
info@pitchpublishing.co.uk

A CIP catalogue record is available for this book
from the British Library.

ISBN 978 1 78531 551 0

Typesetting and origination by Pitch Publishing
Printed and bound in India by Replika Press Pvt. Ltd.

Contents

DEDICATIONS

To Rosemary for her unswerving, selfless,
loving support.

To Matthew for being a good person and
making me proud.

To Sean and Christine for staying strong.

To Mum, with a smile and personality that
will always light up any room.

To Eric Herbert Leaver (5 April 1917–
23 April 2001)

To Charlie, thinking of you.

To all supporters of Alan Gilzean's clubs and
international team – and his memory.

'*Bring back the king to his throne.*'
Sandy Denny

(A pre-eminent singer-songwriter of Scottish descent who was connected to the same 'Maclean Clan' as Alan John Gilzean (1938–2018). Her full name was Alexandra Elene Maclean Denny, 1948-78).

Part of the royalties for this book will go to the Dundee FC in the Community Trust and the Tottenham Tribute Trust.

Foreword

AS A SON I didn't look upon my Dad the way other people did. He was just your dad, not someone's hero to put on a pedestal. He would sit there with us either chatting away or doing his crossword, while having a cup of tea. Or taking the dog out. He was pretty much the same as everyone else's dad, I should imagine. Just because he played football didn't make him any different. He still had to deal with the kids when he got home from work. He wasn't a Superman. He might have been famous for being a footballer – and he played at a bloody good level – but outside of that he was just a normal human being. Alan Gilzean the footballer and father were two separate things.

He didn't really talk about his football career much. I used to ask him a few things. We'd chat about football. Nothing much. Talk about games on the telly while we watched them. He'd come out with something. Or he'd say something about a game he was at with Tottenham when he started doing the hospitality with them, what they were like. He'd give me a rundown of how they had played. He wouldn't say anything like, 'I'll tell you about this game [I was in].' I don't think any normal football person would. Not a lot of players like to bang their own drum. It is up to other people to judge how good they are. You wouldn't go around saying you were brilliant.

When I was growing up, though, I didn't realise how good he was as a player. How good the teams he played in were. You didn't think about it. It was only once you'd finished playing yourself you thought, flipping heck, for him to have achieved what he did as a footballer took some doing. What a player he must have been. You are proud but like any family you have arguments and fall out. It didn't matter if he was a top footballer or not. Flaming hell, it is just normal life. Life that happens anywhere.

What has life been like since Dad passed? It goes on, doesn't it? It's what you do. Of course I miss him. You are going to miss anybody in that situation whether it is your parents, grandparents. There's no magic wand. You have to deal with it in different ways. Some days you'll think, 'Oh, it's a Sunday night. I normally used to speak to my Dad about now.' You try not to think about it.

You can't live in the past. Dad always said, 'You can't do that, you've got to live for the present and future. It's happening. You've got to deal with it and move on.' Otherwise you're not able to function, are you? You try to remember the good times. The laughs. You've got to get on with living with the family, things you want to do. Focus on all that.

There might be times where you watch a game and his name gets mentioned. Or when his face comes up on the television screen, like it did in the 2018 BBC *Sports Personality of the Year* when they were going through sports people we had lost during the year. That didn't choke me, though, because I'd watched that programme since I was young and always knew there was a segment like that. Some who came up you say, 'Didn't even hear about that one'.

I've got to appreciate how it is going to be. I wasn't the only person to lose a father that year. Loads of people did. Look at poor Steve Bruce, he lost both his parents in 2018. It is something that comes to everybody. And we all deal with it in different ways. What happened to Steve Bruce helps put things into perspective.

There was a book out a few years ago which Dad did not want to be involved with, but never, once Dad died, did we think anyone would want to write a book about him. Mike was the first one to come forward. I decided, 'Let's be involved. It will help get things right.' I feel the book reflects the effort to do just that.

Dad came out of Coupar Angus, a small rural town on the east coast of Scotland, to achieve cult status with Dundee and Tottenham Hotspur. Became a folk hero for Scotland, while also experiencing playing in South Africa and managing at

Stevenage and moving into the transport industry. He also dealt with my football career which took me to White Hart Lane and Dens Park too.

This is all covered, so are the decades when he was pretty much out of touch with the game, mostly with Spurs, during which ridiculous myths developed, such as one which claimed he had become a down-and-out. Out of sight out of mind, I reckon. And there were the last few precious years he spent back in football working for Spurs in their hospitality lounges with other club legends and collecting hall of fame awards.

The book also gives insights into my dad's character. How he did not like being the centre of attention but was a sociable, friendly and intelligent person with a big sense of humour when you got to know him. It also tells us how he was as a father and grandfather. Dad's passing came quicker than we thought it would but it was of comfort that his quality of life was good almost to the end. And it is also of comfort to know how much he remains loved in the hearts and minds of so many.

He was a popular figure from his early days as a boy scout right through to working back at Tottenham Hotspur, although it is a shame he did not live long enough for the club to move into their new stadium. Mind you, he did get to see the amazing Spurs training ground where Pat Jennings got him to sign a blackboard. The signature is faded, I'm told, so he'll have to go over it again!

Finally, I would like to thank all the people who knew Dad for giving up their time to help paint as accurate and rounded a picture of him as possible; to reveal insights into him as a person as well as what many view as a football legend from first-hand experience.

Ian Gilzean
Carnoustie, Angus, Scotland
July 2019

Prologue

I AM proud to say I met Alan Gilzean, the King of White Hart Lane and Dens Park. True, I was only 14. A Spurs fan standing by the big wrought-iron gates which separated the world from White Hart Lane Stadium. Clutching a club handbook. I'd seen a signed printed picture of him alongside the other players in the racks on the first floor of the Supporters' Club – there was only one back then – in Warmington House; the organised fans group's attempt at commercialism before the practice took a grip at the Lane on Irving Scholar's arrival in the 1980s. But I wanted to obtain an autograph first-hand.

Gillie appeared from the light of the dressing room into the twilight outside, washed and changed after his latest stellar performance for a team rebuilt by Bill Nicholson out of the ashes of the one which sealed the Double. I coyly asked him to sign over the pen picture printed of him alongside a thumb-sized image of the dark-haired, smiling head and shoulders of a footballer with few equals. I had already got Jimmy Greaves and Cliff Jones to do the same, so when Gilzean willingly obliged with a friendly grin it completed the set. My three favourite players of all time had made their mark in my modestly-sized publication.

I must have seen almost all of Gilzean's Lane appearances in the lilywhite shirt of my favourite team which was, apart from The Beatles, family and a handful of mates, my world. From his debut against Everton in December 1964 to his swansong against Southampton in April 1974 (his testimonial seven months later against Red Star Belgrade was on a school night). His dark, hirsute looks of a matinee idol might have given way to thinning of the hair and greying streaks around the temples. He might have appeared old before his time, but that was an illusion.

He was crowned the King of White Hart Lane early. And one could see why he also earned the royal moniker at Dens Park for Dundee before arriving in London N17. His grace of movement, deftness of touch with either foot and, mostly, trademark flicks of the head, especially when putting Jimmy Greaves in for yet another goal, and his own striker's instinct, was jaw-dropping. Always. A cult figure with class. The template for any Spurs legend. Perfect for playing the Spurs way. A way that entertains by playing exciting football with style and panache in the pursuit of glory.

My best memory of him was when he hit a hat-trick and made the other to help seal Spurs a 4-3 victory over Burnley on a muddy bog of a pitch in February 1966. Especially his volleyed 25-yard winner two minutes from time after Spurs had gone 2-0 and 3-2 down. (It was an occasion which stayed with him, as you will discover.) Conditions didn't have any adverse effect on Gillie. He always produced consistently.

Even when he lost his favourite playing partner in Jimmy Greaves, he formed another awesome twosome with Martin Chivers, claiming another hat-trick of glittering prizes to add to the 1967 FA Cup he won alongside Greavsie.

I can only go on what I have been told, read and seen from old clips when writing of his time at Dens Park, but cannot help discover from all that just why he was deserving of his iconic status back home. He scored four goals against Rangers at Ibrox and led his side to the Scottish title and European Cup semi-finals when only champions competed in the continent's blue riband competition. Gillie also banged in over 50 goals for the Dark Blues in one season.

And he will forever remain in the folklore of football north of the border for scoring the only goal against England, the Auld Enemy, in front of more than 133,000 at a rocking Hampden Park a couple of years before Sir Alf Ramsey's men conquered the world.

Gillie never sought the headlines on and off the pitch, never acted the big-time Charlie. More low-key Charlie. He enjoyed playing his part but happily stepped back to try to lead a normal life away from the trappings of fame.

Of course, when a public figure attempts to maintain a private existence, the curious begin to dig. They can read about those who court fame in the red tops, but what of those with no wish to do so? Out of a bid to lead a normal life away from the flashbulbs and interrogators, Alan Gilzean became portrayed as a hermit, a recluse. Even, fatuously, a down-and-out. Chinese whispers took us down a road he had not trodden.

All sorts of stories cropped up to develop an enigma. It was reported he had lost contact with all who knew him at White Hart Lane, although any estrangement from football seemed to be keener felt in London N17 than Dens Park. The truth was, with his football career finished, he merely mixed with his own loved ones, colleagues in his second career as a transport worker and close friends, trying to live a normal life rather than deal with the abnormal version, with its intrusive stresses, of a public figure.

But in 2012 he returned to the Lane and kept going back for the remaining years of his life. He reconnected with the fans who had never forgotten him, was inducted into the club's hall of fame and became a member of the matchday hospitality team alongside other legends, pals he had lost touch with like Pat Jennings and Phil Beal. He was as alert, vital and sharp-witted as those privileged to have known him during his time with the club had remembered. It followed him being recognised by Dundee, who had welcomed him into their own hall three years earlier, when he also entered the Scottish hall of fame. More belated recognition for a football great.

We discover the legacy he has left behind after his passing on 8 July 2018 just a few weeks after attending his final game. See if comparisons to Dimitar Berbatov – rated a modern-day Gilzean – stand up. And a lot more. Explore it all with the approval of Ian Gilzean, the son who followed his dad into the world of professional football and authorised the biography. The life of a football legend who displayed world-class, entertaining skills on the field and a striking humility which touched everyone he met off it.

I wanted to write a warm, sensitive, affectionate, down-to-earth tome about a much-loved and admired individual through the eyes of friends, colleagues, fans and, above all, his family. I hope I have succeeded.

Mike Donovan

1

Fly High, Grandad

THE WET weather was *dreich* – to use a generic Scottish term to describe dreary and bleak – in Dundee that morning. The two football kingdoms of Alan Gilzean had joined family and friends to pay last respects to their 'sovereign', who had left them, and us, aged 79 as a result of a brain tumour 12 days earlier.

The death announcement had been put into the 12 July 2018 edition of the *Dundee Courier* by the family and read, 'GILZEAN Peacefully, at Greenhill Care Home, London, on Sunday, July 8, 2018, Alan, a dearly loved dad, father-in-law, grandad and brother. A celebration of his life will be held in Dundee Crematorium on Friday, July 20, at 12.30 p.m. All relatives and friends are respectfully invited. Family flowers only, please. Donations, if desired, for Dundee Youth Development Program and Tottenham Tribute Trust will be received at the Crematorium. Black ties not required.'

The coffin of Gilzean – visible through the windows of a black hearse – was transported up the long, straight, residential Clepington Road, en route to the city's crematorium. Behind, the cortége included a black limousine carrying the family of the King of White Hart Lane and Dens Park and swish grey people carriers conveying representatives of the clubs – Tottenham Hotspur and Dundee – which crowned him.

Groups young and old, male and female, had gathered on dampened pavements outside pubs, shops and homes along the way.

Some in replica clothing, some in day-to-day wear. Some quietly clapping, some silent.

Suddenly, one figure caught the eye. It was Doug Cowie, the legendary Dundee and Scotland World Cup defender from the 1950s. He stood outside his home on the road with son Douglas and was waving his walking stick. Cowie said, 'The day of Gillie's funeral I was unable to attend but was told the time the cortége was passing my front door en route to the crematorium and I paid my respects along with Douglas outside my house to a great player and true gentleman.'

He won back-to-back League Cups with Dundee in the 1950s and was in the Dark Blues side which missed the title by a point in 1949. Most pertinently, he was rated by Gilzean as the best centre-half he had ever seen. In his 90s and hard of hearing, Cowie, who also played wing-half, was clearly determined to say his farewells.

Cowie, who made a club record 446 competitive Dee appearances, had been there at the beginning. He was a team-mate when Gilzean made his senior Dark Blues debut in a 4-1 League Cup home defeat against Motherwell on 22 August 1959 and, with the help of his son, it moved those who witnessed his active role at the end. Ian Gilzean, the youngest son of the deceased, said, 'Dad had told me where Doug lived and we realised who it was when we saw him waving his stick as we went by. So poignant. To see the all the people come out for Dad was quite touching.'

Cowie was also noticed by those in the people carrier containing Cameron Kerr, the Dundee vice-captain, director Bob Hynd, one of Gilzean's closest friends, manager Neil McCann, assistant boss Graham Gartland, stadium manager Jim Thomson and former skipper Brian Scrimgeour. As he was by the occupants in another containing other members of the Dundee staff, including director David Grey, secretary Eric Dysdale and chaplain Mike Holloway.

Cowie's gesture was apposite because the previous year multi-tasker Dave Forbes, another friend, unofficial PR, a former Dee director, club reunion organiser par excellence and Clepy Road newsagent, had arranged for Gilzean, whom he'd known since the early 1960s, to visit the former defender at his home. Forbes said, 'It was one of those great moments. Doug is very deaf in one ear so it was better to go to his house and sit with him. I asked Gillie, "Will you come with me to see Doug?" He said, "I'd be delighted to."

'So we went along. I said to Gillie, "We'll probably be about half an hour." We were there for three or four hours. The pair had a great discussion. Doug surprised Gillie greatly with his knowledge of tactics and players. One thing he told Gillie was his lack of understanding as to why players head the ball away. That it would be better to head it down to feet. That was something he did. Could trap a ball with his head, cushion it.

'It was tremendous just listening to them. Backwards and forwards. Wished I'd taped it. Doug's son was there. He asked to be there when he found out Gillie was coming. He'd never met him and was over the moon to do so. Went for a meal after with Alan. We had a good chat about Doug. He was really taken by him. I'd taken a picture of them together and Gillie said to me, "Dave, I've got to have a copy of that picture." I sent it to him. It was a great day for both of them.

'When I spoke to Doug afterwards he expressed his great pleasure at having had the chance to exchange views on football north and south of the border. They both commented on the vast knowledge the other had of the game. Was he a hero to Gillie? Yes. Most people who knew Doug through his days at Dens said there wasn't a better player. Probably one of the finest players Dundee ever had. Dave Sneddon, who also played with Doug, has raved about him. Doug was over the moon Ian had seen him waving his stick at the funeral.'

Hynd added, 'Alan could never work out how Doug trapped the ball with his head! I told Doug that Gillie thought he was the best centre-half that he had ever played with and against. What an accolade. Alan played against the best in Europe.'

Cowie enjoyed the meeting and waxed lyrical on Gilzean the player, mutual respect across the generations. He said, 'When Gillie came to the club he was already playing as an inside-left but he was obviously not the Billy Steel-type of player, which was a dribbler. However, right away you could see he could put the ball in the net. He had something when playing up front that others didn't. A strong physique and a great spring in the air.

'Don't forget Dundee had a good side and players who could play to Gillie's strengths, particularly with Gordon Smith and Hugh Robertson able to swing good crosses in with regularity. Gillie grew in confidence. He knew he was better in the air than opponents and that gave him the belief that every time he went into the penalty box or up for a corner kick he could win the ball. So Dundee played well that way with Gillie up front.'

The evening before, Gilzean's coffin had been laid out in the Alan Gilzean Lounge at Dens Park, minded by a handful of club volunteers, the idea to ease congestion at the Dundee Crematorium the following day. Hundreds entered the room with Gilzean memorabilia on its walls – including a prized Stoke shirt when he performed in a star-studded testimonial for Sir Stanley Matthews – and were able to contain their emotions. But it was clearly all too much for one fan with a London accent and sporting a Spurs shirt and scarf. She broke down in tears when entering the room. It was as if she was shedding them for millions of supporters of the club at which Gilzean became an icon for over ten years in the middle of the home where he first made his name.

Funeral day saw clans in Gilzean's life meet up at Dens in the late morning before making up the cortége; Ian, who followed in his dad's footsteps as a professional footballer with Spurs and Dundee, and elder brother Kevin and their partners Christine and Justine and grandchildren, plus other family members and former colleagues.

The hearse stopped at the main entrance to the Dark Blues's ground as the club chaplain Mike Holloway, having only got back from holiday in Canada in the early hours, said a few words of remembrance to the hundreds gathered in the rain. Hynd, in charge of funeral arrangements, said, 'There were more than we thought. I should have got our chaplain a microphone.'

Spontaneous applause broke out from those present – many with umbrellas up as the hearse eased off behind the 'pager' in top hat and tails ahead of the cortége – in a now common display of respect for a deceased, high-profile footballer, ever since the traditional minute's silence was largely replaced by applause at football grounds across the country following the passing of George Best in 2005.

A middle-aged female threw a bouquet of flowers reminiscent of the gesture enacted during the funeral of Diana, Princess of Wales, 21 years earlier. Well, Gilzean's adopted moniker did more than indicate he was royalty. A group offered more applause as the procession entered through the crematorium gates, having turned off Clepy Road.

The Reverend David Robertson, the former club chaplain and Minister of the St Peter's Free Church in Dundee, who knew Gilzean, conducted the service in a packed building. Bobby Wishart, Gilzean's best friend in football, Bobby Seith and Pat Liney, three of the four survivors of Dundee's only Scottish league championship-winning team, attended the service.

Liney, who kept goal that historic season, said, 'There were a lot of people who turned out for Alan. He was such a popular guy, just for being himself. He was not a show-off. Everybody misses Gillie. I never met one person in all my time with football that didn't like him, didn't get on with him. You can't say that about a lot of people. Such a nice guy.'

Wishart remarked that the funeral helped reveal how his pal 'misread the situation' on how much affection and respect there was for him in the football community, having largely withdrawn from it after his retirement from the game, only returning seriously in his later years. He said, 'Alan told me, "Who wants to see an old guy?" He was very popular. There was a tremendous representation from Tottenham at the funeral. So many of his old team-mates made the effort to come up.'

Wishart had never lost touch with his pal. He said, 'It's the old story. It's what you put into a relationship, but once you lose the relationship there's certainly a hole. He was a special player, a special guy. So many happy memories of the guy. That's what makes it all bearable. I miss him. I miss his phone calls. Anything that was coming up in Scotland, I would phone him. I always had his mobile number. They'll be a lot of friends of Alan Gilzean but next door to his son's I reckon I'd be number one. Nice bit of comfort to take with me.'

Gilzean's former Spurs team-mates flying the flag for his second club across his ten years at White Hart Lane were Pat Jennings,

Phil Beal, Mike England, Alan Mullery, Steve Perryman, John Pratt, Cliff Jones and Martin Chivers. They all helped dreams to come true for the youngster, who wished for Wembley glory as he watched Pathe newsreels at the Queen Street picture house in his native Coupar Angus, a small rural town 14 miles outside Dundee.

The Tottenham contingent – in club ties and smart suits, sponsored by Spurs and organised by the club's senior event venue manager Richard Knott – impressed. Gilzean's former Dundee team-mate Craig Brown, the ex-Scotland manager, said, 'The significant thing to me was every one of them was in club uniform, wearing the club tie. They were immaculate. The respect they gave to Alan and his sons Ian and Kevin was quite noticeable.'

Mullery, Gilzean's captain when Spurs lifted the 1972 UEFA Cup, told Brown, 'They call Alan the King of White Hart Lane – and he WAS the King of White Hart Lane.' Brown said, 'Gillie might have been Scottish and Mullery an England international but he was so respectful the way he said it. And when you consider the quality of players Spurs have had, that is some compliment.'

Perryman, who holds the Tottenham appearance record, said, 'You don't wish to be at such an event but you should be there. We met his sons and other members of the family. The love was flowing out of them for this great man. There's a playing life and there's a life. And it was obvious these people were in awe of this great man and were there to pay their respects as much as we were. We all showed our respect. Credit to Tottenham for paying for the former players to be there. And the measure of the man was the quality of the people who attended his funeral.

'I'd been to Scotland and people spoke to me about him, but they also asked about Dave Mackay, Bill Brown and Alfie Conn [other Scots who played for Spurs]. This day it was purely about Gillie. It was his day. I hadn't witnessed the sort of adulation for him we witnessed as he was applauded through the streets on the way to the crematorium. It was lovely. It was Gillie's day and rightly so. Very honoured to have been there.'

Just three years earlier, Gilzean was part of a similar group which attended the funeral of former Spurs, Hearts and Scotland legend Dave Mackay in Edinburgh – along with Sir Alex Ferguson, the Manchester United icon who had been in the St Johnstone side relegated as Gilzean hit two goals to clinch the 1962 Scottish league title for Dundee at Muirton Park.

Ian Gilzean said, 'One of the former players told me that Fergie went up to Scott Gardiner [the Hearts chief executive who once worked at Tottenham and Dundee] and asked, "Is that Alan Gilzean over there? Would you mind taking me over and introducing me?"'

He added, with a smile, 'Was Fergie a fan? Was he giving us an idea of the esteem Dad was held in? It might have been, "You whacked me years ago and I've not seen you since!"'

The Scottish FA, in the shape of president Campbell Ogilvie, showed its respects by attending the service for the 22-times-capped international who wrote his name into the country's folklore by scoring the winning goal against England in front of over 133,000 at Hampden Park in 1964. Bob Hynd said, 'Campbell was the secretary of Rangers for a number of years. He told me years ago that the first match that he attended was with his father in 1961 when Dundee won 5-1 at Ibrox – and Gillie scored four!'

As part of the service, Reverend Robertson gave the eulogy on behalf of the family. Ian Gilzean said, 'We [the family] were never going to be able to do that. It is tough enough at the best of times. I take my hat off to people who do it. We wrote something down about Dad's life and the minister read it out. Paddy [Barclay, a former journalist author and Dundee native and fan] covered all Dad's football side, which was great.'

Barclay said, 'I was asked to put Alan's playing career in a bit of context for younger people. On the way into the crematorium I noticed that Cammy [Kerr], a local boy, was there representing the players. The manager at the time was Neil McCann and his assistant Graham Gartland, but I kind of directed what I was saying to Cammy. I asked, "How good a player was Gillie?" I said, "If we were discussing now or in the last ten years who was the greatest header, attacking header of a football, it would be a toss-up between Cristiano Ronaldo and Alan Gilzean. That was how good he was as a user of the ball in the air. It was remarkable he only won 22 caps but he was unlucky as he was with a provincial not Old Firm club and his career coincided with Denis Law, one of the three greatest players Scotland has ever produced. If not the greatest."

'I also said a team looks for big performances from its big players in the big matches. That's what Gillie did in arguably the three biggest matches in Dundee's history. He scored four in a 5-1 win against Rangers at Ibrox to convince the whole of Scotland that his team could win the title, the club's only one. Two to kill the game when we beat St Johnstone to be absolutely sure of it. He got a hat-trick in an 8-1 win against Cologne when Dundee began a European Cup run to the semi-finals.

'As a player, certainly, he would be a candidate for the greatest player ever to play for our club but you know he also achieved a similar status in probably more lauded company at White Hart Lane with the best partner he ever had, Jimmy Greaves. Although a goalscorer extraordinaire, particularly at Dundee, he was also a team player as was proved by his complete re-invention at Spurs.

'He dropped off and became a number ten with equal success while still chipping in with 15–20 goals a season. Whatever you wanted, he could do. And he did it with such modesty and style. A wonderful man.'

Cameron Kerr was 'honoured' to represent the current Dundee playing squad. He said, 'It was a surreal experience for me. I remember the day very well. I thought it was important a player from today was there for Alan. Show appreciation. Streets were filled up with Dundee fans waving scarves, reflecting the good times he helped bring. The happiness.'

Kerr was moved by mention of him by Barclay during the eulogy. He said, 'I felt I didn't deserve to be in the same sentence as Alan with the man he was and what I've done in my career. I am a Dundee boy but he was and is a Dundee legend. It was special. I met Alan Gilzean's family, had a chat with Ian and one of Alan's grandsons. Obviously a very emotional day for them. I said to them "I'm honoured to be here."'

Gilzean had split from his wife Irene in the 1970s, but she attended the funeral. Ian Gilzean said, 'What happened happened, but Dad was a big part of Mum's life for a lot of years. They had two sons together, Kev and myself. Nice she turned up? Yeh. Mum wanted to come. Superb she did.'

Ron Ross, a school football team-mate of Gilzean, sat next to her for the service at the crematorium. Ross said, 'I didn't recognise Irene. I saw this blonde woman and there was a seat vacant next to me. She looked on and I said, "Yes, it is free." And she sat down in it. There was a wee while to go before the service started and I said, "I'm here because I was at school with Alan." She said, "I'm here because I was married to him." I said, "I didn't know it was you, Irene. I'm Ron Ross." She said, "I remember you." So we spoke.

'Her demeanour was okay. I wasn't surprised to see her there. I don't know what went wrong with the marriage. They were a devoted young couple. Their families lived in houses about 150 yards apart. In those days you married girls locally. I knew her as a schoolgirl and that was it. I remember her as a young police constable at the top of a busy street. One of the first policewomen in Dundee I would say, especially doing such a highly visible job of directing traffic.'

Invited guests returned to Dens. Wishart had a cup of tea as he spoke to Irene and said, 'It was good to meet her. The club did very well and gave Alan a great send off.' Ian Ure, the fourth survivor of the 1961–62 Dark Blues team, joined the invitees after being forced to miss the service due to public transport problems on his 200-mile round trip from the west coast of Scotland. He said, 'I had a friend waiting to take me to the service off my train. But my train got in so late it was too tight to go to the service and we went straight to Dens. Met Irene. She was very nice. And Ian, whom I've seen at umpteen club dos. Had a good blether with the Spurs players. Good to see them. Everybody was there.'

All the while, flags flew at half-mast in Coupar Angus for the first time since the funeral of the People's Princess. And a rain-spattered Dundee FC flag fluttered at half-mast on the pole erected in town native Bob Hynd's garden.

Kerr appealed in the local *Evening Telegraph* for his club to give Gilzean the 'send-off the Dens legend deserves' in Dundee's first match following the funeral, a home League Cup tie against Dunfermline two days after it. The match programme – which had been handed out to the Spurs eight at the funeral – was given over to articles about the player rated the greatest to don a dark blue Dee shirt in many learned quarters. Even though the team were unable to secure a victory – suffering a 1-0 loss – the occasion enabled young and old to join in embracing the memory of a player who once sprinkled stardust over the same patch of green that Neil McCann's were toiling on. In a more glorious era.

Tributes poured in from old team-mates from north and south of the border before and after that grey day. Dundee stated, 'Everyone at Dundee Football Club are devastated to learn that club legend Alan Gilzean passed away this morning after recently being diagnosed with a brain tumour. The thoughts of everyone at the club are with Alan's family and friends at this difficult time.'

Spurs stated, 'Everyone at the club is deeply saddened to learn of the passing of our legendary former striker Alan Gilzean. Our thoughts are with his family and friends at this extremely difficult time.' Perhaps the most poignant came from Jimmy Greaves, the other half of the G-Men – arguably the most lethal, prolific goalscoring partnership ever seen when they were together at Spurs – and stricken by ill health. It came on the day of Gilzean's passing. Greaves official Twitter feed posted, 'Heartbreaking news today. The great Alan Gilzean passed away this morning. Sympathy to his family. He was a lovely man and obviously one of the all-time Spurs greats … RIP from all of us associated with Jimmy. He loved you and always said you were the best striking partner ever.'

Mullery informed the Spurs official website that day, 'It was only two months ago we were laughing and joking before the games and reminiscing on old times. We're going to miss him, no doubt about that. We missed him for about 35 years but when he came back it was like old times, the stories, the laughter. He wasn't just a good player, he was a genius, untouchable. We joined in the same year, 1964. Gillie joined just after me. He's one of the best headers of the ball I've ever seen, terrific control. I remember playing against him for England against Scotland and he called me all the names under the sun! I thought, "That's not the Gillie I know", but it was England against Scotland!'

The Scottish FA, who had welcomed him into their hall of fame close to ten years earlier, joined in. It said, 'We are fortunate that the history of our game is littered with entertainers who captivated supporters. Alan Gilzean was certainly among them. Our thoughts are with his friends and family.'

And the sentiments were revealed to have spread worldwide when FIFA president Gianni Infantino wrote a letter to SFA president Alan McRae from Zurich dated 7 August 2018, 'Please accept my deepest condolences on hearing that former international player Alan Gilzean has passed away. On behalf of FIFA and the worldwide family of football, I wish to extend our deepest condolences to the Scottish FA and, mostly importantly, to his family, friends and loved ones. We would hope that, in some way, our words of support my help bring a little more peace and solace at this time of sadness.'

Gilzean himself – 'retaining Perthshire lilt' – told *The Scotsman*'s Alan Pattullo, in what he claimed was his first major newspaper interview in 40 years on 14 January 2012, 'I was just a guy whose dreams came true. I have no regrets. I have got friends. I go out. I enjoy myself. You have to at my age. You don't know how many bottles of red wine you have left. You are waiting for the call.'

It seemed he would be accepting of its arrival. It is those who loved and admired him who struggle to recognise it since it came.

'Fly high, grandad', posted Ian's daughter Amy on Facebook. Alan John Gilzean always will be in the mind's eye of those who saw him soar on the field and in the imaginations of those who wish they had.

2

Spiritual Home

ALAN GILZEAN left Coupar Angus physically in his mid-20s. But mentally and spiritually he never departed, reflected in his email address which was 'alanfoxhall@icloud.com' in reference to the town's Foxhall Park where he played his first club football.

Bob Hynd, a fellow Coupar Angus native, saw himself as a reassuring conduit to the small rural town close to the east coast of Scotland for his close pal. The leap from such a place to the brighter lights of the big city of Dundee and even brighter ones of London must have been adjustments for Gilzean, despite him being perceived as self-possessed. And even when he was based in the West Country from the 1990s until his passing, Gilzean welcomed news from 'home', perhaps to allay any doubts and fears he might have had.

Hynd said, 'Gillie never forgot where he came from. Coupar Angus was always in his heart. He always wanted to know what was going on. Who had died, and what so and so was up to. The interest was genuine. He did not ask the questions out of politeness. When he returned to the subject he remembered every detail about it.'

Hynd's son Bobby confirmed this characteristic of Gilzean. He said, 'I never got used to him phoning the house. The first time was the same as the last time. I thought to myself, "That's Gillie on the phone!" Never got used to it. The thing about Gillie was that he never spoke about himself. It was, "How's your job going, Bobby? Your dad was telling me you were doing fencing." You're thinking,

"Why am I speaking to him about this when you could be talking to him about his achievements." But he was genuinely interested in what you were doing. Just a really, really nice guy.

'I remember one game, there was this guy from the band Snow Patrol, Tom Simpson, a Dundee supporter, who had five or six people around him wanting to talk to him. Then we came in with Gillie and everyone moved away. He just got rushed every time he came into a room of people. Don't think he particularly liked it when people were asking, "Can you sign this?" But he did. Was so nice about it. Just stood there and did it.'

It seemed filling his mind with thoughts of Coupar Angus was a constant comfort which kept Gilzean 'earthed'. Bob Hynd was happy to supply the mind-fill. He said, 'To a certain extent I was Alan's connection with Coupar Angus. And because I knew he was so interested in the town, I used to get stories from people. If I came across one I'd tell myself, "I'll need to remember and tell Gillie that." There was one woman – in her 90s – who ran an electrical shop. My wife went in to get some batteries. The woman asked her who she was because you've got to know everybody in Coupar Angus! And then she gave Aileen these batteries and said, "If they are the right ones come back and pay me." She'd never seen Aileen before! I told Alan that story and he just killed himself laughing.

'This woman – I knew her daughter from school – stayed with a guy, Freddie Stewart, who had the florists in the town. One day a couple of a*******s robbed it. Freddie didn't have a till or accept cheques. He just had a big box with compartments where he kept his money. He also never washed the potatoes and leeks he sold! Anyway, these a*******s from outside Coupar Angus asked him for something through the back and when he came back the box had disappeared.

'About a year later – and Alan thought this was a great story – one of the guys had gone back into the shop he'd robbed to buy something legitimately. Freddie recognised him and he and his assistant – both in their mid-80s – locked the door and started beating the guy with their walking sticks!'

Hynd was always astounded by Gilzean's memory. He said, 'Alan was on the phone talking to me about my cousins in a family called Shaw. He would tell me, "Robert Shaw's dead now, Malcolm died this year, Stewart's still alive. Malcolm and Donald played for Kinross FC and they were both good amateur players." He was talking over 60 years ago. His passion for sport was unbelievable and his recall was incredible. He'd remember every little detail of matches. What happened. Who did what. Absolutely incredible.'

As I sat in Hynd's cosy living room sipping a 'wee dram' of whisky and munching, appropriately, Dundee cake, he showed me a series of texts between himself and Gilzean. Many a time the subject was pertaining to Coupar Angus.

The first exchange between Gilzean and Hynd related to a memory from their home town dating back over 60 years.

> BH: Did you play for Errol City Boys?
>
> AG: Sorry to take so long. Just got off the Tube at Oakwood [visiting son Kevin]. I never played for Errol but played against them in a cup final on South Inch for Coupar that we won. I think their captain was called Gordon Kettles. Regards Alan.
>
> BH: Dear Alan, the Evening Telegraph are running an article on the best Dundee XI but have not included you as they say you do not qualify as you were born in CA. Is that correct? (17 June 2015)
>
> AG: Born Perth.
>
> BH: I tried to call you when I left home but you were engaged. I am fishing on the Isla [by Coupar Angus] this evening and will give you a call after 9pm.
>
> BH: Patsy Martin was the next-door neighbour to your uncle Alistair in Trade Lane, Coupar Angus. Your cousin Ann Whitlock would know her well.
>
> BH: Thanks Alan. I have just arrived. I sat and had a blether with Roy Whitlock [a Coupar Angus Juveniles team-mate and close childhood friend with whom Alan stole apples, Hynd understood from speaking to Gillie's old pal] on Sunday and he said he would try and get into a Dundee match the next time you're here.

Gilzean and Hynd became friends after the latter received a phone call from a Coupar Angus resident about 20 years ago. Hynd soon became aware he was to become a member of an exclusive club. The Dundee director said, 'A resident whose family knew the Gilzeans, worked for the council and had dealings with the club, asked me if I could contact Alan's family and let them know that their grave at the Abbey Church in the town needed some repair work to stabilise it.

'I tracked Alan down, through, I think, Dave Forbes. He phoned me and gave me his number and he said, "Don't give this to anyone else. There's only a few people who have got this number." His son Ian told me – and this would not be much of an exaggeration – that if someone got his number he didn't want to have it he would get his number changed and text the new one to those he wanted to have it. He seemed to trust me because I was from Coupar Angus. I knew so many people he knew.

'I offered to pick him up from Carnoustie to take him to a Dundee game when he was staying with his son Ian one time. But I'd been in my bed with a really bad flu. I rang him and said, "Alan there's no way I am going to manage the match. I'll get Jim Thomson, the ground stadium manager, to pick you up." He said, "No, if you are not going, I'll not go." I think he wanted the reassurance of a local Coupar Angus lad to be with him for moral support.

'There is hardly a day goes by when I don't think about him. He used to phone me most weekends. You could just about time the calls. He'd cut off at 58 minutes each time. I assumed he got charged extra if he ran over an hour! He used to tell fascinating stories. My big regret is I never took any notes or recorded anything. I'll forget it all eventually. It was just someone you were friendly with. One conversation we had, I do remember, was when I heard him swear for the first and only time (although others will reveal he did exercise his knowledge of the Anglo-Saxon on occasion).

'He never had a computer but followed what was happening at the Dundee club on his iPhone. And he told me, "I've been reading about the club and a site for the new stadium." I confirmed we'd bought it and he said, "That's brilliant. When will I see a game in

it?" I joked, "I don't think you will. We won't be in it for three years."
He said, "You cheeky bastard, I'll manage another three years, no
bother." Sadly, of course, he won't see a game there but there will
probably be something to commemorate him. His memory will
live on there.

'After Alan passed I learned there was a guy from the builders
yard in the town he was either friendly with or related to who had
just died. I thought, "I must tell Alan." But then you think, of
course, he's dead. It is amazing how he stays in my subconscious.'

Hardly surprising, though, as Hynd's link with Gilzean goes
back a generation. He said, 'My mum knew his mum. She was a
teacher at the school Gillie and I both attended and the pupils
used to get her to go up with stuff for Alan to sign when he was
back in town.'

Alan Pattullo, a gifted writer, brought up eight miles from
Coupar Angus in the village of Glamis, also provided Gilzean with
a comforting link to his home area. Pattullo, employed by *The
Scotsman*, became that rare breed of journalist granted interviews
with Gilzean in the icon's final years, the initial get-together that
first major one with a newspaper in 40 years. He was tolerated and
befriended by Gilzean to the extent he once put Pattullo on his guest
list when attending a Dundee match (a friendly against Everton).

The writer, with his empathetic pieces on the Dark Blues
hero, earned a degree of trust, but knew the foundation for
their relationship lay in the fact his father Sandy, a farmer, was a
talented cricketer. Gilzean harboured hopes of a first-class career
in the sport traditionally rated the nation's favourite summer
sport (discuss). And he earned favourable write-ups in the local
Blairgowrie Advertiser. He was also the shining light when he and
Dundee team-mates took on Coupar Angus. Craig Brown, who
played with him at Dundee, said, 'Alan was a very fine cricketer.
He was captain and manager of the Dundee FC cricket team. In the
summer, we played colleges and clubs. He was a very good bowler
and batsman, he had a terrific eye for the ball. He could play tennis,
whatever. Any ball game.'

Pattullo said, 'I was at a game against Morton with my dad on
Boxing Day in 2011. Gillie came on at half-time out of nowhere and

waved to the fans. It jarred with his idea that he was a recluse. So I thought, "This is my chance. How often am I in the same vicinity as Gillie?" I stayed behind after the game with my dad and waited for Gillie to come out of the boardroom. I introduced myself. Used my dad being a big cricket man. My dad and Gillie struck it off talking about Coupar Angus. All the people they knew. Then I snuck in. Any chance of doing an interview with you? He'd warmed up by this stage and said yes. Didn't appreciate it was such a big thing. Didn't know the extent he'd drifted into the sidelines.

'What struck me was his memory was crystal clear, coming up with number plates for cars he had in the 60s, reeled them off. Must have headed the ball a million times and there's talk of the effect of it on players. But not Gillie, the arch header. His mind was sharp as a tack. We invited Gilzean round to the farm my mum [Heather] and dad ran for dinner one night. It was in 2015 just after Wimbledon. He came. It was lovely. Got pictures. As much as I am heartbroken Gillie has gone, I am glad we had that night. He was great. Just loved it. Didn't talk football at all. Spoke about local matters with my dad. Dredging up names from 50 years ago. People he was at primary school with. My dad knew all these people.

'Picked him up in one of my dad's vintage cars from Ian's house in Carnoustie, brought him back out to Coupar Angus. He seemed to love it. A beautiful summer's evening. I drove him back to Carnoustie. Really nice day. Gillie's aunt, a Mrs Fraser, used to live on our farm. He used to come and visit her. This is what kills me. When he was supposed to have disappeared, he was coming to our farm to visit his aunty! Literally on our doorstep. Dundee's greatest-ever player and I was none the wiser. I was doing a Dundee fanzine. If I'd have known I could have done a great interview, perhaps! He might have broken his own rules for a young fanzine editor.

'A couple of years before his death, I picked up Gillie from Bobby Wishart's house and drove them both to the funeral of Alan Cousin, Alan's old strike partner, in Falkirk and had a great time. I was driving and the two of them were riffing back and forth. Gillie was in the back seat, Bobby in the front, just talking about old times. It was great. What a privilege. My sister Katie had just moved to Tottenham, two minutes from the ground, and Gillie said, "We'll come round for lunch." But he'd passed on before it could be arranged.'

There was a genuine affection from Pattullo. He said, 'I saw his coffin at Dens and went to the funeral. I was emotional, tearful. Had got to know him. I've been to many funerals as a journalist. Often without any personal contact. I had with Gillie. I'd just phone him up for a chat sometimes. We had that kind of relationship towards the end.

'The last time I spoke to him I'd just had a son born [January 2018]. I phoned him up just after to tell him. Glad I did that before he died. I wrote him a letter with a picture of my son Jack when Ian told me where he was shortly before he passed away. Apparently he got it a couple of days before he died. His other son Kevin told me he'd read it and had shown him the picture. Quite nice to know that. I feel I have been robbed. He had so much more to give. So humble, self-deprecating. You could walk past him and not think, "This is an international superstar". It was great for me that he identified with Coupar Angus as I do. We even shared the same doctor. Dr MacPherson was a local legend. Gillie told me he'd go to him for second opinions on injuries.'

* * *

Alan John Gilzean was born a year before the outbreak of the Second World War, on Saturday, 22 October 1938 at the Perth Royal Infirmary, 12 miles from Coupar Angus, the small rural Perth and Kinross town.

Neville Chamberlain, the British Prime Minister, declared 'peace in our time' after the Munich Agreement with Adolf Hitler a few weeks earlier, a claim disputed by Winston Churchill, who would become his successor during the upcoming global hostilities. Actor/director Orson Welles allegedly scared the bejesus out of radio listeners with his narration of HG Wells's *The War of the Worlds* later in the month, like it was needed at such a time.

Coupar Angus is situated south of the meandering River Isla and lies 14.4 miles from Dundee in the heart of the wide, fertile Vale of Strathmore, between the Sidlaw hills and Grampian mountains. Claims to fame were sparse when Gilzean was growing up. It was known for producing fruit and potatoes, installing a communal tradition for picking berries – turned into jam at the Preserve Works, nicknamed locally as the Jellyworks, which closed in the 1960s – and 'tatties', enabling the town folk to pick up an extra few bob through their labour. Also, as the place where the breed of cat known as Scottish Fold – whose ears bend down to make their faces look like that of owls – originated, according to Wikipedia, which also revealed notables were thin on the ground.

They included resident John Robertson, a railway porter, who was an amateur astronomer and lawyer William Clark, who killed a George Johnson in Western Australia's first recorded duel in 1832 and was cleared of manslaughter before becoming a newspaper proprietor. As for sporting heroes, it seemed there was just one Coupar Angus-ite worthy of note, John Bain 'Jock' Sutherland, an iconic American football coach with Pittsburgh Steelers from 1946–47.

Gilzean himself – when searching for links between his home town and football – came up with a tenuous one. He said, 'I remember an old man there [in Coupar Angus], Jimmy White. He was from Edinburgh originally, a right Hearts supporter. He used to go round all the farm cottages, all the cottar houses, in a big van selling things like fruit and tatties. After I signed for Tottenham I talked to him occasionally. He stopped his van one day: "How you getting on down at Tottenham?" And he told me his uncle played for Tottenham when they won the cup in 1901 – a guy called Sandy Tait. I looked it up a long time back and he was right, a full-back.'

Even Gilzean's birth date would not have given you much indication he was destined for sporting stardom. In one list it was revealed he shared it with actors Derek Jacobi and Christopher Lloyd, the former most well known for playing a Roman emperor in TV's *I, Claudius* and the latter played an off-the-wall inventor in the film franchise *Back to the Future*. It all certainly left the way clear for Gilzean to become the biggest name to emerge from Coupar Angus. Period.

He was the fourth-born to William and Barbara (nee Forbes) Gilzean of 25 Strathmore Avenue in the town. Their first child, and only daughter, Thelma (27 June 1928 to 18 August 2012) emigrated to Salt Lake City before Gilzean's rise to renown, working for a bank, involving herself in First Presbyterian Christian Education and teaching the Bible before passing after 54 years of marriage to a fellow Coupar Angus native, Walter Nicoll. The third, William Macrae (born in 1936) died after just 28 days due to infantile atrophy, a wasting condition.

In between, Eric Gilzean, their second, came into the world on Tuesday, 18 June 1929 and found his way across the Atlantic before his sister. He said, displaying Alan's characteristic for fine detail of fellow townsfolk, 'My sister Thelma met her husband in Coupar Angus. He was a carpenter called Walter Nicoll, who was also raised in the town. His parents lived on The Cross right near Davidson's chemist shop. I had a job waiting for Walter when the couple arrived in America, having left for the place in my early 20s.'

Eric had settled in the Utah capital with first wife Betty Jackson in the mid-1950s and eventually traded on his heritage by running a memorabilia outfit, Edinburgh Castle Scottish Imports (established 1987), until into his late 80s before allowing granddaughter Debbie Raskey to take over the reins. But he did have a tilt at the fame game in the entertainment world – in which he met Betty – in Britain in between working for the Wall's ice cream factory in London.

He said, 'Another fellow and I thought we were going to hit the big time. We worked night and working men's clubs. Earned quite good money. I learned guitar and we'd sing cowboy folk songs and old Scottish songs. Looking back I bet people were glad when we got off stage! Met Betty after seeing her feeding lines to a comic on stage in North Berwick. The first time we met she took me to The Beatles' Cavern. A dump. A black, filthy place! We were married 35 years and she died of cancer in 1991.'

As Alan's only surviving sibling, Eric – an extrovert character in contrast to his more reserved brother – was able to give a picture of what life was like for his brother and the rest of the family growing up in Coupar Angus. Delivered in an outgoing, bubbly, friendly, no-nonsense way which belied his years in a largely American accent with shades of his Perthshire roots, when asked about his experience growing up in the town south of the 18th-century Couttie Bridge across the River Isla he laughed, 'Well, I survived!'

Eric painted a bucolic picture of the town, which had 2,262 inhabitants according to a 2011 census. He said, 'It was very rural. Raspberry season in the summer. In the fall, it was the potato gathering. So all the youngsters in the village used to go to pick raspberries and gather potatoes to help the economy of Coupar Angus. I don't think Alan went through much of that, because he was ten years behind me. There were several churches in Coupar Angus, but none were Catholic. The closest Catholic church was up in Blairgowrie, five and a half miles away.'

Alan, Eric and Thelma's parents, William and Barbara Gilzean, respectively born in 1902 and 1904, were well respected in the town. Eric revealed William – known as Willie – Gilzean followed in the family tradition and became a painter and decorator. He said, 'My grandfather had a painting and decorating business in Coupar Angus. Our father worked in the same business. So did his brothers James, Douglas and Alistair. One uncle on the Forbes side worked in the business as well. It was a real family affair. Even my great grandfather was a painter and decorator.'

Mum Barbara (nee Forbes and known as Babs) was a professional cook before marrying William, a freemason who became known for a talent in reciting the works of the world-famous Robbie Burns, the 18th-century Bard of Ayrshire considered Scotland's national poet. Eric said, 'Our dad used to go all over the area reciting Robbie Burns. I attend Burns Nights events local to me now. Our mum cooked on some big estate. So when we ate at home it was like dining at the Savoy. The food was marvellous and my sister inherited the gift. I used to look forward to going over to Thelma and Walter's condominium in Salt Lake City for dinner.'

Barbara was one of eight children to William and Margaret Forbes brought up in the same street as her future husband, Causewayend, he at number 25 and she at 53. Eric said, 'We had a lot of uncles and aunts around. On my wall I have got pictures of where my mother was born, a tall building. There were 10 or 11 people there in two bedrooms. Wow! How did they do it? I asked a famous artist friend of mine in America to take a picture of the cottage while he was on vacation there. He did – and painted it too.'

There were plenty of relatives around for Alan, Eric and Thelma. Eric said, 'I remember visiting farms where my aunts lived. I'd cycle out to one three miles from Coupar Angus after church each Sunday to deliver a paper to my mother's oldest sister Janet, who was married to Chic Brown, and gave me a breakfast which kept coming and coming! Looked forward to that. Another was Lizzie. One cousin became a policeman.'

Alan's dad encouraged his son when he showed an interest in football. But it was clear Gilzean inherited most of his footballing genes from his mother's side. Most of Babs's brothers were promising footballers, particularly Drummond. Eric said, 'All were good at soccer. Played for Coupar Angus Juniors. My mother's eldest brother George Forbes was a good centre-half. And there was Douglas and Drummond.'

Douglas and Drummond helped the club win the Angus Junior League in the season Alan was born with a reported record crowd of 4,000 at their home ground in Foxhall Park to see them clinch the crown with victory against Kirrie Thistle, according to James Morgan's *In Search of Alan Gilzean*. Eric said, 'I used to watch my uncles play for them when I was boy aged five or six. I never went on to play for them like Alan did.'

Drummond, who also played with Alan's other uncles Jimmy, Jock and Andrew, was rated as bright a prospect as Gilzean before the war – with Rangers and Dundee linked with him – but tragedy struck. Eric said, 'When the war came in 1939, half my family were conscripted. They all went to war. My mother lost her brother Drummond just after D-Day. He was in the Gordon Highlanders and killed by a sniper. I got a photographer to go over to France and take a picture of his grave.'

Gilzean's brother recalled his younger sibling had an ability for administration and how it smoothed the way for joining Dundee. Eric said, 'Alan was a kind of secretary for his club (his first, known as either Coupar Angus Juveniles or City Boys). I remember reading in the papers when Dundee were interested in getting Alan. He did all his own paperwork for his own leaving! He was very good at it (skills he employed in transport after his retirement from football).'

The family lived in accommodation rented from the Perth and Kinross Council. Eric said, 'I was born in Teignmouth Place in Causewayend. We lived in two bedrooms up some back stairs. But they built these fancier places just off Causewayend in Strathmore Avenue and the family got a place up there when Alan came along and eventually moved to 2 Stuart Crescent.

'Strathmore? That was nice. There were two families in the bottom part and two on the top. We had people going up the stairs every day and every night. One fellow was a truck driver and he'd leave at five in the morning. We used to get woken up by him having his breakfast. He would smoke cigarettes and we would smell the cigarettes down in our home. They wouldn't tolerate that today with the threat of lung cancer!

'I suggested my parents should buy the place they were living in at the time on a visit home. If you rented for so many years you could do that for £5,000 or so. My dad said, "No, we don't need to." I said, "You can put it in the family, give to Alan, me and Thelma." He said, "No, no , no." I was a bit of a wheeler and dealer and said, "I'll give you the money. Just buy it." The amount it was costing was chicken feed. It was worth five times as much and would get more valuable as the years went on. But they never bought it.'

Eric recalled what life was like in the Gilzean household. He said, 'My father always had a radio on. My Dad loved radios. He was always getting a new version of what was better than the last one. I remember the first television that came out but I don't think we ever had one.' Eric believed, 'Mum and Dad were great parents, providing a great home life.' He said, 'Dad was very easy-going. All the Gilzean family were that way. Jimmy, one of my father's youngest brothers, was one. He was four years in a prisoner of war camp in Germany during the war and months went by before we realised he wasn't killed.

'My mother was the disciplinarian. She would make sure things were done. When my mother said jump you asked "how high?" on the way up. I don't think my Dad ever laid a hand on me. My mother? Almost daily!

'But to tell you the truth, Alan was spoiled. He got away with murder compared to what I did. The things Alan did they'd say,

"Look how wonderful that is." I'd do the same thing and got whacked for it!'

Eric and Alan weren't in each other's pockets growing up due to the age gap between them. Eric said, 'I didn't hang around with Alan when we were growing up as he was so much younger. I was out in America by the time he was doing his thing [in football]. I left for America in my early 20s, 21 or 22 and he was ten years younger than that. I never once saw him play soccer. But I did know he was very involved in scouting and went to a big scouting jamboree [at Sandringham]. And I remember his great sense of humour. He always had it.'

Eric, who played football before his little brother had come of age, described how he was on the receiving end of wry comments from his little brother after Alan had turned professional. He said, 'I played a little soccer but my problem was that I had two left feet. I was with Alan one day. He said to the fella we were with, "This is my brother Eric. He's a much better player than I am. He could have gone better than me if he had kept playing soccer." I said to the guy, "Don't let him fool you." I used to say to my team-mates, "Don't give me the ball because I'll lose it."

'We also both sat and talked to each other at other times when I came home from America and he was home with Mum and Dad once in a while. He told me stories of how just before big games in London he would go and have a bite to eat somewhere with his Spurs team-mates. He'd take the salt shaker and undo the top of it so when someone shook the salt it spouted. He was up to all that kind of stuff. It was to get them relaxed. The young players were so nervous, he'd get them down to square one and to treat it like another game.'

Eric disclosed another light-hearted story revealing Gilzean's sense of fun. He said, 'Alan was comparing what it was like playing for Dundee and Spurs. He told me, "In London, my manager Bill Nicholson would tell us what we had to do, go into detail, but my Dundee manager Bob Shankly would say, "It is a bonnie day lads, let's go out and have a nice time." It was like "you guys know how to play the game, what do you need me for."'

Gilzean used to tell his brother about his on-the-field experiences with Spurs. Eric laughed as he said, 'Alan told me about a team Spurs played and he knocked a guy out. Punched him on the chin. The guy had been tugging on his shirt all the time. They showed the film of the game. That he was justified in doing what he did. I should imagine someone tugging your shirt when you went up for a ball every time would drive you crazy.'

Eric, on one of his regular visits, acted as Gilzean's shield from the media when they were together in the family home. He said, 'I always remember – this'll make you scream – the doorbell was ringing. He was at Spurs and on vacation and, of course, I was over. I'd go to the door because Alan said, "I don't want to go to the door. Find out who it is." Our parents were out the back.

'Outside there'd be two or three guys. All newspaper reporters. And so I'd tell Alan. He'd say, "Chase them! I can't get them to print anything correctly. When I do get interviewed they tell me I've said all this stuff and I've never said any of it. They add to all this stuff to make it more palatable." My job was to go to the door and say, "He doesn't want to see you." Then they started asking me questions. I didn't have a clue what was going on in his life. All the time I was there every hour on the hour someone would knock on the door. I'd say to him, "Jesus, just talk to them for a few minutes, it is not going to kill you."'

Eric revealed how his brother's link with Spurs is known in America. He said, 'I go back and forth to Los Angeles. Have a lot of friends there. One belongs to a health club. He called me up and said, "You know your brother used to play for a team in London called Tottenham Hotspur? Well, the son of former manager Arthur Rowe would like to meet you. So the next time you're in LA we'll set up a meet." The fellow couldn't make it when I did. But we keep talking about it.'

Eric was unable to be at his brother's funeral. He said, 'I got an email telling me he had passed away but I couldn't get over there for the funeral. I wasn't sure when it was going to be and it was all over before I could organise anything. As a brother I remember that, all the time I was with him, he still kept his great sense of humour and was very easy to talk to.

'I'd kept in touch with his ex-wife, Irene. Wrote every now and then when he was playing for Tottenham. I knew her when she was born. Knew her parents quite well. They were lovely people who lived at the bottom of our road. I also keep in touch with Alan's boys. They've got kids themselves. Time marches on.

'I'm into the family history, the genealogy and keep all the correspondence. My dad used to write to me at least once a week. I keep all his letters. I go through them constantly and pick up bits of information – who died in the village and when.'

Bobby Wishart, the Dundee team-mate who became Gillie's closest friend in football, knew his pal's parents. He said, 'I knew them well. They were the salt of the earth. Wasn't surprising he turned out the way he did, someone with no airs and graces. His mum would never have allowed him to be big-headed or anything like that.

'I was there once when Alan showed her his pay packet from Spurs – one of his first pay packets there. Mrs Gilzean said to me, "Bob, these footballers are earning too much. We didn't have enough money when we were young and growing up." I shudder to think what she'd say now.'

3

Coupar Angus Remembers

TODAY THERE have, inevitably, been changes from when Alan Gilzean grew up in Coupar Angus. The railway line which transported him – when he didn't travel by bus – to and from Dundee's Maryfield Station by Dens has been closed to passengers and goods transport since September 1967. Also, the town was bypassed by the A94 Perth to Forfar road. And there has been an influx of Eastern Europeans to add a cultural mix to the native population.

But there remain landmarks Gilzean would remember if he were able to explore his home town one more time. The Abbey Church for starters. A place which provided a beginning and end for him; his marriage to Irene in 1965 and the Gilzean family grave. I looked up at the imposing structure set in a churchyard housing rows of graves, fields stretching out behind them and sheep grazing quietly in an enclosure alongside.

All was still around the parish church established by Cistercian monks – thought to have helped reclaim and improve the land for agriculture – in the 13th century (although there is evidence of settlements in the area dating back to the Bronze Age from 3000–1200BC, including a Roman encampment, according to the Coupar Angus News and Info website which also told of whisky smugglers and the town being 'plundered and burned').

Up the road is the old picture house – in a building converted from a church and now recommissioned as one – where Gilzean saw images of the FA Cup Final at Wembley and dreamed of playing in one there. My reverie was broken by a rattling dog lead. Passer-by Lloyd Brown just happened to be taking his black pet poodle for a walk when I remarked to the total stranger (you can do that sort of thing in Coupar Angus and not be considered strange), 'A beautiful building, isn't it?' 'Och, aye,' said Brown, himself a native. Did he know of Alan Gilzean? 'I knew Alan Gilzean. A nice man. Who did he play for after he went down south?' 'Tottenham.' 'Och, Spurrrrs that's right.'

Everyone seemed to know Alan Gilzean in Coupar Angus. Parking up outside Gilzean's family home at 25 Strathmore Avenue, Bob Hynd, kindly chauffeuring me, I bumped into a middle-aged neighbour who engaged us in Gillie talk as we stood on the kerb, oblivious to the drizzle. With her East Anglian partner, she told of how she and her brethren knew the local superstar and his relatives.

The Gilzeans' old two-floor house is an end-of-the-street, semi-detached building with a beige-painted pebble-dashed style exterior. The main entrance was found around the side, a couple of kids' bikes had been left flat on the small lawn. Your imagination conjured Gilzean honing his football skills in the 1940s and 1950s on that very patch. The dark brown painted front door revealed the number and higher to the left was the black-on-white road sign in capitals boxed off in black. It screamed modest accommodation. And the unprepossessing chicken processing plant built in recent times opposite would be a feature of the area any estate agent could do without.

The family moved to 2 Stuart Crescent, a two-floored sandstone semi-detached which now appears a little jaded, its front lawn left to run riot, one no doubt kept trim for Gilzean kickabouts back in the day.

A short drive to The Square and we arrived at the Coupar Angus Heritage Association based by the bus stop on George Street where Alan Gilzean, aged 15, waited for the bus into Perth where he worked as a clerk for carpet manufacturers Coates, his first job after leaving school.

There we met Jim Thomson, a classmate of Gilzean's who runs the association and not the Dens ground manager, who kindly opened up the headquarters, turning on three fan heaters to allay a winter chill. Thomson has collected a treasure trove of Gilzean pictures from his days in the Coupar Angus Juveniles/City Boys and in the sixth Perthshire boy scouts to his spells with Dundee and Spurs, even the cult hero's wedding to Irene, whose family once used the premises we stood in as a paper shop.

Thomson said, 'Alan was in my class at school, two or three weeks younger than me. A good pupil, didn't get into any more trouble than the rest of us. I wasn't sporty but he was. He played football for the school, the scouts and clubs. I remember he used to join in matches at the back of the school on some grass. Played on it no matter what. Even when rain had turned it into a mudbath.'

His helper, who declined to be named, added, 'Alan's family were friends with my Dad's family. I remember taking a photo album round to show it to his dad because there was a picture of Mr Gilzean in it. And Alan was there. I remember Alan phoning me when he came home from all his football success just for a chat. It was great. He was always the same. What he did as a footballer never changed him.'

She spoke of how most of the families native to Coupar Angus appeared acquainted, giving the town, largely, a 'village feel'. The same lady – as a council worker – also kickstarted the friendship of Gillie and Bob Hynd after the request came through to repair the Gilzean family grave. Everybody seemed to know everybody in the town.

Go to Alan Gilzean's school on School Road, which he attended for ten years, and it is now purely a primary, and a Scotland jersey he wore against Norway is proudly on display in the main corridor. Mind you, another item the player presented to his alma mater, an international cap believed to be from the same game, had gone on the missing list.

Our host Helen Ferdinand, a teacher at the school and a former classmate of Hynd, also my 'tourist guide', was a mine of information. If Alan had been a current pupil, she would have been manager of his school football team.

Pupils in Gilzean's time came from a 'thriving' community and surrounding farms, and were joined by wartime evacuees.

Ron Ross, a classmate of Gillie's, said, 'I'd lived in a little village a few miles outside Coupar Angus but when we moved to the town I jokingly said it was the capital of the world. It was a thriving, busy little place. It's still thriving, but not as much, having been affected by depopulation and lack of jobs. It had a cinema, the railway was still running and it was full of individual shops before supermarkets. An awful lot of the pupils came from agriculture, from families living in cottages on farms which employed four or five workers, although these days they only need one with the machinery they have.'

Alan John Gilzean was admitted to the school – then known as Coupar Angus Public – on Tuesday, 17 August 1943 as an infant aged four years and nine months – admission number 730 – under his Strathmore Avenue address with only his father's name, inserted as 'Wm. John', considered the only parent important enough to register.

About 150 pupils attended and by his leaving date on 2 November 1953 there were an estimated 230. Ferdinand revealed what he experienced through the school log book, with contemporary entries written using a fountain pen. One extract during his opening months read, 'The school closed today [24 September] for Potato Holidays [the time for pupils to boost family incomes by 'tattie picking'].'

HM Inspectors reported on the school's war effort, stating, 'The children have been active in the collection of salvage and have contributed regularly and generously to Red Cross and Prisoner of War Funds.' Gilzean and others in infants were 'entertained this forenoon to a Conjuring Performance – as a Christmas treat' on 22 December. The following June he listened to an RAF talk on 'aircraft production'. 'Some schoolchildren' were injured in a bus accident on 15 November.

On 19 January 1945, 'no meals were forwarded today from Dundee [from where they should have been supplied]. The roads are impassable [snow]. Pupils from a distance were supplied with pies and a hot drink.' On 31 January the milk supply from Perth 'also didn't arrive with stormy, severe weather hitting the area'. Measles (18 May), chicken-pox and colds (11 January

1946) increased absenteeism. And in December that year the 'Headmaster addressed the pupils in Good Manners'. No doubt Gilzean impressed at the Annual School Sports held at Foxhall Park (2 July 1947).

Momentous events such as VE Day, Armistice Day, Princess Elizabeth's marriage to Prince Philip, her accession to the throne as 'Queen of the United Kingdom and the other Commonwealth realms', the death of her father King George VI, and the Festival of Britain Week were noted. In 1945, 8/9 May 'have been observed as Victory [VE] Holidays'. And on 11 November 'all classes observed a two-minute silence while a wreath was placed at the School War Memorial' to commemorate the Armistice for the first global conflagration.

There was a school holiday on 20 November 1947 to mark the royal wedding, and on 8 February, staff and pupils listened to a wireless broadcast from St James's Palace of the proclamation of Queen Elizabeth's accession ('reception of this most impressive ceremony was excellent'). Seven days later 'staff and pupils listened this afternoon to a BBC Broadcast from St George's Chapel of the Memorial Service to his late Majesty – a moving service – reception excellent.'

Gilzean and other pupils were presented with a 'souvenir mug and a box of chocolates' by the local Coronation Committee as part of a Coronation Holiday from 1–3 June in 1953. Ross said, 'There were quite a few significant events while we were at school. I was walking out of the science class on 6 February 1952 and the janitor was up the flagpole. He said, "I'm putting the flag at half-mast. The King is dead."' on 16 August 1951 the pupils were in the local cinema watching festival films.

One intriguing entry on 28 November revealed, 'Mrs Watson, a half-caste negress, addressed the pupils this afternoon on Life On A Cotton Plantation in Slave Days. She illustrated her talk with Negro Songs and "Spirituals".' Visitors from South Africa, Sri Lanka (then Ceylon) and Iraq (Baghdad) also added to the international flavour. There were a whole host of illnesses to deal with amongst the pupils, including measles, chickenpox, whooping cough, colds and even scarlet fever during Gilzean's time.

The school continued to be beset by snow – which prevented delivery of meals and milk on occasion – with the addition of floods. Accommodation problems raised their heads, cramped conditions eased on 15 August 1949 by 'the temporary use of a hut belonging to the Girl Guides, and the following year it was reported 'part of Science Room ceiling has fallen' on 10 November.

Variety was the spice of school life. Church, police, dental, photographic, film, armed forces folk, temperance and Roman history lecturers, and Shakespearean actors (performing *Julius Caesar*) grabbed the attention of Gilzean and his fellow pupils, along with foreign input. Perhaps, given the breadth of what was on offer to Gillie and co, it was no wonder Canadian and even English education bodies sent students there to 'study the Scottish Education system'. One education professional informed me, 'It was considered better than most.' One of the classrooms inside one of two main Victorian buildings in which Alan would have sat with classmates for lessons is now filled with school equipment and adorned by pupils' paintings on the wall.

Gilzean was an 'above average' pupil. He took annual Intelligence Quotient tests run by Moray House, a top teacher training institution, now the Department of Education, within Edinburgh University. He scored 105 in one on 1 March 1949 and only three of the 30 pupils listed scored higher, with a Hilda Gilzean (no known connection with Alan) earning 97. He netted 107 in another on 25 April 1950 but had 11 scoring higher of the 30 (Hilda, out of interest, secured 103).

Alan also might have qualified for a Champions League equivalent with a fourth place in an arithmetic test with 67 in May 1950; an early indication he was predisposed to figures, an ability which served him well at Coates and in his office duties in the transport trade after retiring from football. But the 56 scored for an English test in the same month meant a mid-table finish (14th) among the 30 taking part. 'Looks like the teachers underestimated Alan,' said Ferdinand, who pored over the full details.

It was no surprise he had a preoccupation with sport, especially football. He was reckoned, through his sublime hand-to-eye co-ordination, to also be good at cricket, tennis, golf; in fact, every ball game, besides chipping in on the track during the school's sports day over at Foxhall Park. Gilzean, who partly honed his heading skills against a school shed, himself recalled when the football bug in particular bit during his school days in that major 2012 interview with Alan Pattullo.

He said, 'A lot of my uncles on my mother's side, the Forbeses, they all played football, junior stuff. I remember saying to my mum when I was 10 or 11, and starting to get keen on football, "Mum, how do I go about becoming a footballer?" She said, "Get that nonsense out of your head right away." I thought, "Well, I better not mention that again." So I asked my uncle, "How do I become a footballer?" He told me that you just can't go and walk in and ask for a game. You have to wait until somebody finds you.'

In the 60s, an extension to the school was built incorporating a hall and Gilzean returned in 1964 to give a talk shortly after scoring the winning goal for Scotland against England at Hampden, an achievement for which he received a gold watch from his home town. A picture of the event once hung in the head teacher's office.

Ronnie Ross knew Gillie as a school team-mate, friend and journalist. The retired *Dundee Courier* sports editor welcomed me into his smart new home on a smart estate in Longforgan on the outskirts of Scotland's fourth-largest city. Bespectacled and admitting to suffering with his hearing, he was otherwise as sharp as a pin, intelligent and insightful.

His first thoughts took us back to the time shared with Gilzean at school. Ross said, 'I remember him the very first day I came to the school. The very first playtime at 11 o'clock in the morning. I'd have been 10 and Gillie was 11. There were about 100 boys playing on this ashes-covered playground with one old, scuffed tennis ball. And I saw this little tubby boy making rings round everybody. I thought, "Who the hell is this? He's good." I thought I could play a wee bit but nothing compared to him. He was in a totally different league.

'It used to annoy me when even Dundee supporters – when he was there – would say he's only good for scoring goals. No he wasn't. It was a role he was excellent at but it was just the way

Dundee chose to play him. And he proved that with Spurs, where he was the linkman who could play it around. He scored for the school team but was more a playmaker. People thought he had adapted when he went to White Hart Lane, but he'd just reverted to what he was in school.

'I became quite friendly with him and we were both in the scouts, went on camps together, although we were in different troops. Alan was laid-back, reserved, polite, well brought up in a nice family. Never pushy. Dad was hard-working. Gillie wasn't wild. Possibly had a streak of devilment in him but we all behaved ourselves in those days. His mum used to give us lemonade and biscuits when I went over to play football out the back at his place with a wee ball. It was a thrill for me to have played with him in the school team. He was not tall compared to others in the team – he was, like me, younger than some of them, although he eventually grew to nearly 6ft. But his ability was jaw-dropping.

'I was the secretary of the school football team. I used to have to arrange the matches against other schools. We were playing with 15-year-olds at first. I played at left-half (number six) and Alan at inside-left (number ten) and I didn't hold down a place until my last year. When we did play together we linked up well but he was the one who would say, "Do this, do that." He was always "the voice". In contrast to how he was off the pitch? Yes. His cousin Billy Forbes played on the right wing. Billy was fast.'

There was a memorable time for Gilzean when his school side, resplendent in yellow shirts and shorts and white socks, took on Alyth – from five miles east – in the Napier Cup Final at Foxhall Park in 1952. And 'the voice' certainly came into his own in this decider for a competition between schools in the area. Ross said, 'It was a Saturday morning and we went 4-0 up by half-time. I don't remember but Alan must have scored one or two. He usually did. We began to think it was a cakewalk. We are going to win this cup. Then it was 5-1, 5-2, 5-3, 5-4 with ten minutes to go. It was Alan who said, "Kick it out of the bloody park, never mind the football." We were struggling and tired. Word went round about what Alan had said. So we did what he said. If the ball came anywhere near us we belted it and clung on.

'On the Monday morning at school assembly, when the cup would normally be presented, Mr Eddie Sturrock, our English teacher who took charge of the boys football team, announced that although technically we had won the Napier Cup he did not like the manner in which we'd accomplished it. Therefore, he said, "there will be no official presentation". Imagine that nowadays! He'd wanted us to "play the game" and we hadn't. Funnily enough, Mr Sturrock told us once he'd been friends with Eric Liddell in the army during the war. Liddell was the Scottish runner who refused to race [in the 1924 Paris Olympics 100m heats] on a Sunday [switching to win the 400m], and was the subject of the film *Chariots of Fire*.

'I saw Alan at his peak with Dundee when I was sports editor of the local daily newspaper. It was possibly the biggest thrill to watch him play. It was only ten years after being a wee boy with him at school.'

Jack Scott, Gillie's group scout master, recalled how the sixth Perthshire Boy Scouts troop based inside a Nissen hut in Coupar Angus helped his patrol leader's football career. We sat in the front room of his smallholding in Lintrose in a rural spot a few miles away from Alan's home town and once the site of a camp during the Roman occupation. His charming partner Betty looked on as Scott proved his memory of Gilzean was crystal clear.

Gillie had joined the scout group – with pal Ian McKenzie, who was to be his best man – aged 11 in 1949. Scott said, 'You couldn't fault the laddie. A proper boy. I wouldn't say anything against him. He was genuinely a very nice person for a young lad. Wasn't cheeky. He just loved his football.

'He liked his scouting too. Did his proficiency badges. Mainly outdoor stuff. For cooking, camping and, of course, tying knots when he was a tenderfoot. Liked his camping which we did around the glens in the area. He built himself up into a patrol leader. I think the patrol was called Eagles. His responsibilities were to get the best out of the team; tell them not to be cheeky and to pay attention to the skipper, which was me. Determination was certainly in his brain. It came out in his football. He just loved his football. Very much into that. Part of the reason he came to the scouts, to be honest, was so he could get to play football.'

Scott certainly played his part in Gilzean's football career. He said, 'I tried to teach him what I knew, which was probably not an awful lot. But I gave him a start. He showed his talent at an early age with a strong kick and ability to dribble. He certainly loved to dribble. He would go to the goal, come back and do it again. That was his style. It really was. I was always getting on to him about it, telling him, "Alan, you're a forward, you are going for the goal to score goals. If you manage to overtake a player do so, but don't come back to try to dribble him again." I managed to get him past that, in the main, and he moved on from there. He was wel-built with big muscles.'

Gilzean was dedicated to improvement as a footballer. He developed his heading skills in the scout hut using either a ball or boxing glove attached to rope and slung across a beam of the wooden-floored scout hut, which had been used to house prisoners of war a year or two earlier. Scott said, 'I had the boxing glove or a soft ball for him to use. He'd practise his leap and ability to get more strength behind his heading. Then he would bring the rope down a bit so he could spring higher.'

Gilzean was naturally right-footed but practised with his other foot. Scott said, 'He certainly did and became two-footed. He developed a strong kick with the left foot and scored many of his goals with Dundee, Spurs and Scotland with it.' Practice often took place over at The Common, the patch of green by the school where Gilzean was able to develop his distribution to earn the nickname Peenie, because it was reckoned he could put the ball 'on the equivalent of the head of a pin' (pronounced 'peen' in the local dialect) as schoolfriend Ray Hepburn told the *Dundee Courier*. Scott said, 'We used to go over there in the good weather with a tin can. And the players would try and hit the tin can with their passes. Peenie would do that and it certainly improved his accuracy of passing.'

When asked whether he thought his efforts helped Gilzean become the footballer he became, Scott smiled and said, with a twinkle in his eye, 'I do!' He added, 'Overall I'd say the help he received in Coupar Angus in general made him the footballer he was. I followed his career. I always read about him in the daily papers and occasionally used to go to Dundee to watch him.'

Gilzean's parents supported their offspring's scouting activities. Babs used her culinary skills to bake goodies for the parents' committee meetings and socials and Willie watched Alan march in uniform through the streets of Coupar Angus as part of the Armistice service. And both parents would attend the Christmas party each year. Scott said, 'Mrs Gilzean helped a lot with the baking and that. She was good at it! And Alan's father was always keen on his son doing well. He took an active interest in everything that was running at the time.'

The Red House Hotel is on Station Road – even though, of course, there is no working station these days. Norman Bannerman, whose family run the place, was our generous host, treating Hynd and myself to a free drink in the bar as we sat down to speak. Bannerman defied his eighty-something years, looking dapper in white shirt and tie and dusty blue tank top.

The patriarch of his Coupar Angus clan was a friend of Gilzean's through the scouts, football and by just living in the town, even though a handful of years older.

And he has commemorated Gillie with a museum in one bar. Gilzean memorabilia is housed inside a glass frame stretching the length of one wall. There are autographed Dundee and Spurs shirts, pictures of him with his clubs, clippings and, most notably, a Scotland international blazer donated by the man himself and brought to the hotel on Alan's behalf by Hynd.

Bannerman, also Gilzean's patrol leader in the scouts, said, 'He always kept in close touch with Coupar Angus. When his mum and dad were alive he was up regularly. The last time he was at our hotel was to photograph him with the glass case. His son Ian brought him through from Carnoustie. And he was on great form. When I arrived in the bar where they were he smiled, "Where's my old patrol leader!" The idea for the museum came from a great Dundee supporter, Craig Dunn, who asked my son Alan whether we could do something.'

Bannerman recalled 15-a-side games among the children on The Common close to Gilzean's school and on the opposite side of the road from Foxhall Park. He said, 'There were shoals of juveniles and Alan was among them. Maybe I didn't have the ability but I enjoyed kicking about with them. Alan played for Coupar Angus on well-maintained council pitches.'

The other big interest among kids besides football was the scouting and Bannerman and Gilzean, of course, shared it.

Bannerman said, 'I knew him from school and going on the Alexander's bus to Perth for work, but mainly through the scouts when he joined the patrol I led. Everybody mixed in because it was football and boy scouts. There was not a lot going on in Coupar Angus. After two or three years he became a patrol leader on his own. Friday night was scout night. It is a life that is almost non-existent now as there are too many other things which take youngsters' minds away.

'I remember the jamboree we went to on the Sandringham Estate to celebrate the Queen's coronation. We went down on the British Rail to King's Lynn, which was the nearest station. There were scouts from all over, the West Indies, Bermuda. We all got interviewed by a reporter from the BBC, including Alan. An early media experience for him! We enjoyed camping, in the winter and summer. Alan mixed in well. Very much part of the group round the campfire, wherever. Fully involved. I still see his skipper Jacky Scott. The last time I met Jacky was at the health centre – a regular port of call these days!

'We were all involved in the picking of berries and tatties. Alan's mum was my first boss when I did that. We were all kids and she looked after you. You went to the berries and made money. You went out for tatties for five weeks and did the same. It was part of your growing up. Great time.'

Bannerman disclosed how he personally helped Gilzean's parents in their final years. He said, 'I used to do meals on wheels. Get meals from the factory and deliver them to the housebound. His father was getting on in years but okay. His mum, though, wasn't so well. Men generally weren't great cooks in those days! Alan would be up as regular as clockwork to see them.'

Bannerman, whose brother Telford played for Dundee, used to run a newsagent's from which Gillie picked up the local evening paper on a Saturday night with the football results after he became known, and would often bump into Bob Hynd's cousins and get 'dog's abuse'. Hynd said, 'The Shaws were my father's cousins and were brought up on the neighbouring Peattie Farm. Gillie knew them all well as they were all football fans, played for local teams and were around the same age.

'Stewart is the oldest and is still working in his late 80s. He's a farmer and a hardy individual. He was in intensive care for six weeks after being mauled by a cattle beast and returned to work. The others were Malcolm, Donald and Robert. They had a full-size football pitch with goals in a paddock next to the farm buildings at Peattie. Men from the neighbouring farms at that time used to meet there for a kickabout at weekends and summer evenings.

'There used to be a local sports paper that came out on a Saturday evening around 7pm called the *Sporting Post*. It was part of a normal Saturday to go and watch a team then buy a paper to read the other scores and match reports. At that time, the pubs in Scotland closed at 10pm, so it was traditional to go down to Coupar Angus from the neighbouring farms and have a few drinks with your contemporaries on a Saturday night.

'Gillie said to me that he used to go to Bannerman's shop and jokingly said that he used to dread going down to pick up his paper if Dundee had been beaten as he knew that he would get dog's abuse from "the Shaw laddies". It was all good-natured because they were friendly with Gillie.'

4

'The Man Who Turned Down Alan Gilzean and The Beatles'

ALAN GILZEAN started to play his first club football in 1953 when he joined the newly formed Coupar Angus Juveniles (aka City Boys), who were assisted by the town's Coupar Angus Juniors, the town's grown-up senior outfit. They joined the area's City Boys' League and played home fixtures, as did the Juniors, at Foxhall Park. The side soon started making a name for itself with a clutch of promising native youngsters. In 1955 Gilzean bagged two goals to ensure his team beat Errol 5-2 to lift the Perthshire Cup in Perth.

In the meantime, he had been entrusted with the role of club secretary from the tender age of 15, presumably displaying comparable skills to some of those required as a clerk, his first role in employment on leaving school that year. And the quality of players he signed on seemed to prove him capable of doing a decent job. The club's prospects, which included Gilzean's cousin Billy Forbes, provoked interest from more senior outfits. When those clubs came sniffing around for Gilzean's signature, it placed the hon sec in the unusual position of dealing with any inquiries for it and subsequent transfer.

One club who might have been able to get it was Alyth United Juniors, run by a neighbour of the Ross family who lived in the town six miles from Coupar Angus. Ron Ross said, 'His name was

Finlay Farquharson. He lived right next door to us. I was about 15 and was outside talking to him one night. He was a great man. Very enthusiastic about his club. He said to me, "We could do with young blood, Ron. Do you know any boys who might come and play for us?" I told him, "Yes, there are two in my class in the school team I play in, Billy Forbes and Alan Gilzean. He said, "Can you speak to them. Maybe you can arrange something. We've got pre-season trials coming up next week." I spoke to Billy, who was an apprentice in the same printing firm as I was, and asked him, "Could you and Alan cycle up there?" He said they would.

'I missed the trial – I think I was courting a girl at the time – but the day after it I saw Finlay and asked him, "How did the lads get on, Billy and Alan?" He said, "Mixed results. We've signed Billy Forbes but didnae think the lad Gilzean had got it."

'Then it turned out Finlay also turned down The Beatles (before they became a music and cultural phenomenon). His club ran dances on a Friday night to raise funds for the club. They used to get 700 to 800 people in the Alyth Town Hall. It was the time rock 'n' roll was popular. He said to me, "We got this chance of this band from Liverpool, but they were wanting to be put up in a hotel. I thought that was stretching our budget a bit, so I turned them down." So Finlay went to his grave as the man who turned down Alan Gilzean and The Beatles.'

It soon became apparent Gilzean was destined for higher things in the football world. It was understood Scottish League clubs Hibernian and Cowdenbeath were interested in trying to persuade the player-administrator that his future lay with them in their more glamorous surroundings rather than a youth team based on council pitches.

Hibs seemed a natural choice as Gilzean actually supported them, weaned on the Famous Five. Gordon Smith, Bobby Johnstone, Lawrie Reilly, Eddie Turnbull and future Scotland manager Willie Ormond captured the imagination of the schoolboy enough for him to journey to Edinburgh with pals to see them in action at Easter Road as an impressionable 13-year-old. But Dundee were also in the picture and he signed provisional forms for them in January 1956 following a trial, despite the fact a Dee scout had witnessed

Gilzean's Coupar Angus hit for six by Edinburgh Thistle in the Scottish Juvenile Cup shortly before. He said, 'They were much too good for us. But Dundee's east of Scotland scout seemed satisfied I'd make the senior grade. A week later Willie Thornton sent for me. I did not play trials for any other side than Dundee.'

Even that failed to remove thoughts of a move to Easter Road in Gilzean's eyes when he discovered the Dark Blues boss Willie Thornton had delayed in registering him. He said, 'I signed provisional forms for Dundee under Willie Thornton. But he never registered me with the Scottish Football Association. Hibs got to know about it. So the Hibs approached me. And I was going to go to Hibs. No way would I pass up that chance. But my mother put her foot down. "You have given the man your word," she told me. "You will play for Dundee."' Craig Brown, a Dundee team-mate during the title-winning season, joked, 'Apparently Gillie's mum liked the Dundee scout. Maybe bought her a box of chocolates or something!'

Also, Willie Gilzean thought Dens a better option, partly as it would solve accommodation problems. Gilzean said, 'I was with Coupar Angus Juveniles [aka City Boys]. I had the chance to sign for about four clubs, Hibs and Cowdenbeath were also after me, but father was very keen on Dundee and although I was not a Dundee supporter he reckoned I would not have problems like having to worry about digs.'

Dundee also had leverage because Gilzean's dad had taken him to Dens as a youngster when the Dee were a force, winning two Scottish League Cups. Gillie said, 'I saw Billy Steel play and he was fantastic. [Dad] divided his loyalties between Dundee and St Johnstone, supporting both, but obviously Dundee in the Steel era, there was a charisma about the whole club then. George Anderson was a charismatic figure. The bowler hat, the bow-tie, the cigar and the walking cane and then with Billy Steel in the team, he was the icing on the cake, especially when they won two League Cups with [wing-half] Alfie Boyd.

'When I went there first I can remember Johnny Lynch being in goal, followed by Bill Brown and of course I played with him later at Spurs. Tommy Gallacher. I can remember Danny Molloy before he went to Cardiff City, Ken Ziesing, Jimmy Toner.'

Dundee farmed Gilzean out to Dundee Violet Juniors based at Glenesk Park (where Gilzean remembered seeing Gordon Smith play for Hibs against the Dee at the ground's opening around 1948). As the song goes, 'Roses are red, violets are blue', and that was what Gilzean felt like with the Pansies. He was missing his pals back at Coupar Angus and returned on loan to play for his town's Junior team at Foxhall Park. He had made just one appearance for Violet but thrived back home, playing for semi-pro Coupar Angus in the Angus Junior League for the rest of the season.

Junior level was not far beneath the Scottish League itself. Ross said, 'It was a very successful team. I attended games with 3,000 to 4,000 people. Junior football was much more popular then. Before the distraction of television, it had grown big. Coupar Angus had a very good team. Blairgowrie, a few miles up the road, had an even better one. And there was Alyth also providing local derbies.'

Norman Bannerman, who knew Gillie and was his scout patrol leader, said, 'My old man was involved with the Juniors and Alan was outstanding. A terrific header of the ball. He knew he could do it but was such a down-to-earth guy. Quiet and unassuming.'

The Dark Blues kept a close eye on their prospect. It was clear they liked what they saw and heard, especially when Gilzean fired four goals to help Coupar Angus defeat Arbroath Victoria 5-2 in the 1957 Arbroath & District Cup Final. Gillie and co had landed a big fish, a Junior side which had secured their fourth consecutive Angus League crown the year before, smoked out the team from the town known for its smoked haddock. One which had also managed to remain unbeaten at home from 1952–55. A team from a club, coincidentally, which was formed in the same year (1882) as Tottenham Hotspur, an outfit which eventually played the longest and, according to the man himself in Jim Hendry's *Dundee Greats*, closest part of Gillie's illustrious playing career.

Thornton was sufficiently impressed overall with Gilzean to offer him professional terms and signed the player on full time for Dundee on Saturday, 2 February 1957 with the Dee clearly in need of a goalscorer, having been held to a goalless home draw by Clyde in a Scottish Cup tie on the day.

It augured well for the club's long-term plans as they sought to build a more youthful squad with the halcyon days of Anderson, Steel and Cowie coming to an end. One which would become known as Thornton's Babes and made up the core of the much-lauded playing squad which brought the club's lone Scottish League title success and a taste of European Cup glory; besides Gilzean, the likes of Bobby Cox, Alex Hamilton, Hughie 'Shug' Robertson, Alan Cousin, George McGeachie all emerged from Junior football.

Ross believed Gilzean did not have stars in his eyes when the prospect of playing professionally beckoned. He said, 'I've seen references that he saw football as a job, not a glamour career. That was his attitude. Growing up at the same time as him, I can see it. The ethos was, "Go to school, get yourself a job". That was in my family roots too. I was considered clever and nowadays would have gone to university. But then it didn't matter how clever you were. You all got jobs. Mine was in the print. Economics demanded it.'

The attitude showed itself in Gilzean getting himself that job as soon as he left school. Ross said, 'I remember getting off the bus at quarter to eight in the morning at George Street as he was getting on to go to his clerk's job in Perth.' The former journalist recalled a bus journey a few years later which highlighted how handsomely a switch from a clerical to a spherical object-dominated job had paid off for Gilzean. Ross said, 'I was serving my time as a compositor in the old print trade in Coupar Angus and Alan, by this time, was playing for Dundee. Must have been about 20, 21. We got on the same bus. Me to go and watch a game and him to play in it. The Dee were playing Ayr United. And we got down to talking wages.

'I'd finished my six-year apprenticeship, which involved night school three nights a week and giving up football through lack of spare time. I was on about £15 a week. That was good money back in the early 1960s. He was on £24 or 25. It showed the difference between a tradesman and a professional footballer to be nearly 50 per cent.'

* * *

Glory, though, was far from instant for Gilzean, largely due to receiving a call-up for National Service in 1957. He served as a clerk in the Royal Army Service Corps (RASC) based at the Aldershot Garrison between Aldershot and Farnborough in Hampshire. Private Gilzean had developed typing and shorthand skills while riding what seemed the far-from-magic carpet ride at Coates so slotted in comfortably to his assigned role. Even doing well enough to earn promotion to corporal.

The experience, though, might have stood him in good stead for the trade he went into after his football career finished: transport. The RASC had to sort land, coastal and lake transport for the British Army, supply food, water, fuel and domestic materials and technical and military equipment, deal with air despatch, barracks administration and the Army Fire Service.

One contemporary of Gilzean's, a Sergeant Beck, giving the corps the ironic nickname of Run Away Someone's Coming, gave an idea of what Gillie went through and got out of it. He said, 'Basic training brought out the best and the worst in us. Those who lacked confidence became the victims of those who didn't. I said I would like to drive a lorry; after all, the RASC was responsible for, among other things, transport. In line with what passed for military logic this resulted in my being earmarked as an army clerk! I suppose there were some plus points; some people learned skills they might otherwise not have obtained. For myself, I have never regretted being turned into a touch-typist (would you believe!). Also, I am sure that being uprooted from the home environment eased the passage from boyhood to independent manhood.'

Thornton would have agreed with that sentiment, insisting Gilzean returned to Dens 'a mature character' and went 'from strength to strength from then on', according to *In Search of Alan Gilzean*.

Gilzean, naturally, got involved with his unit's football team. And the side certainly boasted a couple of talented players. Ron Yeats, the legendary Liverpool centre-back, for one. He was the defensive rock on which Bill Shankly, brother of Bob, built his great Reds teams of the 1960s. One which created the high-profile, global image the club enjoys today, especially after sealing its sixth European Cup with a final win over Tottenham in June 2019. A lineage from Shankly to Jürgen Klopp.

Liverpool were a second-tier team with a second-tier reputation until Bill Shankly arrived and installed Yeats as captain in 1961, declaring to journalists while introducing the 6ft 2in defender built like an outhouse, 'The man is a mountain, go into the dressing room and take a walk around him.'

And the extrovert manager, who had a string of one-liners, added that the arrival of Yeats along with Ian St John was 'the turning point' to establishing the Liverpool dynasty after 20 years without a major trophy. Proof came as The Colossus skippered Shankly's side to promotion in his first Anfield season, back-to-back English league titles and the club's first FA Cup triumph, besides runs to the European Cup Winners' Cup Final and the semis of the European Cup. Big Ron's legendary status at the club was cemented when he was made an honorary Scouser in 2009, three years after retiring as the club's chief scout.

Gilzean went on to face Yeats after the centre-back first proved his ability to help other also-rans step on to the big stage. While Gillie was establishing himself at Dundee, his fellow Scot who had worked in an Aberdeen slaughterhouse hooked up with Dee neighbours Dundee United, a part-time outfit languishing in the Scottish Division Two, in 1957.

Three years later he helped the Tannadice outfit secure promotion while on National Service, with the help of manager Jerry Kerr's powers of persuasion in getting him released from the army for Saturday fixtures.

And when Gilzean and Big Ron faced each other in the top flight in 1960/61 it was honours even, with Gilzean helping the Dee beat their neighbours 3-0 at Dens on 7 January to avenge a 3-1 loss at Tannadice on 17 September. They went on to line up against each other when Spurs met Liverpool as the 60s swung.

Alex Young, the Golden Vision, also shared Gilzean's barracks and played centre-forward to his fellow Scot's inside-left in the unit line-up. Young carved out an impressive career with Hearts. He spent the late 1950s helping the club lift the Scottish League title twice, alongside future Gillie team-mates Dave Mackay for the first and Gordon Smith the second, plus the League Cup, while completing his National Service.

The forward was in the opposing team when Gillie made his Spurs debut against Everton in December 1964 after adding to his reputation by scoring 22 goals as the Toffeemen sealed the English league crown the year before. Young, like Alan, was known for his guile, ball-playing and heading ability. The blond ace was, again similarly to Gilzean, 'worshipped' by fans of his clubs and described as 'humble' off it.

When the Golden Vision passed away in 2017 aged 80, Gilzean said, 'He was always the golden boy.' He added it was 'an absolute travesty' his army team-mate only won eight caps (in which he scored five goals) for his country. And Gillie had a personal reason for showering Young with praise – crediting his fellow soldier for the role he played in developing his game.

Gilzean said, 'I was practically an "old soldier" when Alex appeared on the scene. Not only in matches but during afternoon training sessions, Alex showed me how to improve my techniques in so many ways. I felt I learned a great deal more about the game of football when I left the army than I did when I went into it thanks to Alex Young.'

Gilzean was keen to remain on home shores rather than seek a posting abroad, according to Pat Liney, Dundee's championship-winning goalkeeper. Liney and Gilzean first met at Dens in a group with Ian Ure. The honorary Dee club president said, 'Gillie got on with everybody.'

Liney and Gilzean got to know each other while training to do their National Service. The goalkeeper wanted to get a posting abroad so elected not to play football on home soil in the army in case it jeopardised his chances. He said, 'I'd never been out of my own country and thought if I played well they would want to keep me playing for them over here. So I waited until I was posted to Germany and then played for my camp team. It sounds silly but when you are 18 or 19 you want to do things your way. But Gillie wanted to stay local because he'd got in a team right away.'

Ian Gilzean said, 'Dad was quite proud of being in the army. About how he served his National Service and everything.' He added with a smile, 'Don't think he ever did much. I might be wrong but I think some of the players who served it had cushy numbers. Got let off to play. Don't think they were on the front line!'

In March 1958 Dundee sorted a loan so Gilzean could play for Aldershot, who were in the old Third Division South, on £5 a week. It was the last season the level was regionalised, with the Fourth Division being formed for 1958/59. The Shots were struggling to finish the season in the top half, an achievement which would have ensured an escape from relegation to the new division. They had a diamond – albeit in the rough – in their midst who could have shone bright enough to help them to stay up. But The Shots manager Harry Evans chose to limit Gilzean to the reserves and, in the main, the A side which played in the Hampshire League.

Jack Rollin, club vice-president, lifelong supporter, author of *The History of Aldershot Football Club* and respected journalist who was the founding editor of *World Soccer* and football writer with the *Sunday Telegraph*, said: 'Possibly because it was late on in the season, Gilzean did not get a game in the first-team. However, the following season was one of the worst the club had endured, despite the fact we had our highest league win, 8-1 against Gateshead. We had to seek re-election at the end while our visitors escaped. At this distance and with hindsight it would be easy to say he could have made a difference, but a chance in the first-team would surely not have been a waste of time. He went back to Dundee, helped them win the Scottish League title and propelled them into the European Cup, and later found fame with Tottenham Hotspur and Scotland.'

The irony is that Evans was in charge at the Recreation Ground during Gilzean's time, and, like Gillie, was a forward in his playing days with Southampton, Exeter City and The Shots with spells at Woking and Fulham. The same Harry Evans was appointed assistant manager at Spurs by Bill Nicholson in August 1959 after ending his five years in charge of Aldershot. On the face of it, Nicholson's judgement might have been questioned. Evans had just guided The Shots to the re-election zone in his fifth and final year as Recreation Ground supremo. And, overall, had secured 53 wins in 184 matches. But you questioned Bill Nick's opinion at your peril.

Evans went on to help Tottenham's most successful manager lead the north London club – at which Gilzean's star was to burn bright for a decade – to glory. With Evans in harness, Spurs, in 1960/61, became the first winners of the coveted League and FA Cup Double since Aston Villa in 1897 and claimed the cup again while reaching the semi-finals of the European Cup. John White, a member of that great Tottenham team of the early 1960s, became his son-in-law before Evans tragically passed away aged at just 43 on 22 December 1962, during the season the Lilywhites lifted the European Cup Winners' Cup.

* * *

Patience is a virtue, it is said, and Gilzean was clearly, it seems, a virtuous individual when it came to his football career. His time serving the Queen was a major factor in making his entry into the world of the professional game a slow-burner. Gilzean was concerned, at one point, his army career might even end his hope of having one in the ranks of professional football. He said, 'I signed [for Dundee] in 1956 but was called up for National Service the following year. By the time I'd served my two years, guys I started with at Dens – Pat Liney, Alex Hamilton, George McGeachie and Hugh Robertson – had all graduated to the first-team. I was the odd one out, and thought I'd never join them.'

But in between journeys to the home of the British Army, he was able to play in the Dark Blues reserves. And it seemed he was coping with what seemed a frustrating situation. In fact, he seemed to be thriving. Gilzean said, 'During my last six months or so in the army, Dundee used to bring me up from Aldershot on the Thursday night. I would train on the Friday, play on the Saturday and return on the train on Sunday. It was half-time football, half-time army but it was a very enjoyable time for me. When I started playing for the reserves, I began to knock in a few goals.'

John Duncan, who was dubbed the new Gillie on succeeding him in the frontline at the Dee before doing the same at Spurs, remembered watching him in action for the club's second-team at Dens. He said, 'I used to go with my grandfather to see the reserves because the big crowds at first-team games were a bit too much for me. My grandad didn't want to take me among the big crowds anyway. You could go along to where the players came running out of the tunnel on a pathway to the pitch because the attendance was small. I would stand up on a wall by it and as the players, including Alan, ran past I would pat them on the back. Or when they were coming back off the pitch. I always did that.'

Alan's efforts in front of Duncan, his grandad and the diehards who forked out to watch 'the stiffs' earned him his call-up to the first-team squad in 1957. But he would have to wait three and a half years from being provisionally signed to donning a dark blue shirt for the main side.

5

Goalscoring Machine

THE PORTENTS did not look good for Alan Gilzean as he trudged back to the dressing room following a far from auspicious first-team debut for Dundee. The Dark Blues's line-up against Motherwell at Dens on Saturday 22 August 1959 looked strong enough. It was minus Scottish international stopper Bill Brown, who Gilzean would link up with at Spurs having left for White Hart Lane in the summer and was bound for Double-winning success in the English league the following summer.

But it contained his favourite centre-half, the Scottish international Doug Cowie, and Jimmy Gabriel, the blond teenager who would become the most expensive footballer to exit Scotland as a £27,000-signing for Everton the following year and be replaced by Ian Ure. And, more pertinently, there were six of the team that sealed the title in 1962, including Alex Hamilton, Bobby Cox, Andy Penman, Alan Cousin, Hugh Robertson and, of course, Gilzean himself. Yet a 4-1 scoreline against the hosts – with Ally Hill netting their consolation goal – ensured the new number ten would have to hope for better days.

Gilzean said, 'Unfortunately, in my debut for the first-team we were thrashed by a very good Motherwell team, Bert McCann, Pat Quinn and all these guys. It showed me the gulf between reserve and first-team football. Later in my career I would discover there was the same gulf between first-team [club] football and international football. More stamina, more skill. That was always what you needed when stepping up a grade. I had been signed by Willie Thornton and when I played that first game against Motherwell he was still in charge.'

It was his first and last appearance in the club's top team under Thornton. His manager quit in September 1959 after five years of transition for the club due to his wife's ill health. He returned to his native Glasgow to take charge of Partick Thistle having built the foundations of Dundee's most famous team.

Gilzean had to wait until the following February before another look-in under Thornton's successor, Bob Shankly, who had revived Third Lanark and was working with assistant manager Sammy Kean, physiotherapist Lawrie Smith and assistant trainer Jackie Kay. It followed 24 successive games on the sidelines as Gilzean finished off his stint in the army with, in the meantime, George McGeachie, Bert Henderson, Alan Cousin and Jimmy Bonthrone being tried at number ten.

Gillie's return signified his Dundee league debut. It was against Rangers at Ibrox on Tuesday, 9 February 1960. It might not have produced any goals for him, but he was part of a creditable goalless draw in their Auld Firm opponents' backyard. It convinced Shankly to stick with the 21-year-old – now demobbed – for the next game which saw Gilzean notch his first of 169 goals in 190 senior appearances for the Dark Blues on his home league debut.

The strike came with a header as his hours of practising his aerial skills in the scout hut, his family's painting and decorating premises and against the school shed began to pay off on the professional stage – an ability he became universally renowned for, although being no slouch on the deck. His effort helped secure a 3-1 home league victory against St Mirren on 27 February 1960 – with George McGeachie and Alan Cousin completing the Dee scoreline in front of 11,000 who must have boasted 'I was there' at many a bar or dinner party in its wake. He had the opportunity of making it two just two days later against the team he supported but drew a blank as Hibs eased to a 3-0 Scottish Cup victory at Easter Road. And it was the same on 10 March as the Dee were pipped 1-0 at Ayr United.

Gilzean was off the team sheet for the next two matches, a draw at Dunfermline and home win over Partick, but a friendly against

Liverpool at Dens on Wednesday, 23 March 1960 saw Gillie back in a Dark Blues' first-team shirt. He was brought on as a substitute for Bobby Waddell at centre-forward and helped his side to a 1-0 victory over the team Shankly's brother Bill had taken over just four months earlier. (Ironically, Bill, when in charge of Huddersfield Town, had sent a letter of application to succeed Thornton at Dens which arrived a day after his brother's appointment, according to Dark Blues club historian Kenny Ross.)

Reds goalkeeper Bert Slater – who was to replace Pat Liney at the Dee for the European Cup campaign two years later – was reported to have stepped back over his line from a Hugh 'Shug' Robertson corner for the only goal. It was a solid win against a team that included future World Cup winner Roger Hunt and England 1966 World Cup squad player Gerry Byrne. But its major significance for Alan was the effect his performance had on his manager. It seemed a light switched on in Bob Shankly's head as the Dee commemorated the installation of new Dens Park floodlights that night. The boss thought Gillie could switch from number ten to number nine on a regular basis.

Gilzean said, 'Shankly gave me my big chance. We beat Liverpool and I thought maybe I'll get the centre-forward job, maybe Bobby Waddell. He [Shankly] chose me and stuck by it. Played me right to the end of the season and I never looked back after that. It was just the luck of the draw [being chosen over Waddell]. It could have gone the other way.'

He added, 'Obviously I had not done too badly or I would not have stayed in. That was my chance, it was a time Dundee were going through a transitional period. There were still some of the players left from the Billy Steel era, people like Doug Cowie, Albert Henderson and Dave Curtlet [the first two performed against Liverpool]. They were gradually phasing them out and a whole new breed of players were coming in. I always considered it a privilege and a pleasure to play alongside Doug Cowie. To me he was one of the greatest players to have played for the club. He was fantastic.'

The new central striker managed to crash home his second goal for the Dee three days later, against the Hibs team he supported in a thumping 6-3 home win. Gillie switching to number nine continued to prove a fruitful decision for both the player and his boss for the remaining four league games of the season. He netted his first Dundee away goal in a 3-3 draw against Airdrieonians. He scored another first with his debut goal against Old Firm opposition, the opener in a 2-0 home victory against Celtic.

Next up was his first of a club record 17 hat-tricks for the Dee, with Stirling Albion on the receiving end in a 4-1 triumph in the final league fixture of 1959–60 at Dens. And he made it eight in eight as Dundee ended their league season with a 2-2 draw at Third Lanark. Gilzean's debut-season league goals helped ensure the Dark Blues finished fourth in the Scottish League Division One behind champions Hearts, who had lifted the title despite the loss of the inspirational Dave Mackay – a future Gillie team-mate at White Hart Lane – to Spurs the previous term.

Gilzean also chipped in with a couple of goals after his switch to main striker in the non-senior Forfarshire Cup, bulging the net twice in a six-goal mauling of Brechin City at Dens. His abilities in front of goal certainly gave cause for optimism, which was, of course, well founded.

As his future club Spurs were creating history by becoming the first team to secure the English Football League and FA Cup double in the 20th century in the 1960/61 season, Gilzean developed the indelible mark he left at Dundee during his first full season, albeit with either a number nine, number eight or number ten on the back of his Dark Blues shirt, as a goalscoring machine.

Gillie didn't just hit the ground running, he hit it as if turbo-charged at the start of what was, lest we forget, his first complete campaign as a professional footballer. His tail-end-of-the-season scoring streak from the previous term had clearly lifted his confidence. Whatever he did in the summer and pre-season in preparation for the upcoming one proved spot on.

The stats he piled up were staggering. He tucked FOUR hat-tricks under his belt in the first four weeks. He began like he meant to go on with a treble to destroy Raith Rovers 5-0 in the opening game, a League Cup tie at Dens. Gillie managed to do the same in the return tie at Stark's Park, and netted another three in a six-goal mauling of Aberdeen as he secured 14 of his free-scoring team's 23 goals in six straight wins in the competition before Rangers chained him en route to beating the Dee in the two-leg quarter-final.

Arsenal, it was reported in the *Daily Mirror*, caught wind of Gilzean's exploits and cast an eye over him in the second leg in search of a last-four date with Queen of the South. Fortunately for Dundee and, in time, Tottenham, Gillie was off target, even missing a penalty, and the speculation of a move to Highbury evaporated.

Gilzean had bagged hat-trick number four in a 3-3 deadlock with the Dons in the first home league match of the season at Dens. And he went on after the cup exit to help his side seal six successive wins to put Dundee top by 22 October. Alan kept proving himself a lethal finisher by completing the season having scored 32 goals in 42 appearances. Dundee, it had been pointed out, were a good team that lacked a killer touch. Well, it seemed Alan Gilzean provided them with one. He was, of course, not a one-man team, and was swift to recognise it. He said, 'I was one of a number of young players coming through.' The likes of Ian Ure, Bobby Cox, Alex Hamilton, Alan Cousin, Andy Penman, George McGeachie and Hugh Robertson who, with Gilzean, were other Thornton's Babes growing up fast.

Bobby Seith had been brought in at the start of the season, having helped Burnley lift the English First Division crown a few months earlier. Bobby Wishart was signed from Aberdeen – having tasted championship success at Pittodrie – after the Dee went off the boil and failed to win five league games in a row as they slid to mid-table by the turn of the year, while midfielder George McGeachie broke his leg at Motherwell in the December.

Wishart made an instant impact at number ten with a goal double to aid the 3-0 defeat of Dundee United on 7 January 1961, which avenged an early-season victory for their newly promoted neighbours at Tannadice. And a friendship with Gilzean, who played number eight that day, had begun and remained unbroken until Alan died.

Wishart said, 'Well, Alan had been number ten for Dundee. And when I got signed for Dundee, Alan got pushed over into number eight! I joked with him, "You'll have to bloody make way for me!" The first few games I played for Dundee were in his position. We used to enjoy a good banter like that.'

He added Gilzean was part of the reason for him joining Dundee: '[Bob Shankly] "I've got a lot of good young lads [including Gillie] and you can keep them right and push them on. I think you could do a job." I said, "Fine, I'll do that.""

Injuries – Andy Penman broke an ankle – and lack of consistent results might have hampered title pretensions, but it was clear Dundee had the potential to secure their first Scottish championship triumph. There had a blend of youth and experience. The forwards linked well. Cox, Ure and Seith typified a battling spirit. Players, including Gilzean (more later), were internationally recognised.

And 10 of the 11 main men who helped secure the title the following term were already on the payroll, as was manager Bob Shankly. Gilzean said, 'Shankly was an honest man and called a spade a spade, and he quickly gained the players' respect with his knowledge of the game.'

But Alan never forgot Shankly's predecessor Thornton. He said, 'Give Willie Thornton his due. He signed some wonderful players for Dundee. He had a fantastic scouting system. I don't know who his scouts were but I remember my first day at Dens when I reported. Five of us were new boys. Pat Liney, Alex Hamilton, George McGeachie, myself and Shug Robertson. All five made the first-team and about three got caps.'

There was certainly a camaraderie from the off between the players and Gilzean was very much a part of a close-knit group. There were no cliques. It was one for all and all for one. And the spirit developed off as well as on the field helped Shankly develop the championship-winning side which was also to make its mark in Europe.

Craig Brown, former team-mate turned Scotland manager turned Aberdeen director, remembered off-duty bonding sessions between the players when I caught up with him via his mobile phone in the Dons team coach en route to an away cup tie in 2019. He said, 'There was a great camaraderie amongst the players. There used to be wind-ups, of course, we used to wind Gillie up. There used to be speculation in the evening paper, *The Telegraph*. We called it the Tele. There'd be stories about teams wanting to sign him. He was always looking at the paper to see if anything was happening. So was Ian Ure. Both of them. So what we used to do was tear a big hole in the back page. When he came in he asked, "Where's the Tele tonight?" We'd give him the Tele, and he said, "Where's that missing bit? What's in it?" We'd say, "it was a bit about him going to AC Milan or Benfica or something like that. He's convinced and so goes out and buys an *Evening Telegraph*.

'Gillie was very much into team harmony. We went out during the week to a local coffee bar. But there were a few pints consumed as well. Down at Tottenham he got the reputation that he had become a recluse. He was the opposite with us. He was right in the midst of the social. He would like a pint or two, but was NEVER drunk. Socialised very well with the lads. There were three dance halls in Dundee to go to. Complimentary admission as local players. I shared digs at a Mrs Clark's with a few other players. He lived in Coupar Angus but sometimes he stayed with the rest of us. He was extremely popular.

'Gillie had a dry sense of humour. We were all afraid of the manager Bob Shankly; had great respect for him, but he was like his brother Bill. Gruff, aggressive-minded. Rough and tough. But Alan would sometimes get behind him and repeat what he said!'

Brown illustrated how Gilzean, prompted by his sense of fun and nothing else, took a gentle rise out of his manager and team-mate Gordon Smith during the interval of one game. He said, 'I remember one time we were playing Anderlecht in Brussels and Bob was quite disappointed we hadn't shown any positivity. Now Gordon Smith, our famous winger, was aged 37 and couldn't run and Gilzean winked at the rest of us and said, "Listen boss, for the second half I'll just stick the ball inside the full-back for Gordon Smith to cross, and if he crosses it anywhere inside the penalty box I'll head it in." It was a basic pass but I remember Shankly saying, "Christ, Gillie that's way too fucking complicated."

'The manager wasn't supposed to – but we all knew he had two favourites: Gay Gordon, not in the sexual but happy sense, and Gillie. He never called Gillie "Alan" or "Gilzean". It was always "Gillie". When you put "ie" on the end of a name it is a sign of affection.'

Gillie displayed his comic timing at team meetings. Brown said, 'Gillie had had a minor accident with his car [a VW Beetle, which he eventually bought after relying on public transport from his home town] in Clepington Road [near Dens Park] – hit his head on the interior mirror, cut his forehead. He had to get stitches to his forehead, I think. I remember the manager Shankly asking him at this team meeting, "What were you doing in the Clepy Road, Gillie?" He said, "Playing headers with the interior mirror!" All the boys were laughing. Like Gordon, we all knew Gillie was a favourite with the manager and could say things like that. Some guys would say, "I'm not playing because I've got stitches in my forehead." But he just patched it up and carried on. He was so good in the air – and a great, laid-back guy.'

Brown insisted Gilzean's wit remained razor sharp in his latter years. He said, 'I, too, was the butt of one of his famous quips when, during his interview at his SFA Hall of Fame induction at Hampden in 2009, interviewer Dougie Donnelly saw me there and said to Gillie, "There's Craig Brown. What kind of player was he?" He replied, "He was less bad as a manager than he was as a player!"'

Ian Ure remembered 'an easy-going, fun-loving guy'. He said, 'Gillie liked a laugh and a joke and a carry-on.' Ure got to know the Gilzean family socially in Coupar Angus – and received a surprise after staying over one night. He said, 'Gillie's folks were nice people. Lovely. I remember getting up one frosty morning and seeing some pretty-big red stags eating some curly-tailed kale and Brussels sprouts in the front garden. A fantastic sight! We were great pals at Dundee where we were together most of the time at club do's.'

Gilzean and Ure were part of a group led by extrovert full-back Alex Hamilton and known as 'Hammy's Gang'. Gillie said, 'Hammy used to room-up with Urey and I used to room-up with Shug Robertson. We were always up to something. Hammy was great. A wonderful guy – once you got to know him! He could play any sport. Good at golf, snooker. He could do the lot. It was a special group of players. And we were all good mates.'

The bond between the players extended to the backroom staff. I spoke to physiotherapist Lawrie Smith from his Glasgow home while sitting on the bed of my Dundee hotel room, while visiting the area to meet the people in Gilzean's life. He might have been in his 80s but his wits were still very much about him as he recalled Gillie time at Dens Park.

He said, 'It was a happy club. The players integrated with each other. I can't remember cliques. Gillie integrated well. Very easy to approach, very easy to talk to. Very friendly. We had common ground in that Gillie had just done his National Service and I'd done mine two or three years earlier. We used to talk about the world in general and what went on in life.

'He was dedicated to his profession and applied himself to doing the best he could. He was a very, very good player. Oh my goodness, could use both feet, dribble and score lots of goals. Deadly with his head whether the ball came from the right from Gordon Smith or from Shug Robertson on the left.

'Spent very little time with him in the treatment room. He was very seldom injured and an excellent trainer. Didn't like to miss a game just like everybody because it was such a great side. Enjoyed playing football together. Wasn't kick and rush and they scored a lot of goals. Played with confidence but weren't brash.

'Gillie and the others took knocks and bruises in their stride. Had to be really injured before calling off sick. I think he missed one or two games because of flu not because of injury and then he developed a knee problem and missed one or two games.'

* * *

A 22-year-old Gilzean was touted to lead a revival for his country on the eve of the 1961/62 season, one, of course, that is forever etched in the memories of Dundee supporters. Scotland would love to turn up another Gilzean in their desperate search for talent today following the embarrassing 3-0 European Championship qualifying defeat in Kazakhstan which earned manager Alex McLeish pelters – and must have led to Steve Clarke replacing him – in March 2019; the hosts ranked 71 and the visitors 40 in the FIFA world rankings.

But history is merely repeating itself if we analyse the state of the international team north of the border in 1961. Hopes did not seem high when Scotland sought to qualify for the 1962 World Cup finals; proving a realistic viewpoint when, ultimately, they failed to make it to Chile, albeit by losing a play-off to eventual losing finalists Czechoslovakia.

Hugh Taylor, author of the Scottish football book *No.7*, wrote in 1961, 'The real reason Scotland's international prestige has slumped is known to every fan in the land – lack of shooting power. That's why, with the World Cup in Chile looming, the Scottish selectors kept a keen eye on the progress of the first shooting star to appear for years – young Alan Gilzean, a country boy who has become the goalkeepers' nightmare since he joined Dundee. It is refreshing in the days of tip-tap football and insipid shooting to watch Alan spectacularly lashing the ball venomously – and accurately. Of course, shooting isn't Alan's only asset. He looks every inch a footballer and he has craft as well as drive, skill as well as shooting power. He's going to go right to the top.

'There isn't a keener footballer in Scotland than Alan Gilzean. While he is grateful to Alex Young for his help, he is a great believer in self-help. He is naturally right-footed. But he spent so much time and patience strengthening his weaker foot that it eventually became stronger than his right. And to make sure he would get to the top Alan bought himself a ball the summer he came out of the army. He spent it developing his heading, shooting and passing. He enlisted the aid of his cousin Billy Forbes, also a footballer, and every night of the close season the two of them worked long and hard with enthusiasm. We can forecast that Alan Gilzean is destined to becoming a Scottish internationalist.'

Gilzean said, 'When I was a youngster I had two football heroes. They were Billy Steel and Eddie Turnbull. You know how they shoot! I was determined I too would develop a shot. After that it was just a matter of practice – and more practice.' The shoots of Gilzean's international potential were planted when he played for the Scottish League with Andy Penman against the League of Ireland in October 1960 and in an under-23 international debut with Ian Ure in a 1-0 defeat for Scotland against England the following February.

6

Gordon Smith's Red Porsche

ALAN GILZEAN saw a red Porsche parked outside Dens Park when he arrived for pre-season training one morning. He guessed, incorrectly, that it belonged to someone who had just taken over the club. The sports car, in fact, was owned by Gordon Smith, the player who proved to be the final piece in the jigsaw for Dundee's championship-winning team.

Bob Shankly had inherited a promising group of youngsters introduced to the club by his predecessor Willie Thornton, but knew he needed to balance the callow with a bit of been there done that. The Bobbys – Seith and Wishart – had provided it. And Smith, who had won the title with Hibernian (three times) and Hearts, tipped the scales a little more to providing the even distribution of weight required to ensure the greatest prize in Scottish football would be seized by the Dee. He might have been 37 but Shankly knew what he was about as he pulled the masterstroke as Dundee got their man after two previous attempts had failed.

Doug Cowie, the player Gillie hero-worshipped and was honoured to play alongside, had been transfer-listed after 16 loyal years, deemed surplus to requirements. The legendary Dark Blue said, 'I felt I still had a year or two left … however, that was for the manager to decide.' Cowie received a glowing tribute from former team-mate Bert Henderson, who said, 'Cowie was the best player I ever played with – even better than Billy Steel in my opinion.' But it was clearly out with the old, in with the old. And Dundee felt Smith had a few miles left on the clock. Sammy Kean, who had played with Smith at Hibs, said, 'George McGeachie was a tricky little player but Bob Shankly was looking for better service to his big lads, Cousin and Gilzean. Smith was ideal for the job. Unfortunately for McGeachie he was the man to step down.'

Smith was, like Cowie, another player to whom Gilzean bent his knee. Alan displayed his natural propensity to talk about others rather than himself while waxing lyrical about Smith, his arrival and the galvanising effect the winger had on him and the Dark Blues.

Gilzean said, 'I always remember when Gordon came to Dundee. I arrived at training this morning at twenty to ten. There was a red Porsche outside. I honestly thought somebody had bought Dundee Football Club. I never thought it was Gordon Smith. We never knew Gordon was coming. Went inside and found out it was Gordon's Porsche.

'Gordon was an unbelievable guy. A wonderful, wonderful guy. So unassuming. A real gentleman.

'As a boy I was a Hibs fanatic and to me Gordon is one of the greatest players Scotland has produced, because he won five championship medals. Three with Hibs, one with Hearts, one with Dundee. It'll never be equalled again because it is unique for any guy getting five medals not having played for Rangers or Celtic. That record will stand for all time.

'He was such a wonderful player. A natural footballer. So skilful. He was a great boost. Not just to the players in the Dundee team but to the whole fanbase of Dundee Football Club.

'I think he had close to the same number of caps for Scotland as I got in the end [18 to Gilzean's 22]. But he captained Scotland and all that.

'I can remember early on all the big clubs in England were after him. Manchester United, Arsenal, Tottenham, but Gordon stayed true to Edinburgh. We had Sammy Kean [Shankly's assistant] to thank for him coming because Sammy was big mates with him when they played together. That makes you think of the other teams Gordon played for. He played with Busby. All of them. Fantastic.'

The first time Smith showed what he could bring to the party was on a close-season tour to Iceland. He was on target in his first appearance, the opening game, which was a 3-1 victory against KR Reykjavik at the Laugardalur Stadium on 6 July. The Dee beat the country's champions Akranes before, with the help of a Gilzean goal, seeing off their host's national team, whose 2016 equivalent embarrassingly knocked England out of the Euros, with Three Lions boss manager Roy Hodgson resigning after it.

Smith made a goalscoring senior debut in a 3-2 League Cup defeat at Third Lanark on 22 August 1961, with his acolyte Gilzean netting the Dee's other consolation. But the cup competition was to prove a damp squib for the Dark Blues as they failed to get out of their group.

That, of course, allowed the Dee to focus on the league. The opening two fixtures secured wins to put them joint top with Rangers, although Gillie failed to make the scoresheet in either the 3-1 opening victory at Falkirk or the 4-1 Dens derby drubbing of Dundee United, their biggest win over their Tannadice neighbours since 1926. He netted his first of 24 in 29 league games that season in the next fixture but hosts Aberdeen, inspired by future Dark Blue Charlie Cooke, burst the visitors' bubble.

It was a blip as Dundee went on a club-record 19-game unbeaten run in the league; winning 16, the first TEN on the bounce. It proved to be, unsurprisingly, the cornerstone of their eventual title triumph.

Gilzean got into a scoring groove with successive goal doubles against Hearts and Third Lanark, and ensured he made his mark in five matches in a row against Kilmarnock and Motherwell. His last one of the sequence was part of a performance which was eulogised by Gordon Smith as 'the greatest exhibition of football I've ever seen in a club game'.

The Dee were able to show off their A-game of short passing and swift movement developed under Bob Shankly to the nth degree in a 4-2 win at The Steelmen's Fir Park home in front of 15,000 witnesses on 14 October. Shankly summed up the display, said club historian Kenny Ross, as 'our finest all-round display of the season'.

Gillie was not about to disagree with the praise poured on what the classic Dundee XI of Pat Liney, Alex Hamilton, Bobby Cox, Bobby Seith, Ian Ure, Bobby Wishart, Gordon Smith, Andy Penman, Alan Cousin, Alan Gilzean and Hugh Robertson achieved that day. Especially Smith's assessment. Alan said, 'Recalling that, Gordon was a member of the Hibs attack that played so much, that was super-plus, that really meant something to us. We felt pretty good about that victory, for Aberdeen had been the only team to beat us.'

Dundee went into November with a five-point advantage over Rangers, but with their rivals having two games in hand at a time when it was two points for a win, and Gilzean, with Alan Cousin, on 11 goals, thanks, largely, to the service provided by Smith. But the Dee faced back-to-back showdowns with the Old Firm, Celtic and the Light Blues in the biggest tests of their mettle as potential champions.

In these sort of moments such pretenders needed their big players to step up to the plate to show they meant business. Gilzean obliged – and how. Even though he had been on a two-game 'goal drought' during tight wins against Dunfermline and Partick Thistle, Gillie clinched a 2-1 Dens victory over the Bhoys with the second goal (heading home a Cousin flick) – his pal Bobby Wishart netting the first – on 4 November. And he hit FOUR in a 5-1 win over Rangers at Ibrox, that has gone down in Dundee folklore on, coincidentally, Remembrance Day the following Saturday. It was dubbed 'Gillie's greatest game' in a Dark Blues shirt in the official memorial programme for the Dunfermline fixture at Dens Park on Sunday, 22 July 2018. And no wonder.

Dundee, having won their previous seven games, led the table from second-placed Rangers, the reigning champions, League Cup winners and unbeaten in 21. And were boosted facing a team with seven internationals by having won three and drawn one of the previous four seasons in the league at Ibrox.

Dundee fans plotted the journey. British Rail put on a football special from their city's West Station to Glasgow's Buchanan Street, with the fare reduced from 19s 3d (96p) to 15s (75p). And Dicksons Coaches on Reform Street put on buses at a return fare of 12s 6d (62.5p).

But plans were thrown into confusion as Glasgow was blanketed in fog on the day of the match. The rumour mill went into overdrive suggesting the match had been postponed.

The day's equivalent weather forecaster of Carol Kirkwood suggested the fog would clear around midday, three hours before the scheduled kick-off. But the prediction failed to materialise and police turned around the fans' buses under a mile from Ibrox. The rail travellers on the 11.30 out of Dundee, though, had better fortune by default as their return journey wasn't until 6.30.

Ron Ross, Gilzean's friend and schoolmate, said, 'I took the train from Coupar Angus to Glasgow with Alan's cousin Billy Forbes and another guy. Thankfully, we hadn't heard the rumours the match was being postponed because of the fog and saw the game.'

Referee R. Rodger (Stonehouse) only decided to give the match the go-ahead 30 minutes before the scheduled kick-off, deeming the fog had lifted sufficiently. The ground was half empty due to the pre-match shenanigans, but what the 38,000 with enough visibility witnessed was confirmation that Dundee were the real deal in terms of having championship credentials, and that Gilzean had graduated from a prince to a king among the Dens Park faithful who made it to Ibrox's stands and terraces.

It was goalless at the interval. World-class wing-half Jim Baxter had run the Rangers show, moving forward in the opening half. Shankly ordered Andy Penman to attack and force Baxter to chase back at him.

Gilzean put the Dee in front shortly after the restart with the fog drifting back. He headed past Billy Ritchie after drifting to the near post following a Penman cross from a diagonal ball inside the full-back from the breaking, lanky Alan Cousin after Gordon Smith had broken up a Rangers attack.

Soon afterwards Gillie scored his second. Cousin again surged forward to find Penman who slid the ball through for on-running Gilzean to clip home under the onrushing Ritchie.

Gilzean completed his hat-trick with a beauty to light up the gloom after 74 minutes. Unnoticed by the Rangers defence, he ran – first ambling and then darting in that smooth, elegant gait he had – in an arc from the middle of the edge of the penalty area to the near post as Smith swung in a right-wing corner. Getting in front of a home defender, he flicked the ball behind him first time with his right foot, across the back of his left at full speed, facing away from goal, into the far corner. Timing, intelligence, technical brilliance and a killer instinct all combined in a few thrilling seconds.

Ralph Brand pulled one back with a header six minutes from time after a goalmouth scramble following an indirect free kick conceded by Gilzean and Bobby Seith. Gilzean fired his fourth a minute later by seizing on a Penman flick. With his back to goal, the swaying forward allowed the ball to run, drew and dummied a defender as he turned on to his right foot, knocking it to his left and guiding the ball across Ritchie into the far corner. Sublime skill. And Penman completed Dundee's nap hand in what has been rated the greatest league result in the history of the club formed in 1893.

Gilzean said, 'Well, Dundee were really playing so well. Even the year before we won the championship, I thought we had a chance of winning it. And that was before Gordon Smith joined us. We had little guy called George McGeachie who was quick and direct. A very good player.

'We went to Ibrox expecting to win. Whoever we played that season we expected to win. Fortunately the game went ahead because there was the fog that day and all that. We took them apart.

'After that game, there was a break-up of a lot of the Rangers team. Players left the club like Harry Davis, big centre-half big Bill Patterson and Bobby Shearer were more or less coming to the end.

'It was a great thrill to score four. But for me it wasn't the greatest thrill I got. The biggest was when I played for Dundee and we played Hibs at Easter Road [19 October 1963]. I read in Gordon Smith's memoirs that that was his last game at Easter Road. We beat them and I scored all four goals with Gordon in the team. That certainly gave me a bigger thrill than the Rangers game, although the Rangers game was much more important.'

He added, 'It was obviously going to be a hard test for us because Rangers seemed to be our main rivals for the title, but we had a confidence about us and we felt we were as good as, if not better than, any side in the league. We had a run of really good victories behind us and that day at Ibrox we just took Rangers apart. Honestly, it could have been seven or eight. I scored four that day and it was easy to say it was down to me but forwards always get the glory and defensively we played very, very well too. Everything came off for me that day. However, we felt we had better players than Rangers and had gone to Ibrox confident of getting a win.'

Gilzean concluded, 'I finished with four of our five but really it was too easy. I just happened to be there to put the ball home at the end of some great moves. What a topper Gordon Smith was that day. At the age of 37, he was pulling out fleet football skill an 18-year-old would have been proud of. Maybe Gordon was putting on a special show for his wife – it was her birthday.

'As for Alan Cousin, a few years before Rangers had made an offer of £20,000 for him. As he laid on my first two goals they must have had long thoughts!

'I went straight to Coupar Angus from Ibrox and found all sorts of people wanting to shake my hand, saying how glad they were and that sort of thing. When I went for a walk the next day, too, it started all over again.

'But the players who lived in Dundee got it even stronger. Waiting at the West Station were about 500 fans [when most of the team returned to the town]. Many of the people had been to Glasgow, though had not seen the game. They didn't know whether to greet or cheer.'

Ian Ure said, 'My abiding memory of the game is seeing people like Gillie and Alan Cousin coming back through the mist having raided the Rangers goal with their hands up, triumphant, punching the air. I never saw the goals. It was that bad. Just about 30 to 40 yards of visibility. All we could see were attackers disappearing into the mist and coming back with their fists raised. Pumping them in joy. That was quite a victory. A big one. That was the league for us and a great place to do it.'

Goalkeeper Pat Liney also told me how the weather conditions ensured he was blind to Gilzean's goal heroics. He said, 'Gillie scoring four against a team like Rangers was fantastic but I could not see the goals – could only see to the halfway line it was so foggy. I just heard a big roar and finally the players as they ran back into position clapping. We'd just beaten Celtic, now Rangers at Ibrox and I joked to myself, "This is easy, it is no bother getting points off Celtic and Rangers."'

Bobby Wishart said, 'I played in that game. It was very foggy. Dead scared it was going to get abandoned. Somebody in the dark days of television had taken a film of it, and the only time you see me is when a ball is coming down, and I'm missing it altogether! I didn't bother trying to go and buy a copy of the film! Alan's four goals? That was the kind of guy he was. He was a Rangers type of player.'

Even what was rated the most famous league victory in the club's history was not enough for Shankly to consider his talented outfit capable of bringing the title back to Dens by the end of the season. But he was coming round to the idea after a roller-coaster 5-4 home win over lowly Raith Rovers seven days after their Ibrox heroics.

Raith were not expected to give Gillie's boys much trouble given their lowly league position. But the hosts found themselves trailing 1-0 at the interval.

Gilzean netted two in as many second-half minutes and all seemed well. But the Dee defence came apart as the visitors scored three in just five minutes. Five goals had been scored in 13 crazy minutes.

But Dundee showed they had strength of character as Bobby Wishart and, four minutes from time, Bobby Seith put the Dee back level before Gordon Smith sealed the two points seconds from the final whistle.

Bobby Seith said, 'It was a key moment in the title-winning year. Dundee's never-say-die attitude, allied with our undoubted skill, was able to rescue a victory from the jaws of defeat.'

Bob Shankly said, 'It was the season's number-one match.' He added, 'Dundee's terrific fight and last-gasp winner are surely amongst the greatest feats recorded.'

Gilzean never had any doubts about securing the win. He said, 'We just pounded them and pounded them. We got it back 4-3, 4-4 and Gordon Smith hit the winner. The crowd went crazy. It was a great fightback. That was the attitude of the team. We never thought we'd be beat. Even when we were down 4-2 we always thought we were going to win. Guys in the team like little Coxy were so determined. Big Ian Ure was some player as well.'

Dundee sustained their challenge until the end of the year, by which time they had gone unbeaten for 14 games and led second-placed Celtic by six points and were seven in front of Rangers. All, for the most part, with the same XI. Talisman Gillie missed two of those games with a jaw injury before returning for the first match of 1962, a 2-1 win over Falkirk. He wore sandshoes to combat a frozen Dens pitch and was rewarded for thinking on his feet by scoring both home goals.

Gilzean had to keep his sandshoes in the boot room as the frost bit deep enough to cause the opening three games of the new year to be postponed before four league wins on the bounce – extending another victory run to five – maintained progress. The Dark Blues were eight points clear of Rangers at the top on 24 January 1962 when Dundee beat St Johnstone 2-1 at home; Gilzean and Penman on target.

A 1-1 draw with Kilmarnock brought up the 19-game unbeaten in the league milestone after a strained Scottish Cup exit to St Mirren. The invincibles became the not-so-invincibles as avenging Motherwell beat them 3-1. It was the Dee's first league loss in FIVE months. It sparked a losing run of four league games which saw Dundee knocked off the top for the first time since September, falling three points behind Rangers, which left them with no wins in six in the title race. Gillie's goals had dried up. He had not scored since the Dark Blues's last victory, against the Saints.

And he went down with flu on the eve of the return game with Rangers under the lights at Dens on Wednesday, 14 March. It seemed as if things had gone from bad to worse for Dundee. Poor health, injuries and players losing form – plus the loss on occasion of key performers like Bobby Wishart, Bobby Cox and Gilzean – had contributed to what club historian Kenny Ross, borrowing from Shakespeare, dubbed the 'winter of discontent'. But Dundee managed to stem the losing tide with a goalless draw in front of a season's-best home crowd of 35,000. It also stopped Rangers moving five points clear of the Taysiders.

They got back on the winning track, with the likes of Craig Brown and Bobby Waddell coming in and proving their worth. Even with Gillie laid low, they notched successive wins against Raith and Hibs, with Dundee United doing them a favour by turning over leaders Rangers, leaving the Dee just one point behind the Ibrox giants.

And Gilzean returned to help make it three wins in a row, against Stirling Albion, with his first goal in just over two months – one which proved the winner in a victory that restored Dundee to pole position, with Rangers playing in the Scottish Cup semi-final on the day. Shankly restored the main XI for their four-match run-in, with Rangers having overcome St Johnstone to retake the top spot. Dundee beat Airdrieonians as their rivals overcame Dunfermline to go into their Spring Holiday Monday derby against Dundee United at Tannadice one point down on Rangers who faced an Old Firm clash against Celtic at Parkhead. Again, it was Gilzean who proved himself once more the man for the big occasion.

Local pride as well as the title were at stake, but the Coupar Angus native was far from fazed. Even when Jim Irvine put the hosts ahead in front of 20,000 rammed into Tannadice to create an electric atmosphere. Gilzean equalised and it looked as though his side would have to settle for a draw.

But the Dundee talisman belted a 25-yard winner four minutes from time, with the ball bouncing over the head of United stopper Rolando Ugolini. News filtered through from Parkhead, Rangers could only draw 1-1. Dundee were level on points at the top, although second on goal average. Gilzean said, 'That derby win was a huge step for us. It was always going to be a tricky hurdle but, having cleared it, we knew we had an easier finish than Rangers.'

Goalkeeper Pat Liney emerged a hero in the last Dundee home game of the season to help his side move two points clear of Rangers. Alan Cousin had put the Dark Blues ahead against St Mirren, but the relegation-haunted visitors had a chance when Gordon Smith was adjudged to have handled in the penalty area 12 minutes from time. But Liney saved the spot-kick from Jim Clunie, having been told by his Buddies-supporting father that Clunie always hit his kick to the right. Andy Penman sealed a 2-0 home victory.

Rangers losing at Aberdeen the same night confirmed Gillie's would-be heroes only needed a draw against St Johnstone at Muirton on the last day of the season to create club history (nay immortality in the eyes of their supporters).

On Saturday, 28 April 1962, Jimmy Greaves had bagged a couple of goals for Tottenham Hotspur as they sealed a tight 3-2 win against Birmingham City at St Andrew's, having already secured their place in the FA Cup Final for a second successive year, hopes of a successive Double for the north London club having evaporated.

Gillie had come across Greaves first-hand for the first time a couple of months earlier. He was in the Scotland side taking on Greaves's England in an under-23 international at Pittodrie on 26 February 1962. Gilzean got an idea of the goalscoring prowess of the sharp-shooting, quick-witted, jet-heeled striker as Greavsie netted twice in a 4-2 win for the 'Auld Enemy'. Gillie? He drew a blank. When reminded of the details and asked about Greaves being the 'greatest player he played with' he said, 'Yeh. That's right!'

Just over two and a half years later, Alan would forge a prolific goalscoring partnership with Greaves, the pair citing the other as their favourite team-mate to play alongside. But while Greavsie was creating havoc in the Blues rearguard, Alan John Gilzean ensured his Dundee side would rewrite history and secure everlasting fame at Dundee.

No one was making assumptions as the team set off in their bus to St Johnstone's Muirton Park home in Perth, a town where, of course, Gillie was born and headed each weekday morning on a similar mode of transport from Coupar Angus as a 15-year-old clerk.

Dundee dreams of clinching the championship for the first time on the final day of the season had died at Falkirk's Brockville Stadium 13 years before. There would have been many supporters sharing the roads and rails to the St Johnstone ground who had journeyed to The Bairns's base in Hope Street in 1949 and were, therefore, not getting their 'hopes' up.

Gilzean said, 'It was a wonderful day from what I remember. We met as usual like it was a home game. We met at DM Browns for lunch. We set off to Perth. I think it was [in a] Watson's

[bus]. Used to be Dixons and Watson buses. I think we were on the Watsonian.

'I was really amazed with the amount of traffic on the road because we'd left early to make sure there was no traffic but there was a hell of a lot of traffic.

'It was just a wonderful atmosphere. There was tension as always on a big important game. You are nervous. You are not worried because if we played to our ability we felt we were a better team than St Johnstone. We should win. But you can never tell how nerves affects the players.

'We got to Perth. There was a great crowd. A fantastic crowd. And I imagined two thirds of the support there were behind us.'

It was a hot day and most of the 26,500 spectators were in shirt sleeves. Inside the dressing room, Dundee players were dealing with the butterflies in their stomachs. It has also been claimed there was an attempt to 'fix' the game. That word had been passed to the visiting players 'that they could collect £50 each if they made it a draw'. A point would have ensured St Johnstone got the point they needed to stay up. The approach was dismissed 'with contempt' and 'only served to double our determination', according to one affronted player who read the riot act to his team-mates and warned them to pull their full weight. They all did just that. Of course they did. There was never a nanosecond in which they wouldn't. No matter what.

It was a scrappy start on a rock-hard surface. Hardly surprising given what the encounter meant to both sides. But, yet again, it was Gilzean who took responsibility when it mattered most. He gave the Dark Blues a half-time lead by heading home a Smith cross.

Gilzean said, 'I think we just needed one point but when you go one-up they have to get two to beat you. And I didn't think they were capable of getting two to beat us. But yeh, I got the first goal. It was a great cross from Gordon Smith. I got above the centre-half and fortunately for me it went into the back of the net. That settled the whole team. I don't think after that we were in any trouble.'

He said, 'I was told I jumped for joy higher than I've ever jumped to head a ball. Well, I felt great. Next second I was almost bowled over as my mates dashed over to congratulate me. Somehow we knew we were on the way to the title.'

He added, 'My state of mind that day was if you matched them for effort we would get the chances and I was one of the men in the team the rest of the lads relied on to convert these chances into goals. I would back myself to score two out of four and that was how it worked out.'

Just before the hour he made his mark once more to double the Dundee advantage. He latched on to a long Alex Hamilton ball, went round St Johnstone centre-half Jim Ferguson and rifled home. It was his 27th and perhaps most vital goal of the season as it ended the game as a contest. Andy Penman thumped a third – off the bar – in the 67th minute. The Dark Blues played out the remaining minutes in relaxed style before a pitch invasion signalled party time.

There is a famous picture of Gilzean immediately after the final whistle, squashed in by the multitude which squeezed on and obliterated any view of the pitch. Gilzean said, 'It was a wonderful, wonderful feeling you know for the whole city of Dundee because it was the first time they'd ever done it. It was just wonderful.'

He added, 'The scenes at the final whistle were terrific. Within seconds they were on the pitch wildly excited, cheering and clapping us on the back. Others were grabbed and jostled. Bobby Cox and others were grabbed and hoisted shoulder high. Full marks to Rangers too. Soon after we had struggled to the dressing room … the boss read out a telegram from the Light Blues, "Congratulations on winning the league. League champions 1961/62. League champions 1962/63? Rangers." Sure enough, that's how it worked out.'

Gilzean was full of praise for manager Bob Shankly and the experienced heads in the team. He said, 'I was one of a number of young players coming through – Hammy, George McGeachie, Alan Cousin, Hugh Robertson, Ian Ure and by that time we had Bobby Seith from Burnley and Bobby Wishart from Aberdeen and one of my heroes, Gordon Smith from Hearts.

'Bob Shankly had it off to a fine art. He had the nucleus of a good side and brought in the experienced men and, although Cowie was close to a finish at that stage, Seith, Wishart and Smith gave us the experience we needed to make us into a title-winning combination.

'When Rangers whittled down our comfortable lead and moved in front [in the table], Seith, Wishart and Smith calmed things down – their experience meant so much to us during that title run-in. These lads had all been in that position before. They knew what was required. We had a good blend at Dundee. We had bags of skill, we could play football and, if necessary, we could mix it as well.

'We had Ian Ure, Bobby Cox and Bobby Seith who could all look after themselves and we could compete either way. We could do it with brawn, or we could do it with skill and happily it was mostly always with skill.

'Yes, they were exciting days for the club, for the fans, for the whole town because it was the first time Dundee had ever risen to such heights. It was a new experience for everyone and the Dundee public responded.'

But Gillie's euphoria was tinged with sadness due to the result sending St Johnstone down. He said, 'I was a local lad and had a lot of friends who were St Johnstone supporters and the ironic and sad thing for me that day was that poor St Johnstone were relegated. I felt so sorry for them. Our pleasure was their grief.'

Gilzean added, 'Unlike today it was quite common for teams outwith [outside] Celtic and Rangers to win the title. Hibs and Hearts did it often when I was growing up after the war. Then Aberdeen and ourselves and Kilmarnock. It was quite normal. Looking back, Dundee's feat was a bit special. For a start, we only used 15 players during the whole season, most of whom had been signed by Willie Thornton. He must have had some scouting system.'

Cox said in *Dundee Greats* it was his greatest moment in football. He said, 'We knew we had some great players … the youngsters had matured [over the previous two seasons]. Bob Shankly's judgment was sound and he moulded a great team.'

Goalkeeper Pat Liney appreciated the show of affection, which saw players carried shoulder high by jubilant fans at the whistle at Muirton, but suffered. He said, 'I nearly died that night when the crowd ran on the pitch. Jumping on our backs. Round our necks. I passed out. Aye. Terrifying. I thought I was going to get killed! Once they left me alone I came round. It was a great season. We'd got used to winning that season with Gillie scoring loads of goals,

Alan Cousin getting a few too. What a day it was at Muirton. What a celebration.'

Ian Ure recalled in *Up Wi' The Bonnets*, he had a friendly £10 bet with Gilzean before the match that the striker would not score two goals. He said, 'I have never been so happy to lose £10.'

John Duncan, who won that Gillie nickname by following his hero up front at Dens Park and White Hart Lane, was among the crowd swarming and swaying in the giant tidal wave of humanity after that final whistle.

He said, 'My Dad had taken me. It was an unbelievable feeling when we went on the pitch. Phenomenal. And being on the pitch it felt unbelievable. It was just phenomenal for Dundee to win the league as they did. And Gillie had just got two. I remember him scoring a header for the first one he got. A special day. I went to most of the home games as a fan that season, although playing school football limited me for following the side away.'

Dave Forbes joined in too – in between work shifts. Forbes said, 'I was in the police at the time. I'd come off a night shift and went to the game but was back on night shift the same night. But it was tremendous to be a part of it. The team played brilliant football that season. It was a great time to be a Dundee supporter.'

Sir Alex Ferguson, who became one of the greatest managers of all time by guiding Manchester United to unprecedented success, was in the home line-up that day. Beavering away in the St Johnstone forward line without reward, while his opposing number ten, Gillie, was leading his front line to glory. Fergie said, 'Dundee at that time were a team without a conspicuous weakness, an amalgam of all the attributes needed to win a championship.'

* * *

Gilzean missed out on a call-up for the full Scotland team while Dundee team-mates Ian Ure, Alex Hamilton and Hugh Robertson were selected. But in February 1962 he had been selected for a Scotland v Scottish League trial with Hamilton, Bobby Seith, Ian Ure and Alan Cousin. He also gained a Scottish League cap and represented Scotland under-23s.

7

Ahead of Eusébio

ALAN GILZEAN proved himself a world-class performer and goalscorer in the European Cup. He finished as one of the top scorers in the 1962/63 European Cup. He hit a hat-trick on his debut and, overall in the competition, was three ahead of Portugal legend Eusébio, who led defending champions Benfica to the final and vied with contemporary Pelé as the greatest player on the planet.

Gilzean finished among the leading scorers and his NINE goals helped ensure Dundee emulated the run of future employees Tottenham Hotspur to the European Cup semi-finals a season earlier. But when asked to recall the campaign his thoughts went back to Dens Park. He said, 'These European nights were very special. The Dundee public turned out in their thousands and, although we had a very good side, the atmosphere generated by the huge crowds was a tremendous lift.'

But his remembrances also took in the bad and the ugly besides the good as the Dee first dipped their toes into the continent's premier club competition for what has proved the only time to date. The club securing its first – and still only – Scottish League title in 69 years of existence had gained them entry into a tournament then limited to the champions of the countrie's affiliated to UEFA and title holders. The Dark Blues completed the domestic task with class and style, but there were not many predicting they would rip it up against continental opposition.

They were out of touch as they kicked off the 1962/63 season. It was a case of after the Lord Mayor's show. They had been given a civic reception at the City Chambers for their championship success early in the season but lost five of their opening seven games – the first at neighbours United – in a period which sped them to a League Cup group exit. Also, Gilzean was among six of the title side to turn down £25 a week to re-sign (a problem eventually resolved). And new signings, goalkeeper Bert Slater and winger Doug Houston, from Liverpool and Queen's Park, were having to settle in as Shankly tried to refresh his starting XI. Championship-winning stopper Pat Liney, immediately displaced, wondered what he had done wrong while helping create club history. Immortality was always an illusion, mind, but banishment to the reserves so swiftly seemed hardly just reward.

Gilzean said, 'There is no doubt Pat was very unlucky to be discarded, through no fault of his own. I put his plight in the same category as a guy at Spurs, a centre-forward called Les Allen, who scored over 20 goals when Tottenham won the double. And the next season he was in the reserves because the club brought back Jimmy Greaves from Italy. That's what being a manager is all about, making tough decisions. Who's to say Pat would not have performed just as well [as Slater in Europe]?'

Also, their only recent experience of playing European teams had been limited. Over the previous two years they had played Friendship Cup games against Valenciennes (a 1-0 loss away and a 4-2 win at home) and an 8-0 friendly victory against Elfsborg from Sweden. That was it.

Political and economic international ties were not especially close with the continent. The United Kingdom was 11 years from joining the European Union (then known as the European Economic Community) and remaining a member until talk of 'Brexit-ing' it blew up at the end of the second decade of the 21st century. Of course, there was also the added problem of balancing the defence of their title and going after the Scottish Cup and League Cup against forays in foreign fields.

The Dee had to play catch-up and fast with only one player, Gordon Smith, able to boast European Cup experience, with Hibs

– making the last four with the Easter Road outfit – and Hearts. Perhaps Tottenham might have been consulted, with the north London club having established links with the Dee through their 1959 capture of Dark Blues goalkeeper Bill Brown. After all, Spurs were plotting a campaign which would see them become the first British side to lift the European Cup Winners' Cup after securing their second successive FA Cup in the May following their eye-catching continental debut.

Dundee certainly gleaned information on the sort of football they could expect first-hand on a close-to-six-week pre-season tour to the United States. The Scottish League had invited the Dark Blues to represent them in a New York tournament. It was an honour usually given to whichever team was runner-up, but with Rangers favourites to lift the trophy when the nomination went in The Dark Blues got the nod. Results included defeat against West Germany's Reutlingen (2-0) and a draw with Yugoslavia's Hajduk Split, and Italians Palermo (1-1), while also overcoming Mexico's Guadalajara 3-2 and losing by the same scoreline to America from Brazil. But Gilzean believed the 'learning process began' during the trip even though the results were far from impressive.

And Ure remembered the slow build-up of Reutlingen as a lesson learned in how continental outfits played the game. He said, 'The American thing was a real eye-opener, but it served us well for the European Cup.' The opposition which lay in wait, though, might have considered a draw against a team which had been considered relatively provincial, certainly next to the Old Firm, a gimme.

But any in ignorance were made to pay as the Dark Blues marched through their European campaign with a brand of football lauded by respected Scottish commentator Bob Crampsey, who believed it better than the 1967 Celtic team – including future Dee player and boss Tommy Gemmell – which became the first British side to win the European Cup.

And they also had a not-so-secret weapon in Alan Gilzean. Certainly not so secret in his native land and, if Arsenal's interest was anything to go by, south of the border too. It was one thing to be a free-scoring striker in domestic football, but it could be another on the international club scene.

Yet, like the proverbial duck to water, Coupar Angus's greatest sporting export immediately eased into the role. The nine goals he netted on the new adventure seemingly reflected his lack of concern for the reputations of the opposition faced, although there were occasions when his generally unruffled demeanour was ruffled.

First to face the G-Man was Cologne, the West German champions rated favourites along with five-time winners Real Madrid and holders Benfica, who had beaten Spurs in the last four en route to successfully defending the trophy in the previous campaign. Surely it was David versus Goliath? Well it depends on who was playing Goliath on an unforgettable occasion at Dens as the Dee first dipped their toe in European Cup water on Wednesday, 5 September 1962.

Cologne general manager Karl Frolich had come across to find out about accommodation, training provisions and the Dee's on-field form. He was impressed with the first two items, but not the third, having seen their hosts lose to Celtic and Hearts, telling *The Courier*, '[Dundee] were bluffing, and couldn't actually be that poor.' Team boss Zlatko Cajkovski was predicting victory as his side – with ten internationals – played 'decadent' football.

The visiting support – waving flags and banners and blowing trumpets – expected the hyperbole to reflect reality. And, it is understood, Dundee players had to psychologically reassure themselves by reverting back to the V-neck shirts in which they had won the championship, associating the newly adopted crew-neck version with the miserable start they had made to the season.

There were 25,000 crammed into Dens Park as the sides were led up by a pipe band performing the Dee anthem 'Up Wi' The Bonnets'. In the air, there was the resonance of freshly penned lyrics in tribute to the title heroics as captain Bobby Cox led his Dark Blues out, namely:

You can sing of the glories of teams you have seen,
Of the Saints or the Dons up in old Aberdeen,
But in all this fine world there's but one team for me,
It's the bold boys who wear the Dark Blue of Dundee.

(Chorus)

Let the proud Rangers sing of the records they hold,
Let Celtic proclaim all their heroes of old,
We will follow and follow o'er land and o'er sea,
For the brave boys who wear the Dark Blue of Dundee.

For there's many a battle been fought on this field,
And there's many teams learnt that Dundee never yield,
For on all odd occasion defeat we must know,
We will rise up again and we'll beat every foe.

Chorus

Oh there's Robertson, Penman and Alan Gilzean,
With Cousin and Smith they're the finest you've seen,
A defence that is steady, heroic and sure,
Liney, Hamilton, Cox, Seith and Wishart and Ure.

Chorus.

Bob Shankly had decided to put his faith in ten of those players, including Gillie, with Pat Liney still kept out by Bert Slater. It was only the second time he had fielded the line-up that season. The first time saw them defeat Celtic in the opening home match at which the League Flag was unfurled in recognition of the championship triumph, having tried other combinations with limited success during the opening encounters.

It resulted in what few would argue was the greatest result in Dundee FC history. A jaw-dropping 8-1 victory, which created a record for British clubs against German outfits in the European competition, one that still stood when Pep Guardiola's Manchester City went within a whisker of it by crushing Schalke 7-0 in the same competition on 12 March 2019.

Any doubts surrounding Gilzean's ability to rise to the level required were dispelled by a hat-trick of headers with a Matthias Hemmersbach own goal, Bobby Wishart, Hugh 'Shug' Robertson,

Gordon Smith and Andy Penman adding to a scoreline which must have shaken up non-believers on the continent.

Gilzean's first – Dee's fourth – came from a Smith cross. And he completed the home scoreline with two more headers, from Alex Hamilton and Alan Cousin crosses, as the hosts fed the wings and got in 23 shots to the opponents' six.

The Dundee cause was aided by visiting goalkeeper Fritz Ewert being knocked out after colliding with Alan Cousin in the second minute. The brave visiting stopper continued but was clearly not right. After Andy Penman forced Hemmersbach into putting through his own goal for Dundee's first, Ewert saved a divot of flying turf instead of the ball as a Wishart miscue made it 2-0 before Dundee added three more prior to half-time.

Cologne were reduced to ten players when they were forced to substitute Ewert for full-back Tony Regh at the interval with the dazed and confused keeper reportedly believing the score to be 2-0 when it was in fact 5-0 to the hosts, a lead extended by a further three goals before the visitors were consoled when Alex Hamilton diverted a Ernst-Günther Habig cross past Slater.

Spectators poured on the pitch as Gillie and co lined up to clap their opponents off the field at the final whistle. Shankly said, 'I am delighted but the boys rose to the occasion as I expected them to.' The visitors' shocking humiliation dented Cologne's pride and it appeared the Germans were still smarting when Dundee arrived in town for the second leg. They certainly did not appear to be rolling out the red carpet for their visitors in Gilzean's eyes – to put it mildly. It was clear even Cologne's inhabitants were thirsting for revenge.

The hotel attendant taking Gilzean and Robertson to their room at the team hotel 'made the well-known cut-throat gesture, drew his finger across his windpipe'. Gilzean said, 'That was the first indication we had that ahead of us was a frightening football experience. One that made us realise to what depth continentals would go for big-money competition. One none of us will ever forget.' The German media played its part, with Cologne players talking up the 'revenge mission'. And, according to Gilzean's seemingly stylised comments in *The Post*, it had used a picture to 'stir up trouble'.

He reportedly said, 'I'm continually recalling something else that happened – and seeing red as I think about – like the picture in the newspaper. Now there was really something. The paper was laying around in the hotel lounge and I think I was the first to spot the picture on the back page sports section. Now all footballers know how the camera can work remarkable tricks. I often get a laugh at the gestures and attitudes it registers in press pictures. But here was a freak shot being used to stir up trouble.

'Like all continental teams, Cologne had brought a batch of photographers with them to Dens Park. Shooting off pictures all through the game. They must have taken home hundreds of shots, including plenty of the incident in which their goalkeeper Fritz Ewert got an injury which kept him off all the second half.

'One of these was taken at an angle which made it appear that Alan Cousin jumping for the ball was deliberately punching Ewert. And hadn't the Germans made the most of it. It was a deliberate attempt to KO their goalie, they claimed. These Dundee players will go to any length to win, they said. Most of us just laughed about it. And Alan Cousin, the man who never pulls anything in the least shady, took a bit of kidding. But there was nothing funny about it. We were soon to find that out.'

Gilzean revealed the visiting party also had difficulty training. He said, 'When we started to talk about a training session shortly after arrival there came another cold blast. We couldn't have Müngersdorfer stadium where we were to play. It was owned by the city and closed every evening at 5pm. The only other floodlit pitch was ash-surfaced. And Cologne's own training ground was being used by one of the club's minor sides. I could see Mr Shankly was having a hard time keeping his temper in check as all these yarns were trotted out. But there was nothing else for it. We had to make do with a short session next morning – the morning of the game.' Perhaps it was mind games, trying to upset the opposition enough to put them off their game when it mattered.

Gilzean would be the centre of their attention on the field, with Karl-Heinz Schnellinger, who missed the first leg through injury, man-marking him. Schnellinger was recognised as the world's best left-back. He figured in the position representing the Rest of the World against Jimmy Greaves's England as the English FA celebrated its centenary in 1963. And returned to Wembley with a number three on his back as his West Germany lost to the hosts in the 1966 World Cup Final. But on this night against Dundee he was deployed as a right-half to shackle the Dee's main strike threat, Gillie.

Gilzean said, 'I felt this hardy lad was there for my special benefit as I'd managed three goals in that first game.' The plan worked but the hosts were unable to overturn the deficit, having to settle for just a 4-0 win. But beyond the bare scoreline, Gilzean outlined countless negative stories which underlined why he felt the whole experience was like the worst of nightmares.

Cajkovski had been quoted in the German press after the first leg as saying that the unexpected might happen 'if, say, the Dundee goalkeeper was injured'. And when an ambulance was put behind Slater's goal, it seemed threateningly inauspicious. Slater, it was reported, suffered a few clenched fists in the ribs before being caught behind the ear by the boot of Christian Muller as he dived at the feet of the Cologne striker.

Shankly assistant Sammy Kean came on to attend the stricken goalkeeper and, as blood seeped from the injury, called for the bench to treat the keeper. German medics tried to get Slater into the ambulance but the stopper jumped off the stretcher to get to the dressing room and temporarily return on the wing with Andy Penman deputising between the sticks. Gillie described Slater as 'most courageous'. It was damage limitation for the visitors in testing and intimidating conditions in front of a vociferous 40,000 supporters as they were 'kicked and punched' by the opposition.

Gilzean said, 'It was a horror film. X-plus. [After a tackle] they'd lie on the ground. So still I thought we had a fatality on our hands. The crowd lapped it up and screamed their heads off. With a chorus of hate increasing every minute of the game.'

The crowd, realising their team was out, clambered off the terraces on to the track up to the touchline as Dundee tried to play out time, struggling to take throw-ins and having Gordon Smith supposedly tripped up by an encroaching fan.

Gilzean said, 'The officials ignored it. No one did anything. I decided I would dash for it at the final whistle. My team-mates were thinking the same way. All I got was a kick or two on the way back to the pavilion [thanks to the help of hundreds of off-duty British soldiers who volunteered their services as bodyguards to help guide them].'

He reported Bobby Cox and Ian Ure were struck by folding chairs and the Cologne players showered their opponents with water as they went by the home dressing room. And the Dark Blues declined to attend a post-match reception, and that even the receptionist back at their hotel gave them a volley of abuse.

Gilzean said, 'She'd gone to the game. "You dirty dogs", she kept shouting. Charming people. It was a relief to get away from Cologne the next morning. But deep down we also had a wonderful feeling of satisfaction. We had beaten Cologne, one of the favourites for the European Cup. It did our morale a power of good. We felt we could hold our own now with any club.'

Gordon Smith said the match at the Müngsdorfer stadium was 'the dirtiest in my 22 years of football'. Ian Ure described it as a 'right dog fight' but insisted 'we didn't turn up that night, apart from a few defenders. I was f-ing and blinding that night, I can tell you!'

Gilzean found it calmer as the Dee cleared the next two hurdles. Dundee were pipped 1-0 by hosts Sporting Lisbon in front 48,000 fans in the Portuguese capital on Wednesday, 24 October.

But a Gilzean hat-trick sealed a 4-1 win in the second leg at Dens a week later to secure a quarter-final spot, Cousin completing the home scoreline. The Coupar Angus native was a happy bunny.

He said, 'What a contrast to Cologne [when in Lisbon]. The Portuguese people went out of their way to help us. They gave us a practice ground to ourselves – and a bus to get around in. And the game was one of the cleanest I've ever played in. How nice it was too, to be congratulated by the Sporting players in English. They had obviously swotted up their "Thank you. Good game". We reckoned we'd try to return the compliment at Dens Park. We found out that to express such sentiments in Portuguese the word is "obrigado" and that is what we said.' The guests were delighted with their reception, if not the result.

Gilzean led the way yet again with his goals, despite a cut above the ankle which required six stitches as Dundee overcame Belgium's Anderlecht 4-1 in the first leg of their last-eight showdown at the Heysel Stadium in front of 64,703 to earn a standing ovation from the home fans (the same stadium which was the tragic scene of the deaths of 39 fans at the 1985 European Cup Final between Liverpool and Juventus, a disaster which led to English clubs being banned from European competition for five years). Gilzean said, 'The forwards took a lot of credit but defensively we were outstanding.'

Cousin and Smith also scored, as they did in the second leg when a last-four date with AC Milan was sealed. Gilzean said, 'Anderlecht were a delightful team. Technically probably the best we met in the competition. And Dundee folk still remember the sporting bunch of fans they brought with them for the second leg.'

Dave Forbes, Gillie's pal, Dark Blues fan and director and event organiser, remembered a story Gilzean told him about the first leg in the company with Bobby Wishart and Ian Ure over breakfast after a dinner he had organised for the ex-players at Invercarse Hotel in Dundee.

He said, 'You saw the real Gillie. He told how Bob Shankly remonstrated with him at half-time with Dundee 2-0 up. How people defended him and said, "He's scored two goals, boss." And Shankly said, "He wouldn't have f****** scored them if he had played the way I wanted him to." Shankly had tried to play a defensive game as it was the away leg.'

To put the overall achievement in perspective their Belgian opponents had overcome the Real Madrid of Di Stéfano, Puskás and Gento in the previous round. It underlined the quality of a Dundee side proving they belonged in the best of company. Ian Ure was bullish about believing the Dee could get by Milan and make the Wembley final. And no wonder. Unfortunately, for the Dee the wheels came off in front of 78,000 at the San Siro on 24 April 1962. Dundee lost 5-1.

The build-up was not ideal. Dundee were having to play at least two matches a week due to fixtures postponed in practically a 'whiteout' in the opening two months of the year. And inspirational skipper Bobby Cox suffered a torn cartilage at Motherwell four days before the first leg. Hugh Robertson was also injured.

Milan were awash with talent. Italian internationals Jose Altafini, who was to become a two-goal final hero and also play for his native Brazil, skipper and defender Cesare Maldini, father of future Rossoneri icon Paolo, centre-half Giovanni Trappatoni, a Republic of Ireland boss from 2008-13, and striker Gianni Rivera.

And the record books show that Dundee, with Bobby Seith leading in place of Cox, were beaten after going in 1-1 at half-time, with Alan Cousin having struck an equaliser. But, for Gilzean, it was more than just losing a match. He was left with a series of bitter memories.

Dundee complained about flashing cameras distracting Dee keeper Bert Slater and second-half goals against them they felt should not have been allowed. Gilzean recalled a few more grievances – although omitting how he himself was subjected to 'rough treatment' by Milan – in the ghost-written four-parter in the *Sporting Post* in 1964.

That a 'suspicious' and 'voluble' Italian tried to gain entry to the Dundee dressing room shortly before kick-off to 'stage identity passport checks', with Bob Shankly closing the door on him; that the atmosphere was intimidating, the 'amazing feeling' of stepping out 'on to this field … it was like being in giant bowl. Hemmed in by a mass of sound that included trumpets, crawmills [rattles to frighten cows] and an occasional thunder flash. Far worse than Hampden.'

The match provided a litany of injustices in the eyes of the visitors due to the performance of Spanish referee Vicente Caballero who was, according to club historian Kenny Ross, found 'to have accepted extravagant gifts from the Italian club and banned from officiating pending charges of bribery'.

Gilzean said, 'Well, how we lost 5-1 is an old story. We didn't play well, I admit that. But the referee! A lot of hard things have been said about continental referees. Señor Caballero deserved them all. I've never seen anything like what he did. Right from the start he blew for a foul anytime a Dundee man went for the ball. No, I'm not overstating it. That was the state of the party. The least physical contact was a cert for a whistle against us. With the crowd following the lead and howling at us, the effect was so upsetting that before long we were almost afraid to even consider a tackle.

'Ian Ure in particular got a raw deal. Ian always believes in the he-man but fair approach to the game. Señor Caballero had different ideas and they created havoc in our usually reliable defence. High balls, which nine times out of ten Ian would cut out became a nightmare. He was scared to go in for them – particularly when they were landing in the penalty area. And how the Milan wing-halves and backs played on that. Into the penalty zone came long accurate despatches and with forwards bearing down on him, Ian, caught in two minds, often floundered – also unlike himself.

'We were a downcast lot after the game and at the banquet which followed. It lasted until after 1.30 in the morning and gave us a chance of seeing the stern discipline of Italian clubs at work. Around 12.45 one of the Milan players wanted to get away home. He went over to the team coach's table [Nereo Rocco, who had been Jimmy Greaves's nemesis during Gillie's future team-mate's nightmare spell at Milan two years earlier and one reason the Scot was to opt against a move to Italy] and made his request. The coach gave him a mouthful – interpreted later as, "You'll go home when I say it not before" – and a hearty shove into the bargain. That was that. The player stayed put. With morning we felt better and despite that 5-1 against us began to feel maybe we can do it yet with the good old Dens Park crowd behind us.'

The Dundee faithful tried to do their bit for the Dark Blues – 38,000 squeezing into the ground on Wednesday, 1 May 1963 but it proved mission impossible on another evening which left Gilzean with plenty to complain about. This time he did comment about the treatment he received, with the visitors adopting a policy of containment on a hard pitch in blustery conditions.

Dundee, who had upped their game from the San Siro, were constantly frustrated by the deep-lying visiting defence as foul after foul broke up play before Gilzean headed home a Smith cross just before the interval, enough to win 1-0 on the night. But he was sent off for retaliation six minutes from time as the dark arts employed by their opponents appeared to get to a normally calm performer.

Gilzean, in a ghosted interview, said, 'Well, we beat them. The only team in the tournament to do so, but, as it was only by the goal I scored myself, it wasn't enough. But it was another night when things happened that should never happen on a football field. The first time I was on the ball, [Peruvian international Víctor] Benítez, the Italian right-half, gave me a nifty one the referee didn't see. Next time I was on the run he let me pass and then whipped me up. I decided to have no more of it, I'd get in first. From then on we were narking away at each other. Not that we were the only ones. Some of the Italian tackling was as bad as anything in Cologne, with Gordon Smith getting the worst of it.

'After the interval things cooled off. Then I clashed with Benítez once again. [He] went sprawling to the ground. Referee Lucien van Nufell of Belgium came running up to me, turned me round and looked at my number. "Number ten," he said in broken English, "My decision is OUT!!" And he repeated it, "Out! Out! Out!"

'By this time my mates realised I was being sent off. "You can't do that ref," they tried to tell him. "Not after what has gone on before." But Monsieur van Nufell was adamant. "Out! Out!", he repeated. And "Out" it was. Otherwise the game might never have restarted. I went off the pitch to a sympathetic cheer from the crowd, but it was my most humiliating experience. It had never happened. For me, it was a particularly sad end to our European Cup bid.'

Gilzean, like he had done in the previous season, continued to rack up the goals on the domestic front, including a hat-trick against Raith Rovers and doubles versus Dundee United, Forfar Athletic, Third Lanark, Clyde, Montrose and Rangers.

His most notable achievement in Scottish football that campaign was scoring SEVEN goals in a 10-2 crushing of Queen of the South in the league at Dens on Saturday, 1 December 1962. It equalled the club record for goals scored in one match by Bert Juliussen in 1947 and was just one behind the Scottish League record created by Celtic striker Jimmy McGrory in 1928. He also set a league record of six goals in the first half.

Self-deprecating, Gilzean deflected praise away from securing such a haul by saying, 'Mind you, they had goalkeeper George Farm carried off that day [at 3-0].'

He added, '[Farm] dived at my feet to save. His head hit my knee. What a smack. George lay still – out cold. He was carried off on a stretcher and taken to the infirmary. After the game I went to see George. As soon as I got to his bedside, George said, "I've heard the score. How many did you get?" It was just about the most embarrassing moment ever to tell him – seven.'

Gilzean adopted a similarly modest approach in November 2014 when Dave Clarkson honed in on his Dundee record of scoring in seven consecutive matches. But on the eve of Clarkson's bid to do so he rang Bob Hynd. Hynd said, 'Gillie asked me whether I knew Dave and to tell him, "I hope you beat my record". I told Dave, who equalled but didn't beat it. He got seven in seven but Gillie neglected to tell me he'd got 12 in seven [hat-tricks against Motherwell and Queen of the South and two versus Third Lanark].'

Gillie, combined with his exploits in Europe, netted an astonishing 41 goals in 43 games in the 1962/63 season. The Dee's bid to retain the title might have fallen away to mid-table due mainly to the distraction of the continental adventure and the disruption caused by postponed fixtures, but it was clear the Gilzean goal machine remained well oiled.

8

A Man for All Seasons

THE WHITEHALL Theatre in Dundee was built in the roaring 20s as a theatre for 'am-dram' types and those who enjoyed intimate surroundings to watch the new cinema phenomenon of talking pictures in the wake of the release of *The Jazz Singer* the previous year (1927). These days the venue set on Bellfield Street close to the River Tay has offered family, music and professional theatrical entertainment from *Babes in the Wood* pantomime to the edgy comedy of Jerry Sadowitz via evenings with journalist and TV host Sir Michael Parkinson, pop band The Revolvers and SAS leader and sniper Mark 'Billy' Bingham. Variety very much alive.

On Thursday, 20 April in 2017 at 7.30 in the evening the survivors of Dundee's 1961/62 title-winning team took to the stage for the 'Night of Champions'. Among them was Alan Gilzean. The £5 entry fee was probably the best bargain to be had in modern times for the Dee football fans and those who cared about the kudos Gillie and his team-mates brought to the city on the east coast of Scotland.

Gillie was always the star attraction at such gatherings and this night was no exception.

He looked well. Smart, dressed in a dark suit, starched white shirt and a Windsor-knotted dark blue-an-white-striped Dundee FC tie.

It was to be the last major public event in the city for the former Dark Blues striker, so iconic a Dundee fanzine *Eh Mind O Gillie* was named after him when it came out in the 1990s.

Fortunately, the club's television channel was there to record an interview for posterity in a white-walled anteroom; one which was not posted on the Dundee FC website until the 20 July 2018, the day of his funeral.

And Gilzean appeared to revel in the opportunity – albeit probably hiding the traditional edginess he always used to feel when the centre of attention – to talk about his team-mates and what they achieved during their time together in the Dark Blues. His memory was crystal clear when recalling happenings over half a century earlier with great fondness.

We have already revealed his feelings on the momentous moments he experienced with the Dee in the 20-minute chat conducted by club historian Kenny Ross. But it appeared it was the individuals he bonded with to produce them all who mattered most to him.

He sat there intently listening to the questions behind his thin-rimmed spectacles, a wisp of white sideburns peeking out from below their arms. His head moved from side to side as he spoke. Increasing in speed, accompanied by an involuntary licking of the lips and occasional smile, as emotions took a tighter grip.

We have read how Gilzean waxed lyrical about the signing of Gordon Smith on the eve of the championship-sealing season. That he was an 'unbelievable guy', 'unassuming', a 'real gentleman', a 'natural footballer,' 'so skilful', 'a great boost'. He also praised how Smith led the way in adapting diet to suit the professional footballer.

Gillie said, 'Gordon was one of the first guys apart from the Italians who always watched their diet, what he ate and all that. Guys at Dundee used to go into DM Brown's for pre-match meals and that. We had fish. No chips. Or steak. Gordon wouldn't have touched all that.'

But his opinion was equally as positive about his team-mates – although there was an affectionate, tongue-in-cheek negative remark pertaining to a specific area of right-back Alex Hamilton's game – and manager Bob Shankly.

Like Dundonian skipper Bobby Cox, the left-back who had a stand named after him at Dens Park along with Shankly.

Gilzean said, 'Bobby was very similar to Doug Cowie. He never talked much but led by example, was a good trainer. Trained very hard. On the pitch he was a wonderful player, a wonderful full-back.'

Never got a cap? He said, 'When you think of some of the players who got Scottish caps at full-back … some Rangers guys and Celtic guys. You couldn't match Bobby Cox. So sad that Bobby never got a cap. He deserved it.

'He was a wonderful tackler, sliding tackles and all that. I never saw Bobby Cox have a bad game for Dundee, especially if you are up against good wingers like Jimmy Johnstone, Willie Henderson and all them. I never saw anybody who could take Bobby Cox to the cleaners.

'In the [Scottish Cup] final [against Rangers, see chapter nine] they switched Willie Henderson to the other wing so he'd go against Hammy. Hammy's the most capped player for Dundee. He's got about 26 and he was a big pal of mine – we were big mates, but he couldn't tackle. Bobby Cox was a wonderful tackler. And Hammy got about 26 caps and Bobby got none. You see? Where's the justice, eh? A wonderful, wonderful player.

'Big Ian Ure I think had a basic wage would be 28 quid a week. Shankly used to pay around a £30 bonus for some big games. Christ! Urey was nearly breaking down the door to get on the park. That's the kind of guy he was.

'Big Ian, he was some player. As the players went on the field at Dens there used to be two dressing rooms and a wooden area where the guys used to clean the boots. I've seen Ian Ure in there when it was wet and keeping the ball up there for a thousand times in an area [looking around the small room he was in] no bigger than this. Foot to foot.'

Ure won the Scottish Footballer of the Year award – selected by the respected Rex Kingsley of the *Sunday Mail* – for the calendar year of 1962. Deserved?

Gillie said, 'Yeh. When you think of the clubs he had. He went to Arsenal and Manchester United. That's not a bad selection of clubs.

'Alan Cousin and Hughie Robertson were the engine room of the Dundee team which won the championship. Alan Cousin covered more ground than anyone else on the park. A wonderful player. I tell you what, he wasn't half good at shielding the ball and all that.

'When I came in the team at first he helped me so much. He told me what to do. And Shug Robertson was exactly the same. He was just like a little guy who had been wound up before the match. Wind him up and he ran and ran. He was unbelievable.'

How did Cousin compare to Jimmy Greaves as a strike partner? Gilzean said, 'They were different types of player. Greavsie – unassuming like Gordon Smith – was an out and out goalscorer. Alan could defend and everything. When he left he went to Hibs. So shocked when he died [aged 78 on 20 September 2016]. I thought he'd at least go to 80.' And Gillie poignantly added, 'You just don't know what's round the corner do you?'

He described his Dundee team-mates as a 'special group of players and we were all good mates'. Gilzean concluded, 'I've been lucky because I've been with Dundee and Tottenham and with both teams ALL the players got on well.'

The love and respect Gilzean had for his Dundee colleagues was mutual. Pat Liney's views reflected that.

Frank Sinatra's voice was wafting out of small speakers in Liney's front room as I entered the family home, a small, white, neat bungalow bathed in sunshine in the village of Invergowrie four miles west of Dundee, the winter snow of recent days having receded. Dundee's championship-winning goalkeeper was a decent crooner himself judging by the small-framed poster promoting one of his gigs on one of the front-room walls. He clearly wowed them with his singing back in the day. But this day he limited his voice largely to singing the praises of Alan Gilzean after switching the CD player off and boxing the disc.

While we spoke, his delightful wife Ruby – born Rubina – dug out pictures and cuttings from the days her husband was in the spotlight before Bob Shankly thought him surplus to requirements for the first-team, replacing him with Bert Slater for the title defence and the European Cup campaign of 1962/63.

He had been resting his eyes while Ol' Blue Eyes's mellifluous tones filled the room but now he was wide awake. Liney, a gentle, kind and friendly soul, laughed off the suggestion of any bitterness he might have felt at being unable to line up with Gillie in the Dark Blues's continental and domestic adventures.

He said, 'It didn't do me any favours but it didn't hold me back. Just got on with it. Bert wasn't a bad signing for them.' Indeed, Ruby seemed more aggravated by the memory.'

The former goalkeeper loved the time he had with Gilzean from the moment they first played together in a goalless league draw against Rangers at Ibrox on 6 February 1960.

Liney said, 'Gillie had a good sense of humour. Wasn't a show-off. So easy-going and friendly, even in the dressing room before games. He always seemed relaxed. Yet on the pitch he'd give the last ounce of energy to get something good out of a situation.

'He was quite young when he got in the team and we started playing together. Made a big impression very quickly. Some of his goals were unbelievable. [He] was always leading goalscorer from his first full season, seemed to have the knack of putting the ball in the net. Either in the air or on the deck, so good with headers.

'[He] always used to turn up in the right place at the right time. He timed his jump so well when a cross came in. He was up there before the ball waiting to head. A great technique [honed from all that practice back in Coupar Angus, no doubt]. A lot of players jump and it just hits their head and goes away.

'The whole forward line were great at laying on the goals. Alan Cousin was good at long runs, not sharp ones. A fit guy. Two good wingers. The great Gordon Smith. Gillie spoke to me about him. As good an individual player as Gillie, another one-off, he was already so famous but a quiet, gentlemanly guy.

'We had another good inside-forward in Andy Penman. It was brilliant.'

Liney, though, reckoned there was no guarantee Dundee would have won the title without Gilzean. He said, 'It would have been a possibility, but I wouldnae be sure of it because sometimes one man can make a forward line. You can have a team of average players and a good striker and he could make you a winning team. But we had good players all around.

'Beating Celtic and Rangers back to back was obviously a big boost. There were those four goals which I couldn't see against

Rangers and those celebrations at Muirton [the site now an Asda supermarket]. Beating Dundee United. A golden time.'

But Liney confessed to having an inferiority complex when it came to Gilzean. He said, 'I know it sounds silly because he was my team-mate, on the same level as me and the way he was – such a nice, lovely guy in every way – but at the time we were winning the title I felt Alan was a bigger star. To me Gillie was someone to honour. He was one of the best in Britain at the time. The best-ever Dundee player I've seen. Definitely. There might have been some earlier like Billy Steel, but nobody as good since.'

Liney wondered why Dundee made it difficult for Gilzean to leave (more later). He said, 'Gillie didn't really talk to me about it. He'd been a good servant. I'd have thought they'd have encouraged him to better himself. If you are in the reserves you want to play for the first-team. If you are in the first-team you want to get your side higher in the table. It's how you get on in ANY job. It's trying to take the next step up and Gillie was ambitious.'

Liney was delighted Gilzean's career panned out like it did. He said, 'When he first got in the team he scored a lot of goals from crosses. Heading the crosses and corner kicks and things like that. And everybody thought 'he's just a big striker' banging in the goals.

'But when he went to Spurs he was the playmaker for Jimmy Greaves and people like that. And how many people in British football could be a leader at one club and yet when they go to a top club like Spurs could still be their leader. Unbelievable. He is thought of highly at Dundee and Tottenham and there aren't many players who can say they have had the same reaction from all their clubs.'

It seems Gilzean's powers of leadership reflected the sort of characteristics so important to manager Bob Shankly who once said of the sort of player he wanted, 'I look for character. I want lads with guts and go, who won't crumple when things don't go their way.'

The rest of the championship XI – with new signings – continued to play alongside him for the Dee on their European Cup adventure and beyond. Bobby Wishart, who remained a best friend throughout Gilzean's life after they first met at Dundee, believed his pal was the 'man for all seasons'. Wishart was alongside him through the golden years of the club in the early 1960s and saw him play for Spurs.

He said, 'They beheld him at Dundee. He was such a good player. I played behind him. Wore the number-six jersey behind him all the games. And he was probably next to the great John Charles, who was probably the most complete footballer. Alan would have slotted very closely behind him.

'He could do a lot. He did the lot for Spurs. He could lay on goals. He could score goals, he suffered the stigma of "very good in the air" and all that. But he was very good on the ground as well. He could read the game as well. Martin Chivers and Jimmy Greaves got the benefit of his foresight. And he scored plenty of goals for Spurs and Dundee. Yeh, he was the complete article. A modest man. Knew he could play – there was no doubt about that. Never gave you a bumptious impression. He was always just quietly confident.

'There was a journalist who wrote for *The Scotsman* up here, John Rafferty, who was, in my book, a very good journalist. And when Alan signed for Spurs, he wrote an article and said, "It is sad to think that here in Scotland that we've seen the last of the swashbuckling Gilzean". I thought, "What the heck does he mean by that?" But Alan was the kind of player that if you were a goal down he would pick the ball on the halfway line, beat a couple of guys and fire a 25-yarder up into the top corner of the goal. He was so exciting. Swashbuckling.

'He was very instrumental in Dundee's title win and European Cup run. I don't know how many goals he scored. He was the man for all seasons. He could turn on the football. He was well known in European circles in his first season. In the semi-final against AC Milan, that midfield guy Benítez was just there to antagonise Alan. Eventually Alan gave him a belt in the jaw and got sent off! They pinpointed him as the danger man.'

Ian Ure was rated as the other star turn during Gilzean's halcyon time at Dens Park. The centre-half was the first of them to get a big move to the English league, joining Arsenal in 1963 before moving on to Manchester United six years later. But he knew who was number one in the affections of the Dee public. He said with a smile, 'He was the Brylcreem boy in attack, wasn't he? I was the coal-face miner in defence. You always get a better write-up as a forward.

'I signed in 1958 at the time Alan was coming back from his National Service, which I missed as I was slightly younger. First impressions? Awful nice guy. Smashing player. Had a wee bit of everything in him. A great all-round footballer. One of the best I've ever seen in the air. Quite something. He didn't necessarily head for goal all the time. He could direct the ball to a player in a better position –particularly good at that. Great left foot too.

'The team that did well in Europe was very good all round. But he was our main striker. Alan Cousin scored too and they fed off each other. Played brilliantly together. Both good in the air and could shoot. A nice mix that team. We almost played the modern game before the modern game was invented. Short, quick passing in tight areas. I miss the time.'

Ure thought Gilzean joined a more than useful outfit in Spurs. He said, 'The original Spurs team of the early 1960s was probably one of the best club sides I've ever seen. Dave Mackay in particular was something else. A one-man team. There was Bill Brown the goalkeeper who had come from Dundee, of course. We played against each other regularly when he went to White Hart Lane. I was there until 1969. He went a year after me. He wasn't directly up against me. Not an out-and-out striker like he was at Dundee.

'He was in a very much better team than ours. Arsenal were a pretty disorganised team for the first three or four years. We were all singletons. Too many cliques. A "them and us" feel. Attack scored the goals, defence kept the goals out. Forwards could score but weren't trying to stop the other team scoring. War of attrition as to who scored most or gave away most. Until Dave Sexton arrived at Arsenal it was pretty chaotic.

'Alan and I would have a wee blether after the games we played against each other, but he and the other Spurs players went back to the Enfield area, we went back to the Southgate area. There wasn't a lot of contact between Alan and I living in London – never really caught up that much. When I went to Man Utd we played against each other but it was like when I was at Arsenal. We never really came into direct contact on the field.'

Bobby Seith, the other survivor of the early-1960s glory team, insisted his team-mate was a class act on and off the field. Seith said, 'Alan was an exceptional striker for Dundee and Tottenham, but that never changed him. He was always the same nice lad. I think that was one of the strengths of the Dundee team that won the championship – we were all good friends. There were no cliques in the dressing room and none of us let our success go to our heads. I remember when Alan was at Spurs and I was manager at Hearts, we played them in a friendly. He was a big star, but he was exactly the same as he was when we were at Dens.

'Alan was exceptional and a great header of the ball. His timing in the air was the thing and when he jumped he seemed to hang in the air. We knew that if we could get the ball to his head he would score goals. At Dundee he had a fine partnership with Alan Cousin and he would have been the first to say Alan Cousin's donkey work was responsible for him scoring as many goals as he did. With Alan, though, it was not just about his heading, he had two very good feet as well. In fact, I was never sure whether he was left- or right-footed. He had the knack of being in the right place at the right time. He always seemed to know where to be, that's why he scored so many goals.'

Physio Lawrie Smith believed everyone at Dundee got on well with a fearless footballer who felt unadulterated pleasure from performing, hitting the target. Smith said, 'Gillie experienced pure enjoyment from playing good football and was good at what he did without being big-headed. Confident in his ability. Had no fear of anybody. He applied himself by training hard, keeping himself fit.

'The team reflected his confidence in what they were going to do as a team. If they went one down it didn't bother them. A lot of sides went to Parkhead and Ibrox frightened. Not Gillie's Dundee team. I've seen both sides because I was at Rangers for three years.'

9

Times They Are A-Changin'

IT WAS BUSINESS as usual for Alan Gilzean when he started his last full season with Dundee. Goals, goals, goals.

He created a Scottish scoring record by securing 52 for Dundee in 48 games in the 1963/64 campaign. It took a UEFA Golden Boot winner in Henrik Larsson to eventually break it; the Celtic striker netting one more in 2000/01 while securing his continental prize with 35 league strikes as his Parkhead side secured the title.

In all, Gilzean totalled 55 that term including international goals.

His 20/20 vision to aid his focus on the back of the net helped Dundee reach the Scottish Cup Final at Hampden Park, scoring nine in the campaign to match his European Cup total of 1962/63.

Gilzean managed a hat-trick in round two as Brechin City were bulldozed on their own pitch 9-2 after he had netted to help the Dee see off non-league hosts Forres Mechanics, founding members of the Highland League the year Dundee FC was born, 6-3.

He fired a double as Forfar Athletic were flattened 6-1 at the Dens on 15 February. The first equalled the club record of 39 home goals scored in one season set by Alec Stott in 1948/49 before the ace sailed past the milestone with his second and a single in a 4-2 replay victory at Motherwell which helped secure a last-four date with Kilmarnock at Ibrox.

Gilzean converted two chances as the Dark Blues killed off title-chasing Killie 4-0.

Rangers lay in wait on 25 April for the Dee's first cup final since 1952. Stages do not get much bigger with 120,982 packed into Hampden. The gladiators entered the arena in changed strips as their regular colours clashed. Dundee were in all white and Rangers in blue and white stripes, white shorts and red socks. Dundee had more than just hope. They had only lost three in 19 matches since back-to-back reverses at the start of January – and the hottest striker in the land. Yet Rangers had already sealed the championship and the League Cup and could boast one loss in 16 under former Dundee player Scot Symon.

But any hopes Gillie and the boys had of adding more silverware to the Dundee boardroom's trophy cabinet proved illusory.

The Dee began brightly in the rain but Rangers's pressure game turned up the pace and the tension, and upset Dundee's rhythm. And frustratingly for the 25,000 Dundee fans squeezed into the national stadium, Gilzean was tightly marshalled by his international colleague John Greig.

The Dark Blues's outstanding stopper Bert Slater kept Rangers at bay before being beaten by a Jimmy Millar header from a Willie Henderson corner on 71 minutes. Kenny Cameron immediately levelled and it seemed as if Dee would force a replay.

But Millar headed a second from a cross by Henderson, another Scotland colleague of Gillie's, the right-winger having switched flanks to deliver it.

And Dundee were caught out searching for a second equaliser when Ralph Brand made it 3-1 with Henderson again involved.

It might have all been different but for an injury to Gilzean.

Gilzean said, 'I had a good chance to put us ahead but Ronnie McKinnon blocked my effort and unfortunately I injured my ankle. Little Bert played brilliantly that day and he kept us in the match.'

His goal touch was the spark which lit up Dundee's league season. He helped the Dark Blues make an impressive start, taking 21 points – at two for a win – from their opening 14 fixtures by the tail-end of November. Jock Stein, the fabled Scottish manager then with Dunfermline, noticed the Dee had a 'new-found hardness'. It seemed a season without commitment in Europe was doing the Taysiders a favour.

Gilzean was scoring for fun. He had netted 15 in as many games in all competitions when he pulled on his dark blue shirt displaying '10' on its back in the Easter Road dressing room on Saturday, 19 October.

Gillie was preparing for a league encounter with childhood favourites Hibernian, which would give him a bigger 'thrill' than the day he netted his quartet at Rangers on route to the title. He found the target FOUR times in a 4-0 dismantling of the hosts alongside former Hibs favourite Gordon Smith making his last appearance at his old haunt. His third goal in particular stirred up the imagination, showing his delicate touch and cool presence of mind. He got to the ball ahead of home stopper Ronnie Simpson but decided to chip the ball over his own head with his right foot and lob Simpson with his left.

He had helped Dundee to third, one point behind Kilmarnock and three behind Rangers by 7 December. But four defeats in five dented hopes of a second title in three years, before back-to-back defeats after an unbeaten seven-match league run landed the knockout blow to them.

But, whatever, Gilzean carried on scoring. He netted his FIFTH hat-trick against St Mirren as his side secured their second 9-2 victory of the term, although there was an unsavoury postscript with the match featured in a bribery case brought against St Mirren.

Gillie reached 50 goals with another double, in a 5-2 home league win over Partick Thistle seven days before the cup final.

* * *

But times they were a-changin', to quote the title of Bob Dylan's song released in 1964, for the Coupar Angus native turned Dundee icon. May 1963 saw Gilzean unsigned and Ian Ure and Alex Hamilton putting in transfer requests. Ure insisted he would 'never kick another ball' for Dundee after failing to agree terms.

In the close season, Hamilton came off the list, deciding a move might harm his international career. Gilzean? He put his signature to a new Dens deal so his faithful Dee fans still had the opportunity to see him plundering goals once more in dark blue. But the unrest he was part of proved a sign of things to come.

Gilzean saw the title-winning XI begin to break up. Pat Liney accepted he had no first-team future after a season of reserve football and moved to St Mirren and Ure completed his switch to Arsenal for a Scottish record £62,500 on 22 August 1963.

It seemed Billy Wright's Gunners had been impressed enough by Ure from when Arsenal took on the Dee in home and away friendlies in the February and March of the previous year. Wright, though, following the precedent set by George Swindin, sustained a Highbury disinterest in Gilzean – on show in both encounters – for a second time.

Bobby Wishart said, 'We drew 2-2 down in London – they got a soft penalty at the end because it was a friendly and would produce an acceptable result. Arsenal weren't a good side and I couldn't help thinking that if they had any official there who knew a football player he should be making a bid to get Alan Gilzean. Arsenal missed a chance of a lifetime in my opinion as Alan was to show with his performances against the Gunners over the years.'

Another team-mate, Craig Brown, said, 'Alan played very well against Arsenal. He also did the same in a friendly against Tottenham. It gave him the knowledge he could compete at their level.'

Shankly's great squad was cracking up. Gordon Smith, close to 40, and Bobby Wishart had been displaced in the team and the former was granted his request to be released. George McGeachie moved to Darlington in January 1964.

* * *

Full international recognition arrived for Gilzean – belatedly, in the eyes of many experts. His first cap came against Norway in a 6-1 friendly win, alongside future Spurs team-mates Bill Brown, John White and Dave Mackay, at Hampden Park on Thursday, 7 November 1963. The match from which Gilzean donated his shirt – with the number nine on its back, Denis Law taking his now customary position at number ten – and cap to his Coupar Angus school the following year.

But it was not a goalscoring debut. Alan had to leave it to Mackay, captaining his country, to net two and an irrepressible

Denis Law to fire a Gillie-like FOUR. Even so, he caught the eye without bulging the onion bag as he did on his first competitive appearance for Scotland's senior side in a 2-1 win over Wales in the Home International Championship at Hampden on 23 November 1963.

But soaring to head the only goal of the game against England on Saturday, 11 April 1964 assured him iconic status in the whole of Scotland. Most of the 133,245 inside Hampden Park and millions of other proud compatriots watching their television screens and listening to Kenneth Wolstenholme and George Davidson commentate for BBC Scotland experienced sheer ecstasy.

Gilzean glided in a hip-swaying motion rather than merely walking out on to the pitch after the briefest knees-up jog and nerve-easing shake of the arms amidst the Hampden roar emanating from the heaving terraces, with thousands wearing tam o'shanters and waving tartan flags. He looked every inch the matinee idol with his tall, slim build, dark hair and brooding good looks in a tracksuit top over his shirt. Immediately behind him was John White.

He tested Gordon Banks with a cross, which the England goalkeeper let slip, with skipper Bobby Moore saving his stopper's blushes by beating Law to the loose ball.

Gilzean was denied the opportunity to take on Jimmy Greaves and Bobby Smith when the Spurs duo were forced to pull out injured, yet took full advantage of Maurice Norman, the pillar at the heart of the Lilywhites defence, and Banks for the 72nd-minute winner.

He kept his eye on an inswinging Davie Wilson corner from the left, which bobbled in the strong wind, moved forward, sprung into the air and hovered to bravely flick the ball home with his head as Norman and Banks jumped and challenged a fraction too late.

Alan said, 'It was a very, very wet day and a very close game. I had a couple of chances. I hit one really well but Gordon Banks made a very good save. My opponent was Maurice Norman, later a team-mate at Spurs. This corner came over from the left. I got there first, headed it down and it was in the back of the net. That was a great feeling.'

Banks, who went on to win the World Cup with Moore and sadly passed away on 12 February 2019, praised Gillie for his stealth and trademark finish in difficult conditions.

Banks said, 'This was my first match at Hampden, and I had often heard stories that whenever there is a strong wind it gets locked in the Hampden bowl and plays all sorts of tricks with the ball. On this day, there was a gale of wet wind swirling around the game and it was a nightmare trying to decide whether to come off my line for crosses and centres in case the ball suddenly changed course. Davie Wilson fired a corner kick high into the six-yard box.

'It was a goalkeeper's ball all the way and I shouted "mine" as I left my line to collect it. But suddenly the ball was trapped by the wind and stopped as if it had brakes on it. I was left clutching thin air as Alan Gilzean stole it in front of me and nodded the ball into the net with what was his speciality flick header. As the ball went into the net I swear the Hampden roar could have been heard way down over Hadrian's Wall.'

Gilzean's goal ensured a third successive victory over England, the first occasion this had been achieved in 80 years.

Craig Brown, a Dundee team-mate who became Scotland manager, said, 'It was a great header which beat England that day. That gives you a knighthood in Scotland if you beat England. You are a hero forever. I remember it. Oh aye. EVERY Scotsman remembers it. I was just there as a fan. To get a game at that level [as a Scottish League player] and not be in the Old Firm of Celtic and Rangers was a wee bit unusual.'

It was Denis Law, rated by many to be Scotland's greatest player, who was the usual main man for his country, as he had proved against Norway, of course, albeit under friendly fire. But he was happy to be upstaged by Coupar Angus's finest, whose effort proved to be the match-winner on a wet and stormy afternoon against the 'Auld Enemy' in Glasgow.

I caught up with Law at his home in Manchester where he is such an icon from his 60s heyday with the city's team in red, United. There is a statue of him alongside George Best and Bobby Charlton outside one of its two world-famous football grounds,

Old Trafford. Law made light of the recognition, joking, 'I look okay from the back.'

He was equally self-deprecating about an inquiry as to when would be a good time to call him if I needed any more information further than that obtained this day. He laughed, 'About four in the morning – that's usually when I have to go to the toilet!'

Law said, 'Every time I played with Gillie he was fantastic. What a fabulous player he was. It was an honour to play alongside a guy like that. He was one of the best ever to play for Scotland. When you play alongside good players like that the game is easy. When you play alongside players who are not that great it's hard.

'It was always a huge international game when it was against England whether it was in a competition or not. For Scotland to beat England was fantastic. And, of course, he got the goal in front of 133,000! Who plays in front of a crowd that size?

'It was a dream to be selected for the international team as Alan, myself, John White and others were, but to play alongside each other in front of 130,000-plus was a huge prospect for us – and frightening for any opposition. Guaranteed. It was a wet and stormy day? Excuse me! That's Scottish weather! An everyday occurrence! In the game in those days the weather didn't really matter anyway. You were playing for your team.'

Law felt Scotland's victory was against the odds. He said, 'It does make a difference when you only have a population of five million in the country while England's was around 55 million. It makes a big difference. If you get a decent team together you are doing well. It makes playing for them extra special. Alan was very proud of his heritage.

'The home countries championships was a big deal without doubt. It was also a time the English FA Cup was one of the biggest trophies ever. Everybody in the football world wanted to play in the final at Wembley for it. But the game has changed. They stopped the championships because there were less players coming out of the home countries. Players began coming from abroad.

'It was like a World Cup final anytime you played for your country. It was an honour which didn't come to many people. You were just delighted to play alongside whoever it was. But when you played with a terrific player it was even better. And Alan Gilzean was a terrific player.

'We were fortunate to have some good players like John White. What a fantastic player he was. He would have become one of the best ever if he had not been tragically struck by lightning. Another magnificent player for Scotland too was Dave Mackay. A big pal of mine. There were a few of the Scottish guys who played for Spurs.

'Before I forget – because I never liked goalkeepers I played against! – there was Bill Brown, of course, who went from Dundee to Spurs. He was there during Gillie's time at White Hart Lane. It was always a pleasure to play alongside all of them. You always played with good players. You had to be one to be selected.'

In between Gilzean's full Scotland debut against Norway (playing alongside Dundee defender Alex Hamilton, as he did for his first eight caps) and THAT match-winner, Gilzean lined up with future Spurs team-mates (Bill Brown, Dave Mackay and scorer John White) against others (Cliff Jones and Mike England) as Wales were pipped 2-1 in a Home International at Hampden on 20 November 1963.

Gilzean upped his international credibility on 12 May 1964 when he netted a goal double in a 2-2 friendly draw in Hanover in front of 75,000 against a host West German team that included three members of the side defeated by England in the 1966 World Cup Final, goalkeeper Hans Tilkowski, Wolfgang Weber, whose goal forced extra time at Wembley, and two-goal skipper Uwe Seeler.

He was on target in his fifth and final Scotland appearance while with Dundee on 25 November 1964. It sparked a comeback 3-2 Home International victory from 2-0 down against a George Best-inspired Northern Ireland, who had Pat Jennings in goal, in Glasgow.

Gilzean had begun to rub shoulders with players who were enjoying a higher profile with fatter pay packets in the English league while on Scotland duty. He shared rooms with John White, the superstar midfielder whose link play and goals had helped establish Spurs as arguably the greatest British club side to draw breath, beating a glory, glory path to the Double, back-to-back FA Cups and the European Cup Winners' Cup.

White was tragically killed by a lightning bolt on Crews Hill course in north London on 21 July 1964. But his son Rob, a photographer, author and Spurs season ticket holder, is convinced his father played a part in Alan Gilzean signing on at White Hart Lane five months later.

White, who wrote a biography on his dad with esteemed writer and Spurs fan Julie Welch, entitled *The Ghost of White Hart Lane: In Search of My Father,* said, 'As far as I'm aware your story that he roomed with my dad then is correct. Gillie was telling me that when I met him [at *The Spurs Show* podcast at Dingwalls in Camden, north London on Monday, 9 December 2013] and we chatted for about an hour.

'It was the first game my dad and him roomed together, I believe. There was talk. He wasn't being tapped up. But I think Bill Nicholson had definitely given my dad instructions to tell him what a good life it was at Spurs and how he would fit in well to the system. There was definitely some persuasion done by my dad to get him along to Spurs.

'Gillie was looking forward to playing up front with Greavsie but also being supplied with opportunities by my Dad.

'Bill saw Alan play quite a few times, I've been told. He was methodical. Bill was the same with my dad. Knew a lot about him. He asked Danny Blanchflower, "What was John White like?" after Danny's Northern Ireland had played Scotland. Danny said, "He was outstanding." Bill said, "I've got a chance to sign him." Danny said, "You should get up there and do it." The story with Gillie sounds similar.

'I'd been slightly apprehensive about meeting Gillie. Maybe it was from a memory from when I first started going to White Hart Lane in the 70s. I was about ten and might have been with my Mum. There was a bottleneck in the bottom foyer by a staircase leading up to the players' wives tearoom. A scrum. The players entrance was close by and when Gillie came out of the dressing room he said in a real heavy Scottish accent, "It's like f****** Piccadilly Circus in here."

'I told him the story when I met him at *The Spurs Show* (more later) and added, "That was the first time I'd heard an adult swear!"

He could not have been further away from this fearsome character I'd imagined. He was very, very warm. A really good guy.'

Gilzean himself confirmed John White's part in his move to White Hart Lane at *The Spurs Show* his Scottish team-mate's offspring attended.

He said, 'I was John White's roommate with Scotland. It was John who really talked me into signing for Tottenham Hotspur. I was greatly indebted to John for doing that. Unfortunately, I didn't have the pleasure of playing in a white shirt with him.'

And added, 'He [White] would tell me what he was earning and I would tell him what I was getting and believe me there was a big, big difference.'

Ian Gilzean said, 'Vaguely remember learning about Dad going away with Scotland and finding out what players were earning down in England and wanting to prove himself in a different arena. You would have looked at the English league those days and seen it more competitive and that there were a lot of quality British players. He thought, "Hold on a minute, I've got to get down there."'

Denis Law underlined the point. He said, 'I'm sure John and Alan talked wages and what it was like south of the border when they roomed together for Scotland. I think it gave Alan the spur. Don't forget London is a different world even to the rest of England. Completely different. And Spurs had a high profile. To have Scottish players playing down there must have influenced Gillie to go there.'

But it was far from a straightforward transition from Dark Blue to Lilywhite. Dundee turned down his transfer request on 28 June – two days before the end of his contract – and he refused to re-sign for 1964/65. Bob Shankly knew how big money offers had tempted away star attractions Jimmy Gabriel and Ian Ure from Dens Park and was determined Gilzean would not join them out the exit door. There was an impasse. Dundee refused to pay his wages and Gilzean, following a precedent set by Ure the previous season, claimed dole money.

Dundee lost four of their opening five games in his absence. Ian Gilzean said, 'Dad was on a one-man strike. Back then when your contract ended clubs could keep you if they offered you exactly the same terms. Clubs could say "we'll sell you" or "we'll keep you". They kept your registration. You couldn't go anywhere. But Dad wouldn't sign. Terrible system? Yes, but that's the way it was. People find it hard to understand now because of "Bosman". Then there was no Bosman ruling [which came into force in 1995 allowing freedom of movement for players at the end of their deals].'

Gillie agreed a mutually beneficial two-month contract with Dundee later that October, although he was ineligible for the European Cup Winners' Cup campaign – secured as runners-up to Rangers who entered the European Cup as title winners – which faltered at the first fence against Real Zaragoza. He had missed the 15 August deadline and a late Dundee bid to overturn the ruling failed.

Close friend Bob Hynd said, 'Gillie was reluctant to go back to the Dens because he felt Dundee fans would hold it against him that he'd walked out and tried to sign on. Nobody did though. He was just a hero to Dundee supporters. And Dundee had done well out of him, anyway.'

Gilzean used those two months in the shop window to impress any would-be suitors if Dundee relented and agreed to listen to offers.

Gillie hit a goal double for a Scotland XI – including old army mate Ron Yeats – in a 6-2 victory against Spurs in a memorial match for John White on his first visit to White Hart Lane on 11 November 1964. He said, 'I was impressed with the whole set-up both on and off the pitch.'

He added, 'At the next home game [a 4-0 win over Aston Villa] the Tottenham fans had these banners up, "We want Gilzean!" And so Bill Nicholson obliged!'

His impressive performance in a fundraiser for White's family might have made the mind up of Bill Nicholson that Scotland's G-Man might be the player he needed to link up with the English version, James Peter Greaves.

But Rob White, son of Spurs legend John, hinted Nicholson might have been weighing up whether to sign Gillie or his dad's younger brother Tommy, who was with Hearts, and netted a goal guesting in the first half for Spurs before switching sides for the second.

White said, 'There was talk about it. Tommy had been reasonably successful with Hearts.'

Gilzean scored his fourth goal in five international appearances as Scotland defeated Northern Ireland at Hampden Park on 25 November and representatives of Tottenham, Torino, Sunderland, Wolves, Liverpool and Everton were listed as being present to cast their eyes over him.

And, club-wise, Gilzean's mind was firmly made up. He declined to sign another contract, short-term or otherwise, with the Dark Blues. It underlined the player still wanted to move on to the next stage of his career.

He said, 'Eventually you would come to the conclusion that you would have to move and unfortunately that was the break-up of a great Dundee team. At the time there were no long-term contracts and I came to the end of my contract and I had talks with Shanks to see if he could come up with terms that would suit me. But in my heart of hearts I knew I had to go … if you recall the history of Dundee they don't win things on a regular basis … obviously I was an internationalist by then and I thought that might even affect my position with Scotland.'

Dundee caved in and cocked an ear to those interested in signing their prize asset. Spurs manager Bill Nicholson had been impressed with Gilzean's displays in Europe and – with legendary sports journalist Jim Rodger, a Mr Fix It, informing the player of this fact, according to Gillie in *Dundee Greats* – put in an offer which was rejected.

Nicholson said, 'I watched many strikers leading up to Christmas 1964 before deciding on Alan Gilzean. From the moment I first asked Bob Shankly, the Dundee manager, for a price the talks dragged on for three weeks and three times I had to raise my offer.'

But Torino and Sunderland also wanted Gilzean's silky skills and eye for goal enough to put in offers.

Gilzean informed Bob Hynd, the Dundee director, in recent years that Torino had offered him £60 a week, Sunderland £56 – plus reported bonuses of £20 for a win and £10 for a draw – and Spurs £54, while Dundee were willing to give him £48.

Welcome to Alan Gilzean's home town

'Babs' Gilzean, Alan's mum, (bottom row, middle) in the Coupar Angus 'tatty' fields

'Willie' Gilzean (front row, far left), Alan's dad, dressed for a formal function

Gilzean's first home: 25 Strathmore Avenue, Coupar Angus

Gilzean's last family home in Coupar Angus: 2, Stuart Crescent

Gilzean (bottom left, crouching) with Coupar Angus schoolmates

Gilzean's school today

School sign

Gilzean's classroom today

Ron Ross, Gilzean's school team-mate

Jim Thomson, Gilzean's classmate who helps run the Coupar Angus Heritage Association

Gilzean (front, row second right) in scouts' football team

Gilzean (far right) with the scouts

*Jack Scott,
Gilzean's scout
master today*

Foxhall Park where Gilzean first played club football

*Gilzean
with Coupar
Angus
Juveniles /
City Boys
(front row,
second right)*

Gilzean (front row, second right) with Coupar Angus Juniors

Norman Bannerman, friendly with Gillie through kickabouts on The Common in their home town, being his patrol leader in the scouts and his newsagent. He also knew his parents

Gilzean with pupils and staff when he returned to his old school to present his 'alma mater' with one of his Scotland international shirts in 1964

Bob Hynd, a close friend of Gilzean and a Dundee FC director, was a pupil at Coupar Angus school, when 'Gillie' donated the shirt. Hynd displays the top in the playground where Gilzean impressed schoolmate Ron Ross.

Alan Pattullo, brought up close to Coupar Angus and a fine writer who secured the first major interview with Alan Gilzean in around 40 years and got to know him in his final years

Coupar Angus native and Gillie fan Lloyd Brown outside the Abbey Church where the Gilzean family grave is located

Gilzean's iPhone showing text exchanges between himself and Bob Hynd

Coupar Angus today

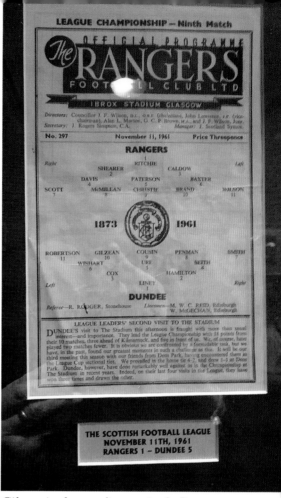

LEAGUE CHAMPIONSHIP – Ninth Match

OFFICIAL PROGRAMME

The RANGERS

FOOTBALL CLUB LTD

IBROX STADIUM GLASGOW

Directors: Councillor J. F. Wilson, D.L., O.B.E. (chairman), John Lawrence, J.P. (vice-chairman), Alan L. Morton, G. C. P. Brown, M.A., and J. F. Wilson, Junr.
Secretary: J. Rogers Simpson, C.A.   Manager: J. Scotland Symon

No. 297   November 11, 1961   Price Threepence

RANGERS
1
RITCHIE
Right   SHEARER   CALDOW   Left
                 2   3
        DAVIS   PATERSON   BAXTER
          4   5   6
SCOTT   McMILLAN   CHRISTIE   BRAND   WILSON
  7   8   9   10   11

1873   1961

ROBERTSON   GILZEAN   COUSIN   PENMAN   SMITH
   11   10   8   9   7
      WISHART   URE   SEITH
        6   5   4
           COX   HAMILTON
            3   2
Left   LINEY   Right
                       1

DUNDEE
Referee—R. RODGER, Stonehouse   Linesmen—M. W. C. REID, Edinburgh
                                          W. McGECHAN, Edinburgh

LEAGUE LEADERS' SECOND VISIT TO THE STADIUM

DUNDEE'S visit to The Stadium this afternoon is fraught with more than usual interest—and importance. They lead the League Championship with 18 points from their 10 matches, three ahead of Kilmarnock, and five in front of us. We, of course, have played two matches fewer. It is obvious we are confronted by a formidable task, but we have, in the past, found our greatest moments in such a challenge as this. It will be our third meeting this season with our friends from Dens Park, having encountered them in the League Cup sectional ties. We prevailed in the home tie 4–2, and drew 1–1 at Dens Park. Dundee, however, have done remarkably well against us in the Championship at The Stadium in recent years. Indeed, on their last four visits to the League, they have won three times and drawn the other.

THE SCOTTISH FOOTBALL LEAGUE
NOVEMBER 11TH, 1961
RANGERS 1 – DUNDEE 5

Dundee goalkeeper Pat Liney holding a picture of the club's championship-winning team, which included himself and Gilzean

Gilzean in the team line-ups in the Rangers v Dundee programme for November 1961

Gilzean heads one of his four goals against Rangers at a foggy Ibrox in 1961

The Sporting Post *reports on Gilzean scoring four goals against Rangers*

Gilzean celebrates Dundee title triumph with team-mates. Back row, left to right: Pat Liney, Gordon Smith, Alan Gilzean, Bobby Wishart, Ian Ure, trainer Sammy Kean, Bobby Seith; Front row: Andy Penman, Bobby Cox, Alex Hamilton, Alan Cousin, Hugh Robertson

Prior to 1961, the maximum wage cap in England was in force.

But the shackles had long been untied by the time Gilzean sat in Bill Nicholson's car by the River Tay talking terms after the Spurs boss had driven the near-500 miles from Tottenham to Dundee.

Bob Hynd said, 'What Spurs offered was a huge amount anyway. Gillie told me the £54 plus bonuses were three times what the average working man was earning. Little compared to now, of course, with players earning five-figure sums a week in Scottish football.'

Fortunately for Spurs money was not Gilzean's only consideration. Even when Nicholson admitted apologetically to him he had misinterpreted the rule book over bonuses, insisting the limit was £4 for a win and £2 for a draw and 'wouldn't go above that' to quote Brian Scovell's *Bill Nicholson: Football's Perfectionist*.

Gilzean wanted to win silverware. Play at Wembley. Taste glory at a club with the best chance of tasting it on a regular basis.

Gillie dismissed the interest from Torino, having knowledge of the negative experiences of British players tempted by the bigger money offers to perform in Serie A. And he felt Sunderland did not meet the criteria of being serial visitors to the national stadium.

Tottenham, steeped in glory during the early 1960s, was his best option for making his childhood dreams come true. Gilzean said, 'Well, first of all I asked for a transfer from Dundee. Because basically, as a young lad, my ambition was to play at Wembley in an FA Cup Final.

'Dundee didn't want to sell me. Then, eventually, they allowed me to leave. But they wanted me to join Sunderland. And I looked down at Sunderland's record of going to [the old] Wembley and in my lifetime they've only been there once [winning the FA Cup in 1973, while excluding the 1990 Second Division play-off defeat against Swindon Town].

'I had the chance. I talked terms with Torino but it was just after Jimmy Greaves and Denis Law had played in Italy. I talked to Greavsie and he said it was like a prison sentence. He didn't like it at all. Also talked with Denis Law [who played for Torino] and Denis said it wasn't for him. And Joe Baker was also there. They didn't fancy it.

'The money they [Torino] offered was very good, but I'd played for Dundee in the semi-final of the European Cup home and away against AC Milan. The tactics they used against us were terrible. They were gobbing in your eye. Horrible. I don't regret turning them down because I had ten wonderful years at Tottenham.

'It was after the great Double side and I wanted to come to Tottenham. I'd been three months on the dole as Dundee wouldn't let me go or pay my wages. Eventually, Bill Nicholson agreed a fee with Dundee and I met him in Dundee to complete the deal. I decided Tottenham was my club.'

Ian Gilzean recalled conversations with his Dad over the leaving of Dundee. He said, 'We asked him, "Why didn't you go to Italy? You must have been off your rocker!" He told us, "I wasn't going to go there." [I] think Jimmy Greaves and Denis Law told him he wouldn't like it, that the football and training was so different.'

Gilzean signed off his Dundee career with a hat-trick at Dens Park on Saturday, 5 December 1964, just three days before Gilzean-less Dee were knocked out of the European Cup Winners' Cup against Real Zaragoza in Spain.

St Johnstone again provided the opposition in a landmark game. And he went one better than the day his two goals clinched the title for Dundee with a headed treble, his 17th Dundee hat-trick, a record. Ally Donaldson, the Dee stopper that day, said, 'I remember playing in Gillie's final game against St Johnstone at Dens. Gillie scored three goals. He was a hero to many including me.'

Gillie put pen to paper at White Hart Lane for a Scottish record fee of £72,500 11 days later – and 48 hours before, Dundee appeased his Dens Park fan club by swooping to sign future legend Charlie Cooke from Aberdeen who eventually joined him in the English capital with Chelsea.

The King of Dens Park had found a new realm after a battle royal in his first one. Bobby Wishart, his best mate in football, was in the trenches with Gilzean throughout it. Wishart said, 'Alan was the kind of guy who needed a bit of support when he was in Dundee in the dark days. When he was being threatened about being put out the game. He went through a rocky period. There was a nasty atmosphere for a while. He needed a friend or two. I was in the twilight of my career and, while Dundee were very good to me during my stay, tremendously so, I had a loyalty to a friend as well.

'I like to think I helped fulfil my role and, as a result, once he got settled down at White Hart Lane, Alan invited my wife Jean and I for an all-expenses weekend to London for giving him that support during the tough times.

'I said to him, "I would be delighted to come down to London and spend a weekend with you but we'll do what we've always done and when the bills come in we'll just split them 50-50. And that way, our friendship will last a lot longer than it would if I was a 'taker' and not really giving all that much." So that was the basis or our friendship.

'We did eventually go down there and went to Alan's local for a few refreshments after a game. And I went on to organise a golfing trip for him and some Spurs players who I'd got to know, at a club in Barnton in Edinburgh.

'So we had a continuing friendship all the way along the line. Alan would phone me up every couple of months and, if he was coming up to Dundee for a function, he always stayed with us in Edinburgh. The kids loved him. And they couldn't understand how this wonderful, marvellous footballer was coming to stay with us.'

Wishart felt Gilzean still needed his support in the wake of his move to London and enlisted another pal who had left Scotland for Spurs to help him provide it.

He said, 'I knew David Mackay from Edinburgh – knew Davey well. I trained with him at Tynecastle when we were young. And of course I played against Davey in my Aberdeen days. I was inside-left. A number ten, and Davey was number four or six for Hearts. He could play.

'When I went down to London, I would see Dave and we would have a night out and a chat. I was able to say to Mackay, because our friendship was the way it was, "Look after this guy because he can play a bit."'

10

A New Kingdom

WHITE HART Lane was bathed in sunshine when Alan Gilzean arrived to sign for Tottenham Hotspur in 1964. An unusual weather condition for London N17 – indeed anywhere in Britain – for the middle of December.

He posed for his first pictures as a Spurs player in front of the fabled West Stand built by compatriot Archibald Leitch, the ground's first and major architect in 1909, smartly dressed in light shirt and dark tie with a tweed jacket and John Motson-esque sheepskin coat to keep out the winter chill.

The footballer we had seen hip-swaying out of the Hampden Park dressing rooms in front of more than 130,000 that damp day in the April – and indeed had had his back slapped exiting the Dens Park changing rooms to perform for Dundee reserves to a meagre gathering only a handful of years before – was instantly recognisable.

Dark, brooding good looks. No hint of a smile. A glint of wariness in his eyes, understandable given his new surroundings towards the other end of the British mainland from Scotland, in the heart of the Auld Enemy's capital. The former Coupar Angus scout was a long way from his rural home. The King of Dens Park had bestrode his realm in a city with an estimated population of around 150,000, give or take.

Would he be able to adjust to conquer and rule another in a town with around eight million inhabitants? One which was at the epicentre of the developing feelgood, multicoloured, vibrant, upbeat social, political and cultural revolution known as the swinging 60s, shaking off the grey, monochrome, dowdy cloak of post-war austerity of the 1950s. Was the youth-with-a-few-bob-and-bright-ideas movement, led by the likes of The Beatles, Carnaby Street, Mary Quant, David Bailey and all, a world too far away for a contemporary of the trendsetters brought up in a small little-known country town on the east coast of Scotland 500 miles north? Even though Spurs had been a part of it with their sexy, entertaining football, which had brought so much silverware to the club's trophy cabinet during the decade to date?

Questions no one could possibly know the answer to – even Gilzean himself. But you had to feel optimistic about his chances.

Dundee had fought tooth and nail to keep their prized asset, especially manager Bob Shankly.

Bill Nicholson, ever the perfectionist, had, as we know, spent months tracking Gilzean to ensure he would be the perfect fit as one of the last major pieces of the jigsaw in his rebuilding of a new Spurs team to follow the Glory, Glory Boys – who sealed the Double, a second successive FA Cup and European Cup Winners' Cup in the opening years of the 60s – before committing £72,500 of the club's coffers on him.

Gilzean had shown himself capable of impressing on the domestic, European and international stages while with a club outside the respected Old Firm in his home country and, perhaps, considered provincial by the less sensitive.

There was a lot riding on the son of Willie and Babs from Nicholson and Spurs's point of view.

The standard set by the first side manager Nicholson had built, and which had collected so much silverware at the start of the decade, seemed out of this world. They were adjudged by many to be the best club team football had yet witnessed – with good reason. They smashed records for fun, playing an irresistible merging of styles. Of Arthur Rowe's push and run – quick passing in player-triangles as mirrored by the Messi-inspired Barcelona of recent years – with more pizzazz and individual flair. Entertainment with results and trophies. The perfect combination. More than 2.5

million around the country flocked to be entertained by them in the year they became the first club in the 20th century to win the English title and FA Cup.

They had been led by Danny Blanchflower, rated the most influential player in Spurs history by *The Times* newspaper in 2009, an inspirational captain utilising his head and heart. Nicholson's voice on the pitch. A voice capable, it is said, of having the manager's ear off it whether the boss desired it or not! An articulate Northern Irishman who defined the club's philosophy with his quote 'the game is about glory'.

The other half-back was barrel-chested Dave Mackay, rated by Jimmy Greaves as the club's greatest-ever player, a bone-shaking tackler with fine distribution and a delicate touch. Above all he was a roaring lion of a winner. Nothing less than victory would be tolerated. Cliff Jones said, 'He turned a good team into a great one.'

John White was part of the engine room. He could run and run. The stamina he built up as a schoolboy cross-country runner enabled him to provide vital links in the chain during build-ups to the opposition goal. And, with his intelligence, he possessed the stealth to drift unnoticed into unmarked positions, hence his nickname, The Ghost. Luka Modric and Christian Eriksen would be the nearest modern-day equivalents in a Lilywhite shirt.

There was the flying machine in Cliff Jones, brave with a spring like a salmon, who thrilled the Lane with his long runs, dribbles and goals.

And the industrious Terry Dyson on the opposite wing was a player with goals in his boots, scoring 17 in the Double season. He possessed the knack of hitting the target when it most mattered, including a Double-clinching second in the FA Cup Final against Leicester City. There were also his two goals and player-of-the-match performance in the 5-1 Cup Winners' Cup Final win over Atletico Madrid in 1963.

Striker Les Allen free-scored in the Double campaign and his illustrious successor Jimmy Greaves illustrated why he was to prove himself the best goalscorer in England, Europe and, arguably, the world, let alone Spurs, while also bagging goals on the big occasion, matching Dyson's two in Rotterdam and opening the scoring in the 1962 FA Cup victory over Burnley.

There was also Frank Saul, Terry Medwin, who replaced Dyson in the season sealed with a second successive FA Cup success, Tony Marchi, the consummate reserve who shone in place of the injured Mackay in the De Kuip Stadium, and Eddie Clayton as back-ups.

Last but far from least, there was Bobby Smith. The player Gilzean was, ostensibly, brought in to replace. Big boots to fill. England international Smith netted 251 strikes in 358 Tottenham appearances, second only to Greaves in the pantheon of top Spurs goalscorers.

And the burly Yorkshireman could produce goals on the big occasion too, as he did in the back-to-back Wembley triumphs and the 1963 Cup Winners' Cup semi-final against OFK Belgrade. He also equalled the goals-in-a-season club record by smashing in 36 in 1957/58, to level things off with Ted Harper who achieved the mark 27 years earlier. It took his partner Jimmy Greaves to beat it. A tall order all the way round. But Gilzean provided a different type of player to lead the front line alongside Greavsie for starters.

And would the neediness of Shankly and the judgment of Nicholson indicate a player capable of performing at a consistently above-average to stratospheric level in the English Football League?

After all, wasn't the bread and butter diet of Scottish League football beneath the standard feasted on by its equivalent south of the border?

Were impressive appearances in a continental club knockout, albeit probably the best of its type in the world, and for Scotland enough to show Gilzean would have the ability to play that well week in, week out?

Eight of the Spurs most famous XI – who won the Double – were still in the club's employ when Gilzean arrived at the Lane: Bill Brown, Peter Baker, Ron Henry, Maurice Norman, Dave Mackay, Cliff Jones, Les Allen and Terry Dyson. (The three no longer on the staff were Danny Blanchflower who had retired aged 38 in the April, the tragic John White and Bobby Smith, who had joined Brighton in the summer when Nicholson decided, briefly it seems, that Frank Saul would be a better strike partner for Greaves.)

Brown, who left Dundee for Spurs two months before Gilzean made his Dark Blues first-team debut in August 1959, vied with rookie Pat Jennings for the number-one jersey.

Baker was generally grounded, with Cyril Knowles, a £45,000 signing from Middlesbrough in the May, largely preferred at number two, although Gilzean was to line up with the blond right-back with the look of an RAF pilot once as Spurs defeated a Blackpool side (containing teenaged Alan Ball, the 1966 England World Cup winner) in March 1965. It was to be the club's longest-serving player's swansong after 13 years as Baker was released in May to allow him to play in South Africa, a route Gilzean himself was to follow.

Norman, an England 1958 and 1962 World Cup international, remained a regular at centre-half, until Arsenal recruit Laurie Brown was tried in the second half of Gilzean's first season. But the East Anglian had his career prematurely ended by a double leg fracture – having broken his leg at the start of his career – in a friendly against a Hungarian Select XI in which Gilzean netted a hat-trick. (Incidentally, the Scot revived memories of his historic four goals against Rangers with a quartet the previous month in another non-competitive encounter against non-league Walton & Hersham, who once boasted Sir Stanley Matthews as their president, swapping Ibrox for The Sports Ground, Stompond Lane.)

Mackay remained at the heart of the club but was sidelined with a broken leg sustained in a comeback match from the same injury – sustained as Spurs's Cup Winners' Cup defence crumbled against Manchester United at Old Trafford the previous season – when he turned out for Spurs reserves against Shrewsbury three months before his international team-mate put pen to paper at White Hart Lane.

Jones and Dyson were still the chosen wing pair and Ron Henry the regular left-back, while Allen had been limited to a run of four successive matches in place of Frank Saul, who otherwise held down the number nine until Alan replaced him.

Bill Nick had already initiated his recruitment drive for players, of course. He wanted to build the second great side of his managerial career at the club he helped secure the First Division title as a player in 1951.

The pragmatist in him knew he should not allow the grass to grow under his feet if this was to be achieved. Laurels could not be rested on.

Anyone who thought Spurs would cash in down the line on their Glory, Glory Boys to help pay for the newcomers were mistaken. Bill Nick seemed more intent on helping those players achieve one more pay day.

Smith went for just £5,000 to Fourth Division Brighton and Hove Albion just a year after winning his 15th and final international cap (his goals helping his new side to promotion in his only season with the south-coast outfit).

And Dyson and Brown were also to go for nominal fees to Fulham and Northampton Town in 1965 and 1966, although Spurs would manage to procure £21,000 from QPR for Allen in 1965 where he went on to lift the League Cup and manage the west London club.

But the manager certainly splashed Spurs's cash in spite of the trickle coming in. In 1964 he made four significant investments. He bought in Alan Mullery – pre-international recognition – for a whopping £72,500 from Fulham in the March, but, it is understood, failed to prise team-mate and right-back George Cohen, whom he felt had an enviable link-up with the right-half and was to be part of England's Jules Rimet trophy triumph two years hence.

Wearing the same number-four shirt worn by Blanchflower, Mullery was viewed as the successor to Spurs's Captain Grey Matter, even though the players were like chalk and cheese in terms of style, Mullery more physical and foraging than the mercurial Irishman.

Two days later winger Jimmy Robertson maintained Nicholson's tradition of raiding talent north of the border by signing from St Mirren for £25,000 two weeks later; someone who had faced Gilzean in the Scottish League.

Knowles, a pit worker and neighbour of cricket legend Geoffrey Boycott in Fitzwilliam, Yorkshire, joined for a hefty £45,000 after just one season in professional football with Middlesbrough following rejections from Wolverhampton Wanderers, where brother Peter starred, and Manchester United.

In June, Pat Jennings, a 19-year-old rookie, was signed for £25,000 from Watford, where Spurs's 1951 title-winning captain Ron Burgess was manager.

The new boys heralded a new era when they all helped Spurs kick off the 1964/65 season with a 2-0 victory against Sheffield United on 22 August while Gilzean was kicking his heels during his dispute with Dundee.

Robertson, reckoned to be faster than jet-heeled Cliff Jones by Bill Nick, showed a few of the flashes that were to help turn him into an FA Cup Final goalscoring hero three years later. But Mullery, Jennings and Knowles all struggled. Knowles, a former left-winger being played at right-back, said, 'I couldn't settle on that side of the pitch. I began to feel shaky and lost my confidence.'

Mullery was given a rough ride by Blanchflower lovers. And Jennings's inexperience led to erratic performances to provoke a similar reaction from followers with a deserved reputation for fickleness. There were the inevitable negative headlines with the media which, having built them up, dealt the 'knock 'em down' card it often plays on such occasions.

Greaves was banging in the goals as per usual but results were up and down. Yet they revived, and the beating of north London rivals Arsenal at the Lane in October, with Robertson among the goalscorers, to go fourth, cheered up Spurs supporters no end. Crisis? What crisis? And the arrival of Gilzean confirmed the next generation of Spurs players were capable of treading the glory trail just like Danny and co.

The first glimpse of Gillie at the Lane in that testimonial for John White's family in November gave the faithful a mouth-watering glimpse of what could follow if he pulled on the white shirt with a navy blue cockerel on its left breast. Two goals and a superlative display. 'Come on, Bill, get him signed up' was the cry.

The team might not have hit the heights of the Glory, Glory Boys but they did not half do too badly once the manager had done just that. It was estimated the average Tottenham home gate back then was 19 times the size of Coupar Angus's population.

But if Gillie was overawed, I, for one, who witnessed most of his Lane appearances over the following ten years, did not detect it. He may have been reserved, wanting to talk about others rather than himself, but there was no mistaking the inner confidence he possessed. That came from knowing you have the ability to not just cope but shine in a big league week in week out. That you put in the hard yards as a kid, albeit in a scout hut, a school shed or your dad's painting and decorating business base, to ensure that ability is shown in its best light when centre stage.

Gilzean had come to Spurs with a reputation as a footballer with world-class potential. A few days after signing on that sunny but chilly day, he was in the home dressing room at White Hart Lane preparing for his debut on Saturday, 19 December 1964. Against Everton. He slipped on the Spurs number-nine shirt – a long-sleeved, crew-neck affair with the proud navy blue cockerel logo in a shield with a navy outline over his heart – pulled up his in-vogue short shorts in navy blue, and sat to roll up his navy blue socks topped in white. He laced up his boots after drenching them in hot water.

Nicholson said, 'Before every match he used to soak his boots in hot water to soften them up. I think that was a legacy from the old days when the toe-capped leather boots would be so stiff that they were painful to the feet unless softened in some way. Some players still did it out of habit.'

He stepped out to the recorded version of 'McNamara's Band', a Lane signature tune. A picture of calm, arms by his side in the pre-match kickabout as photographers buzzed around him getting shots of Tottenham's latest capture for newspapers, magazines and, most likely, the match programme in front of the East Stand.

I watched level with this patient figure from the stand, in front of the famed Shelf, between the halfway line and the corner flag at the Park Lane end. Like the majority of the 41,994 crowd, I was excited about the prospect of witnessing Gilzean in the flesh.

I had read up about Spurs's new striker in my parents' *Daily Mirror* and it had clearly whetted a lot of appetites as well as my own. His goals, his heading, his abilities on the deck, his touch, with both feet, his instinct for finding space in tight spots, his importance to a club attempting to bring back the recent glory days.

It was the only way of gleaning information in the lead-up to matches in those days. There were never any pre-match programmes on the television. Remember BBC's *Match of the Day* had only begun screening highlights from the First Division four months earlier. And it was the only other regular football on the box besides the FA Cup Final in my neck of the woods.

Gilzean took his place in the centre circle and the kick-off was greeted by a deafening roar which echoed around the stadium, creating an intimidating atmosphere from which the meek shrink and the bold stick out their chests and declare, 'Let's have it!'

That was the moment Gillie began to prove he was ready to 'have it'. That he was up to the challenge. Ready to show people the hype had substance.

It was a stern test against opponents who included former Dundee team-mate Jimmy Gabriel and army buddy Alex Young, the fabled Golden Vision, while Bill Brown was in the home goal for, if he needed it, 'back home' comfort. A year previously Spurs had come unstuck in the race for the title with the Toffeemen as the blue side of Liverpool tasted sweet victory, with Gabriel and Young very much a part of it.

As the matched progressed, I was momentarily distracted. The terracing where I stood with my mates Mark and Tony was chock-a-block. So chock-a-block that Mark felt faint. The grown-ups around us youngsters instinctively lifted him and crowd-surfed him down above their heads and plonked him on the track around the pitch where he enjoyed an uninterrupted view of Gilzean and his new mates.

But I regained my focus to see my favourite player Jimmy Greaves, typically, sweep in a couple of goals, while Gillie impressed in his number-nine role in the 2-2 draw. He displayed an ability to lead the line and his link-up play was adept either in the air or on the turf. He showed a few classy touches on the deck, a flicked header here and there, and was robust enough to deal with a physical approach adopted by the visiting defence. Best of all, he gave hope to all of us of a Lilywhite persuasion that he and Greaves could develop a formidable partnership up front, with his new partner crediting him with both his goals.

Greaves said, 'We had an almost telepathic understanding right from the very first game for Spurs in December 1964 when he helped me score our goals in a 2-2 draw with Everton.' Fred Pickering bagged a couple to deny Gilzean a winning debut but a draw against one of the best sides in the league was an encouraging start for the new boy, his new manager and his new followers for a new Spurs.

Gilzean swiftly showed he had not left his unerring eye for goals back in his homeland. He hit the target for the first time with his new club in his second appearance in a fine 2-1 win over high-flying Nottingham Forest at the City Ground on Boxing Day.

And he found the mark for the first time at White Hart Lane two days later as Forest were chopped down again in front of nearly 57,000. It might also be described as the day the G-Men were born as Greaves also netted in a 4-0 win.

Gilzean had performed for just over 140,000 fans in nine days. He also managed a goal on his north London derby debut against Arsenal later in the season, which he finished with a respectable 11 in 20 league appearances. This was no shrinking violet. This was the real deal. He had not only hit the ground running on the big stage, he was speeding like Usain Bolt.

The earliest performances alone gave all Lane loyalists confidence that Gilzean could do more than merely take over from Bobby Smith. Smith did have subtleties of touch, but he was chiefly known for his physical approach – which often intimidated opponents – as well as his goals.

But Gilzean, it seemed, would provide extra dimensions. He could score goals. That was a given. But his all-round elegant game was full of nuances. Qualities, of course, which would allow him to display his versatility over the decade, adapt from centre-forward to deeper and wider roles, one which would allow him to be the architect of a flood of goals for the greatest English goalscorer of them all, Jimmy Greaves.

It was no wonder the Lane faithful were soon singing 'Gilzean Gilzean, Gilzean, Gilzean. Born is the King of White Hart Lane' to the tune of carol 'The First Noel'. And he was just getting started.

He had also made an indelible first impression on his new team-mates too – on and off the pitch. Cliff Jones, who played alongside Gilzean in all those opening games, said, 'I remember him when he came down to White Hart Lane with a Scottish XI to play in the testimonial for John White. That was one reason he came to Tottenham not long after. He settled in quickly after he arrived.

'Bill was changing the team around a bit at the time but Gillie fitted in straight away. Especially linking up with Jimmy Greaves. The G-Men became a special partnership with Gillie's flicks and Jimmy's change of speed [more later].

'He was a terrific player. Could do everything. All-round skill. He had such good movement, great control, a good touch with either foot. Quick over 10 to 18 yards. And he was brilliant with his head, particularly those flicks. He was also a terrific trainer, which impressed Bill, who always said you should train as you play.

'[He] became a big favourite with the Tottenham supporters because they recognised him as a Spurs type of player.'

Alan Mullery was struck by Gilzean's prowess on training runs besides his technique and personality. He said, 'We did a lot of running. On a Monday morning the warm-up was ten laps of the pitch. Alan Gilzean was usually, invariably, the winner. You wouldn't have thought he was fantastic. Like Mo Farah. He could run and run.'

Jimmy Robertson, who played on the right wing during Gilzean's first flourish as a Lilywhite, had, of course, played against his fellow Scot in their homeland.

He said, 'The first time I came across him was when he was with Dundee and I was with St Mirren. It was at Dens Park. Dundee were one of the top sides, had won the title. They beat us by a big score and Gillie got three of their goals.

'There were a lot of good players in Scotland then – not so much now – and he did stand out, was a great signing. Very, very skilful. Good in the air and on the deck. A one-off. [His] deceptive, good first touch, could turn people. [I] like to think that I supplied him with some of his goals. He was a top, top player for me. Not a guy who would promote himself, mind. No image, not fiery, just got on with it. He knew he was good at it. Probably appreciated more by other players than the public.

'Alan was a popular player. The fact we all called him "Gillie" reflects that. Quiet and confident. It was always a happy dressing room with him. Everyone got on well.'

Pat Jennings played with Gilzean for the first time in the home victory against Nottingham Forest on 28 December 1964 and kept a clean sheet while Gilzean, Greaves, Robertson and Double-winner Terry Dyson netted down the other end. He said, 'We were all there when Gillie arrived at the club. Cyril Knowles and myself had signed close together, Alan Mullery a few months before. I'd remembered him from the John White memorial match.

'Bill had fantastic contacts in Scotland. You look at Dave Mackay, John White and Jimmy Robertson. We always had a sprinkling of Scottish players. All the top teams had. And it was clear when he began playing for us that he was a threat. Had a great shot and was brilliant in the air. He had that all-round ability.

'He was fantastic for me. My target man, every time I picked up the ball I hit him and he would just run off defenders and get a little glance on.'

Alan John Gilzean married Irene Davidson Todd at the Abbey Church in Coupar Angus in 1965.

Irene, a policewoman, was brought up just a street or two away from Gilzean's family in the small rural town just outside Dundee. Friends and relations attended the service and reception, including pals of the groom from his world of football. One such friend was Bobby Wishart. Ian McKenzie, a childhood friend from Coupar Angus, was the best man, while Wishart also did a speech.

Wishart said, 'I was involved quite a lot at the wedding. I think I got landed with a speech. Absent friends or something. My wife Jean and I were quite heavily involved when Alan and Rina were courting. They would come down to Edinburgh where we lived to spend the weekends with us. And, of course, we would travel to London when he moved to Tottenham Hotspur and they lived in Enfield. Unfortunately the marriage didn't last – so that was a shame. Just one of those things. But we managed to keep in touch with Alan for the rest of his life.'

Dave Forbes, Gillie's friend, unofficial PR, Dundee FC dinner organiser and former Dark Blues director, worked with Irene.

He said, 'I was in the police for just over two years [in the 1960s] and Irene worked with us. It turned out she was Gillie's girlfriend. It was a well-kept secret in those days. You weren't to be seen to be engaged or anything and they got married later.

'I hadn't seen her for years but saw her at Gillie's funeral and she said to me, "I know your face." I said to her, "You grew up not half an hour from Dundee." Nice lady.'

11

G-Men

ALAN GILZEAN had to accept Spurs were in 'transition'. The Oxford Dictionary defines the word as 'the process or a period of changing from one state or condition to another.'

How long would it be before it is completed for the club to win things once more? How long's a piece of string? It depended on judgement, means and good fortune. Bill Nicholson and Spurs had enjoyed the fruits from those three factors coalescing at the start of the 1960s, but nothing lasts forever, nothing is guaranteed. But there were optimistic signs.

For a start, Phil Beal had become that rare beast, a player to emerge from the junior set-up of a club known for focusing on big names to fill holes in their first-team line-up. The former England youth international was a versatile defender who debuted against Aston Villa on 16 September 1963, the first of over 400 appearances, initially becoming the regular right-back in the 1965/66 campaign with Knowles switching to the left and flourishing.

But ostensibly Bill Nick, as we have discovered, maintained the traditional method of dipping into the transfer market with the capture of Gilzean a prime example.

He spent big money on players he felt had the character – a prerequisite for the Spurs manager of any target – and ability enough to help replenish a silverware cabinet in the now-razed Red House, the former Victorian coffee house turned club headquarters which included the Spurs board and trophy rooms.

If there was space left in it after the prize plundering of the Glory, Glory Boys.

Alan Mullery, Pat Jennings and Cyril Knowles were three examples and had, as we have discovered, needed time to bed in.

Mullery became a trophy-winning captain for Spurs. He said, 'It was tough to start with. Crowds had seen the quality of the Double side and Bill was breaking that side up. He knew his own mind. Later he got rid of Jimmy Greaves, Dave Mackay and Alan Mullery! He wanted to build and build. Wanted Tottenham to stay at the top [for years and years]. A bit like Sir Alex Ferguson in later years with Manchester United. I'd say Alex followed Bill.'

Mullery began to thrive after one incident against Chelsea at the Lane.

He said, 'There were things you had to do to achieve greatness at Spurs. A tough challenge for me, I was a 22-year-old lad taking over from Danny Blanchflower, a legend as a skipper, a legend as a player. The great Double side was breaking up. It took time for the Lane fans to warm to me. I remember the moment they did. I think it was Eddie Baily, Bill's assistant, who told me to give Chelsea winger Bert Murray a dig in the first five minutes. That he wouldn't like it. So I went in with a slide tackle and knocked him into the crowd. A fan called out, "Come on The Tank". The fans' attitude towards me changed from that moment and I had a wonderful career with the club.'

Knowles discovered his mojo when switched to left-back. Jennings found his confidence with a sustained run in the team, enough for Bill Nick to entrust him with the number-one spot when allowing Brown to leave in the summer of 1966.

The new Scots who arrived as part of Nicholson's masterplan continued to settle in nicely. Perhaps, in Jimmy Robertson's case, it was aided by lesser expectations of a player little known outside the English league. The same, as has been made clear, could not be said of Alan Gilzean, given the size of his fee and reputation built up with Dundee through to one match from a European Cup Final while scoring more goals than even the imagined Melchester Rovers ace Roy Race in the iconic cartoon strip.

But Gilzean remained unfazed as he helped Bill Nick begin to reap the rewards for his bold, single-minded attitude with his fresh components gelling, eventually aided by the return of the indomitable Mackay in August 1965. In real terms, Bill Nick's changing of the guard saw respectable league finishes at best leading into the 1966/67 campaign: third, second, fourth, sixth and eighth; the last two with Gillie in the fold. And FA Cup exploits with the former Dens favourite saw successive runs to the fifth round.

The trophy drought was to last four years before Gilzean helped the club secure more silverware and fulfil his Wembley dream. But in the interim he had fun and provided a series of unforgettable moments for his loyal subjects of the Lane who had crowned him their monarch. And how we feasted on them while waiting in hope for the glittering prizes to be collected once more.

He hit a hat-trick on his debut for Spurs in the FA Cup against Torquay United at Plainmoor on 9 January 1965, although their lower league hosts forced a replay. And he did the same in what I consider the most entertaining, gut-wrenching, thrilling match I witnessed at the old White Hart Lane the following year.

It was a grey afternoon as Gilzean and his Spurs team-mates, along with the visiting Burnley XI, stepped on to the muddy White Hart Lane pitch. More than 50,000 expectant fans shook the old ground to the rafters with their collective welcoming roar as the fourth-round FA Cup tie kicked off on the afternoon of Saturday, 12 February 1966. In those days, the world's oldest and most famous national club knockout competition had lost none of its lustre. Yes, continental titles were considered the ultimate test by clubs, but there was nothing like 'the Cup'. You still did not even need to qualify it by putting 'FA' before it.

The match provided twists and turns in the plot more complex than a crime thriller by Jo Nesbo, had the writer and Spurs fan time-travelled to put one together. And drama Tottenham-supporting thespian Sir Kenneth Branagh, who did the voice-over for *The Finale* at the old White Hart Lane, would have struggled to emulate had he been treading the boards.

Spurs trailed to a Willie Irvine goal after just 40 seconds. Irvine made it two in the second minute for the visitors, who included future Spurs League Cup Final match-winner Ralph Coates. Blimey, us supporters were thinking, what is going on here?

Gilzean, keeping his innate calm in what might have been an impending crisis, reduced the deficit with a trademark header from a Cliff Jones cross ten minutes before the interval, and levelled the scores four minutes into the second half, glancing a header beyond Clarets stopper Adam Blacklaw from a ball from strike-partner Jimmy Greaves.

Any thought the momentum had swung back in Spurs's favour was debunked nine minutes on, Irvine completing a treble by beating Pat Jennings from a Willie Morgan pass. Gillie reverted to goalmaker when he combined with Cliff Jones for Frank Saul to make it 3-3 just 20 minutes from time. As the game drifted towards a replay, Gilzean provided the match-winner two minutes from time with a thumping wonder strike after visiting centre-half John Talbot had headed back his long ball forward.

Gillie said, 'My most memorable match [at White Hart Lane] has to be an FA Cup home tie versus Burnley. We got off to a bad start and were soon two goals behind. The game ebbed and flowed and at half-time we trailed 3-1. The second half was a great 45 minutes for Spurs as we won the game 4-3, I scored a hat-trick and Frank Saul got the other one. It was an afternoon that got off to a bad start but had a happy ending.'

But the feature involving Gilzean which remains uppermost in the collective memory of those present during those 'transition' years for Spurs was the formation and development of his partnership with Jimmy Greaves – the much-lauded G-Men. Perhaps the most lethal goalscoring double act known to English football.

It can be argued other footballing duos of more recent times could have given them a run for their money. Liverpool can boast John Toshack and Kevin Keegan, and Kenny Dalglish and Ian Rush. Manchester United once had Andrew Cole and Dwight Yorke. Arsenal? Thierry Henry and Dennis Bergkamp. Even Greaves with Martin Chivers when Gilzean took a more withdrawn role at Tottenham (more later). They all had an understanding which produced the old one-two to sting hapless opponents.

But what gives the G-Men the edge is that they were the first duo to make an impression on me and clearly the perfect foil for others, Gilzean largely supplying the bullets and Greaves squeezing the trigger, apart from the opening three months of the 1965/66 season when the latter was laid low by hepatitis before charging back to finish in his customary position in the club scorers list – top.

The double act underlined just how good Alan Gilzean was as a footballer. His goalscoring exploits with Dundee are the stuff of legend. Quite rightly. But he was always more than a player capable of finding the onion bag at a staggering average of almost one a game. Going back to his wet-behind-the-ears days as a schoolboy, scout and youth player, days when he displayed an all-round ability, he was a maker as well as a taker of goals, whether on the ground with both feet or in the air. Qualities he honed, as we know, through hours and hours of blood, sweat and tears at the sixth Perthshire's HQ, the family's workshop, The Common and Foxhall Park in his native Coupar Angus.

The right-footed Gilzean practised so hard at kicking the ball with his left foot even experts struggled to name his natural peg.

The work he put into springing to head either a hanging football or boxing glove ensured he perfected the ability for which he was most noted, fairly or unfairly given his versatility. It put him head and shoulders over most if not all rivals attempting what is often a crucial element to anyone's game. Head and shoulders being apposite when you think of how esteemed writer and Spurs fan Julie Welch described how he executed one of his many brands of nodding by 'tossing his head like a shampoo advertisement'.

She also described him as 'old-fashioned' and 'almost unwordly', while quoting erstwhile partner Greaves saying tongue-in-cheek, 'He [Gilzean] came from a place called Coupar Angus, somewhere in the back-end of Scotland. As soon as he arrived I showed him all those new sights of London which would seem strange to him – electric lights, carpets, that kind of thing.'

But Gilzean was a sophisticated polymath when it came to making contact with a ball in the air. Nicholson said, 'He was an unorthodox player, different in many ways to Bobby Smith. He was more of a footballing centre-forward and started his career as an inside-left. He didn't head the ball full-on like Smithy, he preferred to glance it as he turned his head. It was not a style you could coach anyone because the margin of error was so small, but it suited him and I never tried to change him.'

He used to have the ability of being able to hover after leaping – a quality possessed by the fabled Tommy Lawton according to my late father – to give himself time to choose to either put in Greaves or another colleague or have a go at goal himself. He worked out his angles to the letter.

Gilzean's aerial prowess was not wasted on Miljan Miljanic. The Red Star Belgrade coach, on a scouting mission with his side, due to take on Gilzean and his team in the last 16 of the UEFA Cup late in 1972, said, 'If ever there is a football university Alan Gilzean should be appointed as the first professor to lecture on how to use one's head and play with one's head.' Alan Mullery said, 'Gillie was not tall but was fantastic in the air. It was as if he had sponges on his feet.'

Timing, intelligence and temperament were other plus points which helped the G-Men work in tandem. Gilzean was reckoned to be 6ft tall, maybe even slightly under depending on which source you use – but seemed to have the better of most opposing defenders even if they towered over him from a standing start because he knew exactly the moment to take off. He remained cool, calm and collected in the tightest of spots, even when suffering the roughest of challenges, always finding space to either find the killer ball or hit the back of the net.

And, ever alert, he would know when and where to move in that deceptively strolling gait he had should a ball come in from far or near, low or high. His touch off either of his hot-water-softened boots was as deft as with his noggin. Ivan Ponting memorably wrote in *Tottenham Hotspur Player by Player*, 'So gently did Alan caress a football that he might have been wearing carpet slippers.'

And his awareness was second to none, especially, it seems, when it came to Greaves. Often his quicksilver compadre was on the run before Gilzean had made any contact. He just knew the Scot would find him.

What gives the partnership more gravitas is the mutual love and respect the two had for each other. They have each cited the other as their favourite player to play with. But they were more than colleagues. They were friends.

Gilzean said, 'When you line up with the guy, he was so unassuming. No big-headedness at all. A right down-to-earth guy, but when he got on the park he was … ah … quicksilver. His awareness, calmness under pressure … and I've said recently that when I watch Lionel Messi now, that was like watching Greavsie all those years ago.

'I can remember watching Chelsea on the television. Their two strikers were David Cliss and Jimmy Greaves and I remember saying to myself [about Greaves], "This guy's some player." A few years passed and I went to watch Scotland playing at Wembley and England thrashed us 9-3! Greavsie ran amok. The following week, he was away to Italy [to play for AC Milan]. And the next time I bumped into him, I played for Scotland under-23s at Aberdeen and Greavsie was in the opposition. And again they beat us.

'So when it comes the time to sign for somebody [when he was leaving Dundee], [it was a case of] if you can't beat them you've got to join them [Greaves at Spurs], haven't you? It was as easy as that.

'It broke my heart the day he left Tottenham. I think he was rushed into leaving Tottenham in a swap with Martin Peters. He seemed to lose faith in his own ability. And that was very sad, because he was one hell of a player.'

'I had FIVE wonderful years with the little maestro. And it was a pleasure to play with him.'

He added, 'Well I didn't see too much of Greavsie off the pitch, because he lived in Essex and I lived in Enfield, but on the pitch it was one of those things. When you line up with somebody your first impressions are normally pretty good. I just got a feeling that we'd play well together and it turned out that way.

'He was a great partner and wonderful, wonderful player. Greavsie was a magician, he could turn games on their head in ten-minute spells. His dribbling ability was second to none. His close possession of the ball, his control, and his awareness of everything around him, especially in the penalty box, was outstanding. He never panicked, just took everything in his stride, and used to stroke the ball into the net, you know? He was just world class. Lionel Messi is the closest to Greavsie in his playing style and ability, with fantastic close control.

'Football was so easy for Greavsie. Other guys had to practise hour after hour, honing their skills, but Greavsie already had these skills when he was 16 at Chelsea. When he started playing with better players, he just advanced and advanced into a wonderful player. They don't come along very often, the Greavsies in this world.'

Gilzean might have scored 169 goals in 190 competitive matches for Dundee, but he was more than happy to take a backseat in the scoring department for the sake of Greaves, reflected in the latter always scoring more goals in each of the six years they were together.

He scored his fair share, though. Having joined halfway through the 1964/65 season, he netted a more than respectable 16 goals in 24 appearances. And when the pair played their first full season together in 1966/67 – with Greaves having been hit by hepatitis for three months in the previous campaign – he managed 21 in 48.

Greaves, naturally, was scoring off the charts, but he knew many of his goals were thanks to the deft skills of a partner who provided him manna from heaven. Gratitude to the Scot was in plentiful supply from the goalscoring master – who topped the European charts for the continent's leading five leagues at 366 until Cristiano Ronaldo of Real Madrid was able to knock him off it in May 2017 – when I asked him his thoughts on Coupar Angus's famous son.

Greaves told me in 2003 that Gilzean was his favourite team-mate and they had a 'telepathic relationship' when going for the opposition's jugular. And, through his spokesperson Terry Baker, after being incapacitated by a severe stroke in 2015, he added, 'Jim loved Gillie. He said that many times, along with Gillie being his favourite strike partner.'

In his autobiography *Greavsie*, he said, 'I was to form a great partnership with Alan Gilzean. I enjoyed a great understanding with Gillie. As a striking partner it was almost as if we had been made for each other ... I don't think I was ever happier than playing with Gillie at my side, he was a tremendously talented player and an unselfish one, too.

'Alan was an unorthodox player very different in style to Bobby Smith. Alan was more of a footballing centre-forward with a great awareness of the play that was unfolding about him. Like Bobby, Alan was very good in the air, but, again, their styles were different. Bobby used to get up and head the ball full-on with his forehead, whereas Alan preferred to glance it with a turn of his head. Alan's style of heading the ball was not one that was coached at the time, simply because the margin for error was small.

'But Alan had this style of heading down to a T. It suited Alan, and Bill never tried to change him, though Bill would, on occasions, chide Gillie about his idiosyncratic style of play. "Where did you learn your football? What were you trying to do out there?" Bill would ask. Alan liked to play the ball up the wing into space and expected someone to tank up from midfield to get on the end of his pass.

'"For heaven's sake Alan. If we don't have a man running, hold the ball up for us, or else play to feet. You're not playing against Partick Thistle now. With the quality we face every week, we need to keep possession," Bill would tell Alan.

'Alan would take all Bill's remarks in good spirit. Alan was easy to talk to and easy to get on with, a very amiable and amicable man. He never moaned and just got on with the job. You could be open and frank with him and he would never go away and sulk. I enjoyed a great understanding with Gillie. As a striking partner it was almost as if we had been made for each other. We had an almost telepathic understanding right from the very first game for Spurs in December 1964 when he helped me score our goals in a 2-2 draw with Everton.'

In his biography, *Natural*, he said, 'I felt he had the ability and it didn't take long for that to develop. He has helped me in so many ways. I can't speak for him, but it helps that I like the fella.'

Spurs goalkeeper Pat Jennings rated the partnership of the G-Men the best he had come across. He said, 'What a partnership. When you look back and think what those two would be worth now as a front two. A fantastic partnership for us. Complemented each other. In the early days when Gillie arrived, he didn't realise how good Jimmy Greaves was. He probably thought he was a lucky player. But as Jimmy – who was in a class of his own – scored more and more goals he realised Greavsie had the art of being in the right place at the right time. Especially playing off Gillie's flick-ons.

'When I aimed for Gillie with a long kick he would get a glance on the ball. Nine times out of ten it would be falling to Greavsie. There was such a good understanding between them. He didn't even have to look.

'I've no doubt Gillie and Greavsie would have been one of the greatest partnerships in the game now. Absolutely.'

Jimmy Robertson was wowed by the G-Men. He said, 'Gillie and Greavsie were dynamite together.'

Cliff Jones uttered the common mantra: 'His link-up with Jimmy Greaves was telepathic. They were called the G-Men and were a great partnership.'

Alan Mullery said, 'He was something special and when him and Greavsie were together, they were unstoppable. The G-Men. They were the perfect partnership, the best strike partnership I came across.' He added, 'To buy those now you'd be talking about the price of a Cristiano Ronaldo for Alan and the price of a Lionel Messi for Greavsie. Gillie and Greavsie were playing against tough guys. Defenders who would kick lumps out of you. They were a great partnership. The side would be playing awfully and one of those two would win the game for you.'

Denis Law knew first-hand how lethal his Scotland team-mate could be playing club football for Manchester United against Spurs. He said, 'Alan had a great partnership with Jimmy.'

Ian Gilzean confirmed his dad's feelings on the partnership he shared with Greaves. He said, 'Dad always said that the two best players he ever played with were Jimmy Greaves and Denis Law and I think Greavsie's the best of the two. He only played with Denis for Scotland, but Jimmy was the one, his favourite. They just seemed to hit it off.

'They had a sixth sense between them? Yeh. You just get that from time to time with players. It just works while with other ones it looks like they've never kicked a ball together before.

'In my day it was Rush and Dalglish. Dad and Greavsie had that at Tottenham for five or six seasons.

'Jimmy saying Dad was the greatest player he played with says something about the two of them. Greavsie was phenomenal. If he'd have stayed fit he'd have played in the World Cup Final. All the players he played with, the career he had – and Dad was his best strike partner. And Dad said the same thing about him. There was something there. The two of them had a special understanding.'

Ian underlined the part his dad's aerial prowess played in the pairing. He said, 'If you time your jump like Dad usually did, it doesn't matter how big the centre-halves are behind you. It allows you to get in front of them. But you need coordination to see the ball, judge how quickly it will reach you and where you are going to put it once it does. That's when you go back to being able to pick up any ball sport. Having that whole picture in your mind before the ball has arrived.

'They had team-mates who could get them the ball and a manager who brought it all out because he believed in that team.

'If you stuck the two of them, say, in a Crystal Palace team, would they have been as good? Probably not. You need the whole thing. That's when the special players stand out.

'Dad became more a creator than he'd been at Dundee. He still scored a few but mainly he was the foil.'

Lane fans enjoyed the whole G-Men phenomena, having plenty of opportunity to chant, 'We've got the G-Men in Greaves and Gilzean. They're the world's best goalscoring machine.'

But Gillie would play it all down. Norman Giller, writer and Spurs supporter, said, 'People did not realise just how sharp he was with his tongue. He used it like a claymore. I once asked him who his favourite partners were. Studiously laconic with his humour, he said without blinking, "Bacardi and Coke."

'Gillie and Greavsie – The G-Men – were a great double act on an off the pitch, Jimmy in-your-face funny and Alan subtle and mischievous.

'I always described Alan as a Nureyev on grass, because he was so balletic. You could have set his movement on the pitch to music. He danced many a *pas de deux* with Greavsie.

'When I tried my ballet metaphor on him, Gillie told me privately, "You're full of shite. I'm a footballer plain and simple." There was nothing plain and simple about Gillie. He was unique and when in partnership with Greavsie, an absolute genius.'

The partnership seemed a football marriage from the off. Greaves, of course, insisted Gillie played a part in both his goals when the Coupar Angus native made his Tottenham debut against Everton.

The dynamic duo put themselves in the limelight once more immediately after each bagged one apiece in the win at Nottingham Forest and shared four at Torquay. They netted all five between themselves (Gillie two, Greaves three) in a 5-0 trouncing of Ipswich Town in the cup, and repeated the trick in a 5-2 league battering of Blackburn Rovers, this time with Gillie netting the hat-trick.

It was no wonder the G-Men dominated the headlines when it came to reports on Spurs.

It was clear Greaves was *numero uno* out of the pair for rippling the back of the net, but increasingly it was Gilzean who was ensuring the player he described as the 'little maestro' maintained his status.

12

Peenie's Picture House Dream Comes True

ALAN GILZEAN had nailed down his spot at centre-forward, but Bill Nicholson continued to tinker and build. Joe Kinnear followed Beal out of the junior ranks and debuted against West Ham on 6 April 1966 when Gillie hit a consolation goal in a 4-1 defeat. (And then took over Beal's shirt when the number two suffered a broken arm in February 1967, the season the trophy cabinet was unlocked for the first time in four years other than for polishing the existing silverware gathering dust.)

England midfielder Terry Venables was bought for £80,000 from Chelsea a month after Kinnear's introduction, with Bill Nick believing his outfit was not the finished article due to it slipping close to mid-table by the close of the 1965/66 season.

John White had not been satisfactorily replaced in the middle of the park, so when Venables made his Spurs debut against relegated Blackburn Rovers it was hoped he would be the belated successor to The Ghost.

But Venables would struggle to appease the Lane faithful. He said, 'The fans may have been heckling me just for not being John White, although I was never a similar style of player anyway.'

Venables got off to a winning start alongside Gilzean as a Greaves goal separated Spurs and Blackburn at Ewood as his new club ended up eighth – while former Dark Blues stopper Bill Brown bade farewell, bound for Northampton Town – and established himself the following season which saw Gillie's Wembley dream come true.

Maurice Norman's leg break – the second of his career – and Laurie Brown's underwhelming efforts to take over the centre-half mantle from the colossus from East Anglia forced Nicholson to invest a record £95,000 for Mike England in August 1966. Wales international England was rated the best in his position in the UK, reflected in his fee, a British record for a defender. Nicholson also had to contend with Manchester United being linked with buying him.

It was a move which was to help Pat Jennings banish his tendency to produce erratic performances and become the club's greatest goalkeeper, for those who would not vote for Nicholson's team-mate and championship-winning stopper Ted Ditchburn. England was to offer the County Down custodian a composed presence, comfortable on the ball and dominant in the air with an ability to stir his mild-mannered ways enough to be the tough guy when required.

England revealed meeting Gilzean was one of the reasons he signed. He said, 'I came to White Hart Lane for the first time and hadn't signed. But on the way to his office, Bill Nick stopped all the players training and introduced them to me. Jimmy Greaves, Dave Mackay and, of course, Alan. It was very crafty the way Bill did it. It was a part of the reason I signed.'

The new team Nicholson had painstakingly constructed consisted of players who would also form the foundation for his third great Spurs team at the start of the 1970s.

It was headed by Gilzean and also included Pat Jennings, Joe Kinnear, Phil Beal, Cyril Knowles, Alan Mullery and Mike England, mixed with those from the recent glory, glory years in Greaves, Mackay, Cliff Jones and Frank Saul.

Mind you, two members of the class of 1966/67 – Jimmy Robertson and Terry Venables – had to settle for that one season in the limelight helping Spurs go close to their second Double in six years, both leaving before the end of the decade.

The Lilywhites had balance. A solid defence with class – evidenced by Knowles's refined left peg, Kinnear's comfort in possession and England's rock-like qualities in front of the come-of-age Jennings. Up front they had the best strike buddies in the English league in Gilzean and Greaves. And the midfield and flanks – with the likes of Mackay, Mullery and Jimmy Robertson – were not too dusty either.

* * *

The sun beat down as Gilzean helped Spurs kick off the season with a goal in a 3-1 win over Don Revie's highly rated Leeds United in front nearly 44,000 at the Lane. (The encounter produced the iconic picture of Mackay grabbing Billy Bremner by the throat following a challenge the Spurs iron man deemed dangerous to his physical wellbeing, not wanting a third serious injury. It is one Mackay did not like as it promoted the misguided notion he was a bully.)

Alan helped lead Spurs to the top of the table by October. He tasted his first victory over the Gunners, who had old Dundee team-mate Ian Ure in their line-up and netted a dramatic winner as Spurs produced a late show from one-down against the Manchester United of Denis Law, Bobby Charlton and George Best.

The number nine bagged a goal in a seven-goal thriller at Fulham and a goal double to stun hosts Manchester City.

He also helped his sidekick Jimmy Greaves secure nine goals in the opening ten fixtures. It seemed Greavsie had not become a manic depressive after being injured in England's third and final group game against France in the World Cup finals that summer. Opposing midfielder Joseph Bonell's rack down his shin required 14 stitches and left a permanent scar to put Greaves out of the quarter-final with Argentina and, almost certainly, denied him a winners' medal despite being fit for the final.

In the meantime, Gilzean suffered a sending off in Spurs's League Cup debut after his club had spent years ignoring a competition which was to give Gillie and themselves multiple glories.

It came on 14 September 1966 at the Boleyn Ground against a West Ham side fielding three of England's World Cup heroes from the summer, Geoff Hurst, who had replaced Greaves and got a hat-trick in the Wembley final, future Spurs midfielder Martin

Peters, the scorer of England's other goal in the decider against West Germany, and national skipper Bobby Moore.

Gilzean was booked for dissent by referee Harry New on the hour, before being ordered from the field five minutes later in a bemused state. He did not know the reason for his dismissal and the official declined to explain his decision when asked to do so by Bill Nicholson. And, ironically, it was Hurst who popped up with the game's only goal. Gilzean said, 'I remember it well – for all the wrong reasons! It's never a great night when we lose and you get sent off.

'But what a dubious decision – to put it mildly. The ball was played up the line and Bobby Moore, who was operating as sweeper, got there at the same time as me, knocking the ball out of play. And the linesman gave the throw to West Ham.

'I asked him, "When are you going to wake up?" Although probably a bit more forcibly than that. And the ref came over and gave me a straight red … not that red cards had even been thought of in those days.

'To his credit, Bobby Moore pleaded with the ref on my behalf. He admitted that he had put the ball out to give his defence time to get back in position, but the ref would have none of it.

'Bill Nick did ask the ref afterwards to explain the decision but he refused. So Bill decided that we would appeal. As a result I went up to Derby for the hearing – where I was promptly fined £100! So I suffered two injustices. I wish we hadn't bothered.

'Anyway, I'll never forget that game – and the moral of the story? Don't use so many adjectives when talking to a lino!

'But on a more memorable and positive note, what a side West Ham had at that time. They had good players throughout the team – and they all seemed to have names beginning with B [Burnett, Brown, Bennett, Boyce, Brabrook – and Bobby, of course].

'Bobby Moore was a great player. He made it all look so easy. And he was a proper gentleman on and off the pitch. He and Greavsie were big buddies.

'And what an honour to captain your side to World Cup glory. Although, as we all know, the first team to beat England after that great Wembley day was Scotland!'

Nicholson said, 'Gillie was reported to the FA and also me but I heard no more about the matter.'

The wheels came off Spurs's title charge. With Gilzean missing, they suffered a shock 3-1 home defeat to Blackpool, who finished the season rock bottom. Gillie returned for the next game but it seemed the Tangerines had squeezed the life out of any early championship hopes. It was the start of a six-match run in which the Lilywhites picked up just one point and they were unable to make up the lost ground as Matt Busby's United sealed the crown, eventually finishing third. An English title to go with the one he gained north of the border would have underlined to Gilzean he had been right to leave Dens for the Lane to pursue his big ambitions.

But Peenie justified the decision by fulfilling the daydream he had had back in the picture house with pals back in Coupar Angus, watching those grainy black-and-white Pathe News films showing highlights of the FA Cup Final at Wembley Stadium, the citadel of football in the country that invented the game – the ones which began, rather aptly as it turned out, with a crowing cockerel in the opening credits.

One of the major reasons he had joined Spurs as opposed to Sunderland was because, he figured, they got to Wembley more often. The stats certainly backed up that statement – just – with the Londoners having made two visits, winning each time, while the Mackems have managed just the one, which was also victorious (mind you, the London outfit have stormed ahead in the head-to-head appearances since – their FA/League Cup combined total is 14-4, and using the rebuilt national stadium for league games over almost two seasons has also bumped up their score).

Gilzean conjured a feature of a British spring – blossom – when he articulated the whole day of the 1967 cup final and the ultimate Wembley triumph as envisioned by his schoolboy self in that darkened cinema on Queen Street back home.

You could see and smell the experience through his eyes and senses. His body was with those present at *The Spurs Show* podcast gathering as he spoke to the audience in Dingwalls, the otherwise music and comedy venue, in December, 2013. But this mind had

hired Dr Who's tardis to travel back to Saturday, 20 May 1967 –
Spurs 2 Chelsea 1.

He tried to be studious and understated to reflect his usual
demeanour, attempting to gently break a stream of consciousness
fighting to flow from his lips. But often the words came out
excitedly in jumbled, though disarming, fashion.

He said, 'The cup final, that was special. Special for everybody.
Come May time and the cherry blossom is out. It is great for
footballers to go down that North Circular Road [to Wembley],
especially from Tottenham. There were blue-and-white flags out.

'It was one of the reasons to sign for Tottenham. That was my
dream. To win it and all that. The camaraderie after the game.
Dave Mackay saying to Joe Kinnear ... Joe kept looking at his
medal. Joe was only 20 and Mackay had three [FA Cup-winning]
medals by then. He said, "Don't worry son, if you lose it, I'll give
you one of mine."

'That was the sort of guy Mackay was. When we came out in
the tunnel with the Chelsea players, he was looking at them and
saying, "You don't fancy it, do you?"

'That was the sort of character we had as a captain. The big
barrel chest used to come out. He just wanted us to play attack,
attack, attack.

'He was the heart of the club – a fantastic leader – a guy
you'd want in the trenches with you. Every game he played in, he
wanted to win.

'We were playing golf once in San Francisco, Jimmy Robertson,
Mackay and myself, a knockout tournament between the three of
us. I was out of it. Coming down the 17th, Robbo and Mackay
were level. There came a downpour. Heavy, heavy rain. Puddles
started appearing on the course. So Mackay got on the green
with his second shot. Jimmy Robertson's second shot stuck in a
puddle short of the green. So he says to Davie, "Water hazard! I
can move the ball."

'Mackay says, "You don't move that ball. That puddle was there
before you played your second shot. Get on with it." That sums
Davie Mackay up. He would never give anything – in practice
matches, on the ball court. I've seen him chin two guys on there.

And that is just in practice! That's how much he was intent on winning. It was never a knockabout with him [Venables has told the story of how Mackay twice "hit me right in the balls with his fist" when he attempted to go by him on his first day at the club].'

He added, 'What was Davey like as a captain? He was the driving force behind the whole club, Mackay. He was one of those who would play with positivity, there were no grey areas with Davey. A born winner.'

Gilzean, despite a cool exterior on the field, confessed to feeling edgy despite Mackay's bravado in front of the Chelsea players before kick-off.

'He said, 'Yes [when asked if he was nervous], everybody's nervous. Most of the Tottenham team, apart from Dave Mackay and Jonesy [Cliff Jones], who by then was substitute, were all new to it. Never had that experience before. Did well to calm the nerves.'

Gilzean recalled Spurs and Chelsea players got together pre-match. He said, 'I remember before the game, because it was the first all-London cup final, the Anglo-American club put on an event at the Hilton Hotel, and both teams were invited along, and we got to know each other. I knew quite a few of the Chelsea lads, but in a cup final you had no friends unless they were in white jerseys.'

But the fact it was a derby, with bragging rights in the English capital, did not provoke any overt naughtiness to 'cause slight or persistent comfort or anxiety'. Even from Chelsea captain Ron Harris, nicknamed Chopper due to his reputation for chopping opponents down (I once saw him booed by his own crowd for taking out Stanley Matthews when the legendary winger visited Stamford Bridge aged close to 50).

That's how Gilzean remembered it. His eyes were on the prize. He said, 'It wasn't niggly. Bringing the trophy home was all-important.'

It was, though, largely, a day when the blossom on any trees or bushes amid the urban symbols of concrete and tarmac on the road from Tottenham to Wembley struggled to provide the image which presented the perfect spring day. The vibrant colours of the flowers in full bloom in bright sunlight were dampened by showers on a largely grey, cloudy day with low pressure dominating a weather front which typified the whole of that month in London.

The Summer of Love, with the cultural revolutionists introducing us to psychedelia in all its forms through art, clothing and lifestyle, was around the corner, but someone had forgotten to tell the weather gods this dull day.

The traditional pre-match community singsong had subsided as the teams emerged side by side behind their managers from the tunnel en route to meet and greet royalty in the shape of the Duke of Kent and get down to business on the famous, wetted turf. There was a deafening roar from the 100,000 who had managed to get a ticket for the game's hottest domestic football event of the time. The world's most iconic stadium with its twin towers shook.

Tottenham were in all white, each player wearing a zip-up white tracksuit top with thin parallel navy blue line around its collar and cuffs. Mackay jutted out his chest and chin behind a smiling Bill Nick followed by Pat Jennings. Each held a football in just one hand in a display, perhaps, of one-upmanship. Terry Venables, Alan Mullery, Frank Saul, Joe Kinnear, Jimmy Robertson, Cyril Knowles and Mike England filed in behind – all displaying an aura of calm.

Chelsea, in blue with matching tracksuits, were more animated and seemingly more agitated behind an uncharacteristically solemn Tommy Docherty. Chewing gum, fiddling with their hair and, in the case of Tony Hateley, even waving at the cameraman, who was capturing the moments on video. It seemed an internal club row over player bonuses in the lead-up might have had an unsettling effect.

It appeared there was less cause for disharmony in the Spurs camp in the build-up, with Greaves subsequently revealing pranks aplenty, including a message to assistant manager Eddie Baily saying, 'Mr Baily, your brother Bill has telephoned to say he won't be coming home,' (in reference to the song 'Won't You Come Home, Bill Bailey'). And another saw the likes of Knowles and Frank Saul left bemused, as shampoo was, unbeknown to them, squeezed on their heads AFTER they had rinsed off what they had already applied.

Most of the Spurs players were spotted, but where were the remaining three members of the Spurs contingent? A long lens trapped them. Cliff Jones, a double FA Cup winner and a sub, was behind England and Jimmy Greaves brought up the rear. Gillie? He was tucked behind Knowles and in front of England, strolling with that familiar hip-swaying gait. A picture of ease like his team-mates, he was idly half-turning his head to the left as if merely giving himself something to do rather than being distracted by any movement or noise, largely obscured by the looming figure of Knowles, a rugby league player's son. It was as if he was determined to make his introduction to the gladiatorial arena as low-key as possible, although no doubt hiding the feeling of butterflies inside his stomach.

One team-mate believed he looked the oldest player in the league in his 20s, while another reckoned he cut an 'ungainly figure with one shoulder higher than the other'.

This day a 28-year-old Gilzean, who was to become known for looking older than his years, still had a black head of hair, although it was receding each side at the front.

And, yet again, it was proved any ungainliness he might have displayed off the pitch was replaced by consummate grace on it. And he was pivotal in the victory with his leadership of the front line and dominance in the air, although Ron Harris's tight attention of Jimmy Greaves limited what the G-Men could achieve.

But he was aided by the decision of fellow Scot Tommy Docherty to abandon a tactic which worked like a dream in the league encounter between the sides at Stamford Bridge back in the October. The Blues boss had employed centre-half Marvin Hinton as a sweeper and it resulted in Gilzean being kept as quiet as a mouse and Spurs suffering their worst defeat of the season, along with a surprise loss by the same 3-0 scoreline against West Bromwich Albion at The Hawthorns. Docherty also retained the system for the draw his young Blues secured in the reverse fixture in March.

Nicholson said, 'When I heard that [he'd abandoned the sweeper system], I told my players, "He's done us a favour." Gilzean didn't like playing against a sweeper.'

165

It left Gillie able to be a big noise in the final, with Hinton part of a flat back four. It was a masterclass of centre-forward play as he beat his opponent in the air and on the ground, while his flicks and tricks found willing runners. Chelsea were, though, as has been said, focused on keeping the G-Men quiet and in so doing gave Robertson and Saul room to pull the necessary triggers.

Spurs also came up with a couple of effective tactics which helped turn the game in their favour. Bill Nick switched the usual full-back roles of Joe Kinnear, who was outstanding, and Cyril Knowles, allowing the former to maraud and the other to hold back. He did likewise in midfield, giving Alan Mullery licence to charge forward with Mackay sticking to more defensive duties such as keeping an eye on Charlie Cooke, who had been signed by Dundee in the wake of Gillie's Dens departure.

It was no wonder Doc's younger side – from which Venables was jettisoned in the wake of a semi-final defeat in the same competition a year before – were unable to get a grip of a match dominated by Gillie and co.

It was Chelsea's first Wembley final – as it was for Gilzean, of course. One Blues – who have been regular visitors to the replacement stadium in modern times – would want to forget. One, naturally, that the former boy scout nicknamed Peenie would never want to.

It was said the Spurs supporters were subdued and I remember. the atmosphere being quieter than I expected, although there was a bell or two rung by individuals and hearty renditions of the Spurs anthem 'Glory Glory Hallelujah'. Perhaps it was the fact there was no north/south showdown to get the entire country excited. But the match itself was a stirring enough affair, even though Spurs never looked in danger of losing with their more creative, ball-playing style.

The sun broke through in the first half of the first all-London final. And the marauding Mullery helped Spurs to shine in it. His shot cannoned off a defender and Jimmy Robertson volleyed home from the centre of the edge of the area five minutes before half-time. Behind the goal, subdued became ecstatic.

Gilzean walked off at half-time side by side with Greaves, both with sweated brows and no smiles. It was clear no chickens were being counted. And Gillie played his part as Spurs doubled their lead. He pressured the Chelsea defence into a hurried headed clearance, which Robertson nodded down for Frank Saul to double the Spurs lead on 67 minutes.

Bobby Tambling pegged Spurs's lead to one with a header from a John Boyle cross five minutes from time, but Tottenham game-managed the remaining time and the cup was theirs – and Dave Mackay's – for a third time in six years. Mackay – the survivor of two broken legs – had taken Gilzean under his wing at the behest of Bobby Wishart, the striker's former Dundee team-mate. Now it was time for the pals and compatriots to celebrate.

It was also a time for the G-Men to savour the moment. Gilzean and Greaves, who had also forged a friendship as well as a strike partnership, walked arm in arm around the track on the lap of honour. Gillie, it is sure, would have appreciated the poignancy for Greaves having been left out of England's winning World Cup team at the same venue a year earlier. And in turn Greaves knew what the achievement meant to his favourite partner in football.

Gilzean had joined the team to climb the 39 steps to the royal box to collect the cup, along with their individual winners' medals, although the thoughtful Scot did reportedly give away another memento, his match shirt, to the son of a Spurs office worker afterwards.

It is for such moments that footballers play the game. And Gilzean, who had his mum Babs and dad William there, was no exception. As he said all those years later, 'It was special.'

One wonders whether he ever went back to that picture house in Queen Street to watch the Pathe News coverage of the time a dream became a reality.

Mike England, Tottenham's genial centre-half with an iron streak, recalled Gilzean's delight. He said, 'Alan joined Spurs because he wanted to play at Wembley in an FA Cup Final and, of course, that is exactly what happened. I remember Gillie walking round Wembley afterwards with the cup on his head. It was very funny. Great. He had a super game. Played really well. It was enjoyable when you won the FA Cup. It was a footballer's dream then. Now it has lost a little of what it used to be.

'I thought I'd have to mark Peter Osgood [who ended up sidelined by a broken leg and was replaced by Tony Hateley]. Bill Nick told me, "Hateley is a big fellow, he's dangerous in the air. You can deal with him." That was a great compliment to me.'

Jimmy Robertson said, 'I remember that cup final! One of the things we worked on was that Gillie would basically mark Hinton. Chelsea played across the back four in the [Italian] catenaccio [a tight man-for-man marking] system and one thing I can remember working on was Gillie standing on Hinton instead of the guy being free. In terms of the game, it meant Gillie would be occupying the centre-half rather than the other way around.'

Pat Jennings revealed Gilzean helped him defend the goal. He said, 'That was the other side of him. He was good defensively for you as he was good in the air. At corners, free kicks into your box, that was the other part we didn't appreciate enough.'

Chelsea captain Ron Harris made no mention of Gilzean when citing the turning point of the final. His focus was on Jennings. He said, 'I thought we were unlucky to be a goal down by half-time. That goal came at just the wrong time for us when we needed to be containing Spurs.

'The ball came off my shin to Jimmy Robertson. He took it well. Disappointing? Of course it is.

'The turning point in theory came with Spurs's second goal. But I think the turning point came just before Spurs scored their first goal. Pat Jennings made a fantastic save from Charlie Cooke. A save that swung the game. We could easily have been one up.

'It wasn't as tough as some people thought it would be. But you can't take it away from Spurs. They were a good side and took their chances well.'

The road to Wembley was a bumpy one for Spurs at first. They were drawn against Millwall in their opening round at The Den. The Lions had just completed back-to-back promotions to the second tier of English football. They were invincible at The Den, having been undefeated for 59 games in 32 months until a loss against Plymouth Argyle the previous Saturday, with the help of the intimidating atmosphere created by their passionate support with their long, monotone roar.

Visitors to Cold Blow Lane clearly didn't like the wind – chilly or otherwise – up 'em. And I detected a feeling amongst the home followers that they suspected the Lilywhites to be lily-livered. Also, the hosts were packed with players who were fast becoming folk heroes to a fanbase from an area considered rough and ready in some quarters – performers such as Harry Cripps and Barry Kitchener.

A literal visit into the Lions' Den was certainly uncomfortable for the glamour pusses from north of the Thames. One story related by Julie Welch in *The Biography of Tottenham Hotspur* illustrates that. She wrote, 'As the Spurs players gathered in the centre-circle before the kick-off, two fans ran on the pitch with a cockerel and a set of gallows, from which they proceeded to hang the unfortunate fowl.'

Perhaps my protective Dad had taken me to the loo, but that incident escaped my attention. Yet there was no question the hosts had created a mood which tested the mettle of Gilzean and the rest of my favourites.

But the 'glamour pusses' proved they had a bit of the lion in them as well, showing pride in the shirt. They displayed the required bottle to withstand everything that was thrown at them by hosts who limited the visitors' more expansive, sophisticated style as the tie ended goalless.

And a Gilzean goal ensured Spurs got the job done in front of a sell-out 58,189 crowd under the Lane lights nights later, myself being one of many locked out.

The path smoothed out as draws continued to favour Spurs, with three more Second Division outfits pulled out of the hat at FA headquarters by nondescript officials of the governing body rather than celebrity players in front of television cameras at a venue to suit the companies that own those cameras. In the initial two at home, Gilzean notched a couple of goals to help see off Portsmouth 3-1 before a crowd close to 58,000. The pulling power of the cup was evident when the Scot's strike partner Jimmy Greaves netted a double to defeat Bristol City 2-0 before a crowd getting on for 55,000.

Gilzean and his Lilywhites were a major attraction on the road too, with Birmingham City's biggest attendance of the season

(51,467) witnessing the visitors fortunate to earn a goalless draw. But Spurs hit City – who had Gillie's future Highlands Park team-mate Barry Bridges in their line-up (more later) – for six in the replay of the sixth-round tie on a boggy pitch played out before another 50,000 fans who saw the Scot hit the mark from a Robertson cross.

Spurs ran out of relatively easy options in the semi-final. Opponents Nottingham Forest – second to leaders Manchester United in the title race – were considered favourites for the Hillsborough meeting on Saturday, 8 April 1967. But Gilzean literally used his head to help them stand up to be counted as the G-Men combined in typical fashion to give the north Londoners the lead against the run of play on the half-hour.

Gillie was considered, euphemistically, to have a 'threepenny bit' head. The opinion was based on the fact that as the old British coin had 12 edges it was comparable to his bonce, given the player was capable of angling a ball to his whim off it, rather like Kryten in TV science fiction comedy *Red Dwarf* might have done if his character with the multi-angled head had been cast as a footballer rather than a 'service mechanoid' onboard the spacecraft Nova 5.

And Alan's cranium was in full working order inside and out as he followed a long ball from centre-half Mike England to the edge of the penalty area just to the right of the semi-circle. He spotted Greaves more centrally placed a few yards behind him and, gently, deliberately guided the ball back into his partner's path. And Greaves volleyed beyond Forest goalkeeper Peter Grummitt with his left foot into the corner of the net.

The Gillie-Greaves one-two dealt a fatal psychological blow to Forest. The bright start Spurs's opponents had made gave the impression that Johnny Carey's men had gotten over the loss of influential Joe Baker, the former strike partner of Denis Law at Torino, to injury in their quarter-final win against Everton. Not so, it seemed.

Frank Saul sealed a final date with a cracker 20 minutes from time – with Terry Hennessey heading a late consolation for the deflated opposition – but it was apparent Forest had been chopped down by the G-Men, most notably Greaves who had the sign over them. Gillie's pocket-sized genius of a partner scored more goals against Forest for Spurs than against any other team, totalling 29 – including three lots of four goals.

The surprise victory came in the month 100-1 Foinavon upset odds in the Grand National at Aintree with the aid of a pile-up at the 23rd fence of the toughest steeplechase of all.

It might not have registered as high as one of sport's biggest shocks, but Gillie and his men in white could not have cared less.

Gilzean said, 'Forest were a good side. We had a difficult tie against Millwall. Neither game was a good one and we scraped through. We didn't play well, but after that we started to play. I remember we drew at Birmingham and thrashed them six or something at White Hart Lane.'

13

I Predict a Riot

ALAN GILZEAN was at the centre of an extraordinary moment as he helped Spurs grab a share of a second trophy in three months.

It was his club's first big match since they equalled Wanderers's number of five FA Cup wins by beating Chelsea; an achievement completed, of course, in a professional era rather than in the amateur world prevalent in the Victorian one lived in by a team largely made up of former public schoolboys.

The moment? It came in the annual season curtain-raiser between the cup winners and the league champions for the FA Charity Shield at Old Trafford on Saturday, 12 August 1967.

Spurs already led hosts Manchester United 1-0 thanks to a Jimmy Robertson goal from a deflected low Jimmy Greaves cross when visiting goalkeeper Pat Jennings launched a huge, seemingly sky-scraping, punt forward.

Gilzean's reactions were razor-sharp and he was off on his toes to get on the end of it, a tactic he and Jennings regularly employed. He ran in behind the home rearguard as the ball fell. But there was no opportunity to get a contact either with his head or any other part of his anatomy as it dropped high and wide of his right shoulder and bounced just outside the penalty area.

Alex Stepney had advanced around 15 yards from his goal. The spherical object he had hoped to gather looped up again and arced over his head with the United goalkeeper caught in no-man's land. The ball bounced once more – inside the six-yard box – as Gillie, running left to right on an angled run across Stepney, followed the ball in as it nestled in the corner of the net. It was a Dambusters-like raid on the home goal, with the bouncing bomb replaced by an inflated leather projectile.

BBC commentator Kenneth Wolstenholme, who had become famous for his 'they think it's all over' phrase as Geoff Hurst sealed the World Cup for England the previous year, hesitated. Perhaps he thought the laws would not allow it, that he would be mistaken in declaring a goal. Gilzean seemed to have no doubts as he jumped in a half circle while his raised right arm windmilled round to spin his body to face back to the field, although he did glance across to the official then known officially as the linesman rather than referee's assistant.

Jennings admitted to me that he was unsure of his effort's legitimacy. He said, 'I was basically trying to hit Alan that day. There was a free kick to us just outside our box. Dave Mackay ran up to take it. I said, "Give it to me, Dave. I'll knock it up." And he gave it back to me and I was, as I said, trying to hit Gillie up front. I think Alex Stepney came up the back of Gillie thinking he would pick up a miscontrolled ball that had travelled the length of the field. Of course, it has missed Gillie, and Alex is in no-man's land. With the next bounce it is in the net. Everybody, including me, is saying, "What does the referee give?" We'd never seen it. I can still picture Gillie jumping! I have to tell you, Mackay claimed an assist – for giving the ball back to me!'

Bobby Charlton, a World Cup winner, blasted United back into contention with two thumping efforts, the second made with the assistance of Alan's second-favourite player, Denis Law.

But Gilzean popped up on the left to cross for Frank Saul, holding off a challenge from another of Alf Ramsey's heroes, Nobby Stiles, to head Spurs back in front before Law made it 3-3 to ensure both clubs shared the trophy.

Denis Law had a soft spot for Gillie's Spurs team as the pair went head to head while developing a growing rivalry between their clubs.

Gilzean's debut against Law's United had seen them secure a 1-0 win with nearly 59,000 squeezed into a sell-out crowd at White

Hart Lane on 6 February 1965. The G-Men were in action, as were United's Holy Trinity of Law, George Best and Bobby Charlton, but home full-back Ron Henry was the unlikely match-winner.

A Gilzean prod as the ball rebounded off the bar set Spurs on the way to a Holy Trinity-dismaying 5-1 victory at the Lane eight months later. He also combined with Greaves to set up a Neil Johnson goal. And chipped in a superb assist for the final strike from Jimmy Robertson by wriggling clear down the left on a slippery surface. It was a match most famous for arguably Greaves's greatest goal, a turn and a run through the United defence like a knife through butter.

But Gilzean had to suck it up as Scotland team-mate Law bagged a double as United reversed the score in the reverse fixture a week before Christmas.

The G-Men each netted in the last five minutes in a dramatic comeback Spurs victory after a Law goal had given United a first-half lead at the Lane on 10 September 1966.

In the wake of the six-goal Shield thriller that season, in which United lifted the European Cup, Gilzean and Law each scored as United beat Spurs 3-1 at Old Trafford 12 months later. And the friendly rivals helped their sides battle out a 2-2 FA Cup thriller in front of 63,500 at the same ground in the January. Law missed the replay, which Gillie helped Spurs win. But he returned in Gilzean's absence to inflict a league defeat on their London hosts in the third meeting between the teams in seven days.

There were to be more high-profile White v Red clashes in front of massive crowds involving the Scottish duo.

The following season they each hit the mark in a 2-2 Lane deadlock – it was the final Spurs appearance for the other home scorer Cliff Jones – after United had secured a home victory.

The next Gilzean-Law showdown came on 5 December 1970, each scoring in a Lane draw eight months after the Spurs ace had converted a match-winner against the Law-less visitors.

Honours were even in 1971/72, with both helping their teams win at home, although Law could claim the edge by scoring twice at Old Trafford.

Spurs's 2-0 win at the Lane on 4 March 1972 was the last time they locked horns in the club rivalry.

Gilzean missed the memorable day when Martin Peters scored all four in a 4-1 win over Law's United at Old Trafford on 28 October 1972. And neither Scot took part in the drawn Lane fixture the following March. (Note, Law moved to Manchester City for the following season and scored a famous goal against United, mistakenly believing it had sealed relegation for his former employers when their fate had been sealed elsewhere on the day.)

Alan was to play only once more against United, who were en route to their demotion. And it was a winning experience in front of almost 43,000 at the Lane on 10 November 1973. He came on as a substitute for Martin Chivers, with whom he enjoyed his second prolific strike partnership at the club (more later).

Law admired the Tottenham side his international team-mate shone so brightly in.

He said, 'Gillie played for a magnificent Spurs side. They were one of my favourite teams, although we didn't like playing them because they were so good. It was a huge game.

'I used to enjoy going down to London to play them. And if we got a result against them it was even better!

'The beauty was that both mine and Alan's side hopefully played exciting football.

'The fact Spurs had fantastic Scottish players besides Alan, like Dave Mackay, helped make them so good. John White had been another and would have become an all-time great for Scotland had he lived. His death [just before Gilzean arrived at Spurs, of course] was so tragic. They also had Jimmy Greaves in that great partnership with Gillie too.

'It was hard to play against players you played with for your international team in club football. But playing against them could give you an advantage as you knew what they could do!'

Law enjoyed being part of the Holy Trinity with George Best and Bobby Charlton, who got together regularly to take on Gillie and co. He said, 'It was a nice thing to have in your life. It was a lovely time for football with some very good teams and some very good players.'

Gilzean might have been relieved to learn Spurs would not have a commitment in the League Cup for the 1967/68 season after the team's and his disastrous debut against the Hammers the previous term.

The league campaign got off to a bright start with Spurs winning five and drawing one of their opening seven fixtures. Spurs were second. Any optimistic thoughts of a title bid were soon scuppered. They hit the buffers with back-to-back defeats, the first an embarrassing 4-0 loss to their fiercest rivals Arsenal at Highbury, followed by that Old Trafford loss in which Gilzean managed to hit the target. They tried to rally and goals by Gilzean secured impressive victories against Chelsea and, even more satisfyingly, the Gunners.

But his goals were few and far between. Maybe he was over-concerned about keeping the still-potent Greaves with enough ammunition to slip into his six-gun. Maybe not. But he failed to get into double figures by the end of the league campaign for the first time since he arrived from Dens Park.

There were also moments of frustration away from the task of finding the onion bag. Gillie's normally phlegmatic disposition was understood to ruffle as it did at West Ham. It came in a 1-0 reverse against Don Revie's high-flying Leeds United at Elland Road on 17 April 1968. Reports had it he aimed a boot at home left-back Terry Cooper with play 40 yards away and received his marching orders and a one-match suspension for the start of the following season (thus missing a 1-0 home defeat against Arsenal).

One presumes his England international opponent had rattled his cage. The Leeds website oz.whitelufc.net opined, in what seemed exaggerated tones, 'Spurs boasted the reputation as one of London's glamour sides and had a fine pedigree for "playing football the right way". But that reputation was seriously tarnished at Elland Road as an intense rivalry was born. Tottenham gave away an incredible 19 free kicks and saw Scottish international Alan Gilzean sent-off ...'

The second half of the season was further complicated for Gilzean when Bill Nicholson began to experiment with him in positions other than centre-forward. He wore the number-eight, ten, eleven and seven shirts rather than the number nine. He even had to pull on the number-12 top against Stoke City and Coventry, coming on in both wins for Martin Chivers.

It was deemed Bill Nick was tinkering to find a regular place for him in the front line while trying to accommodate central striker Chivers, who was signed for £125,000 from Southampton in January 1968.

It could have been argued that Chivers was casting a giant shadow over the long-term future of Gilzean had not the Scot's manager tried so diligently to find him a spot, even if it was coming off the bench.

All in all Gillie, who finished with just eight goals in 32 league appearances, helped Spurs finish seventh, 11 points off champions Manchester City, with Greaves rattling in 23 in 39.

The league campaign was a let-down as the previous season had promised so much. An unbeaten run of 16 matches to finish off the 1966/67 season might have even allowed those of a Lilywhite persuasion to believe a second Double in six years was possible had it not been for injuries and a few mistakes.

But more than a morsel of positivity came out of the FA Cup for Alan Gilzean and Spurs in 1967/68. Jimmy Robertson saw Tottenham into the fourth round with an extra-time winner against Manchester United in that replay previously mentioned. And goals by Greaves (2) and Chivers against Preston sealed a 3-1 home win before Liverpool, led by Gilzean's old army pal Ron Yeats, ended Spurs's hopes of a Wembley return in a fifth-round replay at Anfield.

But it was the first match of the cup campaign – the 2-2 draw with United at Old Trafford – which shone a light into Gillie's future at Spurs.

Bill Nick had opted to play Gilzean up front alongside Martin Chivers, with Greaves left out, for the first time after trying all three in Chivers's initial Tottenham appearances, against Sheffield Wednesday and Arsenal in the league.

The new duo caught the eye after combining to secure a last-minute equaliser in United's Theatre of Dreams. Gilzean flicked a Mike England free kick into the path of Chivers, who converted his second goal of the match to force the replay, although mistaken anticipation of disgruntled Stretford Enders paying the travelling support a visit at the away end to duff us up limited my celebrations.

One prescient national scribe, the late and legendary Desmond Hackett of the *Daily Express*, stated, 'Alan Gilzean, who was becoming a problem player, is now thriving in the company of Martin Chivers. They could develop into one of the greatest scoring acts in the First Division.'

The hopes of Gilzean and Spurs revisiting former European glories proved illusory this season.

It had been all smiles and tears of joy as Gillie and co made their lap of honour at Wembley after ensuring a place in continental competition by winning the FA Cup Final against Chelsea.

But it was more all scowls and tears of frustration as the reality kicked in at the end of what was a third Cup Winners' Cup campaign for the Lilywhites. They had won it at the first attempt, fallen in the opening round of their defence against Law's Manchester United – during which Mackay suffered his first broken leg – at the second. But the third tilt was far from lucky.

Glory, Glory Nights were replaced by Gory, Gory Nights as Spurs and Gilzean were edged out in the second round.

Gilzean had taken Europe by storm in his only previous European adventure, with his nine goals helping Dundee surge into the semi-finals of the European Cup in 1963 while Spurs completed their Cup Winners' Cup triumph.

But an unwanted history repeated itself for the former Coupar Angus schoolboy turned superstar. His first journey had been largely fun as he underlined his credentials as a world-class footballer. But the overall experience, as we have discovered, had not been all sweetness and light given the intimidation and physical abuse endured in Cologne and Milan, with Gillie losing his cool enough to get sent off against the Italians in the second leg of their last-four tie.

There were similar tests of self-control required as the 1967 FA Cup winners returned to European competition. It all looked good on the surface when Gilzean helped Spurs defeat hosts Hajduk Split 2-0 in the first leg of the opening round on 20 September 1967, but dig deeper and there were frustrations for the visitors. And not just the hot, humid weather conditions and rock-hard surface.

The now-Croatian club were named after bandits considered Robin Hood figures for stealing from the rich and giving to the poor, and it might be deemed the referee may have had sympathy with that philosophy, judging from the comments of Geoffrey Green, one of the most respected and eminent contemporary football writers. He wrote in *The Times*, 'All that spoilt it [a Spurs victory] was the incessant whistle of the Bulgarian referee who had eyes only for the Slavs, an official who must have learnt the rules from a book unknown to the original lawmakers.

'Still Tottenham kept their heads calmly turning away from every frustration in the match played out to an incessant screech of whistles in the crowd and to a non-stop rocket barrage ... More than once, in fact, Greaves and Gilzean – often caught offside – stopped in their tracks thinking the referee was playing his usual serenade, only to find too late it was some joker up on the open terraces.'

Phil Beal, so often the unsung hero, marked the home dangerman Miroslav Vardić out of the game and Robertson and Greaves, following a 40-yard run, netted the goals.

Gilzean found the target as sluggish Spurs went through with a 4-3 win at the Lane despite allowing Hajduk three late goals, but the achievement ensured another more-than-merely uncomfortable experience in the next round.

The Kaiser Chiefs rock-pop band sung 'I Predict a Riot' in 2004. You wondered whether one could have been predicted prior to Spurs's second-round tie with Olympique Lyonanais. Well they got certainly got one, according to reports.

Bill Nicholson said, 'The match was a disgrace and this Lyon side played more like rugby league than football league. They pulled and shoved all through the game and yet the referee let them get away with it.' Even opposing manager Louis Hon said to John Oakley, 'He [the referee] lost control altogether at times.'

London Evening News reporter John Oakley labelled it the Battle of Lyon, with five Spurs players injured. And Gilzean was right in the middle of it, sustaining a bruised side on the field and worse off it.

The encounter which produced what the *Daily Mail*'s Brian James described as a 'riot', could hardly be classified as a crowd-puller, with the Gerland Stadium of the hosts almost three-quarters empty. But those who were in the stands and on the terraces certainly made their presence felt with a series of pitch invasions, one sparked by a 33rd-minute bust-up between Alan Mullery and Lyon player Andre Guy.

Mullery was left 'unconscious' on the turf and said Guy had 'kicked me full in the mouth' and added, 'I retaliated. I punched him.'

James wrote that 'the teams fought with fist and foot' for eight 'appalling' minutes in the aftermath as home fans joined in. The outcome saw both players eventually sent off by Czech referee Josef Krnavek. Gilzean got involved in the interim to the chagrin of Guy.

Gilzean said, 'What happened was, Mullery and a guy called Guy clashed and they both got sent off. And the referee was going to be sending the wrong guy off. I pointed out to the referee it was Guy who'd clashed with Mullery. Eventually he sent Guy off.

'Coming down the tunnel there was an atmosphere there was going to be trouble. I said to Pat [Jennings] as he came off at half-time, "Can you be my minder?"'

Jennings took up the story. He said, 'Gillie was waiting on me when I was coming off the pitch at half-time and he said, "I think there could be trouble here, can you keep an eye on me?" So we are walking through. The next minute it is "bang" and this fellow [Guy] has hit Gillie. I was looking the other way and the guy has read the situation. They were out for Gillie. And the next thing I'm seeing Bill Nick on top of this bloke who hit him! And me supposed to be doing the minding because I'm the big guy.

'On the field, Gillie took a lot of stick. Their defenders got away with ridiculous challenges. But you couldn't kick him out of the game. That was one of his strengths. Kick him and he'd be back at you.'

Gilzean smiled at the memory, laughing, 'An enjoyable match.' There was also irony in his voice as he recalled the second leg at White Hart Lane when he scored one of four goals Spurs netted that night. He said, 'It was really funny. Guy couldn't play and unfortunately Mike England was injured. We beat them 4-3 but on away goals they are going through. I remember coming into the dressing room afterwards. Bill got hold of Greavsie and me and gave us a right rollicking. We [the forwards] had scored four goals [Gillie and Greaves three between them] and the defence had lost three and Bill Nick blamed the forwards! Funny old world, isn't it?'

* * *

The Scottish contingent in the regular Spurs line-up was numerically reduced by a third at the end of the 1967/68 season when Gillie and Jimmy Robertson waved goodbye to Dave Mackay. In terms of the hole Mackay's departure left it was, of course, far bigger. Bill Nick had replaced ten of his Double team, but not the iron man from Edinburgh, the player he considered his best signing when he shelled out £30,000 for his services to Heart of Midlothian in 1959. Mackay was considered by common consensus to be as close to irreplaceable as you can get. No one had the fire of Mackay. No one had the heart of Mackay. No one had the will to win of Mackay. He had, as Cliff Jones told me, turned a good side into a great one.

It was Gilzean's pal, the guy who had kept an eye on his friend when moving from Dundee, who forced Nicholson's hand. He wanted to take the rap for an underwhelming season, insisting he was finished after 12 years of glory and pain at the Lane.

Mackay and his manager made plans for a return to Tynecastle as player-manager. Out of the blue, Brian Clough of Second Division Derby County defied the perceived wisdom of perhaps the two most important individuals in the history of the club and argued Braveheart had more to offer – and after changing Mackay's opinion of himself, got his man. And Mackay proved this brash young manager was right by leading Derby into the First Division and earning the Footballer of the Year award in his first season at the Baseball Ground. Alan Mullery said, 'It took another three years to build a side without Mackay as captain.'

Graeme Souness might have had a similar influence to Mackay and made Bill Nicholson's third great team even greater had he not been lost to the club after just one first-team appearance – in the UEFA Cup in 1972 – and twice being named an unused sub.

Souness had a stellar playing career with clubs Middlesbrough, Liverpool, Sampdoria, Rangers and Scotland, one rewarded when he accepted his induction into the Scottish hall of fame on the night Gilzean was inducted in 2009 (more later).

But he was the player at White Hart Lane with a bit of the Mackay about him.

And Gilzean it is understood offered the young Souness encouragement after Spurs signed him as a 15-year-old apprentice in April 1969 before taking him on as a professional the following May. Pat Jennings, who was at the club with the two, said, 'Gillie would have loved Graeme for being Scottish. Although he didn't spend much time with him as a player, he knew plenty about him. Graeme might have cleaned Gillie's boots when they were at the club together.'

James Morgan wrote in *In Search of Alan Gilzean*, '[Gilzean] pulled him [Souness] aside and told him the two Scots had to stick together.'

Gilzean's former Dundee team-mate Pat Liney, said, 'Gillie would have helped Graeme. He would help anybody in any situation. That was the type of guy he was.'

Souness has said he benefitted from Gillie being around with him at the Lane. He said, 'Gillie is a marvellous player and I'm not saying that because we both come from Scotland. Any youngster can learn an awful lot just by watching him.'

Certainly, it is understood Bill Nicholson saw Souness as a 'possible successor' to Mackay. Nicholson said, 'There was no mistaking his ability. He was a strong lad, but the problem was he could be spiteful in the tackle. He didn't get on with [assistant manager] Eddie Baily, who would throw his coat across the dressing room and curse. I said to him [Baily], "Souness will become a great player one day and it's worth being patient with him." He could have been Dave's successor, but he wanted to progress more quickly than I had planned for him.'

Souness said, 'There are times when I think I should have stuck it out at White Hart Lane. If I had done that, I could have shown Bill and the fans that I turned out to be a pretty useful player.'

Pat Jennings confirmed Nicholson's opinion of Souness. Jennings said, 'Bill fancied him. Graeme was some player – won the FA Youth Cup when he was at the club alongside Stevie P,

Johnny Pratt and Clarkey [Ray Clarke, who went on to play with Johan Cruyff at Ajax]. But Eddie Baily used to knock Graeme back at every opportunity. Eddie used to like doing that kind of thing to people.

'Knowlesy [Cyril Knowles] and myself were in digs together and we got a call one night from Harold Shepherdson [Middlesbrough trainer who did the same job in England's World Cup win]. He said, "We're interested in this lad Souness. What's he like?" We said, "Phew … what's he like? He can play, this kid. He's a bit flash." Harold said, "Don't worry, we can handle that." And the next thing Middlesbrough had bought him. And he went on to Liverpool and more. What a career.'

Souness went back home to Scotland before all this. Jennings said, 'He must have got the needle with us because he was saying players that weren't as good as him had got in the team in front of him. He took off. But Bill went and got him back.'

14

'We Got On Well, Martin and Me'

ALAN GILZEAN, his dark hair thinning and grey, remained one of Bill Nicholson's regulars in the Spurs starting XI during a second transition period for the team following the Scot's arrival in London N17, with the manager breaking up the 1967 FA Cup-winning team.

Final goalscorer Frank Saul departed to Southampton as a makeweight in the Martin Chivers deal for a British-record fee in January 1968. And Wembley sub Cliff Jones, a survivor from the Double team, was offloaded to Fulham in the October.

In the same month, Jimmy Robertson – who scored one and made the other in the final – did what might have been considered the unthinkable and joined Arsenal.

Bill Nick was pinning a lot of hopes on Chivers, who had made the Saints first-team aged 17 and banged in 97 goals in 175 appearances. Ten goals from 23 games in his first season was promising, but a twisted knee which severed the lower patella ligament against Nottingham Forest ended the following campaign for the central striker after just 11 games, in which he scored six including a League Cup hat-trick. Frustration could not have begun to describe the feelings of both the player and manager.

Gilzean himself only managed a worst-in-career-to-date total of seven goals for the entire campaign, although there was more emphasis on him as a goalmaker in a season Bill Nick tried to reignite the G-Men, with the Scot returning to number nine in the absence of Chivers.

There was encouragement, though, as Greaves was still proving a regular source of goals. Greavsie netted a hat-trick just two matches after Chivers had been sidelined, which at least gave Bill Nick an excuse to display a glimmer of a smile. It came against Leicester City and one of his treble was arguably the best goal he ever scored for Spurs. With Gilzean and the rest of his team-mates mere spectators, he set off on a run after collecting a punt from Pat Jennings out wide on the halfway line, past his marker, beyond three more defenders and goalkeeper Peter Shilton, who was to become England's most-capped stopper, before tapping the ball into the net.

Another sign that that were nuggets of positivity to collect for Gilzean and his increasingly merry men despite the setback with Chivers was a run to the semi-finals of the 1969 League Cup; admittedly, on paper, a seemingly comfortable cruise past Aston Villa, Exeter, Peterborough United and Southampton. But the last four provided a north London showdown against Arsenal over two legs.

Spurs were 1-0 down from the first when they took on the Gunners on 4 December 1968 to try to come from behind to seal a return to Wembley.

The bid was unsuccessful, with a Greaves goal in a 1-1 draw not being enough to see them through, although Cockerel fans were able to crow when the Gunners were stunned by Third Division Swindon Town in the final.

But behind the bare facts the encounter was a brutal one that embarrassed Bill Nick and had Gunners goalkeeper Bob Wilson writing, 'It was like sitting on the edge of a volcano. For those playing it was unabashed hatred. Never before or since have I experienced the elbowing, disgraceful tackling and foul language that erupted out of a long-standing rivalry that was a north London derby. The stakes were too great – a Wembley place, local prestige and a passport to Europe. The 22 players kicked lumps out of each other ... experienced players lost their senses in the heart of the battle ... the game was too tense, too physical.'

185

And an action from Gilzean involving Wilson during it seemed to illustrate the goalkeeper's point. Team-mate Phil Beal, who was to act as Gillie's matchday chauffeur on car journeys from the West Country in latter years (more later), said, 'Bob used to roll the ball along the ground and pick it up again – something you could do in those days. Gillie saw him doing this one time and turned around quickly and got into a tackle with Bob and got the ball off him.

'A few years on [42 to be precise] Bob was doing a charity cycling event [Wilson's daughter Anna died from cancer and Wilson was intent on raising funds for the Willow Foundation he set up with wife Megs by pedalling to every Premier League ground] and they checked everyone beforehand.

'They said to Bob, "You've cracked a bone in your leg, haven't you?" Bob said, "No." They said, "You must have done when you were playing football. It is just showing up from the X-rays."

'I believe Gillie had a disliking for Bob [born in Chesterfield, England] over the fact somewhere down the line he had a relation in Scotland and that enabled him to play for Scotland. And Gillie said, "He's not Scottish at all. Why should he play for Scotland?" But Gillie never bore grudges. When he did corporate hospitality [in his later years] at Tottenham, Bob was in one of the boxes and Gillie said, "Oh, I'll go down and have a chat with Bob." They got on like a house on fire. That was Gillie all over. There wasn't a nasty bone in his body.'

Gilzean, who played up front with Wilson in a charity match at Barnet after they had both retired as players, was asked in recent years if he recalled the moment he broke Wilson's leg. Alan, who admitted he should have been sent off, said, 'I remember whacking him, but I had no idea I'd broken it, and he didn't know until umpteen years afterwards that was broken. But I talked to him once he'd heard it was broken and that he thought I had done it, and I've given belated apologies, as he's a hell of a nice fella.'

Gillie played down the perception that there was ever a mutual hatred between himself and Wilson. He said, 'It was my fault. I made a statement – and I still believe this, and my own son, Ian, was born in England and played for Scotland [under-18s] – saying you should play for the country where you are born, and Bob was born in England. I said it shouldn't be allowed and everyone said I hated him because of that.'

Gilzean, with seven, ranks highly in the list of Spurs's top scorers against Arsenal, with Bobby Smith (10) and Harry Kane (9) leading the way as this is written. He only missed three of the 21 played during his time at Spurs.

Gillie netted his first on his debut appearance against the Gunners, although it was a consolation in a 3-1 defeat at Highbury on 23 February 1965. He made it two in two in a 2-2 deadlock in the September at the Lane with old Dundee mate Ian Ure in the visiting side (they were to face each other eight times in total during the derbies). Gilzean helped Spurs complete the double over their neighbours the following season, bagging his third in the away fixture.

His fourth was the only goal of the game in front of nearly 58,000 fans at the Lane on 20 January 1968. Goal number five came in another away victory the following year. He made it six with a header against Wilson in another 1-0 Lane win. His final goal in the showdowns came in a 2-0 Spurs victory on 13 October 1973, Chivers netting the other. His final appearance in the derby came in the reverse fixture when Spurs completed the double over their rivals.

He said, 'I remember one of my first games against Arsenal at Tottenham, and we beat them 1-0 on a really muddy pitch, and I scored the only goal of the game, and that gave me a thrill, because it was a really hard game. I think that was Martin Chivers's [home] debut for Tottenham that day. It's always good to win the derbies, and it's always nice to beat Arsenal.'

But his view of the north London derby overall mirrors the one expressed by Wilson in that cup semi-final before 56,000, a typical Lane attendance for the meetings. He said, 'I don't think I ever played in a classic north London derby, there's too much at stake, a lot of hard tackling and nastiness.'

One that Gilzean lined up in that particularly sticks in the craw of Spurs fans was when Arsenal completed the first half of the Double – which was to emulate their own club's feat – at White Hart Lane on 3 May 1971 in an otherwise positive season (more later). It was an occasion in which, as reported, Gilzean missed a chance – that would have given Leeds the title – and Arsenal's Ray Kennedy took one.

* * *

An 'angel' appeared to Gilzean when Bill Nicholson decided Steve Perryman should become his roommate on away trips. The decision to hook up the teenage Perryman with the now been-round-the-block Gilzean surprised Martin Chivers, who was to help form the Scot's second great striking partnership at Spurs.

Chivers said, 'We thought, "Christ, you [Nicholson] are killing him. Gillie was a late-night merchant, a man-about-town." Gillie would leave me standing if it came to socialising with him. We thought that it was the worst partnership you could ever do. But it worked. Worked incredibly well.'

It worked despite their differences – that Alan was 30 and Perryman 17, that Gillie and his family owned a semi-detached house in well-heeled Enfield (worth £12,000) while Perryman lived in his parents' Northolt council house, that the Scot drove around in a Jaguar, while Perryman had a Ford Cortina, that Gilzean was on a much bigger wage, that Gillie's politics were Conservative and Perryman's Labour.

Indeed, Gilzean – whose experience was exemplified by that thinning pate (and straggling sidebits) – was able to play a part in what the Scot perceived as either a spiritual body or someone of exemplary virtue spreading his wings, having already impressed an impressionable with his playing skills when the schoolboy Perryman first arrived at the Lane in 1967.

He was indeed 'from the realms of glory' as he became the most consistent and loyal of stalwarts in Spurs's history over 19 years – the winner of the most medals collected by a Lilywhite, the club's appearance holder in every competition with a staggering total of 1,014 first-team starts and perhaps sacrificing a full England career beyond the one cap he was awarded to aid the Spurs cause. He provided support to Gilzean and every other team-mate, support to Bill Nicholson and his other Spurs managers. That he was a Captain Fantastic, guiding Spurs to back-to-back FA Cup triumphs and a League Cup Final, while helping the side lift a few more pots along the way. That he was named the Football Writers' Footballer of the Year and a recipient of the MBE.

Some 'angel'.

And one with the face to match as a teenage prospect as he began his stint with an individual with a more lived-in look due to a loss of follicles.

Perryman, in the same FA Youth Cup-winning team as Graeme Souness, made his first-team debut in a Toronto Cup match in Canada in May 1969. His first league start was alongside Gilzean, with the G-Men present and correct against Sunderland, one of the clubs the Scot rejected in order to sign for Spurs, on 27 September. It was a losing one, the Mackems, to be relegated at the season's end, returning to the Wearside glorifying in a 1-0 victory.

And he remained grateful that Bill Nick paired him with the Coupar Angus native who shared his thoughts on football, the Spurs team, manager, family, life and whether a pot of tea was needed to wet their whistles. And the deeper connection brought out the paternal in Gilzean, who would complain to whoever dished out rougher treatment than he deemed was necessary on the field to his roommate.

Perryman said, 'When I first came to Spurs I had no link with anyone apart from Bill Nick, his assistant Eddie Baily and Charlie Faulkner, the chief scout.

'Just trained there once or twice a week over the course of my under-15 year at school. Didn't have anything to do with the top players.

'Then I signed apprentice [terms] and, of course, I would stand there and watch them train, Gillie and Greaves. A practice match, a finishing exercise. I can't believe Gillie was aware of me other than Tottenham had signed an England schoolboy international.

'I broke into the team quite early and Gillie was in that team. From that moment he was more aware of me and I was more aware of him!

'But it goes deeper than football because you get to know the players on a personal level. With Gillie part of that came from Bill Nicholson, in his wisdom, deciding to room us together.

'It felt like the oldest player with the youngest one when we roomed together on away trips. Whenever you room with someone you become that little bit closer to whoever it is.

'Gillie said he used to room with Dave Mackay and that Dave Mackay was so untidy. And that if they spent more than two or three days in a hotel room – albeit on tour or whatever – then any roommate would go on strike because the room would be so untidy.

'All of a sudden Dave leaves for Derby and an "angel" appeared – which was me! That was Gillie's take on it. Seventeen years of age. Was it, "Clean my shoes?" "Wash the bath out?" Gillie adored a bath but I never cleaned his shoes or ran his bath. Yet I would probably have got on the phone to order a tea or coffee and a plate of sandwiches. I'd have done that bit for him!

'But when he told the story – everyone gives it legs – he was putting the untidiness of Mackay against the respect I would show him.

'Of course Gillie had a different relationship with Bill than I did. He was around 30. I remember rooming with Gillie for my third or fourth away game. After breakfast we all had to report to Bill's room at 11.30. It'd have been a typical talk and maybe naming the team. Bill Nick added, "The hotel just want to apologise because on the third floor where you all were there was a lot of shouting and screaming, banging the doors and all of that. Maybe they were worried that your sleep was interrupted. So was anyone's sleep interrupted?" And Gillie said, "Aye, me." I'm thinking, "What's he talking about?" Gillie carried on and said, "Bill did you say three o'clock?" Bill replied, "Yes, Gillie." Gillie joked, "Yes. Three o'clock, two dolly birds were 'bang, bang, banging on me and Stevie's door – to get out!" Bill would have said, "You'll be lucky!" I didn't know anyone else who would have made that comment in front of Bill. I had been worried about what Bill Nick was going to think of me, but Alan made up the story, making light of the situation. Fantastic.

'Gillie was there to help and advise you, spend enough time with him outside of football helping each other along the way. Top player and a quality friend.

'As a bloke, he was genuine. If Gillie said he was going to do something he did it. For instance, there was a club I was attached to for a number of years, Yeading, on the borders of Hayes and Southall in west London. Friends of mine and my brother's friends all played for it and helped turn it into a junior status club. They eventually got to the Conference with a lot of hard work.

'Over the course of the years they would have said to me, "Steve, could you ask Gillie to do an end-of-season presentation?" And I'd think, "That's a long journey for him. I do that journey every day." But when I asked Gillie he said, "Yeh, Steve, I'll do that. Would love to be there."

'Gillie would be the perfect gentleman. Polite to everyone. Humble. All of Gillie's class on the football field was matched by his class off it. Just the perfect role model for a younger player growing up in this wonderful game.

'What a role model for me. People would fall at his feet for an autograph at a hotel on a Friday night [before a game]. They'd be, "Oh, it's Alan Gilzean!" Just to see how he dealt with them. A master at his job. It wasn't an act. He was being his natural self.

'He was a famous footballer but you never knew it. He'd never say who he was if someone didn't know. A wonderful, wonderful man. He believed in living his life. Enjoying himself. But not treading on anyone or being bolshie. Just a nice guy who had a special ability to play football.

'And by Christ could he play. As graceful as Nureyev on grass, journalist Norman Giller wrote once: "I like that elegant man, elegant player." He just oozed class. Everything about Gillie was class. Whether he was flicking the ball on or laying the ball off. Or you were meeting him.

'Of course, I have played with a lot of great players and normally the greatest players are the best people. And Gillie is in that category. Super talented.

'When you think of someone you think so positively about Alan Gilzean. I knew his son Ian from his Tottenham days and now fortunately I've met his family and close friends. They all match up with Gillie. Proper, solid people.'

The feelings were mutual with Gilzean, who delighted in his roommate going on to have one of the greatest careers at Spurs.

Gilzean said, 'As Davey finished, Stevie was the heir to the Dave Mackay throne really and took over as the driving force at the club along with Alan Mullery. Stevie Perryman's appearance record will never be beaten. He confirmed, 'Stevie was my roommate as well. I lost Mackay and I got Stevie. I was as surprised as anyone when I got Stevie. But what a wonderful little guy. I knew his father and his brother, he's a really lovely guy, Stevie Perryman.'

* * *

A second son, who was to follow in his father's footsteps at Spurs and Dundee, provided an early Christmas present for Alan and Irene Gilzean of Enfield, north London, on 10 December 1969. And Ian Roger Gilzean's arrival came a couple of years after the first-born, Kevin.

Dad completed a commitment to play for Spurs against Manchester City three days later. The match was rather less momentous than the pulsating, roller-coaster in the same city against Pep Guardiola's super-rich superstar-soaked City on 17 April 2019 when Spurs sealed a European Cup semi-final spot for the first time in 57 years.

But surely Gilzean must have felt as buoyed as any of Mauricio Pochettino's Lilywhites were by giving themselves an opportunity to go at least one better than Bill Nicholson's pre-Gillie Glory, Glory Boys of 1962. Just ask any new dad.

And he was able to help his side earn a respectable point – home product Neil Johnson on target in the 1-1 draw – against the 1968 champions under Joe Mercer and Malcolm Allison, who were to lift the FA Cup that season and the European Cup Winners' Cup the following term.

The team, despite the injection of youth in 17-year-old Perryman, who managed 28 appearances in his first season and proved his versatility in a string of positions, was not pulling up trees. Forests worried about being denuded seemed safe with Spurs destined for its lowest league position – 11th – since Bill Nicholson took over a decade earlier.

The manager decided to become the tinkerman again mid-term to see if he could enliven the campaign and get on track to building the third great team he envisaged – one that was proving difficult to complete in changing times. The likes of reserves such as Graeme Souness had become less patient waiting for their opportunity, as we have noted. Bill Nick also saw possible signings not up to the standards his double outfit had set. And football itself was changing from the more free-flowing to the more pragmatic. The game was becoming less about glory, more towards boring people to death with defensive attitudes, to twist Danny Blanchflower's famous quotes.

And it would come at Gilzean's expense, among others.

Nicholson swung the axe in January 1970 after a disappointing FA Cup exit against Crystal Palace in a fourth-round replay at Selhurst Park in January after a goalless draw, this after the Lilywhites had taken two matches to dismiss third-tier Bradford City.

The G-Men, Cyril Knowles and Joe Kinnear found their heads in the basket, metaphorically speaking, of course.

Gilzean, Knowles and Kinnear, it was considered by Nicholson, had heeded the wake-up call and came back into the side. Bill Nick clearly felt his master goalscorer Greaves had not. Yes, he might have banged in three against the Bantams, but what would he be like with Spurs left with only heavyweights to deal with in the First Division for the rest of the season? Bill maintained his reservations.

Nicholson left Greaves to score goals for fun in the reserves' Football Combination, despite the media pressing him to recall the striker. But the G-Men were dead. Greaves, who only turned 30 in the February, had made his last appearance for Spurs's first-team.

In March, after nine years and a staggering 306 goals in 420 games for the Lilywhites, Greaves became a makeweight in the deal which brought West Ham's World Cup Final goal hero Martin Peters to White Hart Lane.

Greaves was upset. He said to me, 'I didn't want to leave Tottenham. It was the worst time of my life. People talk about missing the World Cup Final in 1966 but I felt worse when Tottenham got rid of me.'

193

Gilzean ploughed on without his old partner. His link-up with fit-again Chivers was a work in progress, but there were indications something good was around the corner, like when the pair each hit a goal double in a 4-1 home win over Nottingham Forest in the month of Greaves's departure.

Alan seemed to have rediscovered his goal touch, bagging five in the final eight fixtures. Also, Peters, with his subtle skills and late runs into the box, seemed to be bedding down.

Perhaps Gilzean, now a thirtysomething, might enjoy collecting more silverware to go with his increasingly silver locks.

'When the Year Ends in One' was a song written and performed by Spurs supporters Chas and Dave with the players. It refers to the fact that the club tend to hit the heights in the first year of the decade, as was proved – before Gilzean's time with the club – in 1901, 1921 and 1961.

The fact Gilzean was 31 at the start of the 1970/71 season added to the symmetry. And it was a campaign when clinging on to such superstitions proved worthwhile. They finished third in the league, reached the quarter-finals of the FA Cup and lifted the League Cup for the first time. It seemed Bill Nicholson was getting close to completing the hat-trick of serial trophy-winning teams he sought.

Much of it was down to Gilzean and Chivers producing a partnership which was a worthy successor to the G-Men. The pride of Coupar Angus had largely played a central role up front with the darting Greaves alive to his every nuance in the air and on the ground. But he played a more withdrawn role, with Chivers able to use his strength, pace and eye for goal as a number nine. His partner used his physical advantages as a big strong lad, something Bill Nick had become frustrated in coaxing out of an individual described as 'moody' and lacking the 'fierce-mindedness' that ran through his previous sides. Chivers said, 'I'd always been a timid player.'

But all that had changed as Chivers showed himself to be world class, liaising with a player who had long proved himself in that category.

There were also the effective tactics the pair employed, like the long throw Chivers produced, with Gilzean flicking on near to the far post for Peters to float in undetected and nod home, or for big Mike England to attack the goal from a more central position.

Gilzean said, 'I went more towards the right wing with Martin. He was completely different from Greavsie. Jimmy was a more natural talent whereas Martin was training ground. If you persevere and persevere you come good. Martin had a fantastic shot, was strong, could hold people off the ball. Jimmy was lightning fast with dribbling skills. We got on well, Martin and me. Big strong guy.

'Martin Peters also came on the scene. We were more or less playing three forwards at that time. Obviously, we won the three cups in four years. It was a good team. And Martin Chivers had two wonderful seasons. He was hitting them from everywhere. And they were going flashing into the net. And he was just great to play with.'

He added, 'Martin Chivers was a very important player for Tottenham. He was good in the air and had a great shot with both feet. He was a terrific servant for Tottenham and instrumental in us winning three trophies. A fantastic player. His record speaks for itself.'

The partnership was certainly helped by Gilzean playing a supporting role, just like he did with Greaves. Chivers said, 'We only played with one main striker and that was myself. Once I got confidence I took everything from the back. Gillie would track up and down the wing. Bill played three of us across the front and when the ball came in from the other side Gillie would move in behind me. He scored his quota of goals.

'I didn't know what an incredible goalscorer he was at Dundee until I went up for his funeral, but he scored his fair few for Tottenham, didn't he? Up in the hundreds.

'I must have set some goals up for him but he set up a lot of goals for me, although I had to read what angle that ball was going to come off that shiny bonce of his. He was balding wasn't he?! But he always got his head to it. He caused havoc in the opposition's penalty area.

'Decent understanding? Yeh. You can't put a finger on it and say we were friends because it just wasn't like that. It was that when we were on the football field we played off one another and it worked.

'We used to practise the long-throw routine until we were blue in the face at Cheshunt. No wonder I've got bad bloody shoulders! I've had one replaced and I'm getting the other replaced as well. But I used to hurl the ball in. It was a good attacking ploy. I threw the ball low and hard rather than looping it and it came quite firmly to Gillie, who flicked it on. That was the easy job. The hard job for us was to find someone who could get on the end of it.

'Funnily enough, Mike Summerbee of Man City always said we were the best partnership in the First Division, that his side didn't know how to cope with it.

'I put it down to Bill. Bill was the one who picked the team. I read Gillie and Gillie read me. We worked very hard together, especially in European games. It was incredible.

'As a footballer, he was always very confident in the dressing room, geeing people up to get them into the right frame of mind to go out there and play. More vocal, saying things like what he was going to do to the opposition. He always gave me that confidence because I was quiet in the dressing room.'

Pat Jennings, who played behind the dynamic duo, underlined how fortunate Spurs were to have a second great strike pair involving Gilzean. He said, 'Gillie had a good partnership with Martin? Yes. Martin was another great player. A powerful player. A great striker of the ball. Good in the air as well. Quick. Powerful.

'It was a different partnership to the one Gillie had with Greavsie. They used to drift into different positions. I would kick it to the corner flag and Alan would just nip across the front of the defender before it got to them to give it a touch on. We had a really great team.'

Peters ably backed the pair with his stealthy late runs into the box catching defences on their blind side. He was an all-round talent, able to work hard, run swiftly, make things happen, provide a decent free kick and could score goals, netting one on his debut against Coventry, the club against whom Perryman and Souness had lifted the FA Youth Cup. It seemed he was worth the British transfer fee Spurs had paid for him.

In midfield, Alan Mullery was an inspirational skipper in word and deed alongside a fast-emerging Perryman, with Nicholson retaining faith in wingers, something his old team-mate Alf Ramsey had rejected with England. Jimmy Neighbour, who has sadly passed on, Jimmy Pearce and Roger Morgan, a £110,000 signing from QPR, vied for a spot before Ralph Coates was added to the mix in 1971.

The back four impressed. It was superbly marshalled by rock-solid centre-half Mike England with the diligent, ever-reliable Phil Beal at his side, with Cyril Knowles and Joe Kinnear still providing oodles of quality at full-back. And behind them there was Pat Jennings, who had developed into the finest goalkeeper in the English league and arguably Europe, possibly the world.

Gilzean's tally of scores in the league emphasised the role he was capable of filling when a member of the sixth Perthshire troop in the eyes of his scout leader Jack Scott: a goalmaker. He netted just nine in 38 games while laying umpteen for Chivers, who averaged a goal every other game. And Peters fed off his near-post flicks from Chivers's windmill throws while scoring nine.

The double Alan got as Spurs kicked off their league season with a 2-2 draw with neighbours West Ham flattered to deceive. He did not hit the target again until aiding a home win against Manchester City with one of his nine league goals that term. He also scored in Spurs's biggest league win of the season – 4-0 against Burnley. A consistent term saw Spurs edged out of the title race after an injury to key defender Mike England.

A 3-0 home win over Stoke City in October 1970 has been cited by Chivers as the game which saw his partnership with Gillie take off, with the big striker finally able to pull his full weight after an erratic season following his long-term left-knee injury.

He said, 'I had been nearly written off. Out for almost a whole year and returned the following season. I was super fit because I'd been doing weights and running. The only thing that was lacking was the confidence of somebody whacking me on my leg and me getting through it.

'Eventually it came to me one special game. It was against Stoke and Gillie was out there that day. He scored one goal and I got two.

'I beat Gordon Banks for my last goal by bending it around him from about 30 yards after a real big tussle with Denis Smith. Denis was a very physical player and had been pushing and knocking me all over the place. I'd had a ding-dong with him, so for that goal I bundled him off the ball and nearly off the pitch. When the ball went in the whole bloody stadium erupted. That was the day the Tottenham crowd said, "He's back." From that day on I didn't stop scoring goals. Every striker needs a boost of confidence. I certainly needed it.'

And Gilzean was able to indulge in the goalscoring past-time which had Scottish League opponents running for the hills in the FA Cup, although strangely he drew a blank in the four Anglo-Scottish encounters in the Texaco Cup. He scored four goals in ties against Sheffield Wednesday, Carlisle United and Nottingham Forest, before Spurs were squeezed out in the last 16 by Liverpool after a replay at the Lane in which future Spurs keeper Ray Clemence was outstanding for the Reds.

Wearing the number-seven shirt, Alan was magnificent in the League Cup as he helped Spurs return to Wembley.

The long-throw tactic involving Chivers, Gilzean and Peters worked like a dream, especially in the last-16 home tie against West Bromwich Albion. Spurs's World Cup hero guided home a Gillie flick from the Chivers Exocet as part of a hat-trick by the midfielder. The Scot also made another for Peters and managed to convert two chances in an impressive 5-0 home win.

The draw favoured Spurs as it was their third on the bounce at home following wins over Swansea and Sheffield United. And they secured a fourth which saw the Gilzean-Chivers dream team in perfect harmony as Coventry City were brushed aside 4-1, the former on target and the latter completing a hat-trick.

The pair were at it in the semi-final against Bristol City of the Second Division, with Gilzean on the mark in the drawn first-leg at Ashton Gate and Chivers grabbing one of two in extra time to see Spurs scrape through at the Lane in the second, with the help of a stunning double-save from Jennings in normal time.

Spurs, on the face of it, seemed to have more good fortune when Manchester United lost their last-four encounter with Third Division Aston Villa. But nothing could be taken for granted, with QPR (1967) and Swindon (1969) upsetting the odds against top-tier opponents in West Brom and Arsenal in two of the competition's recent finals.

Gilzean looked the picture of confidence as he joined in the snakeline of players making their way out of the tunnel at Wembley before another 100,000 crowd on Saturday, 27 February 1971. His entrance might have been low-key when he came out with his team-mates to win the first London FA Cup Final. But this time he made more overt gestures to imply he was feeling good about Spurs's chances by bobbling the ball on top of his now relatively hairless cranium as he hip-swayed on to the pitch.

It was believed if Spurs matched Villa for effort that their class would shine through, but they dominated at a strolling pace and Gilzean, twice, Chivers and Peters missed opportunities.

Villa came out of their shells and Chico Hamilton hit Pat Jennings's bar and Steve Perryman had to clear off the line from Andy Lochhead.

But Gilzean helped to shake Spurs out of their lethargic state with a crucial role in the breakthrough goal for his partner 17 minutes from time.

Buccaneering indomitable skipper Alan Mullery charged forward and aimed a high ball to Chivers who knocked it down for Gillie. The Scot, with his back to goal, spun marker Keith Bradley to caress the ball outside him with his left foot for Jimmy Neighbour. The overlapping winger had his effort half-saved by Villa keeper John Dunn and unmarked Chivers tapped home the rebound with much-loved TV commentator Brian Moore telling his viewers, 'Spurs are ahead but they really don't deserve to be.'

Celebrating Gillie immediately gave Chivers a big hug as he leaped up on to the big striker, wrapping his arms and legs around the number nine's upper torso.

Chivers said, 'Gillie was always the first one to jump at me and congratulate me for scoring a goal. A great team man.'

And Mullery found Chivers, who wrapped up the 2-0 win with his second thanks to a superb first touch and turning two defenders inside out eight minutes from time.

Chivers said, 'We didn't play that well in that League Cup Final. We rode our luck. Stevie [Perryman] cleared off the line. I was lucky to be the man to lift us with a couple of goals. I was lucky in finals [more later].'

The most significant consequence of the victory was that Spurs had sealed a return to European competition in the UEFA Cup, something Bill Nick always felt would provide the greatest test of his side's mettle.

The manner and size of the success could hardly compare to any of the achievements of Nicholson's early 1960s side with its one-touch, entertaining, attacking football which had certain experts claiming the Spurs team were the best club team yet seen.

But the 1971 triumph reopened the door to the continent in a time when defensive, winning-is-everything football ruled in place of the style the Double heroes excelled in.

Bill Nick knew the third team he had built was less about individual flair, particularly after the sale of the remaining Glory, Glory Boy, Jimmy Greaves, than a cohesive unit, with the manager giving up a few of his perfectionist principles for the sake of victory. As the football romantic reluctantly admitted, 'A bloke is measured by what he wins.'

But all the while Gilzean was around the Lane you had a reminder of the flair and class once possessed in spades by those wearing a Lilywhite shirt in the previous decade.

* * *

The curtain fell on Gilzean's international career when he earned his 22nd cap against Portugal on 21 April 1971.

His swansong struck the wrong note as Scotland suffered a 2-0 defeat against their hosts in what was a European Championship qualifier. At least he could say it took the likes of Eusébio, rated one of the world's greatest footballers, to help see off his side. The African-born striker, outshone by Gilzean in the 1962/63 European Cup, scored his country's second goal. He was also in the Benfica side which knocked Spurs out of the continent's premier club competition the season before the Dee's odyssey.

Gilzean's first cap after joining Spurs came in a goalless friendly against Spain at Hampden on 8 May 1965. He was joined in the side by new team-mate Bill Brown and friend and club rival

Denis Law. He managed a goal double with Dave Mackay and Brown alongside, as Jock Stein's Scotland were pipped 3-2 by Pat Jennings's Northern Ireland, who also played George Best, in a Home International at Windsor Park in the October. A World Cup qualifying debut for Gilzean ended in a 2-1 defeat against Poland 11 days later in front of 107,580 at Hampden. But another six-figure Hampden crowd saw Gillie help Scotland to a superb 1-0 win against Italy in another group game a month later.

Then 15 days later he guided his country to a 4-1 Home International victory over Wales in Glasgow.

Gilzean made a goalscoring return for Scotland after a two-year absence. He netted the first in a 3-2 success against the same opposition – who included Cliff Jones – in the same competition at Hampden in November 1967.

Gillie came on as a sub for marksman Denis Law as Scotland overcame Austria 2-1 in a World Cup qualifier before 81,000 at Hampden 12 months later. And he netted a goal double to help crush World Cup qualifier hosts Cyprus 5-0 a month later.

Alan also helped his country secure a solid 1-1 draw with West Germany in another qualifier in front of almost 100,000 in Glasgow the following April. He chipped in with one in a 5-3 Home International triumph against Wales in Wrexham the next month, but a week later his side suffered a 4-1 defeat against England, who included Alan Mullery, at Wembley in the same competition.

Gillie was unable to hit the target in an 8-0 World Cup group demolition of Cyprus at Hampden seven days later. A Gilzean goal consoled Scotland in a battling 3-2 qualifying group defeat against West Germany in Hamburg in October 1969. But he was unable to prevent a 2-0 defeat in Austria the following month. Scotland had failed to qualify for the World Cup finals for the second time in a row.

He earned his 20th cap in a 1-0 Home International win over Pat Jennings's Northern Ireland in Belfast on 18 April, 1970. And he helped seal a joint-championship title success with England and Wales as a substitute in a goalless draw against the Auld Enemy watched by a staggering 137,438 inside Hampden a week later.

Gilzean said, 'My biggest regret at that level was not getting to the World Cup finals. I always felt we had the ability, but perhaps lacked the teamwork or pattern. Germany knocked us out to go to Mexico in 1970; we played well in Hamburg that night but Tommy Gemmell unfortunately gave away a silly penalty.'

15

Euro Glory

ALAN GILZEAN was to celebrate his 33rd birthday in the 1971/72 season and there were hints he might be drifting beyond his sell-by date at White Hart Lane. His balding pate gave the false impression that Gillie was getting fit for the knacker's yard, particularly when he was considered among the fittest players on the staff.

Modern football has seen thirtysomethings ripping it up in the Champions League – evidenced by the performances of Lionel Messi and Cristiano Ronaldo. But the adjective 'veteran' – implying past it – could well have been applied to English league footballers of Gilzean's vintage once they had turned 30.

Outfield players, as a rule, had shorter careers during his time as it was before sports science educated the likes of Messi, Ronaldo and every other top footballer who had departed his 20s in ways of extending their careers through nutrition, technology and increased knowledge. A more analytical approach, but one fervently adopted as we move into the third decade of the new millennium.

There was speculation (in James Morgan's *In Search of Alan Gilzean*) that he might link up with Dave Mackay, now at Swindon Town, in a cut-price deal to secure himself a last bumper payday as a professional footballer. Just like Mackay himself, Bobby Smith and other Spurs heroes did.

It was thought that he might jack in the game altogether and become a real-life Basil Fawlty – without the hang-ups! – and run a hotel, although one wonders if anyone resembling 'the Major' character in the television comedy from the mid-1970s would have popped up to remind him of an officer back in his National Service days.

There were even suggestions that Ralph Coates, signed for £192,000 from Burnley, might trouble Gillie for his spot should he stick around.

But Gilzean abided by the maxim 'you are as old as you feel' and he felt as fit as the fittest fiddle. And he proved his opinion was not based on self-delusion when he shone brightly – scoring 22 goals in 50 appearances – throughout a campaign that brought him European glory for the first time nine years after he went so close to it with Dundee.

It seemed his propensity to largely avoid injury helped his cause in the eyes of Bill Nicholson, who dumped Alan Mullery in the reserves after his loyal captain had recovered from a long-term pelvic strain sustained in the month the midfielder became a thirtysomething.

The Gilzean-Chivers axis went from strength to strength, right from the off. They were each on target in the season's opener against Wolverhampton Wanderers at Molineux, the first of four encounters in that campaign with the Black Country outfit who were to provide the opposition in the UEFA Cup Final.

Gillie and Big Chiv each managed a goal double as Huddersfield Town were hammered 4-1 at the Lane. And Spurs were unbeaten in four with six from eight points when Gilzean managed to secure his 100th goal for Spurs in a 1-1 deadlock against eventual runners-up Leeds United on 25 August 1971.

The strike at Hull City's Boothferry Park – with Elland Road shut down because of hooliganism – fitted the milestone of reaching three figures for the Lilywhites. Again it saw him link up with Chivers to thump home from distance.

The *Tottenham Herald* reported, 'Alan Gilzean was out of this world. Gillie was playing his 300th game for the club, but it was surely his best. He improves with age – just like good wine.'

Gillie and Chivers were at it again in front of goal in a comfortable 4-1 home win over Wolves.

The dynamic duo – with Chivers the more deadly and en route to 44 goals in 64 games that season – continued to thrive as Spurs maintained an unbeaten home record until West Ham fans sang 'I'm forever blowing bubbles' as their team burst Tottenham's in the final Lane encounter of 1971.

But inconsistencies in the league cropped up for Spurs. With Gilzean, they failed to win their first three fixtures of the new year. They then won three on the bounce and went on to win five of their opening ten games of 1972, scoring 12 and letting in seven.

The roller-coaster of form infuriated Bill Nick and the board as Spurs finished sixth. Chairman Sidney Wale told all who would listen that the league was the club's 'bread and butter'. But Spurs, as they often did during Gilzean's time, feasted on the haute cuisine – to a greater or lesser extent – supplied by knockout competition.

Gilzean helped Spurs make a fist of their League Cup defence before Chelsea ended it 5-4 on aggregate in a tight semi-final.

The exit choked up the offspring of Willie and Babs. He said, 'Ask anyone at Spurs to name the most disappointing matches of 1972 from the club's viewpoint and he will certainly include the League Cup semi-final against Chelsea at White Hart Lane. Some – myself included – rank missing that final at Wembley as one of the biggest disappointments of their careers. Defeat at that last hurdle before a second Wembley final in two years is a hard pill to swallow. But the manner of our exit was what sent everyone on the staff into a state of depression, which took weeks to wear off.

'With the aggregate scores of the two-leg semi-final level in the dying minutes of normal time I was already anticipating the extra time which I was sure would go in our favour.

'Then Chelsea were awarded a free kick after a foul by Mike England on Alan Hudson on Chelsea's left flank near the corner flag.

'Four of our defenders lined up in the six-yard box and there was not a single Chelsea forward in sight as Alan hit a hopeful cross towards the near post.

'Cyril Knowles stepped out to clear an apparently simple ball but somehow missed it completely and the ball bounced under his foot and past Pat Jennings into the net. Ninety-nine times out of a hundred Cyril would have planted the ball firmly towards the other end of the pitch. Unfortunately for him – and the rest of us – one lapse of concentration came on the threshold of Wembley.

'Let me say straight away, however, that to blame Cyril for missing Wembley would not only be unfair – but foolish too. Well as Chelsea played in the second leg we should have sewn the tie up in the first game at Stamford Bridge.'

And the Coupar Angus hotshot had a series of goalscoring field days in the FA Cup, netting in all of the matches – against Carlisle United, a home draw and replay victory, Rotherham United and Everton – which helped his team make it to the quarter-finals, where they were pipped by eventual winners Leeds United at Elland Road. One moment, when he laid on one of Chivers's goals in the second game against Carlisle, displayed one of his multitude of qualities. The *Daily Express* reported, 'Gilzean, who seems to collect seconds all to himself to decide what to do next, coolly delivered the ball to Martin Chivers.'

Gilzean even found time to show Torino what they had missed by guiding Spurs to two wins over the Italians which enabled the north Londoners to lift the Anglo-Italian Cup Winners' Cup, netting in the home leg.

* * *

The greatest feat of the season, naturally, came in the UEFA Cup. It took 12 games to lift the trophy and become the first British side to win two cups in a major continent-wide inter-club competition, scoring 30 and letting in only six.

Gilzean – who played in 11 – certainly broke the ice with a hat-trick in Iceland as Spurs opened their campaign on 14 September 1971.

He had travelled in a 16-strong party to the edge of the Arctic Circle – around 25 miles off the north coast of singer Björk's homeland – to face amateurs Keflavik in front of 10,000 at a cold and blustery but attractive venue. The group decided against sampling the warmth of the geysers on a visit to the country's tourist attractions before the encounter, but were clearly too hot for their hosts who were memorably described by author and *Daily Mail* reporter Brian Scovell as like a 'Southern League conference side without the gale force winds and the ice', one which 'had to pay for their own meal before the game'.

Gilzean refused to be blown off course. Besides his treble – his best a glancing header from a long throw by Chivers – he made goals for Ralph Coates, the former Burnley midfielder's first for Spurs, and Alan Mullery.

A shot and a header gave Gilzean a double – and he made one of three for Martin Chivers – as Spurs completed the formalities with a 9-0 win over Keflavik at the Lane, their 15 goals over the two legs one short of the British record in Europe held by Leeds United.

Graeme Souness made that single first-team appearance in the first leg of the tie alongside Alan, the figure he so much admired at the Lane.

Souness displayed the self-confidence and willingness to express an opinion, which has aided careers as a player, manager and pundit when he said, 'I had already played in Iceland with the Scottish Youth side, so I was able to tell the lads what it would be like … I came on as a second-half substitute [for Alan Mullery] with about 20 minutes to go. It is hard for anyone to be a sub because you have to struggle to get into the game. You can't seem to get involved but I don't think I did too badly.'

Gillie and co flew to France to take on Nantes in the first leg of round two. Pre-match, the players whinged about the hotel, the food and an alcohol ban Bill Nick had imposed. A dressing room lacking ventilation did not help the mood and when the players returned after sealing a goalless draw a displeased manager had, according to Hunter Davies in *The Glory Game*, a major bust-up with Chivers.

Gilzean missed a couple of chances in the second leg but Spurs edged into the last 16 with Martin Peters, skipper in place of the absent Mullery, scoring the only goal.

Geoffrey Green of *The Times*, describing how much Spurs dominated, wrote, 'Jennings – a lonely figure at the other end might well have laid himself a table and helped himself, cross-legged, to a bottle of aperitif.'

Gilzean helped make two goals, one for Chivers, against Rapid Bucharest in the last 16 as Spurs went to Romania holding a 3-0 advantage. But an apparently smooth road into the quarter-final got bumpy. Very bumpy. It proved time for tin helmets and self-control beyond self-control in the second leg, which was dubbed 'The Battle of Bucharest'.

Gilzean received physical abuse that would have had his attackers up on charges of GBH had the incidents occurred on a British street, while managing extraordinary restraint to set the perfect example, one generally heeded and needed to ensure the last four was reached.

His kidneys were the first part of his body to be assaulted. Hunter Davies wrote in *The Glory Game* how Bill Nick 'was on his feet, tearing towards the touchline, shouting and screaming. Gillie had been brutally and openly punched in the kidneys by the Romanian number four, unseen by the referee who was at least 50 yards away.'

Eye-witness Davies added, 'As they stood shouting, ignored by the referee, it happened again. This time the number four took a running jump at Gillie, going through the air and bringing both his upturned boots down against Gillie's legs. Again it had been completely unprovoked, yet once again, he did nothing in reply.

'Slowly, Gillie shook his head and moved out of reach of the number four, shrugging his arms to Bill on the touchline, signalling there was nothing he could do. A younger, less experienced player would certainly have retaliated. Yet Gilzean, miraculously, stood there, taking it.

'Bill and Eddie [Baily] were hysterical. I thought they'd both have heart attacks. The powerlessness of their position made them both froth at the mouth. It had been Gillie's brilliant back header in the first minute of the match at Tottenham that had led to Rapid's downfall. There had obviously been instructions this time to get him.

'Play moved on, the number four had to run for the ball and Gillie escaped, limping. Bill and Eddie [Baily] collapsed back on the bench, their heads in their hands, moaning.'

Gilzean needed his ribs strapped, as did defender Peter Collins as the doctor attended the walking wounded, and was sent out for the second half. Eventually he had to come off to have treatment on both legs and his back. Steve Perryman, who sustained a dislocated shoulder, also had to be replaced.

Gillie's sub Jimmy Pearce scored and saw red and Martin Chivers belted a second to seal a 2-0 win.

Geoffrey Green wrote for *The Times*, 'The Romanians threw everything at them [Spurs], except the giant floodlights.'

Pat Jennings, who had both arms trodden on, said, 'Gillie could play under any circumstances. Whatever the opposition put up against him he could handle.'

Defender Phil Beal, another survivor of a match against opposition described by Nicholson as the 'dirtiest' team of his experience, said, 'Gillie used to take some batterings but used to just get up, wipe himself down and get on with it.'

Norman Giller wrote in the *Daily Express* that Spurs were, 'hacked and kicked about like rag dolls.'

Peter Batt of *The Sun* described it as the 'most shameful exhibition of thuggery I have ever seen' from Spurs's opponents. Jeff Powell of the *Daily Mail* described it as one of the most 'savage matches in European football history.'

But the upshot was a quarter-final spot against more Romanian opposition in which the former despatch clerk with a Perth carpet manufacturer helped account for Unizale Textile Arad. Gilzean glided home a late equaliser with Spurs facing a first home defeat in a European tie after a 2-0 win behind the Iron Curtain.

Gilzean said to Giller, 'I was beginning to wonder if one would ever go in.'

It ensured a semi-final against AC Milan, who had ended the Scot's dream of European glory with Dundee in 1963 and gone on to lift the European Cup at Wembley.

Gillie had suffered from the dark arts employed by the Italians – most memorably by Peruvian international Victor Benítez, back then, when he failed to maintain his cool and was ordered off.

The San Siro giants, it seemed, had not changed their approach in 1972, judging by a contemporary report by Jeff Powell in the *Daily Mail*, who felt Spurs were 'shamefully brutalised by the hatchet-men of Milan'. As if Gillie and his pals had not had a basinful of it in Bucharest!

But it was hardly surprising as Neoro Rocco, who coached the Italians nine years before and Jimmy Greaves's bête noire, was still in charge.

Gilzean, though, was able to taste victory a decade on with the help of two goals from roommate Steve Perryman.

Milan's Romeo Benetti, more hard man than soft romantic, put the visitors ahead. But Alan helped conjure an equaliser when he combined with Martin Peters for Perryman to volley home from 20 yards.

Milan, who included Karl-Heinz Schnellinger, Gillie's man-marker in Cologne, had Riccardo Sogliano sent off. The Italian had clashed with inspirational Alan Mullery, who had been recalled from a loan spell with first club Fulham due to an injury crisis and his own fine form.

And Gilzean was in the Spurs line-up as they battled to hang on to a 1-1 draw in Italy and move into the final. All rather different from his San Siro nightmare with Dundee in terms of the result, although not too dissimilar when it came to the physical assault he sustained.

The heroic Mullery gave the visitors an early lead before Gianni Rivera equalised 22 minutes from time.

Perryman said, 'When I scored my two goals from outside the box it probably was the only way we were going to score because Gillie, Martin Chivers and Martin Peters – all our big soldiers – got such buffeting. The closer they got to goal the more their bodies got buffeted. And that's a nice word for what that sort of team could do to you. Over the two games Gillie took it and came back for more.

'I remember the battering Gillie used to get in these games. Despite his class, Gillie was a very, very strong competitor. It was a competitive age when you are playing against teams like AC Milan and Leeds United. If you were a shrinking violet they soon smelt it. And Gillie was certainly not that. He stood his ground. Could compete in the air with anyone.

'I used to be asked to take near-post corners. Just float them in for Gillie to flick it on. I could deliver the ball and he could find the space to get his head to it to flick it on to where it was needed across goal for someone maybe on the far post to put it in.

'Even if I hit some bad ones, Gillie would get there. He found a way to the ball. I always say his ability to get the ball first is not thought of enough. Loved him.'

Perryman also appreciated the experience and nuances Gilzean's game brought Spurs abroad as well as at home.

He said, 'We did great things in Europe. Great things. But Gillie had already done great things in Europe before he even came to us, even reaching that semi-final with Dundee. He was vastly experienced. He had Scottish international experience, although his number of caps was hampered, I believe, as he was what was called an Anglophile – for going to England.

'What a player! He was an intelligent guy. Intelligence came out in different ways for Spurs over the years. We had Martin Peters drifting into space or, later, Ossie Ardiles picking up the ball and running at opponents to put them out of the game. With Gillie it was a shrewdness, a cleverness of movement. He could read situations and react to the reading of them.

'A lot of Bill Nick's way – not sure if that was consistent with the Double team or whatever – was a ball up to the frontman in a quality way and back to midfield and then play forward. The targetmen were so important to it. So that was Gillie's starting position.

'Gillie was perfect for Bill and it was obvious Bill loved Alan Gilzean.

'Don't think Bill ever let us know that. It was an era where you didn't get too many "well dones".'

Gilzean's friends and family might have wished for something more glamorous than a European final involving two English clubs. Spurs versus Wolves would almost certainly not sound as attractive as Spurs v Real Madrid or Spurs v Johan Cruyff's Ajax to them. After all, the away legs could be spent enjoying the tourist sights of Spain's capital or Amsterdam.

Wolves ensured the first all-English decider in Europe's major tournaments by seeing off sexy Turin outfit Juventus in the last eight and Hungarian side Ferencváros in the semi-finals. But those sorted tickets for the first leg at Molineux on 3 May 1972 and the second at the Lane two weeks later by Gillie would have been delighted when European glory became a reality for the Coupar Angus native.

Spurs had never lost a major final and, of course, had been unbeaten throughout their maiden campaign in the UEFA Cup.

And with Gillie's help it looked as though both those stats would remain unchallenged following the first leg on a damp Black Country night. He was the victim of a reckless Gerry Taylor challenge 12 minutes into the second half. And from the free kick Mike England placed the ball on to the head of Martin Chivers, who nodded Spurs in front.

Wolves pushed Spurs back but found Pat Jennings in unbeatable form until Jim McCalliog equalised from a quick John Richards free kick which caught the visitors out in the 71st minute. Spurs were not best pleased with Russian referee Tofiq Bahramov, who, as a linesman, adjudged Geoff Hurst's second goal had crossed the line in the 1966 World Cup Final.

But Chivers made sure Spurs would take an advantage into the second leg with a stunning winner just three minutes from time. He gathered a ball from Alan Mullery, moved in from the left and rocketed the ball into the net from 25 yards. Chivers said, 'I've never hit a ball better.'

Spurs were able to boast they were the first British team to win two European finals in their 66th match of the season.

Gilzean with Chivers looked to provide the cutting edge and Gillie twice went close, but it was Mullery who extended Spurs's advantage from the first leg close to the half-hour. He hurled himself at a Martin Peters cross to the near post to head home, getting knocked out on colliding with Wolves goalkeeper Phil Parkes.

The Tank recovered to keep Spurs rolling until David Wagstaffe levelled for the visitors. The boots were on the other feet and the likes of myself and most members of the 54,303-strong crowd were suffering high anxiety as the visitors searched for a goal that would level things up overall. Fortunately, Pat Jennings showed yet again why he was rated the best goalkeeper across the continent.

Gilzean and team-mates did a lap of honour in 'Mullers's Final' to celebrate a feat in which they had gone more than the extra mile as they had travelled 10,238 miles by air and 7,500 miles by train. Bill Nicholson dampened the party by telling his players the best team lost. Pat Jennings said, 'We were swigging the champagne that night. The door opened and Bill came in and he said, "I've just been in to tell the Wolves team the best team lost." So that was us getting knocked back. Cheers Bill!'

But another dream had come true for one of the most elegant players ever to don a Lilywhite shirt.

Gilzean's first thoughts when recalling the final were not of clinching his first European trophy and the burst bubble of a celebration, his mind went back to the first leg.

He said to Spurs club historian John Fennelly, 'My outstanding memory was one of the two goals which Martin Chivers scored. It was a horrible night at Molineux, and Chivers hit one from about 35 yards, and it just flew into the net. What an unbelievable goal that was.'

Mike England said, 'European competition suited Alan. Very much so. Very comfortable against foreign teams. He quite enjoyed it, particularly playing away. Played at some pretty good grounds on decent pitches you could play football on. White Hart Lane's one was not always the best. Got heavy and rain didn't help. But we had plenty of success. Beat a lot of top teams and won the UEFA Cup, which was a great achievement.'

Gilzean's consistency of performance was noted. Phil Beal, the defender often the equal of his team-mate in such a quality, said, 'Every game you took him and his contribution for granted. That was it. [He] wasn't one of those players who played well one week and then you didn't see him for three or four games. He was there every week. Week in, week out. Game by game.'

16

Behind the Scenes

ALAN GILZEAN was featured in *The Glory Game*, the ground-breaking, behind-the-scenes story of Tottenham Hotspur's UEFA Cup-winning season.

Author Hunter Davies, a journalist allowed access all areas, including the normally sacrosanct dressing rooms throughout the 1971/72 campaign, tells how he wrote what he saw, heard and sensed in a groundbreaking book considered one of the game's classic tomes.

Davies attempted to give his readers a few insightful clues as to what Gilzean was all about away from the public arena. But of course the Scot was just one of many who came under the Davies spotlight.

It was, overall, a fly-on-the-wall glimpse of a year at a top football club – warts and all – and a few of its subjects, not for effect but to reflect the reality, like the hours of boredom. Charlie Watts was once asked what it was like to be a drummer in the Rolling Stones as the band celebrated its 25th anniversary and he replied, '20 years of hanging about.'

Gilzean and his team-mates must have felt similar feelings when on the road with little to occupy their time, judging from Davies's observations.

The tedium factor could, it seemed, permeate training with Davies writing about Gillie being caught yawning by Bill Nicholson during exercises on the first day of pre-season.

The hot-under-the-collar verbal exchanges were reported, particularly the one with Chivers after the Nantes game. As were the moans, thinly veiled as jokes, by Bill Nick, sporting his never-changed short back and sides, about the in-vogue-amongst-the-young long-hair styles sported by his players, although Gilzean must have escaped the manager's barbed comments given his lack of follicles.

The banter was touched upon with Gilzean quick to join in, reflecting the sense of humour his brother Eric told me he had had as a child growing up in Coupar Angus. Before the first game of the season against Wolves at Molineux, Cyril Knowles's brother Peter, who had once played for the old-gold-shirted hosts and was now a Jehovah's Witness, came into the dressing room, and Davies wrote:

> 'That's your brother then, Cyril?' said someone when Peter had gone.
>
> 'Yeah,' said Cyril. 'Still got a lot of skill.'
>
> 'Must have,' said Alan Gilzean. 'Takes a lot of skill to read the Bible.'
>
> Everyone laughed. Bill Nicholson even smiled. He asked Gillie if it was the London Palladium he was going to today. Gillie said yes. Top of the bill.

There was also a safety issue touched upon when Gilzean displayed his wry wit, judging by a quote attributed to him by Davies.

The Spurs team coach was inching through the traffic jam – with a cacophony of car horns blaring – en route to the San Siro for that UEFA Cup semi-final in front of nearly 70,000. And it is reported youngsters 'screamed and spat at the windows, banging so hard that the players took cover' and that Gillie remarked, 'It'll be bricks on the way back.'

Gilzean, Davies informed us, wasn't always up for a quip, such as following the goalless UEFA Cup draw in Nantes. Davies wrote, 'On the plane next morning, only Gilzean was moaning, at least moaning on about France, saying it was his third French trip and he still didn't like it.'

There was the involvement of family. Gilzean, by then a father of two, it was noted, 'did the doting uncle bit' when an injured Alan Mullery introduced his two-year-old daughter Samantha to him. Davies wrote, 'Gilzean, in true Scottish fashion, did the doting uncle bit and pressed a ten-pence piece into her hand.'

The book gave an idea of the depth of desolation, hurt and sense of loss felt by players following a defeat even though it only came as a result of a football match. And it was all epitomised by Gilzean.

An unwanted health bulletin was issued on Gilzean's behalf by a doctor in a largely silent dressing room of stunned players and management after the League Cup exit against Chelsea. Davies described the scene:

> Gillie was in a daze, his head going from side to side, struck dumb with disbelief.
>
> The doctor came in from the treatment room, all jaunty and chirpy. People avoided his gaze and his remark. He checked on Cyril, Ray [Evans] and Gillie, all of whom had colds in the chest before the match... 'I've never known a time when we've had so much chest trouble. Do you know that Bill ... well I'm going to the reception. Get a few noggins in.' The doctor went out, still smiling. Nobody moved. There was silence again.
>
> Gillie, speaking for the room rather than the state of his medical condition, was quoted saying, 'Fucking tragic ... I'm definitely not going upstairs. They can stick their reception ... I couldn't stand seeing anyone. I'm going straight home.'

On a lighter note, albeit on the evening after a home loss to Derby, Gilzean was observed by Davies as he turned up for a swish house party of 60 guests – including Australian singer Olivia Newton-John and an individual claiming to know Prime Minister Edward Heath – put on by Mike England and wife Gwen. Davies wrote:

> Alan Gilzean arrived late, looking, as usual, unlike any of the other footballers. He was in an old-fashioned two-piece dark suit and white shirt. He slipped quietly in as if it was a

216

business call, and he had come to read the meter. There were none of the quick smiles or hurried glances in the mirror to check his hair and shirt, the way the younger ones had done. He was hardly noticed a he picked a vacant seat and went straight to it, drink in hand. You could feel he'd been to many parties and had his priorities right. He wasn't going to waste time on any social chit-chat.

Mind you, Gillie's neat, classic look would now surely look less embarrassing in any photographs than the one adopted by colleagues slavishly following the fashion trend of flared trousers, floral shirts with giant collars and big hair. His lack of vanity no doubt down to the fact he had every confidence in how he appeared and, maybe, a lack of hair to comb. And, perhaps, his decision to avoid 'chit-chat' was purely down to his innate reserve.

Ian Gilzean said, 'Dad wore what he was comfortable in. He wouldn't try to be someone he wasn't. He only got into wearing jeans for the last ten years.'

It can be seen from a 1972 photograph that, like his football, Alan was consistent in his dress sense. Smart-casual. As if about to play golf.

He is pictured on the sofa with his family in Enfield. His wife Irene is by his side. He holds eldest son Kevin on his left knee. The couple's youngest, Ian, has Mum's right arm around him as he balances on her lap while stretching his left leg over Dad's other knee. Look closer and you appreciate Gillie's preferred appearance. He has a light V-neck jumper over a dark shirt with neat, sharply-creased trousers. One presumes his shoes would also be as neat and tidy had they not been cropped out. He looks like he might be dressed for a round or two on his favourite course.

Davies certainly gives his readers noteworthy, chunky morsels of the man behind the shirt, but there is nothing extensive on Gilzean. Manager Bill Nicholson, rightly, and a few players had chapters devoted to them. Gilzean has bit parts, entering stage left when prompted.

But yet it is revealed on *The Glory Game*'s pages that Gilzean, who attended supporters' functions, is the fans' favourite player.

The original King of White Hart Lane. Another reporter David Leggat, who covered Spurs for the *Tottenham Herald*, told of how Gillie's social skills helped firm the bond he always had with the Lane faithful.

David Leggat said, 'He went to a lot of supporters' events. I think that's why they identified with him so much … He was quite happy to mix with the fans.'

Davies seemed to take his life in his hands and boarded what was dubbed 'the skinhead special' on the train's journey to Coventry for a league fixture. The skinhead had been a breed of youngster known for donning Dr Martens, using the boot to kick people as well as walk in, with, as the name implies, cropped hairdos. Hippies had been a target. Now the skinheads had morphed into 'smooths' – with slightly longer hair and still heavy footwear – with opposition fans their sworn enemy, with whom to engage in a 'bit of bovver'. A bit of hooliganism.

Davies got talking to the cult group about the Spurs players. He wrote:

> They seemed knowledgeable but completely uncritical in their loyalty to Spurs. They hadn't a bad word to say about any player. They loved each and every one. There was no one they wouldn't have in their team. But Gilzean was clearly the most popular player. At the mention of his name, they burst into his song, to the tune of the Christmas carol Noel Noel. 'Gilzean, Gilzean, Gilzean, Gilzean, born is the King of White Hart Lane'.

Still, Gilzean, from what I have gleaned from those close to him, would not be 'bovvered' by the general lack of attention paid to him in the book. In fact, he would probably have welcomed it with that reserve of his.

Davies delved into Gilzean's social life as well as his popularity with the supporters. There was a drink culture among footballers of Gillie's era, by common consensus. It didn't mean to say they were alcoholics or borderline alcoholics. They just liked a drink to wind down after a game, often with fans in pubs close to White

Hart Lane like the Bell and Hare (now renamed No.8). They also got together for club functions, or away from club functions.

Gilzean himself made no secret of enjoying a social gathering. He said during an interview with Alan Pattullo in a north London bar called The George enjoying a breakfast with other customers already supping pints, 'We used to have some nights in here.'

There was a story of a supporter complaining to Bill Nicholson that he had seen Gilzean coming out of a nightclub at two o'clock one morning.

Norman Giller, a journalist the player came to trust, said, 'Gillie replied with that poker face he always had on the football field, "Well he's mistaken. I was going into the club."'

Former *Daily Express* journalist Giller, who worked for the newspaper Gillie read each day, added, 'He delivered his lines in the style of Chic Murray, the deadpan Scottish comedian, and people often didn't realise he was joking.'

Gillie said, 'I got a reputation. I've got to admit I did my share of nightclubbing, that's for sure, but I don't know. He [the supporter] probably did see me. I wouldn't argue that one.'

But it seemed his goat was got during the preparation of *The Glory Game* by what he viewed a contrivance of a social situation. Davies wrote:

> On the train home [from a game] they had dinner and plenty to drink, half of them ordering lagers and limes, two at a time. Steve Perryman stuck to Coke. By the end of the journey Gilzean had several empty lager cans stacked in front of him.

The author added in a 2001 edition:

> … I suppose a superficial reader could see lots of references to, say, Gilzean having lots of empty bottles [described as cans elsewhere] in front of him, and be led into thinking that the book must be full of footballers boozing. Tut tut. Footballers drinking? What an allegation.

Gilzean said, 'Some players weren't happy about it [*The Glory Game*] … obviously if you [write] run-of-the-mill things fans wouldn't buy the book. They want the naughty stuff. They want people getting drunk and all that. Parties with women and all the rest of it. What you didnae see he made up. That's how I feel.

'I can remember him saying in the book [that] on the train back we were only allowed lagers. We always had cans of lagers. And we had a card school going. Mackay, Knowlesy, England and me, we used to play cards.

'And a photographer came on with Hunter Davies, who did the book. There were a load of empty cans of lager. And they put them all in front of me and took a photo of me. I'd drunk my share. But not that lot. That was a lot.

'But that's how things happened. They make headlines of it and into the book it goes. And there you go. What can you do?

'Personally, if I had been Bill Nicholson I would never have allowed the book. The guy must have sold a lot of copies.'

Gillie had another bone to pick with *The Glory Game*. He was quoted as saying in the dressing room while on the sidelines, 'You better win this one lads, I need the bonus. I've got a wife, two kids and a budgie to keep.'

Gilzean said, 'I've never had a bloody budgerigar in my life! We had to let him [Hunter Davies] come to our house. A couple of the lads wanted to chin him. Mike England wanted to – and if you get hit by big Mike you stay hit.'

Gilzean was a popular member of the Spurs playing squad and enjoyed 'socials' in restaurants, on golf courses, and in pubs.

Steve Perryman and his wife Kim used to go out for dinner with Gilzean and his wife Irene – and smash a few plates. He said, 'Gillie would sometimes say to me, "Steve, after the game Saturday, we'll go out somewhere." It was normally with our wives. But also on our own. He had a favourite restaurant. It was a Greek restaurant. He loved smashing the plates [a tradition associated with such eateries] and all that. He'd do that.

'Gillie could have fun. There was no doubt about it. He was up for fun. There are certain times you've got to relax and enjoy yourself. It was never stupid, never childish. It was a proper,

proper man going out to enjoy other people's company. That's what he was.'

Perryman confirmed there was a drinking culture in football, but adamant in refuting suggestions it might have been a problem for Spurs. He said, 'You could not play for the very professional Bill Nicholson if you weren't right. You could not. Anyone who is even thinking about that is being a bit disrespectful to Bill Nick, but especially Gillie. He was a cross-country runner, could outrun anyone on the track at Tottenham. His hair would have suggested that he was getting on but he wasn't as old as he looked. And his legs said it at times. I was supposed to be fit, but, by Christ, he could run me on that track.'

Defender Phil Beal remembered how Gillie voluntarily did extra running to keep in shape following a social occasion. He said, 'Gillie used to enjoy himself. He used to drink with the likes of Dave Mackay after games. It was a form of winding down. What was good about him, though, is that if Gillie felt he had had a drink over the weekend, a bit of a session after a game, he used to come in and run it off. He used to do things like that of his own accord. His long-distance stamina running to work off what he'd been doing. You had to do that else Gillie wouldn't have been at the top of his career. He was very, very fit.' Mike England said, 'Gillie liked his golf. Played with him a lot.'

Pat Jennings, a goalkeeping coach under Mauricio Pochettino at Spurs in recent years, remembered golfing and drinking with Gillie. He said, 'Loved to play a lot of golf with Gillie once or twice a week most weeks at Crews Hill, where John White was killed. We had an associate membership up there. All the Scotsmen we had seemed to be good golfers. Brought up with the golf in Scotland, I would guess. He loved it. His handicap was pretty low – 10, 11 – something like that. Good player. Mackay was the same. Think some of the boys still play up there.

'He liked his drink the same as all of us. He didn't like the drink any more than the rest of us.

'That was the way it was in those days. You had a players' room after the matches. You went in and had a drink with the opposition. That's all changed now. All gone.

'The Bell and Hare was our port of call after matches. We went to a pub – I don't know the name of it – in Enfield, which was just around the corner from where Alan lived, a couple of nights a week, usually. Gillie would have been there. But, as I say, he was no different to the rest of us for drink. And NEVER over the top. Just the drink and that was it.'

Jennings also recalled how Gillie and Jimmy Greaves joined in singsongs on away-game trips and tours.

He said, 'There was partying in those days. A drink after a match. Gillie loved the singsongs. His tune was "Campeltown Loch" [a Scottish folk song popularised by contemporary performer Andy Stewart and, incidentally, named after the beauty spot close to where Beatle Paul McCartney bought a farm]. The lyrics included, "Campeltown I wish you were whisky, Campbeltown Loch, och-aye, Campbeltown Loch, I wish you were whisky, I would drink you dry." Did Gillie have a good voice? You knew what he was singing, yeh.

'Greavsie's was "Maybe It's Because I'm a Londoner". They all did their little bits. Their own tunes.'

Cliff Jones said, 'He was a lovely easy-going bloke. We all got on so well with him. I remember when we were abroad once. He hadn't been with us long, not that long after he had scored the winning goal for Scotland against England at Hampden [1964]. So he was a bit of a legend to the Scots. We were sitting around at a café when the Black Watch marched by and spotted him. Next thing he's joined up with them and marched back with them to their headquarters.'

Jimmy Robertson said, 'We got on like a house on fire from the start at White Hart Lane. Was always pleased to see him. We moved into a house in Enfield, north London, and he came round a few times from the halfway house he lived in close by. Good company. An intelligent guy. Great character, great company. Liked a laugh ... Good sense of humour. We liked to drink together occasionally. When you played football there was always some function going on. He was one of the boys, but he was quite reserved, didn't seek the limelight and not a big socialiser.'

Manchester United's Denis Law, his Scotland international team-mate, confirmed he enjoyed a 'social' drink after a game against Spurs with Gilzean and other international team-mates. He said, 'Did I meet up with Gillie socially? Yes, absolutely. Just have a couple of beers after the game on a Saturday or in the week. That was the beauty of those days. If we were staying in London I went out with Dave Mackay and that and had a beer. It was the same when we were playing Arsenal or Manchester City. During the game you wanted them beaten. They were the enemy. But you were still friends with them after the game and you enjoyed a beer. There was a drinking culture but we'd only have the one or two. And you also met with supporters. Don't think all that would be allowed today. It's a different world.'

Bill Nicholson was aware Gillie and his other players enjoyed a drink. Nicholson said, 'Most of them took a lager. I know Alan Gilzean was a drinker. He liked Bacardi and Coke. There is a lot of free time in football and a lot of energy expended. It is normal to drink and I let them get on with it as long as it was done in moderation and didn't affect their performance.

'I made a point of never listening to gossip about my players or spying on them outside of working hours. I reminded them that they had a reputation to maintain and I trusted them to keep it. I don't believe they let me down.'

Gilzean used to occasionally go out to a pub with Jimmy Greaves. He said, 'Greavsie would never go to the Tottenham pubs, he would go to the Old Hall Tavern in Chingford. During the week I would sometimes go with him. Greavsie would only drink beer at that time – half-pints of bitter. He was a typical Cockney boy; he was always good for a laugh.'

Yet an independent streak was detected by his first strike partner at Spurs.

Jimmy Greaves wrote in his autobiography, 'I don't think I was ever happier than when playing with Gillie. He was very honest both as a player and a man but there was also something of the loner about him.

'Gillie would join the rest of us for a few beers, but after that we never knew what he did or what his interests were. He didn't talk much about his life outside football, and I took that as a sign I shouldn't ask.'

And Ian Gilzean insisted his dad's close friends during his playing days with Spurs were outside the club.

Ian Gilzean said, 'I think he had his own mates. He'd go out with the players but I don't think he went out too much with the football lot. He saw football as his job. His work. He'd get himself away from that. I don't think they were the main people he would hang about with. He'd be out with his own mates, especially in London.'

Would I be able to get hold of any of those friends beyond the game?

Ian said, 'They might be dead. They were all older boys. I heard Dad talk about a Ricky Prosser. There was another boy he used to know called Capo. He'd play golf with him. He'd be dead. He was a lot older than Dad. Used to call him Captain Jim or Capo. He was from Edmonton.'

James Morgan, the author of *In Search of Alan Gilzean*, revealed in the book he had spoken to Prosser in May 2010.

Prosser, who ran a haulage company, said, 'We were great, great friends. He never acted like a star, he was just an ordinary bloke. But I've not seen him for over ten years.

'My wife and kids used to play football with Dave's wife and kids [the Mackay family] in their living room and Dave was big friends with Gillie.

'We had some good social times together [naming venues such as the Starlight Rooms in Enfield, linked to Enfield Town FC, and the Bushey Hill Country Club with singers, comedians and variety acts].

'He was good fun to be with. He liked a drink; we used to go to Newmarket races. I'm not a betting man, but I liked going along to watch.

'We used to have a day out golfing every year at Beckenham in Kent or the Isle of Sheppey. He was friendly with Mike Madison, my transport manager. Gillie and him were out all the time.'

David Leggat, who covered Spurs for the *Tottenham Herald* in 1972/73, said, 'Jimmy Burton, who was Dave Mackay's partner in his tie company, was also part of the scene. He was a bit of a ducker and diver ... Gillie took me out with these guys ... I was a friend of Gillie's and that's all that mattered.

'A few weeks before England played West Germany in a European Championship game ... Gillie took me to this restaurant in Soho. Sitting at the table opposite me were Franz Beckenbauer and Bobby Moore. A couple of minutes later, they were over and sitting at the table with Gillie and I'm thinking, "fuck me, its Franz Beckenbauer." But that was Gillie. Wherever you went, everybody knew him and everybody loved him. He had a shyness and he didn't hog the limelight. He was just a nice guy, because there was no side to him.'

17

Tweet

THE NOUN 'tweet' means a post made on Twitter, the social media application, to many in the modern day. Alan Gilzean, according to close friend Bob Hynd, was attempting to get his head around such things after becoming the proud owner of an iPhone in his later years.

But the noun meant something rather more 'back to nature' long before Jack Dorsey, Noah Glass, Biz Stone and Evan Williams's brainchild became a global phenomenon which attracted more than 320 million active users by 2018 while becoming a major source of breaking news worldwide. It was the chirp of a small or young bird. Perhaps a canary.

The moniker of the songbird from the finch family with origins in the Canary Islands was adopted by Norwich City as a nickname as East Anglia had been known to have bred them.

And it was the Canaries – rather than any budgies, if you recall the quote credited to Gilzean in *The Glory Game* – which provided the last chapter of a tale that saw Gilzean seal his final trophy-winning moment with Tottenham Hotspur in the 1972/73 season, with the World Wide Web, let alone the website just referred to, yet to be invented by that clever chap Sir Tim Berners-Lee.

It was a period in which many male pop musicians applied makeup and donned loud glittery clothes in the name of glam rock. The one with the most credibility to these eyes, David Bowie, released his ground-breaking album *Ziggy Stardust and the Spiders from Mars* just prior to the start of a season which saw Gillie and co lift silverware for the third successive campaign.

But the times were far from colourful and tuneful in other areas of UK society with a strike by dockers following one in the coal-mining industry, a second Cod War over fishing rights in the North Atlantic sparked by an Icelandic gunboat sinking two British trawlers and the government bringing in price and pay freezes to counter inflation.

Football was being adversely affected as the country's economy was moulding into a pear shape. Bigger wage demands and increased overheads ate into any profits and clubs in the red just got redder.

To pile on the negative, spectators voted with their feet with the beautiful game becoming more and more about pragmatism than entertainment. Spurs were no exception. Gates averaged 38,000 in the season that sealed their second European triumph and it was en route to declining to 26,000 by the end of the 1973/74 season. The rise of hooliganism didn't help.

Playing ugly and seeing violence to match in and out of grounds were anathema to the idealist in Bill Nicholson, of course.

He struggled on, becoming more and more a bemused man out of time, but still managed to help Gilzean and the club he had devoted his life to since 1936 become the first club to lift the League Cup for a second time.

The club even made a £300,000 profit on the season, although it would drop to £35,000 for the following campaign with forecasts of a £250,000 loss the season after with no revenue from Europe for the first time in four years. And the club had to bite harder on the bullet, being committed to spending £200,000 to refurbish the Lane.

Gilzean was fundamental to the cup win, in that intelligent, elegant way he always possessed.

There was the hoopla which surrounds all finals at Wembley. And, despite the lowering attendances elsewhere, the meeting with the Canaries of Norwich on Saturday, 3 March 1973 attracted a full house. One hundred thousand were expectant, despite the apparently lopsided contest – promoted Norwich destined for relegation in their first season in the top flight – that was about to unfold in front of them. Some were there for the occasion – not as many as the FA Cup Final where the 'prawn sandwich' brigade, as Roy Keane once had it, attended in force – but the vast majority were there to roar their team to victory, hopefully in style. Or at least that was the hope from those of a Lilywhite persuasion.

Hopes were heightened by the choice of kit. Against Villa two years previously it had been as if two kits had been thrown together to make one, with white shirts, navy blue shorts and yellow socks. This time it was all white – the Real Madrid-style kit, through which Spurs had enjoyed so much success in European competition. The teams walked on in the traditional fashion, side by side.

Gilzean's gait was characterised with that familiar swagger, his long arms swinging back and forth each side. Even thinner on top than when doing his two previous pre-match Wembley walk-ons, the number seven was wearing the hair he had around the back and grey sides a little longer. He appeared relaxed.

He and his colleagues shook the hand of the royalty present and removed their white tracksuit tops with navy blue edging ready for action.

But they found a canary-yellow wall blocking their path when the encounter kicked off. Norwich were known to be fit and it seemed they were determined to use their energies on keeping Spurs out.

Spurs had never lost a major final and were desperate to extend an unbeaten run to eight, although recent favourites, such as West Bromwich Albion, Arsenal and Chelsea, had had their backsides bitten by underdogs Queens Park Rangers, Swindon Town and Stoke City.

Gillie, bright as a button, was in the mood for the wish to become a reality.

His ability honed to produce the unexpected with his unorthodox style which relied on stealth and awareness rather than huff and puff.

Facing the left-hand touchline, he performed a backward flick behind him, sensing Jimmy Pearce was behind him on a run. Unfortunately the winger found his way blocked.

He helped Pearce again when flying in for a header, forcing Norwich captain Duncan Forbes to head the ball at the number 11, who hit the post. And he laid an opportunity on for Mike England which the defender hit over.

Gilzean also produced a piece of wizardry which almost got himself a goal. He controlled a long Martin Chivers throw, bamboozled his marker Dave Stringer on the turn, which allowed him space to get a shot away. Unfortunately for the Scot, Canaries keeper Kevin Keelan, all in green, saved it.

Then came a crucial piece of intelligence to alter the point of attack which opened up the Norwich wall 18 minutes from time. A long throw by Martin Chivers was headed towards goal by Martin Peters at the near post toward Gilzean. The forward, instead of trying his luck close in while surrounded by three defenders, shielded the ball and, hopping gently backwards, carefully spun the ball with the instep of his left foot towards Mike England, having spotted the defender making a late run into the box. A Norwich defender managed to get a toe on the ball before it reached the defender but was unable to control it and the spherical object ran loose to sub Ralph Coates who volleyed the ball into the corner of the net like an arrow from the edge of the penalty area.

Gilzean queued in his polite way to congratulate Coates, offering him applause, a hug and several pats on the back. He was clearly delighted for the winger, who had become Spurs's first substitute in a major final.

He also stood up to be counted as Norwich searched for the equaliser. He put in two tackles – one after the other – any of his defenders would have been proud to have made to help Spurs clear their lines. Gilzean even helped produce a break from which overlapping left-back Cyril Knowles hit the post. Mind you, it seemed Phil Beal gave Gilzean a flea in his ear for not picking up Duncan Forbes after the Norwich captain headed just wide late on.

A muddied Gilzean picked up the match ball as referee David Smith blew the final whistle after Knowles had aimed a long ball towards his head. He held it in the crook of his left arm as he shook the hand of Dave Stringer, future manager of the Canaries who had spent much of his time trying to nullify the Scot's effectiveness, before throwing it to the Gloucestershire ref. Job done.

As a spectacle, just like the 1961 FA Cup Final in which Spurs completed the Double by beating Leicester, it was lacking.

As television commentator Brian Moore said, 'It was a big match … which didn't quite fulfil all the expectations. Spurs just about had the edge.' (Others would be less kind, using words such as 'tedious' and, in the case of respected writer Brian Glanville of the *Sunday Times*, 'awful'.)

The Wembley scoreboard lit up, declaring, 'Hard luck Norwich, you put up a brave fight.' And then replaced it with, 'Congratulations again to Tottenham Hotspur – still unbeaten at Wembley.'

Meanwhile, Gilzean, immediately behind captain Martin Peters, trooped up the famous old 39 steps to the royal box just like he had done two years earlier. As Peters held the cup aloft, Gillie collected his winning silver tankard and tucked the cup's plinth under his arm for the journey down the steps and the lap of honour.

Gilzean was strolling, looking to his right, when he sensed something coming up behind him. His instinct was right and after a quick look back over his right shoulder he ducked and stepped backwards under an arch formed by the left arm of Martin Chivers and the right of Mike England with the cup its centrepiece, making sure to look up to take a look at the pot as his team-mates jogged on. Ralph Coates took England's place as Gilzean displayed his reserve, fading into the background by briefly continuing his stroll before joining in the jog-in.

The television cameras went inside the Spurs dressing room as the players, led by Bill Nicholson, sung 'Glory, Glory Hallelujah' in between sups of champagne. But those cameras did not pick up Gilzean. Maybe he was avoiding them so others could bathe in attention. Certainly the likes of stalwart defenders Mike England and Phil Beal, goalkeeper Pat Jennings and, of course, Coates, were among the players who deserved it. Or maybe he'd merely popped to the loo while the cameras were rolling. Whatever, he had relived his Wembley dream, and won his last major trophy as a professional footballer.

Gilzean, though, looked back more fondly on his first taste of League Cup success. He said, 'I wanted to beat Villa more than Norwich. Norwich weren't a big club, but Villa's always been a big club. Villa Park's a wonderful stadium. It's funny because when I played for the under-23s for Scotland, there was a guy called Charlie Aitken, and he played in that Scottish team with me, and he was marking me in that final against Villa.'

Gilzean had every right to take centre stage given his contribution on the path to Wembley. He netted in each of the opening rounds of the League Cup at home to Huddersfield Town and Middlesbrough and guided Spurs through in the last 16 against Millwall, which is something, you may remember, he did in the FA Cup six years earlier.

And he was integral to the most impressive result of the run in a 3-1 fifth-round replay win for Spurs over Bill Shankly's Liverpool, who were to end the season with two other trophies (one at Tottenham's expense), under the White Hart Lane lights on Wednesday, 6 December 1972; a victory secured just two days after he had aided a 1-1 draw at Anfield.

It assured Spurs a semi-final spot and Gilzean was in the line-up for both legs of it against Wolves, helping his side win through 3-2 on aggregate. It was never easy against those Black Country chaps (wouldn't be much easier now, come to think of it).

* * *

Gilzean went close to a second piece of silverware in the same campaign as Spurs defended the UEFA Cup.

He proved his worth with a couple of goals in a 6-3 win against Lyn Oslo in Norway in their opening match of it, before assisting Martin Chivers to the first of a hat-trick in another six-goal demolition in the second leg (an encounter, incidentally, which saw roommate Steve Perryman, 13 years his junior, named as captain for the first time, in place of the injured Martin Peters).

Alan withstood a physical clobbering to set up a goal in a 4-0 home victory against Olympiakos Piraeus and played his part as his team clinched the tie in Greece.

He created the first and netted the second in a 2-0 home win against a team which would provide the opposition for his testimonial, Red Star Belgrade, with Spurs completing the task of reaching the quarter-finals without him.

Gilzean assisted Spurs's path into the last-four on away goals against Vitória Setúbal and figured in two monumental showdowns against Liverpool in the semi-finals. But he was unable to prevent Shankly's team going through on the away goals rule and lifting the trophy against Borussia Mönchengladbach as they took over the baton as the dominant British club in continental competition, establishing the reputation it enjoys today.

Reds goalkeeper Ray Clemence, who was to join Tottenham, said, 'Spurs had a bigger reputation in Europe than ourselves.'

Gilzean believed the Spurs team, which won three trophies in back-to-back seasons in the 1970s, differed going forward to the previous Lilywhite line-ups he was in. He said, 'Defensively it was much the same. Very similar. Okay, Mackay had left but defensively we were more or less the same outfit. Pat Jennings was in the goal. Joe Kinnear and Cyril Knowles. Alan Mullery, Mike England and Philip Beal. They were the stalwarts of the team. It was just, more or less, the forward line that had changed. And we had to change our style because at the beginning when I went there we had two flying machines on the wings in Cliff Jones – Jonesy was fantastic – and Jimmy Robertson.

'These two guys could take the ball from just outside their own penalty box and go the length of the park with it. That was a great pressure reliever for the likes of Greavsie, me and that.

'We played more high balls into the box. Martin Peters, Martin Chivers and myself were good in the air.'

Pat Jennings agreed. He said, 'We played more direct football. That is where Gillie was brilliant for me as a target man. Everybody played long balls. None of this short ball you play now when it is 20 passes to get into the other half. But we were one of the first teams to use full-backs going forward, with Cyril Knowles and Joe Kinnear. Still played good football, though. That's what Bill Nicholson encouraged. If you couldn't play he wouldn't have bought you. So he knew what he was buying in Gillie.'

Unfortunately, the FA Cup campaign in 1972/73 was a disappointment.

After non-league Margate were defeated, Gilzean was on target in the fourth-round replay against Derby County. But

Spurs threw away a 3-1 lead with five minutes left to lose 5-3 in extra time in an extraordinary tie I witnessed squashed in the Park Lane End terrace with nearly 53,000 packing out floodlit White Hart Lane.

The league campaign was also a case of 'could do better', with Spurs lacking consistency, often reliant on the brilliance of Pat Jennings – he saved two penalties in a league draw at Anfield – and ended eighth. And Gillie only contributed five goals in 35 starts wearing the number-seven shirt.

But Gilzean had once more proved his staying power, while maintaining his subtle qualities. His efforts – a season after receiving the Spurs President's Award and, perhaps in recognition of his decade of loyalty, consistency and brilliance, saw him voted third behind winner Pat Jennings in the Football Writers' Association's Player of the Year award.

Like with Coates at Wembley, it seemed he was delighted his team-mate was in the spotlight. No hint of 'why not me?' Typical Gillie. Just like the kindness he displayed helping out a local journalist before the League Cup Final.

David Leggat said, 'Gillie was very kind to me. The editor of the newspaper said he wanted a first-person piece but, of course, this was a small newspaper and there was no money to spend. So I asked Gillie if he would do it and he said, "What will I get?" I told him I could buy him a drink. He did that for me.'

Gilzean certainly backed up his belief, he remained capable of performing at a high level – and enjoying his football.

He said, 'Once you get past 30, people start writing you off. As far as many are concerned I have been surviving in soccer for the last four years on borrowed time. Well, I don't feel finished, but I must admit, the refs' revolution has helped! I never was overkeen on a hard, physical game – it wasn't my style. Now, the referees' campaign to clean up soccer and clamp down on the dirty players has helped me last the pace better at an age when a tough, tiring match is the last thing I need. Extra protection gave George Eastham the chance to parade his skills in Stoke's fantastic League Cup march last season – and he was another player supposed to be too old.

'This season I have felt as effective as ever and enjoyed my soccer as much as ever. But being realistic about it, the "pudding" pitches are now here. The mud, snow and slush that we get after Christmas could slow me up. Last season I was quite often the Spurs man to be subbed late in a game when the old legs weren't taking the strain as well!

'Another factor to consider will be the increasing chance of tackling two matches a week. The UEFA Cup and the League Cup have already given Spurs a busier programme than some clubs and I can't see our season getting less crowded. Nor do I want it to.

'Extra games are caused by successful cup runs and I really believe that winning is the best cure for tiredness. Nor do I ever get bored with training if Spurs are on a winning streak. Morale is high in the whole team and training seems easier. I have had around 15 years in top-class soccer and keeping fit is not more difficult now than it was as an eager young kid. Once the season is in full swing you are almost playing enough matches to be in perfect trim all the time.

'At 34 , I can still finish in the middle of the pack in the training sprints. I find weight-training and distance running enjoyable. Always have done. I suppose running is what I enjoy best nowadays. Ten-lap races around the ground – lovely! We used to do a lot at Dundee and I have developed the right mental attitude for settling into a stride and churning out the laps.

'During matches, though, I now try to conserve energy. Experience can save you yards. Think a move out and you might not need to make it. Nor has getting older lessened my heading ability. My main fear is that knocks won't mend so quickly as I get older. Other than that I honestly don't worry about my age; no extra training on my own or special precautions. When my soccer days ARE over I expect I shall devote more time to my golf handicap of 14. As a true Scot I have a healthy regard for the game but I don't play as much as I would like.'

* * *

Gilzean's Spurs career tapered down dramatically to a stop by the denouement of the 1973/74 season.

Coincidently, there was a parallel with Bill Nicholson, who continued his downward path to the end of his 15 years in charge. It was to be the last full campaign of an individual rated the greatest manager in the history of the club. He said, 'It was the most disappointing season since my first as manager.'

It was a campaign that provided further proof of the team's Jekyll and Hyde tendencies; reaching the UEFA Cup Final while skirting with relegation before pulling their collective socks up to 11th in the league.

As ever, Bill Nick put the club first and searched for a formula which would see Spurs firing on all fronts. One step he took was to turn Gillie into a regular for the reserves. It came after a disappointing first half of the season run of results in the league, a first-round exit in defence of the League Cup against Queens Park Rangers at Loftus Road and a fall in their opening FA Cup tie against Leicester at Filbert Street. Even though an operation early in the new year for a cyst behind his right knee proved nothing to worry about.

It must have been a hard decision for Nicholson, who saw Gilzean as a 'natural' with 'instinctive' abilities to 'thrill the crowd' – qualities which symbolised his ideal Spurs player given his edict to his players that the fans are 'the most important people at the club' and should always be supplied with an enjoyable product.

But these were changing times. Other pillars of Nicholson's 1970s triple trophy winners, Cyril Knowles and Joe Kinnear, also involved in the 1967 FA Cup win of course, discovered they were no longer so vital. Youth products Ray Evans and Terry Naylor were tried at full-back. Another youngster, forward Chris McGrath, was given a run as Bill Nick tried to freshen-up an ageing side.

Yet the team lacked firepower in the league, netting only 45 in total, equalling the club's worst return in 1912/13; a factor in the falling gates.

Nicholson struggled to find the right blend as well as a big name to provide a long-term replacement for the likes of Gilzean. Spurs were no longer the attraction they once were and the manager considered there was a dearth of talent available.

Fortunately, Gilzean and others of experience came in handy as Spurs progressed in the UEFA Cup after sealing their spot by lifting the League Cup the previous term.

He came off the subs bench to provide the nous and skill, plus a couple of goals, to turn the opening tie against Zurich's Grasshoppers in Switzerland to Spurs favour, before helping the Lilywhites complete a 9-2 aggregate victory.

Gilzean made the Spurs goal for Ralph Coates as his side drew 1-1 with Aberdeen in the first leg of the second-round tie against the old club of his Dundee team-mate and pal Bobby Wishart at Pittodrie before being part of the team that completed the job at the Lane with a 4-1 win.

It was to be Gillie's last bow in European competition. He was unable to share in an impressive run to the final which saw Spurs beat Dinamo Tbilisi, Cologne, against whom Gilzean's star had shone so brightly in the European Cup for Dundee, and FC Lokomotive Leipzig.

Feyenoord, who included members of Johan Cruyff's Holland side which reached the World Cup Final that summer, was always going to be a tough nut to crack. And when Theo de Jong netted a late equaliser to make the first-leg score 2-2 at White Hart Lane there were those around me with a sinking feeling about the second leg.

No one knew that Spurs's reputation would plummet even deeper than suffering their first loss in a major final in the second leg. It was due to the hooliganism which erupted among those purporting to follow Spurs on the De Kuip terraces. Even Bill Nicholson's half-time pleas for a cessation of the violence fell on deaf ears; violence which continued post-match.

Nicholson was to have another row with Chivers – this time over pay – on top of the other attendant problems. But the behaviour of the spectators in the same stadium that bore witness to arguably the greatest moment of his reign and the club itself – lifting the European Cup Winners' Cup in 1963 – appeared the straw that broke the camel's back.

He limped on – without having the services of Gilzean to call on if required into the following season – before throwing in the towel, resigning in August 1974 after a poor start to the 1974/75 season.

Gillie ended up with just three goals in a mere 23 appearances and finished seven short of becoming the first player to score a century of league goals in both England and Scotland, but did have the satisfaction of scoring the final goal of the season on his final competitive appearance in a 2-0 win over Newcastle United at St James' Park on 11 May 1974. It was his 133rd goal in 429 first-team games, a record which put him seventh on the all-time Spurs goalscorers list, although pushed down to ninth by Jermain Defoe and Harry Kane in the new millennium. Tellingly, his two main partners Jimmy Greaves and Martin Chivers were rated first and third when Gilzean ended his time at the Lane.

There had been suggestions in the February he may choose to go abroad, with clubs from South Africa and the United States of America purportedly interested in him. After all, it seemed as if his career at Spurs was drawing to a close. He refuted such suggestions as 'nonsense' at the time.

Gilzean said, 'I don't want to make any decisions until the end of the season when my contract runs out – that will be the proper time. Then I will look at any offers and make up my mind.'

Speculation was ramped up when Bill Nicholson revealed Spurs would be giving Gilzean a free transfer, which would allow the player to sort a decent deal for himself with whatever club he joined.

Nicholson said, 'We shall be letting him go and I should imagine he will have a crack at playing in South Africa.' Furthermore, the manager revealed the club were writing to the powers-that-be for 'permission' to stage a testimonial.

He said, 'Spurs need the go-ahead, because he is just four months short of completing ten seasons with the club.'

Gilzean, though, was still around when Spurs went on their summer tour.

He had been on several with the club, enjoying the differing cultures and standard of football from west to east, from tortillas to sushi, to lifting minor silverware such as the Toronto Cup and the Costa Del Sol tournament trophy. He was in the parties for Holland, Israel and Spain (1965), Bermuda, North America and

Mexico, and Spain (1966), Switzerland (1967), Greece and Cyprus (1968), North America (1969), Malta (1970), Spain (1970), Japan (1971) and Israel (1972).

But his final one saw him pull on the Lilywhite shirt one last time on a volcanic island nation paradise called Mauritius in the Indian Ocean just off the south-east coast of Africa, a continent to which Gilzean was soon destined.

Spurs vice-chairman Charles F. Cox quoted American author Mark Twain in the club handbook for 1974/75, 'God made Mauritius first and then Heaven. Heaven being copied from Mauritius.'

The former British colony looked breathtaking with its lagoons, palm-treed beaches and coral reefs around much of its coastlines. Mauritius's tropical climate was almost as far away as you could get on a winter's day of rain and snow in Coupar Angus. An extra attraction for golf fan Gilzean was a course on white sands at the Spurs hotel. All in all, a place to rejuvenate the body, lift the spirits.

And it certainly lifted Gillie and the rest of the touring party headed by Eddie Baily – with Bill Nicholson head-hunting for players and securing his last signing, Alfie Conn – on their arrival from London N17, having flown the 6,000 miles from Heathrow on Sunday, 2 June. They were in need of a little R&R. It had been a frustrating season of decline domestically and disgrace internationally through the misbehaviour of supporters in Rotterdam.

Just how perked up was displayed in their opening tour match against a Mauritius Select XI at the King George V Stadium in Curepipe on 8 June. There were 18,000 there to see Gilzean net two goals and Martin Chivers three in a 5-0 victory.

The Scot repeated his feat against another Select XI as Spurs came from 2-1 down at half-time to secure a 6-3 win in the same town five days later, although only 5,000 bothered to watch the action.

But Gilzean had saved his best until last. Literally. He hit a hat-trick in the third and final game of the visit, again against a Select XI, on 16 June 1974. It helped secure a 6-0 win (a scoreline, according to Jennings in *Pat Jennings: An Autobiography*, bet upon to pay off a drinks bill the club baulked at paying).

The rumour mill, understandably, had it that this would be Gilzean's last club trip. And the emotion was, stated reports, palpable on Gilzean's face as Perryman and Martin Peters presented him with decorative cockerels, the symbol of the club, of course, before kick-off, after Eddie Baily had formally introduced him to the players as a brass band played 'For he's a jolly good fellow'.

Afterwards the players put Gilzean on their shoulders for a lap of honour in front of the 10,000 around the 'uncovered brick' stadium.

Reporter Harry Harris, writing in the *Tottenham Weekly Herald*, said that it was a 'final tribute to a great player and friend' after it was confirmed by Nicholson that Gilzean would get a testimonial, with the English powers-that-be granting the Scot special dispensation to have one.

He added that the bright, warm weather and prolific goals return on the tour 'could well have made him decide to end his playing days in the sun with a South African club.'

Harris could well have had a point, with Gilzean having revelled in the warm climes of a country not too far away from the republic. His career wasn't as dead as a dodo in the land where the extinct flightless bird was once endemic.

For the following month he signed a two-year deal with South African club Highlands Park.

18

'The Saddest Day of My Life'

ALAN GILZEAN was hurting the day he left Spurs.

And that hurt remained in his voice, eyes and body language when he recalled it almost 40 years later.

He sat onstage alongside former team-mate Pat Jennings at *The Spurs Show* podcast in Dingwalls, north London, in December 2013, seemingly wrestling to subdue his inner emotions, describing how he felt about ending his top-flight professional career with one of the leading clubs in the country, one respected throughout Europe due to its exploits on the continent.

Gilzean said, 'Football breaks your heart when you've got to leave it. I can remember going to collect my boots at White Hart Lane. It was the saddest day of my life. You know you can no longer play the game to that high standard. It takes so much away from you.'

He pinpointed the moment he knew his time was coming up and said, 'The decision came pre-season the previous season. We'd get hard training. It was at Cheshunt those days. It was really hard training. We were getting in the laps and I was always good at distance running. I could go on forever. And the legs seized up. Eddie Baily, the assistant manager, used to shout, "Gillie, what's wrong with you?! You've been out drinking and all that." I said, "My legs have seized up."

'Bill Nick took me aside and said, "Right, don't do all the heavy training. Do what you feel like." And I'll be eternally grateful to him for that because he must have gone through it himself. When you get to 35, 36, 37 your brain is sending down the messages but the legs are not relaxing. That's the first time you realise you are on your way out.

'I had ten wonderful years at Spurs but when it is time to go it is time to go. You've just got to accept it.'

It was clear Gilzean's affection and respect for Nicholson remained as strong as it ever did.

He said, 'I never really had that much to do with him. I was only in his office twice in ten years. That was to re-sign. It's impossible to say [what he was like]. He moaned a lot. After games it would be, "Christ, Gillie, you should have been doing this and you should have been doing that." But he was a very honest man. You knew where you were with him. He laid down what he expected of you.

'I had it a wee bit hard to begin with. He expected me to go round like Bobby Smith and knock people for six and all that. And that wasn't my style. He kept on saying, "Bobby Smith would have had that goalkeeper in the net." Things like that. I said, "Well, I'm sorry. You'd better go and get Bobby Smith back again."

'To be fair to him, he was always good to me. He listened to me. But, as I say, I was only in his office twice in ten years so he must have liked me.'

Gilzean added, 'Bill was a very fair man. What he promised you, you got, you know? In the ten years I was at Tottenham, there was never a cross word with him. In my eyes a wonderful man.

'Bill Nicholson and all the staff there were just one big happy family. When we got beat we cried together, and we all partied together when we won.'

Ian Gilzean revealed his dad told him about Nicholson. Ian said, 'Dad spoke highly of him. He spoke highly of his two managers – Shankly at Dundee and Bill Nicholson at Tottenham. Both were great guys who wanted the game played in a certain way. If you worked hard and gave it your all that was it. Didn't get many pats on the back from the pair of them. But they had a way. And the players played for them. It worked for them.'

Gilzean reckoned Bill Nick's assistant Eddie Baily was a 'hard taskmaster'. Baily was a team-mate of the manager when they played together in the Spurs team which won back-to-back titles in 1950 and 1951.

He said, 'Eddie played in that great push-and-run Tottenham team with Les Medley, Ron Burgess and Bill Nick. That was a superb side in those days. Baily was one of the playmakers. He was the John White of his day and was a wonderful passer of the ball, and even when he was training us in the gymnasium he could still do the ball skills.

'You have to admire people, when you're young and have just joined the club. You have to take notice of what he said, because he's been there and done it all. There was one experience Eddie would never like talking about. England played the USA [in the 1950 World Cup] and got beat, and Eddie was in that team. That was a very sore point with him. But Eddie and Bill naturally wanted the best for Tottenham. Tottenham was their life.'

Gilzean has revealed his feelings on his striking partnerships with Jimmy Greaves and Martin Chivers, the influence of John White in his move to Spurs, the driving force that was Dave Mackay and roommate Steve Perryman.

But there are many former Spurs team-mates who meant a lot to him. Pat Jennings for one. He rated his friend and Northern Ireland World Cup international the best goalkeeper on the planet. He said, 'Pat was a quiet guy, he never said much before a game, but everybody would wish everyone a good game before you go on the pitch, and Bill Nicholson would do his thing; wind you up, and get you ready for the game.

'But Pat, he was the best goalkeeper in the world, there was no doubt about that. When he used to come out for crosses and take them one-handed. What a goalkeeper he was. I've talked about Stevie Perryman making all these appearances for Tottenham, well, if Pat hadn't have gone to Arsenal, he probably would have had that record. For some crazy reason he was allowed to leave though. Unbelievable really, but there you go.'

Cyril Knowles, the classy full-back who inspired the song 'Nice One Cyril' and sadly passed away of cancer in 1991 aged 47, was another pal and respected colleague. Knowles earned four England caps but Gilzean insisted he deserved more.

Gilzean said, 'Knowlesy was a very good player and great tackler, but I felt sorry for him because I thought he should have got a lot more England caps. The two full-backs were very good going forward, both Joe Kinnear and Knowlesy.

'He was a very good guy. There were four of us: Mike England, myself, Pat Jennings and Knowlesy. We used to play golf together during the week. Toss up for partners. We all lived in the Cheshunt and Enfield area so I got to know these three especially well.'

Gilzean was full of praise for Martin Peters, the World Cup goal hero for England. Peters was part of the treble-trophy team in Gillie's second decade at Spurs. He even skippered the 1973 League Cup winners.

He said, 'Martin was wonderful. He had all the skills. He was good in the air, a good passer of the ball, had a good shot with either foot, and his blind runs were fantastic. He used to appear from nowhere in the box and score from headers or side-footing in shots. He was like Greavsie in that he had a wonderful awareness in the box. That special skill, that he could time his runs perfectly. You don't get World Cup medals if you can't play.'

As the original King of White Hart Lane, Gilzean built up a rapport with the supporters which was sustained down the generations.

How would I describe your relationship with the Tottenham fans?

Gilzean said, 'Very good. They were fantastic to me; the Tottenham fans were marvellous. They used to sing my name, and I had ten years of wonderful support. I could never remember them really giving me stick.'

Gilzean clearly had no regrets about joining Spurs.

He said, 'For me Tottenham have always been a big club, and have been a good club to me. When I came down first there were five top clubs, Tottenham, Arsenal, Everton, Liverpool and Man United.

'When I left Scotland I was only going to join one of these five. I wouldn't have joined Sunderland or Wolves or any of them.

For me Tottenham have always been a big club, and have been a good club to me.'

It was a love-in all round with his team-mates appreciating what Gilzean brought to the party.

Pat Jennings said, 'One of the loveliest blokes. Just unassuming. Never got above his station. One of the lads. Lovely lad. Great team-mate. Let his ability do the talking. Brilliant.

'He was quite laid-back in the dressing room. Wouldn't be running around encouraging people. The way it was in those days was for Bill Nick to come in literally 20 to 25 minutes before kick-off. He would be around the team. Told each of us the strengths and weaknesses of our opponents. Whether they were right- or left-footed, good in the air, whatever.

'Nowadays you get videos an hour before the game. Every throw-in. Every corner. Bill got that sort of information into us within that 20 to 25 minutes. Probably more beneficial at that time.

'The fans loved Alan. I suppose it helped we had a good team in those years.

'He began to look older than his years when the old hair had gone. He used to say, "Lend me your comb and I'll leave a few [hairs] in. Greys are better than nay hairs."

'I'm sure he improved. With respect to the Scottish players he played with, he played with better players. That partnership was there with Greavsie.'

Jennings refuted claims made by Hunter Davies in the *New Statesman* in March 2007 that Gilzean had 'little interest' in football and saw it as 'just his job'.

He said, 'I don't think you could have contributed what Gillie contributed if you didn't love it. He must have done.' The goalkeeper agreed with a Gilzean quote from the book that although he still enjoyed football that that enjoyment was diluted because 'now the object is not to get beat at all costs'.

Jennings said, 'In the early days when you played for fun you probably enjoyed it more. The minute you turn professional everything changes, especially for a goalkeeper and a forward as well. If you are not scoring you are not winning. The name of the game is to draw at least and hopefully win.'

Defender Mike England remembered Gilzean as 'very bright'. He said, 'Gillie was a smart cookie. A little smarter than the average footballer. In his early days he did a [clerical] job that showed he was good with numbers. He looked to entertain. Did clever, skilled tricks with a coin. He'd throw a coin in the air, catch it on his head, let it drop to his knee and flick it back up into his top pocket. Always remember watching him do it. So I went away and practised and practised and practised so I could do all his tricks!

'He was laid-back, just an average Joe. Really good company. That's why he was so popular. The supporters loved him because of the skill he had. He made things look easy, which good players do.

'Awareness of people in the box was his forte. Very clever at getting in front of defenders, getting his toe in, side-footing the ball into the net. Made it look easy. Had the skill to get away from a defender and into space and – bang – it was in the net. Opponents must have wondered, how did he do that? All about the timing.'

England contrasted Gilzean's spells north and south of the border. He said, 'Gillie adapted his game. But also, and I'd better be careful how I say this, but at Tottenham he was playing against better players. When he got to Tottenham he had moved up a notch.'

England was convinced Gilzean's laid-back image was beneficial to his performances for Spurs. He said, 'I found Gillie a nice person. Liked him very much. His temperament helped him as a player. Off the pitch, he was very casual. You wouldn't think he was playing for a big club. A very special person not just a good footballer. Well respected.

'Bill Nick knew what he was doing when he signed him. Blooming heck he used to do things. Few performances that weren't clever, great. He had class. That is one of the nicest things you can say about a footballer.

'Alan joined Spurs because he wanted to play at Wembley in an FA Cup Final and, of course, that is exactly what happened. When you are a young lad you need to try and win things. The league, the FA Cup, in Europe. Win this and that so you can look back and see what you've achieved. That's why players love winning trophies. We didn't do too badly and that meant Gillie didn't do too badly either.'

England felt Gilzean was underused by Scotland. He said, 'Gillie didn't receive enough recognition for such a talented player. The fact he only played 22 times for his country surprises you. It might have been the fact he went to England instead of staying in Scotland. Might be similar to Mackay. Gillie and Mackay. Oh my God, incredible players. I must have played against Gillie for Wales and most probably kicked him up in the air!'

Phil Beal, a member of the treble-winning team with Gillie in the 1970s, reckoned Gillie was king of the header as well as White Hart Lane. He said, 'What a great player. He was the best header in the game. I've never seen a better header of the ball to the near post for a flick-on than Alan Gilzean.

'When I see all these present-day players try and do it – and even players in my era – no one could head a ball like Gillie. And even now no one could flick a ball on like Gillie.

'He had incredible ability. Combined so well with Jimmy and Martin. Gillie provided memories for life with what he did on a football field. Very fit, lots of stamina, rarely injured. Easy-going on and off the pitch. Took his knocks in an era of hard tackles.'

Alan Mullery, who captained Gillie's Spurs to the 1971 League Cup and 1972 UEFA Cup, rates Gilzean among the 'legends' he played alongside.

He said, when I asked him for a list of his top team-mates for *Glory, Glory Lane*, 'All of them. Couldn't pick one. All extremely good if not great professional footballers. Pat Jennings is one of the best goalkeepers of all time, Mike England one of the greatest centre-halves. Bobby Smith? Marvellous. Alan Gilzean, Jimmy Greaves, Cliff Jones … you were playing with legends.'

Cliff Jones provided pace, flair, goals and bravery to aid Gillie's Spurs after supplying the same qualities to the club's greatest-ever team; more than a mere illustrious predecessor to the likes of compatriot Gareth Bale at the Lane. He knows a player when he sees one and certainly recognised it in Coupar Angus exile Gilzean.

Jones said, 'Gillie was a lovely guy and a special player. All-round ability. So skilled at heading the ball. Great control, quick over 10 to 18 yards. He became a big favourite with the Tottenham supporters. They recognised him as a Spurs type of player. The main thing they loved was his link-up play with Jimmy Greaves. Was a terrific trainer. That impressed Bill who always said you should train as you play.

'Contrast to Bobby Smith? They were both stylish and skilful, although Bobby was more known for being tough, strong and physical.'

Martin Chivers remembered how Gilzean was in the dressing room as well as their on-the-field partnership.

He said, 'He wasn't loud at all. Just confident. He used to talk himself into a game and talk about the other team. Some of us were probably a little bit more nervous and thinking about how we're going to get on. I was going to get goals and people think it's easy, but they don't know. All players are thinking about their opposition. Even the night before you think about how am I going to get around this fellow?'

The last word among his Tottenham colleagues comes from his manager throughout his decade in London N17.

Bill Nicholson said of Gilzean, on the eve of the 1974/75 season, 'He has been a great player for us and has played a vital part in helping the youngsters fit in the side.'

Nicholson also wrote, 'I liked Gillie. He was easy to talk to, never moaned and got on with the job in an uncomplicated way. I never had any problems with Gillie and … he wasn't greedy when it came to money.

'I could be open and frank with him and he wouldn't get angry or sulk. He was very trustworthy and likeable. Away from football he was something of a loner, a quiet, unaggressive man. It was a tribute to his fitness that he was still playing for us at the age of 36.'

19

'That's a Scottish Legend, Son'

RICHARD GOUGH, who captained Spurs to the 1987 FA Cup Final and skippered Scotland, remembered how he woke up with a start one morning as a 12-year-old. Across the other side of his bedroom a somnolent figure reclined in the spare bed, his head poking above the top of the sheets.

It was Alan Gilzean.

Richard's dad Charlie had helped recruit the King of White Hart Lane and Dens Park for South African serial trophy winners Highlands Park.

It was all with a view to the Scotland international perhaps reigning at the Park's Rand Stadium in Johannesburg. The King of the Rand?

Charlie Gough, the Park assistant manager and player from 1965 to 1973, and former team-mate-turned-boss Joe Frickleton, both Scots, wooed Gilzean on a scouting mission to Britain.

And a place in the sun won over cold winters in the English league when their compatriot signed a two-year deal in July 1974, ensuring glorious Highveld sunsets would provide the perfect backdrop as the sun set on the playing career of a true great and reluctant hero.

I spoke to the much-travelled Gough, born in Sweden before his dad was bought out of the British Army by Charlton Athletic, from his home in San Diego, California. He was 'relaxing' and 'knocking away at a wee business'.

Gough was full of questions of his own. Did Gillie do okay in his transport career after football? Where did he live? Was he married?

I managed to squeeze in a few of my own, starting with the spare bed episode.

Gough said, 'I saw this guy was sleeping in the spare bed and said to my Dad, "There's a strange guy in the room." My Dad just said, "You'll never have a more famous man in your room. That's a Scottish legend, son. That's Alan Gilzean." I couldn't believe it.

'I didn't know then of course, aged 12, that I was to go on and have a decent career and play for Tottenham and Scotland as well.

'They must have had a good night. One on the tiles, maybe! My dad must have got on well with Gillie. My Dad was a bit of a social animal as well. Probably they had been drinking. My Dad had a pub in the house, a wee bar. Probably spent time there. Maybe my Dad didn't want to let him drive home.

'We lived in Glenhazel in Johannesburg, just down the road from Highlands Park, while Gillie lived in the inner-city residential neighbourhood Hillbrow.

'Did I form an impression of Gillie as an individual? No.

'I would've seen him play for the club but can't remember his performances. I was too young. I am close friends with Martin Cohen, one of Gillie's team-mates at Highlands Park. He told me he was a great player but he didn't play that many games. Maybe about ten.

'I never met him after Highlands Park, which was a shame because we could have spoken about my dad, who has also passed away unfortunately [in 2015]. But when Alan passed I read a lot of the stuff in the obituaries and it was good stuff. I wanted to speak to his son. But sure you could pass on the message.

'There were a few parallels between myself and Alan. He scored for Scotland in a 1-0 against England at Hampden Park in 1964. I did the same against England in 1985 [with, like Gillie, a header from a left-wing cross. Graeme Souness skippered Scotland that day].

'We both played for Tottenham, of course. He was a Tottenham hero. I was only there one season but like to think I was well remembered there. Johnny Wallis [part of Spurs's backroom staff] always used to say, "I hope you are as good as that Gilzean." Tottenham always used to do well when they had a Scotsman playing for them. Mackay, Gilzean, then [Steve] Archibald [who was in that 1985 victory over the Auld Enemy]. We did quite well.

'I played against his son Ian for Rangers. He was with his father's team Dundee. Small world! They beat us in a famous game. You must look into that – August 1992 at Dens. I'm sure he scored a couple of goals. He was quite a good player. Centre-forward. I was marking him. Think he gave me a torrid time. We got beat by them 4-3, which was unusual. We went on an unbeaten run of 44 games after that.'

Gilzean left his family – wife Irene and two boys Kevin and Ian – behind in Enfield for the latest chapter in his football career.

His youngest son Ian said, 'I don't know whether he and Mum talked about going out there at that point. We never went anyway but I don't think it was going to happen. I think at the time apartheid was still around.

'Dad quite enjoyed the football and a few players [from England] used to play out there for Highlands Park [like former Chelsea and QPR striker Barry Bridges] but don't think he could handle the different buses for the different ethnicities and stuff. You can't have a civilisation working like that.

'He did talk about his time out there, but not much. Some things, as a kid, you don't take in anyway.'

It is understood there was another negative which might have led to Gilzean cutting his stay to just three months in the republic, where Peter Baker, Spurs's Double-winning right-back, settled, initially to play in Durban and then run an office and stationary firm.

Highlands Park's players had to take a regular daytime job during the week as they were part-time professionals. It must have taken an adjustment for Gilzean who had not had to do that since getting on the bus from Coupar Angus to Perth as a teenager to fulfil his clerk's role at Coates and Co. To make it seemingly trickier for an individual known for his reserve, he was employed in sales at Rex Evans Motors, the firm named after and owned by the club chairman. (Mind you, his employer was an individual of lofty ideals which would have met with Gilzean's approval given the Scot's discomfort with the overt signs of legal racial segregation. Evans was to be hailed as an individual who helped change the face of South African football by negotiating the introduction of non-racial professional football in the country in 1978. Indeed, it could be argued he was the Nelson Mandela of South African football.)

Brad Kaftel, chair of the reconstituted Highlands Park and managing director of a car sales firm in the republic, took time out to answer my queries on Gilzean's time at the Park.

The high-flying business operator has a special affection for the club dubbed the Lions of the North based in Johannesburg. He grew up watching the team win most things in sight as they totted up a record eight South African National Football League titles and six cups.

Alan Gilzean emerged before him during Kaftel's early teens. He said, 'I remember watching Alan playing for Highlands. I was a very young teenager, probably only about 14 years old. He was a terrific addition to the squad.'

Gilzean must have felt strange wearing the team's red tops as it was akin to Arsenal, although their kit was a copy of Manchester United's.

Alan played in the 1974 NFL Cup Final under lights at a packed Rand Stadium, Park's home venue. It was against Arcadia Shepherds, whose kit resembled that of West Germany, World Cup winners a few months earlier. Arcadia won 2-0 and finished the season also tucking the title under their belts (although the following year, minus Gillie, Park took revenge by winning the league and cup, while making the Shepherds feel 'crook' in the final).

Gilzean's Lions went in as holders but their opponents took the initiative, according to one commentary. In fact, it seemed the commentator was glorying in their struggle, stating Arcadia were 'outplaying Highlands Park's sophisticated and star-studded side, driving forward with great panache.'

Gilzean got amongst it to try to turn the tide. One time he made a prodigious, well-timed hanging leap from a long ball, the momentum moving him from left to right in the air to get in front of his marker. He beat his opponent and headed the ball. But he was unable to guide it with his subtle trademark touch to a colleague and collided with the challenging full-back, lost control of his body, fell backwards and crashed on to the bone-hard surface with a thud. He seemed to literally bounce before settling in obvious pain.

And his reward for this physical torture? He witnessed future Coventry City winger Steve Wegerle, brother of Roy, who played for Chelsea, QPR and others in the English league, put Arcadia ahead with a scrappy effort.

Gillie picked himself up to try to carve out an equaliser. A run and cross he made from the right almost did the trick. But the team-mate who connected with the ball had his header saved by the Shepherds stopper. Arcadia completed the scoreline seven minutes from time.

Gilzean said, 'My team, Highlands Park, reached the final of the cup, but we lost. Our keeper made a couple of errors which cost us the game. It's a shame I couldn't take Pat Jennings out there with me. At one time it looked as though we would clinch the league, but eventually finished third.

'I had many happy days at Tottenham and regretted very much the time I had to leave. Yet the prospects look good out in South Africa. We play in front of an average 15,000 people. But in some of the really big games, particularly when two of the top "black" teams meet, the gates swell to 60,000.'

Kaftel kindly gave me contact details of two of Gillie's Park team-mates, Hennie Joubert and Martin Cohen. He said, 'They are quite active with hosting lunches for some of the old-timers and I am sure they could give you plenty of information.'

I was unable to reach Joubert but tracked down Cohen, who also played and was friendly with George Best – and Phil Beal – when at Los Angeles Aztecs. He also faced the likes of Pelé and Franz Beckenbauer of the New York Cosmos in the North American Soccer League.

Cohen's day job on Gilzean's arrival in Johannesburg was running his late father Jack's paint and hardware firm, eventually turning it into a mega franchise across South Africa. And he took time out to recall his time alongside Gillie. He said, 'Maybe he came because of the Scottish connection with our management.

'All the players knew of Alan. He had been a legend at Tottenham.

'When Alan came out for August, September and October in 1974, he was fantastic. He was a striker and scored quite a few goals in those few months. His other attributes, also, were his first touch and getting up and hanging there to head the ball.

'He was good for the changing room as well because he was quite funny in certain situations.

'He was a character on and off the field. All the players got on well with him. He was an asset to our team. We also had players like Chris Chilton from Hull. We had a good side.

'It was just a pity he only played the three months. He was supposed to come back for the next season. I don't know what went wrong but he didn't come back.

'In South Africa around that time there were some unbelievable players and not only playing for Highlands Park. Many British players were coming out. Gordon Banks I think was one, Bobby Moore another. Big-name players getting into their 30s and a little bit past it to play the [English] First Division.' (Note, other British players involved in football in the republic during this period included George Best, Sir Bobby Charlton, Geoff Hurst, Kevin Keegan and Sir Stanley Matthews.)

What was Gilzean like as a bloke? Cohen said, 'I got along with him.' What about where he lived? He said, 'Most of the players stayed in a place called Hillbrow. Lot of hotels and nightlife. I was a young player around 20 and stayed with my Dad. Most of the foreign players, especially Barry Bridges and Alan, who weren't there with their families, stayed, I think, at a hotel.'

Cohen guessed Gilzean might have not warmed to having to do a day job away from the game. He said, 'Maybe it was a little bit strange. I never really mixed with Alan in the day because I was running my business and didn't speak to him except at training between 6pm and 8pm.

'I don't know how that affected him because he was used to football as a full-time profession.'

Could disaffection with the day job have been a reason for him not returning to the club? Cohen said, 'Maybe. It might well be.

When you are accustomed to a certain lifestyle, getting up and going training rather than working all day.'

In between, Gilzean was on the blower from Johannesburg to the UK. There was the testimonial match in recognition of his ten years' service at White Hart Lane to sort out. It was a time when these sort of non-competitive matches were vital to elite players. More than vital. A necessity rather than a financial token pat on the back by club owners to help departing players readjust to the outside world.

Six-figure weekly pay packets – which have become a reality in the English Premier League – would not even have been thought, let alone dreamed, about in 1974. Testimonials in the modern day for Premier League players are clearly superfluous unless, perhaps, the recipient is planning to banish world poverty and ensure a cure for cancer is found. But back in Gillie's day wages did not amount to a king's, queen's or even an agender ruler's ransom. A bit more than their predecessors had had to endure with the £20 maximum wage limit in force before Jimmy Hill, George Eastham et al. came along on their white chargers to smash through such a ceiling, maybe. But nonetheless nothing that would enable them to save enough to keep a roof over the heads and food in the bellies of dependents once playing days were over.

Certainly, there was, generally, no way Gillie and his contemporaries could avoid having to go out and do a nine to five to survive once boots had been hung up, unless they hailed from family or friends with a bottomless pit of money.

Pat Jennings had been the first person for Gilzean to get onside. Jennings was first in the queue for a testimonial with Spurs in the 1974/75 season. But the Irishman was only too happy to oblige his main target man.

Jennings said, 'Gillie was ready to go for a testimonial and because he was leaving Spurs I let him go in front of me. So I went back to 12 years then [eventually staging his own testimonial against Arsenal in November 1976 when Jimmy Greaves scored twice in a 3-2 Spurs win]. But it was a pleasure to be able to do it for him. Testimonials meant something in those days. The money wasn't that great. It was a nice little send-off.'

Spurs swiftly agreed to Gilzean being able to stage the match at White Hart Lane, once dispensation had been granted from the Football Association despite their loyal servant coming up a few months short of the requisite ten years' service.

The stage was set for Gilzean to bookend his life at the Lane after taking his first breaths of it to raise funds for the family of former Scotland team-mate John White in 1964. The Gillie hotline from the South African capital remained hot as he liaised with Frank Hampton, the chairman of his testimonial committee, and Bill Nicholson when he learned that his only Spurs manager had resigned.

Red Star Belgrade – the team Spurs beat on route to the 1973 UEFA Cup semi-final – agreed to provide the opposition free of charge for the testimonial match at White Hart Lane on Wednesday, 27 November 1974. And Gilzean wanted Nicholson there.

His Spurs manager had stayed away from the club after taking charge of Gillie-less Spurs for the last time in a 4-0 home League Cup defeat against Middlesbrough 46 days earlier after five defeats in the opening six league fixtures. But Bill Nick popped round the corner from his Creighton Road home to join the 22,239 crowd – which also included Cohen and other Highlands Park colleagues – in paying tribute to the King of White Hart Lane.

Nicholson said, 'Don't kick up a fuss because I'm returning. This is his night. I don't want to be noticed. I just hope he gets the kind of crowd he deserves. If every manager had a team of Gilzeans then I'm sure football in this country would not be in the state it is in. Not just from the point of view of his football ability but also because of the way he honoured his contracts. He was wonderful. He never argued. Once he signed, that was that. Greaves was the same. He never got a penny more from Tottenham than he was entitled to.'

It is clear Bill Nick rated Gilzean among his best signings, and not only that. He said, 'He was a likeable fellow.' But why did you come back for him? He said, 'Well, he's a bit different to most, and he loves Tottenham.'

The tributes flooded in. Miro Radojcic, a writer on the Serbian daily newspaper *Politika*, said in the match programme that

Gilzean was an 'apostle of Total Football'. *News of the World* writer Reg Drury, who ghosted Pat Jennings's autobiography, remarked that Gilzean 'retained his popularity with the White Hart Lane crowd right until his final appearance.' Frank McGhee, with the *Daily Mirror*, effused, 'Take a good, long lingering look at Gillie in action tonight. You may never see another exactly like him.' *Sunday Mirror* writer Ken Jones, a cousin to Gilzean team-mate Cliff Jones, wrote, 'There is no need to apologise for including Alan Gilzean among my favourite footballers. What really appeals is the quality of instinctive football intelligence.' *Daily Mail* writer Jeff Powell wrote, 'Alan Gilzean brought grace and touch to an age when football was overshadowed by the cloggers and the grafters.' Brian Glanville of the *Sunday Times* opined, 'It is not often that you get a Players' Player who is also, and emphatically, a Fans' Favourite. Alan Gilzean, however, is that rare bird.' But the writer who got to Gilzean the bloke was Tommy Gallacher.

Gallacher, writer on *The Courier* in Dundee, wrote, 'When Alan Gilzean phoned me from London wondering if I would contribute a word or two towards a brochure for his testimonial game, my immediate reaction was to say of course I'd be delighted. On my daring to pose the question, "Exactly what sort of stuff did you want?" the answer was so difficult. "Och, just say a few words about whether you thought I was a good player or not," all of which just serves to show that Alan Gilzean, the boy who joined Dundee from the tiny Perthshire town of Coupar Angus, had not allowed the bright lights of London or anywhere else that football has taken his talented feet over the years change his down-to-earth attitude.'

Frank Hampton, the chairman of Gillie's testimonial committee, wrote, 'We can all remember those players that for you and me had that special flair that makes some of them great. I wonder how many of us would list Gillie as one of those great players. Probably all of us because he is one of those players who are easy to remember. He *does* something on a football field – you notice him. He doesn't have to try to play. It just happens and it happens well … we are here honouring one of the greats – one who had helped to make football the art that it is.'

Gilzean lauded in a cartoon strip displayed in the Coupar Angus Heritage Association centre

Gilzean flanked by Dundee manager Bob Shankly (to his left) and Spurs boss Bill Nicholson

Gilzean (front row, third from the right) at Dundee's Centenary Dinner

Gilzean (left) reunited with former Dundee team-mate Doug Cowie in 2017

Dave Forbes, former Dundee director, dinner organiser and friend of Gilzean

Gilzean with Dundee club historian Kenny Ross

Gilzean in the team line-ups for his Spurs debut against Everton

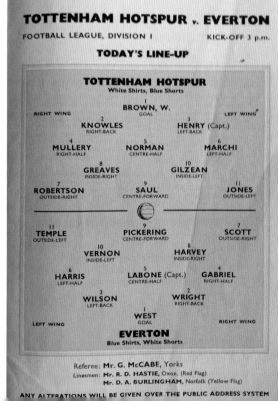

The Tottenham Weekly
Herald *report on Gilzean's*
first Spurs appearance, at
White Hart Lane

The G–Men: Gilzean and
Jimmy Greaves

Gilzean marries Irene Todd at the Abbey Church in 1965

Gilzean (left) and Martin Chivers, with whom Gillie enjoyed a second great strike partnership at Tottenham

Gilzean, rated one of the best runners in training at Spurs, proves the point by stepping it up round White Hart Lane with Greaves (right) and Cliff Jones

*Gilzean climbs
above Manchester
United's Denis
Law, his pal and
Scotland team-
mate*

*Gilzean, seated
with Greaves
(to his left) and
Jones in dressing
room with Stanley
Matthews before
the wing wizard's
testimonial in 1965*

A dream comes true: Gilzean celebrates 1967 FA Cup glory at Wembley following victory over Chelsea with Dave Mackay (holding trophy) and Pat Jennings

Gilzean (No. 9) celebrates goalkeeper Pat Jennings' goal against Manchester United in the 1967 FA Charity Shield match at Old Trafford

Bob Wilson, with whom Gilzean clashed in the 1968/69 League Cup, is challenged by the Spurs forward

It was clear Gillie was looking forward to the occasion. He said, 'I just can't wait. The prospect of playing for Tottenham again makes me tingle with excitement. I've really enjoyed my first season in South African football and I intend to give it another season out there – but there's nothing like playing for a team of Tottenham's class. Everything is so different playing for Spurs.'

Prior to the kick-off, Gilzean handed out a football to each of the winners of a competition to write essays about him run by *The Herald* in the company of Harry Harris, the newspaper's Spurs reporter who went on to the nationals and authorship. Examples of the best entries, which were printed in the programme, proved Gilzean was popular with young supporters.

Mandy Stanton, a 15-year-old from Tottenham, wrote, 'I think Alan Gilzean is one of the greatest footballers of his time ... he's put his heart into every game ... not a man easily provoked and Alan is quite prepared to help young and new players.'

Paul Murphy, 12, from Cheshunt, wrote, 'He was never selfish with the ball and he did not get into trouble with the referee or the management.'

Terry Hill, 15, also of Cheshunt, wrote, 'The classic, magical performances had the crowd stunned.'

During the prize-giving, one fan dashed on the field to kiss Gillie's feet, Harris recalled in his *Tottenham Greats* book.

Gilzean led Spurs to a 2-0 win with the loudest roar on the night when he converted a Cyril Knowles ball to complete the scoring. He did, however, have an earlier opportunity to get his name on the scoresheet when Spurs were awarded a penalty, but disappointed the crowd by displaying his modest self and giving the spot-kick opportunity to Knowles, which the full-back stuck away on the rebound.

Gillie lined up with Pat Jennings, Ray Evans (Joe Kinnear), Cyril Knowles (John Pratt), Neil McNab, Mike England (Mike Dillon), Terry Naylor, Steve Perryman (Chris McGrath), Chris Jones, Martin Peters (Jimmy Neighbour) and Alfie Conn (Ralph Coates). He came away with an estimated £12,000 from the event and unforgettable memories. He knew what he meant to the fans the moment that kiss was planted on his boots.

Meanwhile, Gilzean crossed paths with John Duncan, who had left Dundee for Tottenham the month before the testimonial, down in London. Duncan watched his old Dundee boyhood hero against Red Star from the sidelines just three days before his third goal in his first six Spurs appearances and got to know him.

He said, 'I got to know him reasonably well without really being one of his mates. Alan was a great bloke. I remember one time when my car had broken down near White Hart Lane and I happened to meet him. He quite generously just said, "Look, John, take these keys [to his own car]. Off you go. Get yourself home. And bring it back to this address in Enfield tomorrow." Thought that was fantastic. Obviously I got home and dropped his car off at his home later on.'

Duncan, the striker dubbed Gillie at Dens, had spent seven years attempting to convince the Dark Blues faithful he was worthy of the label, with great success, having scored 109 in 188 appearances, including 40 in the 1972/73 campaign. And he had just started to do the same thing in London N17 on becoming Terry Neill's first signing after the Irishman succeeded Bill Nicholson, costing a princely £140,000.

He said, 'I suppose we were going to get compared because I was Scottish, from Dundee. There was comparison there, but he'd done so much I wasn't going to establish anything like that, of course. He'd been a big success and helped win a few trophies.

'It wasn't a direct comparison. I was a forward and enjoyed heading the ball like Alan did, but wasn't quite the same type of player as Alan was.

'I didn't see myself as replacing Alan. I was a goalscorer. That was my role, whereas Alan had to adapt from what he was at Dundee and played as a partner to Jimmy Greaves and Martin Chivers. More a provider, sometimes playing a wide striking position at Spurs. Something I never had to do. I was judged on my goalscoring.'

20

Managing

THE PLAN seemed to be that Alan Gilzean, now 36, would be heading back out to South Africa for one more season as a player after counting the funds raised from his testimonial match.

You could see the smile on his lips as he said, 'I'm looking forward to the new season which gets underway at the end of January, which means I'll be back there at the start of the month for training. While you're all freezing in winter, I'll be lapping up the sun.' He confirmed, 'The next season will probably be my last.' But then Gilzean threw in a couple of curveballs.

He said, 'The game has given me so much I'm seriously thinking of trying to give something back by becoming a coach or even a manager. But more than likely I'll settle for a business partnership with my brother [Eric] who is doing so well in America.'

These considerations were in marked contrast to the opinions he was quoted as uttering in *The Glory Game*: 'When I've finished playing, that's it. I couldn't stand the aggravation of being a manager, having fans, directors, press, everyone after you. No thanks.' A hot seat in football appeared to hold zero appeal and, by inference, the hassle of the commercial sector did not either.

It seemed, though, that he would not miss his return flight to Joburg. But reports in late January 1975 more than suggested Highlands Park would kick off their new season without their cultured international. Why? Because, they told us, Gilzean was still in the UK.

Tommy Gallacher, the *Dundee Courier* reporter and former footballer Alan had contacted for a contribution to the testimonial programme, revealed on 24 January in his newspaper that there was the 'distinct possibility that the former Dundee, Spurs and Scotland star may not, after all, be going back to South Africa.'

The journalist seemed close to him judging by the sentiments expressed for the Red Star fundraiser. He certainly had a handle on the modest tendencies of the individual from a small town who hit the big time, and revealed how he had had a conversation with Gilzean at the footballer's Enfield home, where Alan informed him he was still 'tying up all the loose ends' linked to the testimonial.

He estimated it would take two more weeks 'and even after that he still wasn't sure what he would be doing football-wise'. Quoted by Gallacher, he said, 'I am in no hurry to decide where my future lies. I have had offers from America and Australia and, of course, Highlands Park want me back in South Africa to play for them again. But I haven't made up my mind and won't be doing so until everything in connection with my testimonial has been settled.'

The waters were further muddied with Gallacher putting forward another option, the possibility of Gilzean returning to Scotland to play for Arbroath. The Smokies had been 'foiled' in their bid to get a few games out of him before returning to the republic due to the player picking up a groin strain. But he might be tempted to have a second bite at the cherry with Gilzean having 'second thoughts' about going back to South Africa.

Stevenage Athletic threw their hat into Gilzean's ring in the spring of 1975.

The club chairman Jimmy Burton was on the lookout for a big name for the non-league club, based in the new town 33 miles north of London (one that was to become the home of Double-winner Terry Dyson, whose former Spurs team-mate Johnny Brooks played for the new town's original club).

Burton might not have been Elvis Presley's lead guitarist like his American namesake, but he could certainly pull a few strings. He had the reputation of being a 'wide boy' and well known within football. Pertinently, he was a business partner of Gillie's old team-mate and friend Dave Mackay selling ties (Stevenage club historian

Lloyd Briscoe, son of founder Jim, said, 'As a kid I remember my bedroom being full of ties. My Dad kept bringing home these boxes of them!').

Most pertinently, of course, he was a pal of Coupar Angus's reluctant hero himself.

The trail to Gilzean taking his first and only managerial role started when an announcement over the tannoy echoed around at Broadhall Way on Monday, 3 March 1975. The voice was that of Bill Coldwell, who told the 352 spectators he was stepping down as team manager and managing director of Stevenage Athletic after three years.

It was a double whammy for his listeners on the night they witnessed another reason why the (red-and-white) Stripes's Southern League Division One North promotion bid had gone south, their favourites losing 3-2 to Cambridge City in their own backyard.

He said to them, 'When I came here three years ago I promised promotion to the Premier Division in three seasons. I believe in honouring that promise and I feel it's best that I leave the job to someone else.'

Jimmy Burton, the chairman, and Ronnie Duval acquired Coldwell's majority holding jointly and the latter filled the managing director's job. Roy Johnson, Coldwell's assistant, took over the managerial hot seat. But he scurried off to Cambridge City to join their new boss, one Bill Coldwell, within a fortnight. Burton himself took charge of the team for one match – which they won at Banbury with a goal by Steve Mahoney (more about him later) – before former Cardiff City defender Trevor Peck took charge in what was a mad March for the Hertfordshire outfit.

Peck, it was reported, believed he would be in charge for next season with the current campaign petering out. But Burton refuted Peck's claim which led to the club losing their third manager in as many weeks. The chattering classes began to believe Gilzean would be the fourth when he attended a 1-1 draw against Witney Town in April.

But the *Stevenage Comet* had suggested he was merely being sounded out as a player and director by old pal Burton who was quoted as saying Gilzean told him he was 'too old and that his best days were behind him'. But the former international, according to the *Stevenage Comet*, 'expressed an interest in Stevenage's offer,' which was ostensibly a seat on the board.

But he was then provisionally offered and provisionally accepted the role of team boss subject to ironing his contractual commitments with Highlands Park. It followed a five-hour meeting with Gilzean after he had watched Stevenage defeat Chelmsford City – a club Jimmy Greaves was to join two years later – in the wake of Peck's departure a week earlier. And he even attended the reverse fixture against Chelmsford midweek.

Burton, understood to be helped by another old Gilzean friend Ricky Prosser at the club, said to the *Stevenage Comet*, 'These [Highlands Park contract complexities] are not insurmountable problems and there is plenty of time to sort them out. The important thing is that Gillie has given a conditional yes.

'Alan has already indicated to the board the amount of money he feels he needs to build a promotion-winning side here, and he said how impressed he was with certain of our current players. This area is desperate for a footballing personality and I and my fellow directors believe that he can stimulate the team and the town to great things. We have even had offers of cash donations to help the club afford him.'

It seemed he was proved right, with Gilzean agreeing to take on his second office job – after clerking for a Perth carpet manufacturer – on 1 July 1975.

Gilzean tantalisingly left the door ever so slightly ajar when he spoke of whether he would combine his off-the-field role with one on it as he outlined his plans.

He said to *The Comet*, 'I was at Tottenham for ten years and I thought it was time to look for something else instead of struggling to find a place in the team [having gone to South Africa]. I felt it was a good opportunity to become manager at Stevenage. You are limited in non-league football by how much money you have available.

'But I just hope to get a good team together and see them enjoy their football and start winning games. I will see how it goes, but at the moment I am not considering playing. I shall get the players together four weeks before the season begins and possibly we will have a weekend get-together as well.'

Gilzean had jumped from inhabiting an other-worldly world of the top flight to what is now the eighth tier of English football, and was reminded of the chasm when asked which player he most admired. He said, 'In my time I always admired Denis Law and Bobby Charlton. I thought they were great entertainers. I am a Bobby Moore fan as well – I think he has given fantastic service,' (presumably it was a given that Jimmy Greaves was already top of that list).

Although not officially starting until the following month, Alan got involved in the nitty-gritty of preparing for the 1975/76 season. He swiftly arranged a glamorous pre-season friendly with Dave Mackay's Derby County who were fresh from lifting the First Division title. Gilzean said to *The Comet*, 'Dave Mackay is an old buddy of mine and he was pleased to give us a game.'

He also began sorting his playing staff, hinting teenage goalkeeper Steve Anscomb, formerly of Luton Town, might have a first-team future after understudying Mick Gevaux throughout the previous season in which Stevenage ended 11th. He said, 'I don't think it's fair to go out and sign another keeper until the lad has had a chance to show what he can do.'

'Mr Gilzean' invited defender Hugh Pratt to stay after presenting him with Stevenage's player of the year award in May. He also offered deals to two unnamed Football League strikers. Fans were told the price of admission would increase to 35p – compared to 45p in the Southern League Premier and 65p in the Football League. But it was hoped by Gilzean, Burton et al at Broadhall Way that they would get value for money.

Burton, whose persistence was credited with landing a big name, also helped convince Javier 'Joe' Revuelta, a property tycoon based in Bournemouth, to help sooth any palpitations over financial security.

But Gilzean's lone experience of the manager's hot seat was to prove far from smooth. Bumps in the road were plentiful, starting with the gaoling of Burton a month after Alan agreed to take on his part-time role in between a job with a 'big haulage firm in Enfield'.

It was reported Burton 'wept in the dock' after being sentenced to two years for financial irregularities.

There was a light side, with Gilzean involved in a game inside the walls of Burton's Grendon Underwood prison near Aylesbury, according to his number two Jim Briscoe. Briscoe said, 'Jimmy Burton knew everyone – and I mean everyone – from show business to sports personalities. Jack Chisholm [ex-cricketer for Middlesex, ex-Sheff Utd player and ex-manager of Plymouth] put together a team for Jimmy to play the staff in a benefit match at the prison.

'Boy, what a team! Frank McLintock had to play in goal, because Bob Wilson couldn't make it. Terry Venables, Malcolm Allison, Dave Mackay, Alan Gilzean, Danny Blanchflower, Dave Webb, Martin Chivers, Ralph Coates, Jimmy Greaves, just to mention a few of them. I was nominated as the "manager" because I had brought a kit with me from Stevenage Athletic.

'That evening was spent in the Prison Warders Club, and was one of the funniest and most drunken evenings I have ever spent in my life.'

Burton's incarceration was a test if Gilzean harboured any disquiet over the trials and tribulations of becoming a manager. But he was not about to have second thoughts.

Stevenage director Ernie Ward said to the *Stevenage Comet*, 'Alan has got down to the task. He has expressed a willingness to stay and make Stevenage a club to be proud of. Much at Broadhall Way will revolve around Alan – he's a very important man to us.

'There is no doubt that Jim Burton will be missed at the club. He has done a tremendous amount for Stevenage Athletic and has asked for little in return. All of us at the club have now got to give 100 per cent and pull together to help the club in every way possible.'

Gilzean might have come in as a favour to a mate but was making all the right, positive noises in word and deed. After meeting up with the retained players, he revealed himself 'impressed' with their attitude.

Revuelta took over the chair in Burton's absence but there appeared to be no improvement in the playing budget for Gilzean.

Gillie stuck with it but a lack of funds and quality players hindered his ambitions, which was evident in a five-month run without one league win. In one dire sequence, Stevenage lost 11 on the bounce in February and March, leaking 34 goals and hitting the target on a meagre three occasions.

Club historian Lloyd Briscoe said, 'They weren't a good club. That wasn't a good team. It was a shocking pitch in those days.'

Things seemed no better in the boardroom, with Revuelta leasing the ground from the Stevenage Development Corporation. Briscoe said, 'Jimmy had arranged for Javier Revuelta – or Joe as we called him – to take over the club while he was in prison. He was a multi-millionaire businessman originally, I think, from Malta. He was not a football man. He was after the freehold of the ground, I think, to turn it into something else. But the ground was owned by the council.

'There were all sorts of ructions and he got a JCB and just got the pitch dug up at the end of the 1975/76 season. No football was played there for four years until it got sorted. That's when the current club my Dad helped found moved in after playing on a roped-off playing fields pitch since 1976.'

Briscoe pointed out Gillie 'recognised that the club was in turmoil' but 'agreed to stay on' with the club historian's dad remaining his assistant. But he added, 'The writing was clearly on the wall when, in April, owing to a secretarial oversight, the club was delinquent in issuing retention notices to the playing staff commensurate with the rules of the FA.

'The consequence of this was that a number of prominent and key players left Stevenage, and there was nothing that the club could do about it.'

Athletic's final humiliation occurred in the last game of the season, with an 8-0 drubbing at Merthyr Tydfil on Friday, 30 April 1976. Gilzean was not in charge of the final game in the history of Stevenage Athletic. His farewell was a 1-0 defeat at Bedworth in the penultimate fixture on Monday, 19 April 1976. For the record, the Stevenage team was: Fisher, Riolo, Kerr, Noble, Hull, Whishaw, Hamilton, Montgomery, Mahoney, Weilbonelski, Oxley. Sub: Fricker (not used).

Jim Briscoe, Athletic's and subsequently Stevenage Borough's first manager, revealed Gilzean was told by Revuelta after the game that 'effective immediately the club no longer existed'. And it left Briscoe in charge of a ramshackle outfit for the final fixture, which included Sunday footballers scouted the previous weekend on Stevenage park pitches.

Briscoe, a former Sheffield Wednesday striker, wrote in his memoirs, 'Gillie received a phone call from the club's owner, Revuelta. He told Gilzean that, effective immediately, the club no longer existed. Gillie told the team what had happened.

'The team's response was that if the club no longer existed, then they would not be prepared to travel to Merthyr Tydfil to complete the last fixture of the season.

'Virtually everybody had left the club, with the exception of Vic Folbigg [a former manager] and myself.

'We both knew that if we did not send a team down to Merthyr, then there could be serious ramifications from both the league and the FA. We [Vic and I] had just two days to get a team and transport them to Wales to fulfil the fixture. We contacted anyone who could play from the local Sunday league.

'One volunteer called Fred drove his Marley Tile van all the way to Wales and back with 16 people inside it.

'When we arrived at Merthyr, it occurred to us that we hadn't registered any of our players with the authorities. In order to compile the team sheet, I had to put down false names such as Johnny Brooks [a former Spurs and Stevenage player) and Ray Peacock.

'After I had submitted the sheet, I later received a tap on my shoulder. I turned around to see John Charles, the ex-Leeds, Juventus and Wales international. He was involved with Merthyr Tydfil at the time and was enquiring as to where Johnny Brooks was because they were old friends.

'Squirming, I had to "come clean" and explain the situation to him. His response was quite frivolous, calling me a "cheeky bugger". We both had a good drink in the bar after the game together though.'

Stevenage finished rock bottom, 11 points adrift of Wellingborough Town, collecting just 18 points from 42 games, six wins, six draws, 30 losses, scoring 46 and conceding 109. They resigned from the league on 13 August. The club were no more.

Lloyd Briscoe hinted the experience might have made Gilzean feel he was not cut out for management. Briscoe said, 'He knew he wasn't a manager.'

He claimed Gillie once turned up at the wrong ground. Briscoe said, 'One occasion he said to my dad and the rest of the team, "Next Saturday the game's at Ashford. I'll meet you down there at the ground." Fair enough. The team bus has gone down to Ashford in Kent and Gillie had gone to Ashford in Middlesex. Gone to the wrong bloody ground.'

Whatever the results, the politics, the manager's sense of direction, it was clear that Gilzean was popular with the players. Forward Steve Mahoney said, 'Do you want the truth? There's loads of stories because he was a character. A lovely lad.

'You couldn't help but admire him because of what he'd done. He was a megastar. My dad was one of six boys, three supported Spurs and three Arsenal, and the Gunners had the edge for me, but I remember watching him in action with his flicks and that. It was great for us to have someone like Alan as a manager. He stimulated a lot of interest in the club that suffered from being so near London and people who came to live there supported the likes of Chelsea, Arsenal and Tottenham.

'He wouldn't have had a lot of money to buy players and couldn't pay for big players from other clubs. He was getting local players play that didn't cost any money because he had a budget and it saved him money. So there was a few of us. I was young – about 19 – but doing okay. I was seasoned as I'd been there for three years. Peter Shreeves, who went on to manage Tottenham and Wales, was there. Peter played full-back and managed Stevenage. He was a taxi driver at the time.

'But we had a lot of the local boys who didn't have the experience in that league who played. The league was too high a level for them. Don't get me wrong, we were doing all right but it was a funny time for him [Gilzean], I think.

'Training was not that inventive. A lot of running. Sometimes up and down the steps at the ground. A lot of fitness. But that's what we needed because we were quite young and inexperienced generally at the time so we had to work hard to get anything out of it for him.

'Alan Gilzean was great to be around. Loved a game of cards. We'd play cards every away trip. He was good fun. If I look back I don't think he was seriously a manager at the time. We had a laugh.

'He did his tricks in the bar. Get a two bob and flick it up from his knee to his head or shoulder and into his top pocket. Really a fun, nice guy.

'It was a time I think which was difficult for him. A bit strange. We became quite friendly and I think he was going through a hard time in his personal life.

'Wouldn't ever say anything bad about him. He was an extremely nice man.

'Barry Fry signed me for Barnet from Hitchin when [ticket tout] Stan Flashman was chairman at Underhill. Jimmy Greaves had just left and I played down the middle up front, but I did play against Jimmy a few times.

'Forget the playing, it was the characters I was with or met socially that form the biggest part of my football memories.'

Ian Gilzean said, 'I think one of his mates was involved and said, "Would you come and do it?" And he soon realised it wouldn't work for him.'

Whatever people may think of Gilzean as a manager, the Stevenage episode gave us a final opportunity to witness Gilzean the player for the very last time.

He turned out in a benefit match for Ray Dingwall, a captain and centre-back who had to have a cancerous leg amputated. And Alan ended up 'rolling back the years' when he scored with a glancing header from a Cliff Jones cross for a Stevenage All Stars XI, which included Dave Mackay and Steve Mahoney, against Ron Atkinson's Cambridge United in a 2-2 draw at Broadhall Way on Monday, 1 March 1976.

The *Stevenage Comet* reported, 'Almost 1,700 people – Broadhall Way's biggest crowd for two seasons – turned up on Monday to honour Ray Dingwall ... The goal that brought the greatest cheer came when Cliff Jones made a fine right-wing run and cross and there was Alan Gilzean rolling back the years with a flashing header that billowed the net and signalled a pitch invasion.

'But even that had to take second place to the reception received by the night's hero Ray Dingwall when he came on to the pitch five minutes before the start to meet the teams.'

Self-deprecating Gilzean I am sure would have appreciated the greater emphasis being rightly put on Dingwall in the summation. Kind-hearted Gillie also used his Spurs contacts for a second benefit game for Dingwall at Stevenage the following month. His old club sent a strong side to take on a North Herts XI on Thursday, 22 April, attracting a bumper 3,500 crowd.

Gilzean sat this one out but the visitors included first-teamers Martin Chivers, Ralph Coates, Gerry Armstrong, who scored, Don McAllister, Willie Young, Chris Jones and an 18-year-old Glenn Hoddle, who was named player of the match and destined to succeed Gillie as the King of White Hart Lane. But the Lilywhites were beaten 2-1 by opponents who included Barry Fry, the former Manchester United youth player who became Jimmy Greaves's manager at Barnet. North Herts were able to have the last laugh with a winner from Paul Giggle.

Gilzean, as well as helping Dingwall, proved himself ahead of the curve when it came to women's football, which has enjoyed a huge upsurge of interest with the 2019 World Cup in France (although he would have been gutted by Scotland's early exit). He was president of Stevenage Ladies and supported them from the sidelines as they took on Spurs Ladies to raise further funds for the stricken defender.

It seems apposite a Dingwall helped Gilzean draw the curtain on his time in football and a Dingwall – where he did *The Spurs Show* Podcast in 2013 – helped him raise it nearly 40 years later.

21

Dad

IAN GILZEAN entered the Carnoustie Golf Hotel through the glass double doors and spotted me, offered a huge smile and a firm handshake as he removed his flat cap and sat on the comfy chairs in the foyer, the very spot where his dad had conducted his first major newspaper interview in decades seven years earlier with *The Scotsman*'s Alan Pattullo.

He had similarities in looks to his father, especially around his dark eyes. But he still retains a decent head of hair, unlike Gillie, who was clearly losing his follicles by the age of 30. Ian said, 'Dad looked older than he was as a player. My Grandad, my Dad's dad, was bald. Fortunately I've escaped so far!'

He had finished his shift working in further education, eaten dinner with his family and was of a friendly disposition as he began talking about his father.

Ian had lived – with his wife Christine and their two children – in the small coastal east coast of Scotland town famous for its golf course for years but his London accent remained uninfluenced by any hint of the Perthshire lilt his dad possessed. He was also taller, certainly at least 6ft – and sturdier set.

We began with early memories linked with Stevenage Athletic. The Broadhall Way Stadium was an alternative playground for Alan Gilzean's sons. It was relatively handy, just over 20 miles from the family home in Enfield. For Ian it marked a humble beginning to him following in his dad's footsteps into professional football, in reverse, going from Spurs to Dundee. Ian said, 'I remember going there [Broadhall Way] a couple of times [for matches], me and my brother [Kevin, who went on to play for Cheshunt]. I don't think we watched much football. We'd be mucking about. Running around the ground. Kicking a football probably, not really watching the game. I'd have been about five or six. Kev would have been seven or eight.'

It was around the time Gilzean parted from Irene. Ian said, 'I was only five or six when Mum and Dad split up. It was in the 1970s. You get on with it. People make excuses for everything if they want. But you just deal with it.

'If it didn't work, it didn't work. It didn't work for a lot of people. That's what happens. You can't make excuses and stop living through bad times. You still know the difference between right and wrong. Bottom line.

'We still saw Dad once a week. He still lived in London. Remained in London for quite a few years. We went to Tottenham games with him. When his dad got ill he'd come up to Scotland.'

Gilzean involved his boys in sports. Ian said, 'We played badminton and football in the back garden when we were younger. Dad used to play a lot of golf. We used to get taken to the golf on a Saturday in the summer, pushing the trolley around or hunting for golf balls. When we were old enough we got a half-set of clubs each. You'd go to the golf range and progress on to a golf course.

'Never went to the cinema – I'm not a massive film watcher even now. It was lots of sporty stuff. Two brothers growing up. It was all sports. We'd play anything and everything. Football, cricket, tennis, athletics. Do everything. If a parent is a sportsman you are going to be more into sport than playing the piano or whatever. We got bikes when we were 13.'

Gilzean's mum Babs, as we know, was the disciplinarian when he grew up in Coupar Angus. And history repeated itself when Gilzean had his own family, although circumstances were different. Ian said, 'It was difficult because we stayed with Mum and when they split up Mum was the one who provided the discipline because we lived with her.'

Ian remembered spending time with all his grandparents. He said, 'We knew both sets of grandparents equally as both used to visit us in London every year and we would holiday with them. When went to Coupar Angus, we'd ride bikes, play pitch and putt, play football in the back garden or over the park. We also used to pick raspberries. We'd just run about and play.'

Golf matches in Scotland became a source for bonding between Gilzean and Ian. Ian said, 'I used to come up golfing with Dad when I was about 15 or 16. We'd come up for a week. Play four or five days of golf and that was good. We'd tee off about nine o'clock. Go in for lunch then go out and play in the afternoon. We did 36 holes a day.

'Can't remember what we talked about, but it was good having quality time with Dad. Trying to beat your dad at golf is a big thing. Dad used to beat me. He wasn't the biggest of hitters but the ball went straight down the middle of the fairway, while I was hunting for my balls in the rough or in the trees. He just ground me down! My boy now beats me. I don't beat him anymore.

'Dad played a bit of cricket up in Scotland. He liked a bit of cricket. He batted and bowled. Unusual because Scotland is not a cricketing nation, especially years ago. But all the villages had teams.

'If you have good hand-eye coordination you pick up ball sports easily. Dad certainly had and did. Golf, cricket, football, anything. He was a natural. He never got lessons, just picked it up and went for it. Others try but it never happens. God-given ability. But you need determination as well as talent – a bit of everything.'

Gilzean supported Ian when his youngest son wanted to be a professional footballer. Ian said, 'Dad – and Mum – would have said, "Go your own way". If I wanted to do it and had the opportunity to do it they wouldn't say, "You are not going to do it".'

Ian attended Raglan in Bush Hill Park as a junior and Edmonton County was his secondary school, and he was a member of Sunday league club Enfield United. He said, 'We were lucky. We played in good school sides, good youth sides. Probably won more games than we lost.'

Ian first played with Spurs aged 12 to 13 years. He said, 'That's when I started training with them. You didn't get associated seven-, eight- and nine-year-olds and all that years ago. I was on schoolboy forms. Then they'd decide whether to take a punt on you.

'Dad would watch a game and give you a few tips about what, maybe, you can improve on. You see some parents on the sidelines watching kids football who are quite embarrassing. Who run up and down the sidelines telling their children what to do. It's not right. When you turn pro you can't be standing on the sidelines shouting at your kids about what to do anyway.

'Dad wouldn't have been one of those embarrassing parents. He'd come and watch games, but be well away from anything. Right at the back of a stand, or round somewhere else standing. Not getting involved, so he could just stand and watch me from there. Or, when I played for the school, he'd watch while sitting in his car parked on the road. He could see the pitch from where he was.'

It was the same low-key approach when Gilzean turned up when Ian played for Spurs reserves at White Hart Lane. Ian said, 'Quite something to play at White Hart Lane. Just to be good enough to be a pro was quite something. Not many people get to do that.'

Was being the son of a famous footballing father a help or a hindrance? Ian said, 'Both. Obviously there's a name there, but if you are rubbish you don't get a look-in. If you can't control and pass a ball, they are not going to take you on just because your dad used to play. You have to have something to get offered to play there. If you ain't any good, you ain't any good. That's it.'

Ian never had charges of nepotism thrown at him by the Spurs coaching staff. He said, 'Nah. None of that. John Pratt [who attended Gillie's funeral] used to coach us. He'd coach at the school on Tuesdays and Thursdays. When I was a YTS, I was coached by Keith Blunt [who passed away in August 2016] and Keith Waldron.

'Those were the boys we were working with. It was in their best interests if they could push boys into the youth, reserves and first-team. It looked good for the set-up. Dougie Livermore was in charge of the reserves and David Pleat had just taken over as first-team manager in 1986 when I was there.'

Ian made it into the first-team squad, but appearances were limited. He said, 'I got into the league squad – once I think. A few of the big boys were either suspended or injured for a game against Sheffield Wednesday. In those days you only had two subs and I was 14th man. I got injured a couple of weeks after that and that was it, although I did play in end-of-season friendlies [against Bordeaux and Cardiff City], testimonials and matches like that. Tough period? Yeh. That's what happens in football. Some are luckier than others.'

He did not expect his dad, who had relatively few injuries, to provide a shoulder to cry on. Ian said, 'I was about 19 or 20, big enough. You get on with it. I'd done my knees, had the operations and tried to get back. In those days the operations weren't as successful as they are now. Medical science – as well as the football – has come on so much. At least I had a go. Managed to play for 15 to 16 years until the knees packed in.'

Ian moved to Dundee under new manager Simon Stainrod – with Spurs duo Gary McKeown and Jamie McGowan – on a free transfer in the summer of 1992. It was an opportunity to boost his career 30 seasons after his dad had led the Dee to the semi-finals of the European Cup, in a campaign which would see the club celebrate its centenary. And one in which there was a mood of optimism, with the club fresh from celebrating promotion after winning the First Division title for the second time in 13 years.

Ian said, 'To me it was just a move. It just so happened Simon Stainrod was the manager of Dundee. Simon played for Terry Venables at QPR. Venners was the manager at Tottenham when I got released.

'They probably spoke about players and the move might have come about through that. It was probably the best offer I had. Probably that or play in the bottom league in England or even below, but with Dundee I could play in the top league in Scotland. It was a no-brainer.

'The fact Dad played for Dundee never came into it. It was the best option. If it would have been St Johnstone I'd have gone there because it would have been the best level to be playing at.

'What was the reaction of the fans given my name was Gilzean? If you play well the fans like you. If you have a few bad games they let you know. We managed to win a few and stay in the league.

'Lot to live up to? Yeh. But the game had changed from when Dad played, like it has changed massively to where it is now. I couldn't have turned it down given the other offers on the table. It would have been stupid if I had picked somewhere else.

'Did I discover how revered my dad was? You sort of knew that, growing up. Some Tottenham fans probably think he started at Tottenham. But we knew he played at Dundee when they won the league, got so close to winning the European Cup four years before Celtic actually did and made the Scottish League Cup Final. They had a bit about them.'

The 6ft powerhouse, who had gained Scotland under-18 recognition at Spurs, made his competitive first-team club debut as a professional against Falkirk in a 2-1 league defeat at the Dens on 1 August 1992; wearing the number-nine shirt his dad wore when making his breakthrough appearance for the Dee as a sub against Liverpool in 1960.

Ian tasted his first victory when Rangers visited Tayside 14 days later. And he was able to repeat the feat of his dad and score – with his head – against Ally McCoist's Light Blues in a high-scoring win (4-3). He also made two for Billy Dodds, the match-winning second after winning a penalty when impeded by Richard Gough. He went on to net five in 25 appearances (six as a substitute) in his only season at Dens.

He said, 'It was my first season playing after my injuries, so that was quite tough. It was what it was. You do your best. No player goes out to play badly. Some days you do better than others.'

Ian continued his football travels back in England with Doncaster Rovers and Northampton Town. Gilzean also returned to Scotland to play for Ayr United, Elgin City and, where he finished his playing career in 2003, Montrose. He made a scoring League of Ireland debut for Sligo Rovers and hit a hat-trick on his first game for St Patrick's Athletic at Sligo.

He also turned out for St Pat's in a UEFA Champions League qualifying defeat against Celtic in 1998/99, and in two losses against Moldovans FC Zimbru Chisinau in two more qualifiers in the elite continental club competition the following season. Ian hit the only goal of the game to help Glentoran beat Portadown in the 2000 Irish Cup Final. He also played a fourth Champions League qualifier while at Shelbourne.

Ian also turned out for Drogheda United and all told he netted close to 100 goals in more than 250 senior appearances. Like his dad, he was tempted into management and bossed junior club Carnoustie Penmure, where Gillie's team-mate Bill Brown had kept goal, for three years from 2010.

Pat Jennings knew about Gillie's offspring, although it was his old team-mate's eldest Kevin, rather than Ian, who triggered one memory for the goalkeeper. Ian said, 'Kev won a competition taking penalties against Pat in 1979 [when Jennings played for Arsenal]. Our school versus another. Whoever scored the most got tickets for the FA Cup Final, the Arsenal v Man United game.'

Jennings, who helped the Gunners win the final, said, 'They used to invite kids to take penalties.' Jennings also revealed his son Patrick Junior crossed paths with Gillie's youngest in Ireland. He said, 'It is hard following a famous dad.

'My boy was a good golfer. I thought he might reap the benefit of being in an individual sport but, no, he told me, he wanted to be a footballer. And worse, he wanted to be a goalkeeper.

'In the early days I used to go to matches and say to him, "Patrick, forget about goalkeeping and play golf," but to be fair to him he was better than the other goalkeepers at his club. But he was up against people telling him, "Your dad would have caught that cross with one hand."

'He was also clever and walked through his exams but thought he could always go back to studying. I didn't have the heart to knock him back.

'Patrick started at Tottenham, went to Wimbledon, Vinnie Jones's QPR, and Cardiff. He was in the reserves as Cardiff got relegated and decided not to have a reserve team.

'He had the chance to play at the University of Dublin where he took more exams and finished up going around Ireland, playing for Derry and Shamrock Rovers. He and Ian would have known each other. Patrick's now a goalkeeping coach and runs a gym.'

In the meantime, Alan Gilzean was carving out his post-football career in haulage.

Pen-pushing in an office might be in stark contrast to being a football superstar, but Gillie knew he had to eke a living given what he earned from football was not going to sustain him through to his pension, even with the windfall from the testimonial match against Red Star Belgrade.

Ian said, 'Yeh, it is a big difference then to now. In those days you had to work, didn't have the money to retire. There weren't the roles in the media that there are now. So what do they do? Still needed something to live on. That's just the way it was. Unless you could stay in the game by being a coach or something in a period when backroom staffs were small, like in my dad's time. A manager and a trainer and not many others! Quite different to what it is like today.

'Dad wasn't stupid. He'd probably have said he was brilliant at school. But you didn't need to have loads of qualifications to be clever or speak well. He was good with words. I know he was good at crosswords, that's something he always did even when we were young, and well up on current affairs.'

There was an unconfirmed suggestion in the *Glasgow Evening Times* in April 1980 that Gilzean fancied being a pub landlord when he quit playing football, confirmation Ian was unable to give, but haulage proved the greatest attraction when it came to a new career.

The Glasgow paper's report stated, 'Now he's manager of the Blue Dart in London. But it isn't a pub, it is a transport company.' Gilzean's quote on the matter in the paper was, 'I wouldn't have a pub now. You're tied to it seven days a week, whereas at present I start at 8am, finish before 5pm, Monday to Friday, have a very good salary and few problems.'

I tried to piece together Gillie's career in the transport trade and found, via the TrucknetUK website, information which pointed to the footballing superstar being in the employ of Blue Dart on the A10 trunk road in Enfield in 1975 before a mid-1980s stint at Leggett Freightways, and the fact that he was popular with the truckers.

'Formertrucker' posted on the thread related to Enfield and Lea Valley Hauliers for 'mushroomman' on 12 December 2016: 'I do remember Leggett Freightways of Chingford in the days when they were just on the crossroads. I drove for them for about six months back in 1982 on night trunk from the depot to Charnock Richard and back, driving one of their Sedaks. At the time I was there the transport manager was Alan Gilzean, who used to play for Spurs alongside Jimmy Greaves, a great man to work for. In the office was Harvey Chown, son of Roger who was also one of their day drivers.'

'Mushroomman' replied, 'Well there ya go. Alan Gilzean was one of the transport managers at the Blue Dart Enfield depot on the A10 in 1975 shortly after he finished playing football for Spurs. As "formertrucker" said, he was a great bloke to work for and got on well with all the drivers.'

The exchange was provoked by a 2009 email by the intrepid author James Morgan, who uncovered a third firm who purportedly hired Gilzean, Langham Transport.

Pat Jennings said, 'Gillie became a transport manager when he finished playing. I was lucky to be able to stay in the game with Spurs as a goalkeeping coach and I still come in to help the young keepers. Most players had to get another living after football. You didn't earn enough money to do you for the rest of your days. These days if you sign two- or three-year contracts and are clever with your money that'll do you.'

22

'I've Never Been a Recluse'

THERE WERE fewer reasons for Alan Gilzean to stay in touch with football when the Stevenage episode ended.

He had his career in transport to keep him occupied each working day. His children and, of course, his close circle of friends were generally outside the game. But a 'few bad experiences with reporters' sparked what was judged an 'exile' from the game, oiled by a near-40-year media blackout which ended when he gave his first major newspaper interview in four decades to Alan Pattullo of *The Scotsman* in January 2012.

The worst of these 'experiences' came when he was questioned by a journalist about Bill Nicholson early in the season after the player left Spurs, who were to be relegated in 1976/77.

The subsequent reporting of that conversation mortified Gilzean, who loved Bill Nick because of who he was, what he did for him and what he did for Spurs.

He said, 'This reporter had me saying it is time Bill Nicholson left. He was more than a manager to me, he was a friend.'

Ian said, 'He fell out with this reporter, who misquoted him about Bill Nick. He didn't have a high trust of journalists after that.'

It followed his not being best pleased by the 'stage-managed' picture being taken of him with a pile of empty beer receptacles for Hunter Davies's *The Glory Game*. He decided enough was enough and withheld his thoughts from the media. And the time, it seemed, was right anyway. Ian Gilzean said, 'I think he just needed a break from the game.'

So, as can happen, his profile was reduced to close to a footnote at best as James Morgan discovered when trawling newspapers and the internet while researching *In Search of Alan Gilzean*. Dribs and drabs related to the King of White Hart Lane and Dens Park. It was as if the greatest Spurs player in his position of my close to 60 years of support for the club – with the feeling no doubt mutual with any comparable Dundee supporter – had destroyed his own legacy by having the temerity to keep his mouth shut in front of members of an industry he no longer trusted.

He had become perceived as British football's most well-known recluse. It's Lord Lucan, if you will. It is an image he totally rejected. He said, 'I have never been a recluse. I always enjoyed myself.'

But, with former Dee team-mate Bobby Wishart the only player he maintained regular contact with, he added, 'I have always been a bit of a loner. I became more of a loner at Tottenham. You are better that way. I wasn't a loner so much in Dundee, because I used to knock about with Hammy [Alex Hamilton] a lot and also little Shug Robertson. They are both gone now, unfortunately.'

Gilzean said, 'I lost interest in football. You lose interest in things. It's like taking up a hobby, the easy part for me was playing. That was the part I loved. It was taken away from me. The legs were not doing what the brain was telling them to do.'

He appeared to strengthen the argument that he was distancing himself from the game by being a reluctant spectator. Ian Gilzean said, 'He did go to games and sign programmes and that when people asked, but he wasn't overly bothered about going or not. He didn't like it. Don't think he was a great watcher. You get a lot of players who are not because they want to play. When you think of it there is nothing worse than sitting there watching it if you feel like that.'

Wishart has a unique viewpoint on the 'years of exile' as Gillie's lone contact in the game through decades of establishing the lowest of profiles from one that was one of the highest. He said, 'I was always very close with Alan, even during his "beachcombing" days when he disappeared out of football for a while. He was always in touch with me. I think at one stage only three people had his mobile phone number. His two boys – Kevin and Ian – and myself.

'He didn't like the way his words were twisted when that newspaper reporter had asked him, "What do you think of Bill Nicholson at White Hart Lane?" Alan always had a great word on Bill Nick, and told the guy that. The journalist turned things round and more or less intimated that Alan thought Bill Nicholson should go. And I think Alan got so sickened with that he just turned his back on the football. That lasted for a year or two you know. Aye. It was a job getting him back into the football.

'I said, "You should get back into the football. Visit Dens and White Hart Lane." He said, "Who wants to see an old guy of 70?" That's what he used to say to me. I said to him, "You'd be amazed how many folk want to see an old guy who had brought great credit to his clubs. You've got to understand the mentality of football fans. It's more than life to a lot of them." And Alan couldn't get that into his head to start with.

'He thought, "I've played my football. It's all in the dim and distant past." I kept trying to get him back, of course. Any time he came up to Scotland he always stayed over with us. He was a friend of the family, Alan. It was more than just a footballing connection.

'What did we do? He was a great boy for walking. He had a tummy problem. Had to watch himself. He became very abstemious as far as drink was concerned. He made friends quite easily, Alan, but wasn't the kind of fellow who sought company.

'He landed up in Weston-super-Mare [in the late 1990s], but he didn't travel to any of the local games. Didn't get himself tied up with a Bristol club or any of that sort of thing.'

Wishart disputed Hunter Davies's submissions in the *New Statesman* of 26 March 2007 that his friend had little interest in football and, although he was good at it, appeared not to enjoy playing or talking about the game. Submissions made during the period when, to many, the icon had turned his back on football.

Wishart said, 'Gillie was always keen to chat to any of the old players at all times So we used to contact some of the old players. Alex Young at Everton, who was in the forces with Alan. We met up there. One or two of his old pals; he was never the kind of guy who wanted to detach himself from football. Our conversation, most of the time, was football.'

It seemed the 'estrangement' was more keenly felt at White Hart Lane. Gilzean's youngest offspring, though, questioned whether his dad's media silence was indicative of a conscious attempt to exile himself from Spurs, with his former Lane clubmates seemingly – in general – more vociferous than their Dundee counterparts in asking, 'Where's Gillie?'

Ian Gilzean said, 'Dad probably stopped going to football with me and Kev. But did he lose contact with Spurs, that's the thing? He always knew where they were. They didn't move. Tottenham Hotspur Football Club was always there.

'Because he didn't want to get involved with it, he probably didn't speak to people there. But he knew where they were. All he had to do was pick up the phone. It was his choice what he wanted to do. It's hard to explain. He finished. Went back for a few games. Stopped going to games and then probably didn't bother.

'It was ,"Why should I go?" There wasn't the hospitality he ended up doing then, don't forget. Probably wasn't high on his agenda of what he wanted to do. The last game I can remember him taking me to at that time was the League Cup Final against Liverpool at Wembley in 1982. He might have gone with Kev to the FA Cup Final replay against QPR that season. I went with the club that night because they used to take some of the young schoolboys there and back in a bus.'

Did he have an appreciation of how much he was loved? Ian said, 'It is not something you ever asked. I wouldn't have asked him. If you've played and won the medals he won I think you must realise that fans would hold you in good regard.'

I pointed out Wishart's comment about no one being interested in an 'old guy' like him. He said, 'Yeh, that would probably have been Dad's answer to a lot of the stuff. He'd probably come out with a remark like that. Probably didn't even mean it. But Dad was, once he'd stopped playing, like, "I've had my time. Done my bit. It's someone else's mantle now to take on. They don't need me."

'He'd been out of the public eye since the mid-1970s. It's not like he was right in it for the 1980s, 1990s, even the 2000s. When he finished in football he'd gone and done other stuff. As has been said, he had to go out and work, had other things going on.

'I think things changed when the Premier League came in and former players started to do the hospitality. Some people started to ask, "What's he doing? Why is he not doing this? Why's he not in the Spurs hall of fame?"'

Gilzean had been living in London – understood to be in Daines Close, E12 – when he upped sticks for the West Country, specifically Weston-super-Mare, in the late 1990s.

He said, 'I went down with my work, and I liked it. I worked there as part of the Ocean Group. They had a factory at Avonmouth. I didn't work in Weston but I lived in Weston and came back to London at weekends. But I liked it down there so I stayed down there. It's like the seaside. It's got the pier – well it burnt down a few years ago, but it's back up now. And you don't get the blooming snow. I couldn't live back up in Scotland now with the cold weather, and that wind.'

Gilzean underlined the point to Bob Hynd. Hynd said, 'I wondered to him, if he had such an affection for Coupar Angus, why didn't he go back. He told me, "Ah, I couldn't cope with the weather. It is generally colder up there than it is down here." I had an aunt down south and she felt the same!'

But myths developed. The keyboard warriors which spread gossip and unsubstantiated facts on the internet had a field day. Folk love a good mystery, reflected in the current UK obsession over crime dramas in books and on television. From Lee Child to *Line of Duty* to *Where's Wally?* Even when there isn't one beyond the prosaic.

That Gillie's whereabouts were unknown publicly – the move to Weston was not mentioned in the press until Alan Pattullo revealed it in 2009 – fuelled the over-fuelled brains of those tapping out their chatter.

One post on a Spurs messageboard in 2005 stated Gilzean had fallen on hard times and was a down-and-out in the West Country, with others hinting alcohol had been a contributing factor. (These were a series of Chinese whispers which piqued the curiosity of James Morgan, a Spurs supporter and *Glasgow Herald* journalist, into investigating what had happened to his dad's hero, and producing that book, *In Search of Alan Gilzean*, five years later, a tome which reawoke a hero slumbering in the minds of many.)

Ian said, 'These sort of postings are what some people will do. It's rubbish. Take the way Dad dressed. It was always smart, in trousers, shirt and a jumper. He always wore a pair of nice shoes. He wouldn't pay £100 for a pair of shoes – he knew the value of money and never thought they'd be worth that much – but was always well presented.'

Gilzean himself dismissed the posting of him being destitute. He said, 'Someone wrote that on a Tottenham website. It was probably an Arsenal fan. I don't know how you control these websites. I don't do computers. I stopped at bloody spreadsheets when I worked in the transport industry. My son says, "I will get you a laptop." I said, "Don't bother, I will never use it."'

Gilzean – apart from his smart, fit, healthy appearance and razor-sharp recall – revealed a string of reasons why the very suggestion of him being a down-and-out was ludicrous during his two-hour sit down with *The Scotsman*'s fine journalist, who produced an article of heart, warmth, compassion and delicacy.

He would return the £20 notes included with stamped addressed envelopes posted to his Weston-super-Mare home by a vicar each time the person of the cloth requested an autograph, asking, 'Why would I keep the money?' (Mind you, Bob Hynd added, 'He was sending the vicar signed photographs and the guy goes and puts them on the internet. He really resented that.') He would send a card to then Dundee manager Barry Smith for saving his old club from relegation despite a 25-point deduction. He would show pictures of his grandchildren on the mobile for whom only a handful had the number. He would hang on to medals, signed shirts – including the one of Sir Stanley Matthews – and general memorabilia worth a few bob. He said to Pattullo, 'I would never have sold them. I have been asked to sell them, I have been approached. One of my grandsons will get them. I don't know which one yet. There will be a riot. Maybe I will have to sell them to keep everyone happy!'

Proof he hung on to the keepsakes came from close friend Hynd, the Dundee director. One was the Sir Stanley Matthews shirt he wore representing a 'Stan's XI' with Jimmy Greaves and Cliff Jones against an 'International XI' which included Ferenc Puskás and Alfredo di Stefano; a memento now owned by son Ian and hung in the Alan Gilzean Lounge at Dens Park.

Hynd said, 'He wasn't as bothered about his own medals and trophies. He asked if I could get an evaluation on the shirt. He wanted it insured. I understand 120 million people listened to Sir Stan's match around the world on their radio.' (Gillie made the first goal in a 6-4 win for the opposition in front of 35,000 at the Victoria Ground, home of Sir Stan's first club, on 28 April 1965. Greaves was among the scorers.)

Hynd was discharged to take care of the metal stuff to prepare it for display at Dens Park. The Dundee architect got the medals and trophies in blue wrapping out of the dusty boxes Gilzean himself had sorted for his own memorabilia, spread them over his firm's huge dark wooden table in the classy offices of Leadingham, Jameson, Rogers and Hynd. I felt a poignancy handling and reading the inscription on each artefact as Hynd removed the wrapping paper. And it gave me a thrill to see each one with its inscriptions such as:

'FIRST DIVISION SEASON 1961/62 D.F.C', 'SCOTTISH FOOTBALL LEAGUE FIRST DIVISION CHAMPIONS 1961/62' and 'WINNERS INTERNATIONAL FOOTBALL LEAGUE CHAMPIONSHIP SEASON 1960/61 A GILZEAN VERSUS THE FOOTBALL OF IRELAND'.

There was also the 'SCOTTISH HALL OF FAME 2009' award to excite among the collection.

Hynd said, 'When Alan gave me the medals and trophies, they had not been out of the loft since he'd been there [perhaps because of his propensity not to show off his achievements].

'They weren't corroded but badly needed cleaning. [I] was told about this jewellery repair business in the centre of Dundee run by a Dundee fanatic. It was December and he told me he was up to his eyes with Christmas offers, repairs and adjustments and said they wouldn't be ready until well into January. I said, "No problem." He said, "Bring them round."

'It was like a Dickensian workshop. Wood panels, wooden desks. I handed the medals over. He saw Alan's league championship medal among others and said, "Where'd you get these?" To kid him along I said, "I just picked them up and read up about Alan Gilzean on the internet." He said, "I might be interested in buying these from you."

'I couldn't keep it going any longer and said, "I'm friends with Alan." He said, "Do you know something. As soon as you'd have walked out of that door I was going to phone the police." He phoned me two days later and said, "Come and get your medals, they're done. Just tell Alan, no charge." He didn't know Alan had asked me to put them on display at Dens!

'Alan came up for a pre-season friendly – think it was against Rangers – and I invited this guy who had to come with a friend because he was so shy and they met him. Alan was unbelievably gracious. They were delighted. The guy would probably have remembered Alan playing.'

Dave Forbes, a friend from the 1960s, former Dundee director and newsagent, acted as Gilzean's shield when the media attempted to get a comment out of him during his 'silent' period.

Forbes said, 'I got a phone call from some guy who had heard someone on the Alan Brazil programme saying Gillie was a down-and-out. I phoned the programme to tell them, "Gillie's a friend of mine, that's rubbish." They asked me, "Can he come on." I said, "I can tell you now Alan won't come on but I'll speak to him and I'll get a statement."

'[I] spoke to Alan and told him, "You are a down-and-out in the West Country, just a recluse." He just laughed. I'd prepared a statement with Gillie saying, "I'm fine thank you. Had some ill health but I'm on the mend. Definitely not a down-and-out."

'A couple of months later I got a call from John Brown, with DC Thomson, who says this guy from Ireland is writing a book and wants to meet Gillie and you are the guy to do it. I said "Fine, okay."

'So I spoke to Alan who agreed to meet him. Afterwards he said, "I want nothing to do with the guy. He says he's been out to

Coupar Angus, been talking to people without my permission. Actually been doing all these things."

'I told the guy [James Morgan] he wanted nothing to do with it. Not answering any questions.

'He wasn't happy with the boy's attitude. Interfering without his permission.

'Alan wasn't trying to be insulting by his attitude. He'd had his career and wanted other guys to get on with theirs.'

James Morgan said, 'My intentions in writing *In Search of Alan Gilzean* were honourable from the start and my aims were clear: I wanted to find out what had happened to him given the rumours surrounding his name. I felt it was a terrible shame that he had not had greater recognition and I helped to secure that by nominating him for entry into the Scottish Football Hall of Fame; I also hoped that he would one day return to White Hart Lane. Of the first, I soon established that he was living in Weston-super-Mare and in good health. Naturally, given the rumours about Alan, I was forced to ask some difficult questions but I believe I did so respectfully and transparently.

'As for the second aim, I achieved what I set out to do when Alan was inducted into the Scottish Football Hall of Fame in 2009. Of the third, more hopeful, aspiration, I had less of a part to play. Nevertheless, I was delighted to see him return to the bosom of his old club and colleagues as a matchday host at White Hart Lane in subsequent years. Indeed, I had tears in my eyes on the day he went back to the club in 2012. A fourth aim had been to write the book in tribute to my late father, who was a devotee of the younger Gilzean during his Tottenham days. It was a hugely emotional and conflicting process from start to finish.

'Alan did not see the need for a story about his life, nor did he want to cooperate with me, but I made that clear to every single person that I spoke to from the outset. I even make it clear in the book; Martin Chivers tells me he does not want to speak to me if Alan is not involved and similarly Pat Jennings is reticent about conducting an interview with me when I arrive for my meeting with him in a Waterstones in Enfield at Morris Keston's book launch.

'I was also unaware until recently that Gillie was unimpressed that I had been to his home town of Coupar Angus and spoken to his friends. I made it clear to those I interviewed that either I had not spoken to Alan or he was not on board with the idea. In my conversations with Ian MacKenzie, Alan's best man and lifelong friend, it was referred to more than once in our regular email correspondence.

'Alan subsequently spoke to me after that and again on further occasions such as the night he was inducted into the Scottish Football Hall of Fame. At no point did I get the impression that there was any ill-feeling on his part. We chatted amicably, he asked about my son. There was no hint of anything other than goodwill.

'Only once, in 2017, did I receive an angry call from Alan after I had made some enquiries about updating the book. He requested that I did not and I agreed at that point and ceased work on the update immediately. In that call, he made reference to the fact that I had never once offered him money for the book. This was not correct. Alan had been made an offer which he refused – again as documented in the book. And, as I pointed out to him then, sports books are not written as part of a get-rich-quick scheme – they don't actually make that much money – it had been done for a nobler aim.

'Whatever else, we resolved our differences on that call; he told me it was "a good book" and that he had always signed it whenever asked. We agreed to have a drink the next time we were both at a Glasgow Spurs function, although that point never arrived because he died before we got the chance to meet again. But that suggested to me he was at peace with it all.'

Gillie's Spurs team-mates largely confirmed they fell out of touch with Gilzean. Cliff Jones said, 'I'm not sure where he went when he left Spurs. Do you know?'

Pat Jennings said, 'Everywhere we went people were asking, "Do you know about Gillie? Anybody seen Gillie?" And we hadn't heard from him in years. When he left the Tottenham area and moved down to Weston-super-Mare he couldn't have heard or read much about Tottenham.'

Steve Perryman said, 'I don't think Gillie saw anyone. Because if he had have done they'd have done what I did [on his return to the fold, see later] and let him know how much people were missing him. I can't imagine he thought they didn't want to see him. I never asked him anything about that period when he was completely out of the limelight as such, was outside of the group. It wasn't to do with anyone. He hadn't fallen out with anyone, with the club. But I never deemed to ask him because I thought it would be disrespectful. Gillie didn't want to be a part of it. That's enough for me.'

Perryman, like Forbes, dismissed the myths that circulated while Gilzean was out of the public eye. He said, 'If someone had asked me, "Have you seen Gillie?" the truthful answer was, "No I haven't." "Do you know where Gillie is?" "No."

'If someone on the odd occasion suggested Gillie was struggling, I'd say, "I'd be careful about that if you are thinking about passing it on." Any story can be made up with lack of knowledge. Uninformed opinion. Do they call it fake news? I call it people talking out their arses.'

Phil Beal said, 'I suppose the sad thing is we lost touch with Gillie as soon as we packed up playing together. Nobody but nobody could get in touch with him or knew where he was.

'I can remember Tony Galvin [a UEFA Cup and two-time FA Cup winner with Spurs in the 1980s] telling me he had a friend who lived down in Weston-super-Mare he was visiting. He said, "I was walking along the seafront the other day and I'm sure I saw Alan Gilzean walking along." So I said, "Did you speak to him?" He said, "No because I wasn't sure. He never recognised me because I had a hat, scarf and coat on because it was cold. But I'm sure I saw Alan Gilzean." We then found out he was living in Weston-super-Mare.'

Martin Chivers said, 'After he left us he used to pop into my hotel with his two boys a few times in Brooklands Park. And then suddenly they were gone and we heard that he moved down to the West Country.'

Jimmy Robertson said, 'I'd lost contact with him. Hadn't seen him for a number of years. Dropped off the map to a certain extent. I found out he was living down in Weston-super-Mare when somebody contacted me about it. He'd just decided he wanted to live his life. Which I could understand to a large extent.'

Mike England added, 'It was great playing with Gillie for ten years but we'd lost touch.'

Ian Ure, the defender who was a team-mate in Gillie's Dundee sides which won the championship and got to the semi-finals of the European Cup, said, 'He kind of went missing for a while. I never got any information about that. It used to trickle back, "Where's Gillie? Where's he gone? Where's he disappeared to? I don't know."

'I think his health took a turn for the worse after he finished playing. I don't know. Then I heard he'd gone to the Weston-super-Mare area. I thought, "What's he doing down there?" And then someone said he'd taken up a job after he finished playing at a transport company and the company had a base in that area and he took up that job.

'He went to ground for some reason. At the funeral I was speaking to some of the Spurs players and they said they couldn't trace him [during his time out of the spotlight]. Didn't know where the hell he was. He wasn't in contact with the club and they wanted him to contact them. It was, "Where's Gillie? Where's he gone?" Years had passed. That was a mystery period.'

But Pat Liney, Dundee goalkeeper in the title-winning team of 1962, underlined the theory that Gillie was seen more of an exile south of the border.

Liney said, 'I didn't particularly keep in touch when he left Dundee but if he was up visiting we'd make a point of seeing him. He would pop in to see us. For such a top player, he was never stand-offish. It was a nice way to be.

'Gillie never changed from being the shy guy he always was. People couldn't understand it for someone as talented as he was, but he didn't let fame affect him.'

Maybe, unlike Ure, Liney remained in the Dundee area and would therefore have been better placed to see Gillie on his return to it, while the Ayrshire-born defender was based in Kilmarnock on the west coast of Scotland. Near Troon rather than Carnoustie.

Ian Gilzean, a resident of Carnoustie, confirmed his dad did not lead an hermitic existence in Weston-super-Mare, that he regularly visited family in Scotland, with Ian, with his wife and children, settled in Carnoustie from the 1990s. Ian said, 'He'd come up for three or four weeks in the summer.

'Yes, he was a doting grandad. The grandkids loved him as they would their other grandparents. Kev's boys and my two adored him.

'He'd come down with me and my son on the golf course and walk around with us. My son's more into golf than football. He's out on the golf course most of the summer and a bit afterwards too.

'I was in charge of Carnoustie Juniors and Dad would watch a couple of games. If he couldn't be bothered he'd go to the top of the road and watch amateurs Carnoustie Panmure YM, just stand there and watch the game with our dog. He'd talk to anybody whether it was there, in the supermarket or just generally walking the dog. That's the way he was. He'd just blend in.

'He would look after our dog when we went on holiday for ten days during the time he was here.'

It seems Gilzean revelled in his time back in Scotland, especially in the loving company of his youngest's family and the laid-back lifestyle it afforded him.

Ian revealed also how he himself loved life in the small town at the mouth of the Barry Burn River on the North Sea coast.

The London-born Ian Gilzean said, 'You don't miss the big city. The weather is not always great. But the way of life, it's easier.'

23

The Last Suppers

IT SEEMED ALAN Gilzean's move back into the public consciousness was more to do with re-establishing links with Tottenham Hotspur than Dundee. Sure he had spent time away from the game for decades – with the Dark Blues, apart from Bobby Wishart, seemingly joining everyone else on Gilzean's back-burner.

But by the time of a much-heralded return to Spurs in the second decade of the new millennium, there was evidence he had, without public fanfare away from north of the border, been returning to his Scottish football roots for at least close to 20 years.

Wishart said, 'There were a lot of good people who worked hard to get Alan to go back up to Dundee, like Dave Forbes and Bob Hynd. To dinners. That's when it started.'

Gilzean was contacted by Dave Forbes to attend Dundee's Centenary Dinner at the now-demolished Angus Thistle Hotel in the centre of the city on 25 April 1993, the year Alan's father died.

Dundee fan Forbes, you may remember, was a friend from the early 1960s who also worked with Irene Todd, Gilzean's then partner, and helped form a board at Dens after a period of financial turmoil. He had been charged with organising the shebang because his little black book contained contacts of most of the survivors of the good and the great from the Dee's past, including that of Gilzean.

Forbes rung Gillie, living in London, about attending the occasion, along with his title-winning and European Cup quarterfinalist team-mates. He said, 'I phoned Gillie a couple of weeks before the dinner. Somebody wasn't well in Coupar Angus. Anyway, I phoned the day before and he said, "Och, I'm not sure, Dave. What's happening?"

'I said to him, "I want you here for about six o'clock because things start at 7 for 7.30 and obviously I want pictures of the team together, so if you can be there for six o'clock we will get the pictures done and if you want to get away after that, that'd be fine. I think the guys would be delighted to see you." He said, "Right you are on." He arrived at 6pm – and left 3 o'clock the next morning!'

There was clearly a lot of catching up to do. Forbes said, 'I'd always assumed the players met up regularly. When Gordon Smith arrived I was talking to Ian Ure. And they were pleased to see each other as they hadn't met for years. It was a tremendous night.'

It cemented hopes Gillie would return into the gaze of the football fold. Forbes said, 'Once it was going with the guys and stuff, he never ever let me down. Any dinner it was, "I'll definitely be there. Just tell me when." It was easier once I got his number. He wasn't a great one for giving his number. Once he left Dens there was a gap until I started putting on these sort of events. Those dinners helped us form a friendship that lasted until the end.'

Gillie joined his old team-mates for the night at the Invercarse Hotel on the Perth Road in Dundee in 2002 when Dundee celebrated the 40th anniversary of the title triumph.

And that was despite the logistics being trickier as he had moved further away from his homeland, deep into the West Country of England at Weston-super-Mare. Bob Hynd smoothed the way.

Hynd, from Gillie's home town, had got to know him by then through helping sort repairs for the Gilzean family gravestone at the Abbey church in Coupar Angus. He said, 'I sorted his flight from Bristol to Edinburgh. I was going to arrange to pick him up at Edinburgh too but he said, "No, I'll get Bobby Wishart [who lived in Scotland's capital] to pick me up."'

Gilzean joined old team-mates at the July 2006 funeral of Bert Slater, the Dee goalkeeper for the run to the last four of the European Cup who signed from Liverpool. But he was unable to attend the first Dundee Hall of Fame induction back at the

Invercarse Hotel on 3 April 2009 when he was admitted along with Doug Cowie, William Longhair, Claudio Caniggia, Barry Smith, Billy Steel, Jocky Scott and Bobby Cox.

The programme's author wrote, 'There have been some great forwards in Dundee's history but none have had the strike rate to match Alan Gilzean, the Coupar Angus-born hit-man delivering 169 goals in 190 competitive appearances in the club's colours.' But an ailing Gilzean sent his son Ian in his stead to accept the induction.

A few months later he was inducted into the Scottish FA's Hall of Fame. Gilzean made it back across the border for this one held at the Hilton Hotel in Glasgow on Sunday, 15 November 2009.

He shared the night with fellow inductee Steve Archibald, a Spurs striker when his son Ian was at the club, and the player he helped as a youngster at White Hart Lane, one Graeme Souness, who was belatedly accepting his induction after being unavailable to do so five years earlier.

But it was an occasion he might have missed without the persuasive powers of Bobby Wishart. It was more to do with stage fright than any suggestion of wilfulness.

Gilzean's reserved self did not enjoy being the centre of attention, as we know. And he only went after Wishart agreed to go with him. Perhaps he needed his pal's reassurance. Remember, he had turned down an invitation to a Dundee game because a flu-ridden Bob Hynd was unable to be his reassurance policy.

Wishart said, 'I got a phone call from Alan. He said to me, "I've been invited to enter into the hall of fame by the Scottish FA." So I said, "Congratulations! That's marvellous. When's the event?" "Oh, it's November or whatever it is. I don't think I'll be going to that." That's what he said to me. Aye. I said, "You can never not go to that. That's the highest accolade you can get. Being chosen by your country to go into the hall of fame." He said, "I'll go on one condition." I said, "What's that?" He said, "That you come through as my guest." I said, "If that is what it takes to get you there I'll come through as your guest."

'I met him at the hotel in Glasgow. My son-in-law drove me, and Alan was a bag of nerves. He was so nervous. He said to me,

"I don't know what I'm doing here." I said, "You are here to get the biggest honour you can get as a football player, a Scots lad." He said, "I shouldnae let you talk me into it. Coming to this."

'He was down in the dumps. And when we went downstairs to the reception, the first person we met was Craig Brown, so that settled him a bit, to see another familiar face.

'The thing that clinched it was being inducted into the hall of fame at the same do as Graeme Souness. When we sat at the table, Souness's table was quite near ours and Graeme came across and saw Alan, gave him a big hug because when he was at White Hart Lane Alan was a senior member of the club and looked after him. Graeme was only about 16 or 17 at the time.

'Graeme was inducted before Alan and he made mention in his speech of what Alan had done for him. And that warmed the crowd tremendously towards Alan. Most of the folk there were Rangers supporters anyway. Souness had the big connection with their club as a manager and player there and all that. I took Alan asking me along as a bit of an honour, but he took it as a bit of an ordeal.'

Gilzean, though, managed a few words to sum up the playing career which had earned him his award. Words uttered, of course, during his apparent long-term disassociation from Spurs. Words which must have made it even harder to understand for any already baffled Lilywhite, kept largely ignorant of the facts given his unwillingness to discuss anything directly with the media.

Holding his hall of fame memento on stage, he said to those gathered, 'Going to Tottenham Hotspur was the best move ever for me. When you are in football, you've got to go to a club you feel is right for you and the two clubs I played for, Dundee and Tottenham Hotspur, everything was right for me. I had great players around me.

'I had seven fantastic years at Dundee. When I joined Spurs I wanted to go because it was my dream to play at Wembley. I can remember Dundee wanted to sell me to Sunderland. I said, "I don't want to go there, they don't go to Wembley too often."'

His innate humour continued to display itself when he added, 'Another reason I went to Tottenham is because I knew I only cost £72,000 and Greavsie cost £100,000 so you can point the finger.'

And he reached out to Spurs fans who put him on the throne as their King of White Hart Lane through with that warm quote, 'Through the years you set up a rapport with the fans. If you give 100 per cent, try and train hard, the fans – who came to watch us train – begin to realise you are 100 per cent for the club.'

Gilzean might have missed his own induction into Dundee's hall of fame, but he attended the next one the following March to witness his pal Alex Hamilton posthumously admitted to it along with Jim Duffy, the player and manager who compered the first event, and Gordon Wallace, while Bob Shankly won a heritage award and Georgian midfielder Giorgi Nemsadze the international prize.

Gilzean also made it to a mega-celebration to mark the 50th anniversary of Dundee's much-fabled championship success in the city at a packed Caird Hall, containing nearly 700 people, on Sunday, 29 April 2012, the same year Dundee named a lounge after him.

He said, 'I wouldn't miss this gathering for anything. Dundee's still the first result I look for, closely followed by Spurs. I've always retained a soft spot for Dundee.'

Just six members of the eleven carved in stone in the minds of all true Dark Blues remained alive: Pat Liney, Bobby Seith, Ian Ure, Bobby Wishart, Alan Cousin and Gilzean, along with squad members Craig Brown, Bobby Waddell and Alex Stuart. Skipper Bobby Cox, Gordon Smith (Gillie's hero), Andy Penman and Hugh 'Shug' Robertson had passed since the centenary gathering, with Alex Hamilton having died in 1990. Gilzean said, 'It's a shame the whole lot of us can't be present.' No doubt he was also thinking of his Dundee manager, the late Bob Shankly, too.

He said, 'Shankly was a real hard taskmaster but he knew the game inside out. He also kept things straightforward, insisting football was a simple game. He came into the treatment room once when Alex Hamilton and I were injured and started to reminisce about his boyhood growing up in Ayrshire. His family were so poor his mother used an old boiler to do the weekly wash on a Monday – then made soup in it to last the rest of the week.'

Gilzean joined in the applause as Wishart and Bobby Seith received awards as they were inducted into the club's hall of fame. And he clapped with the crowd as Gordon Smith's son Tony and Hugh Robertson's offspring Derek received the mementoes which commemorated both their late fathers' admission.

Gillie's hands must have been close to red raw, with award trophies presented to the 1962 physio Lawrie Smith, the late manager and coach Bob Shankly and Sam Kean, represented by their daughters Margaret Briggs and Maisy Scott, as well as the awards of freshly cast title-winning medals to Craig Brown, Bobby Waddell and Alex Stuart with one of the event organisers Dave Forbes collecting one on behalf of the remaining squad member George McGeachie.

But there was no questioning who was the main focus of attention, unwanted as it may have been to the recipient – Gilzean himself. As the queues for his autograph testified; bees around a honeypot.

Bob Hynd said, 'It was the biggest event of its type that had been put on for Gillie's team. It was rowdy on occasions. Perhaps because people there had been drinking. But when Alan spoke to them in that high-pitched voice he had there was complete silence. It was very emotional.'

Wishart said, 'From about our centenary time, there was a good excuse to have dinners and civic things. Of course, he was like the number one, Alan. If all the players at that time lined up and 44 went with their autograph books, 35 of them would be going to Alan.

'The players understood that Gordon Smith, the great Hibs, Hearts and Dundee winger, played until he was 40. He was a marvellous player and a freak. A Scottish Stanley Matthews. Gordon had a following. A lot of people admired him so much. And Bobby Cox, the captain, always got a bit of support. But people love goalscorers. Fans love them and Gillie was champion of that at Dundee.'

Gilzean instigated the last reunion dinner of the Dundee championship squad during his lifetime at the Invercarse Hotel in the city on Sunday, 27 November 2016.

Dave Forbes, organiser of the Sportsman's Dinner, said, 'I was talking to Gillie about different things and he said, "Bobby Seith and Bobby Wishart are in their 80s. You've kept us together all these years so how about another dinner for the guys who are left?" I said, "Yes, as long as you sanction it."'

Sadly, Gillie's Dark Blues team of legend lost another of its number, Alan Cousin, a polymath who became a teacher having studied Greek and Latin at St Andrews University, a month before the event. Forbes said, 'I'd spoken to Alan Cousin just a few weeks before it.'

Five months later, Gilzean was back in Dundee for that final major public appearance in the city, the Q&A at the Whitehall Theatre.

By then, Gilzean had finally made his White Hart Lane homecoming. An emotional-with-bells-on homecoming. Pat Jennings and Steve Perryman were at the heart of it.

He said, 'Pat was the reason I came back down the Lane. Him and Stevie Perryman.'

24

'I Need Your Grace to Remind Me to Find My Own'

I ARRANGED to meet Pat Jennings at Spurs's state-of-the-art-and-then-some training ground in Enfield that knocked the one which Alan Gilzean and he knew at Cheshunt into a cocked hat. It was, ostensibly, to discuss his part in ensuring the original King of the Lane returned to his subjects. But the conversation was to pan out to cover a whole lot more.

The facility is just by the A10, the main highway that has led up north through Tottenham from the City of London since the Romans popped over for a spot of invading 2,000 years ago to establish it. I have time to observe the 80-acre complex set in green belt land stretching out from beyond the security hut by its entrance adjacent to a piece of topiary shaped into the club's emblem of a cockerel. Jennings's presence was being sought to confirm I did indeed have a meeting arranged with the greatest goalkeeper I had ever seen turned goalkeeping coach to Spurs's youngsters.

It is like a rural oasis in comparison to the urban existence prevalent with cars, trucks and the occasional bike trundling up the Great Cambridge Road, aka the A10. I espied in the distance giant space-age buildings dotted in between plush, manicured pitches and a road system for the luxury vehicles of choice driven by the staff and to others allowed access. One cheery receptionist, whom I had seen at the gate, rubber-stamped my authenticity by finding the greatest living Irishman – in my book – and I was allowed to enter the 'haloed' world in which Spurs prepared for matches in the 2018/19 season which ended with them playing their first UEFA Champions League Final.

I found my way to one of the glass-fronted hanger-like buildings, which housed indoor training facilities, offices and an auditorium for press conferences. I opened its main door into the open-plan entrance hall and made my way to reception, was given my clip-on accreditation card and asked to wait for Pat upstairs. I stopped to chat to a few journalist colleagues, researching at tables and chairs provided while awaiting the arrival of manager Mauricio Pochettino for his latest briefing inside that auditorium before striding up the stairs for my own 'summit'.

Jennings, as I expected, was welcoming, easy-going, warm, friendly, classy and open. He mentioned how he had somehow hurt his foot, he knew not how. And how his wife Eleanor sung at the London Palladium, remarking to me, 'You're showing your age now, son!' when I told him I remembered seeing it on television.

I must have detected a wistfulness in his eyes as he reflected on the day Gilzean had come up on 7 July 2017. How, during it, he had taken his old pal and colleague down into the kitman's room to sign a blackboard with a gold felt-tipped pen along with other superstars of Spurs past such as Cliff Jones.

And there was more sadness in his body language when recalling a meeting he and Alan had had with Jimmy Greaves after Greavsie had suffered a stroke which left Alan's former strike partner in a wheelchair.

He said, 'I'd been telling Gillie about the training ground, the set-up and that. I said, "Alan, I can't start to tell you how good this training facility is. It is a different world to what we had. You really need to come. I'll pick you up and show you round the place." So he came.

'We got a call from the chairman's wife Tracy about inviting Jimmy Greaves to take a look around and suggested a date and I said, "Yes, definitely."

'I took Alan and Jim in one of the little carts the club have at the training ground. Must have spent an hour taking them around.

I remember Alan couldn't get over the facilities. He said, "I know what you mean now. And why you couldn't start to explain how good the place is." He would have had a similar reaction had he remained alive to see the new ground [the Tottenham Hotspur Stadium which opened in April 2019]. That it was another world to what he knew.

'I took Gillie to the kitman's room. The kitman's got a board there. And I said to the kitman, "We've got another signature for you," and I got Gillie to sign this board. Maybe you can take a photo of it [I did]. That would be nice. We'll see if we can walk through and take a look in the room later.

'Gillie and I had been up to visit Jimmy. He'd been back at the club for about a year and we got talking one night about Greavsie. I said, "Would you fancy coming to see him?" He said, "Absolutely." So I said to Gillie, "Let me know what day and I'll make arrangements. I went and picked Gillie up on the day and we went to Greavsie's house in Essex. We spent – not wanting to outstay our welcome – about 25 to 30 minutes with him.

'Jim still knew everything you were saying. But it took him a bit of time to respond. He loved the fact we'd been to see him. It was emotional. So sad to see him in the situation he was in.

'Jim was everybody's favourite player? Yeh. He was brilliant. Fantastic to me.

'A year before I joined him at Spurs I was playing for Watford just a few months after playing Irish B league football. In those days we didn't have any goalkeeping coaches so you just had to learn through your mistakes. And I'm sure I would have cost Spurs in my early days at the club. Cost the team their bonus money. You'd have heard mutterings in the back seat, "The keeper should have done better there." But Jim used to come over and put an arm around me and say, "Keep going, son. You are going to be the greatest." I've never forgotten that.'

Seeds for a Gilzean return to Spurs were planted by Scottish rock musician Tom Simpson on a Hertfordshire golf course when the then keyboard player with Snow Patrol approached Spurs legend Jennings. Simpson informed Jennings that he 'hoped' to 'see a pal of yours, Alan Gilzean …'

Jennings said, 'I met Tom – and I don't know how many times I've seen the brilliant Snow Patrol since – at a golf day. He said, "I'm hoping to see a pal of yours next week." So I said, "Who's that?" He said, "Alan Gilzean." I said, "You'll be lucky. We haven't seen him for 30 years." But I added, "If he turns up, please give him my number and ask him to ring me."

'The following Wednesday night there was a message on my phone. "Missed call. Alan Gilzean". But the message said he'd ring me back at 8 o'clock the following night. Sure enough, I was waiting on the call. Couldn't wait for it. It came. So I said, "Gillie where have you been? Everybody's asking?" He said, "Oh, what do they want to know about me for. I'm an old man. I'm gone." I said, "We're all old but still working at the club, doing the legends stuff and that." He said, "Are you serious?" I said, "Of course. Why don't you come and get involved?"

'I think he was due a little operation at that time. Whenever I got talking to him, he said, "Well, maybe I'll think about it."'

The timing of the story has proved difficult to pin down. Jennings told me the golf course meeting with Simpson was just prior to Gilzean's 2009 Scottish FA Hall of Fame induction. It is understood the musician gave Alan 'an extra nudge' towards getting back in touch with Tottenham in the Dundee boardroom on Boxing Day 2011 when the Dee lost 1-0 to Greenock Morton and the icon was introduced to rapturous applause to the crowd at the interval.

Simpson, after a brief initial contact, proved elusive as I attempted to add salient details.

Gilzean said, 'He [Simpson] came over to me and we were chatting. He told me he was a friend of Pat Jennings, played golf with him. I tried to test him out; which course did you play on? He said Brickendon Grange, he had Pat's phone number, and he gave me it.'

All that matters to those in London N17, though, is that the king rang Jennings.

Simpson's old band – formed at the University of Dundee – had had a hit with 'Chasing Cars' which included the lyric, 'Show me a garden that's bursting into life.'

302

And as far as all at Spurs were concerned they entered a Garden of Eden with Gillie back inside the fence for a few precious years largely as a result of Simpson resting his digits from pressing white and black keys and developing 'green' fingers. He made a lot of people happy.

Spurs folk thrived as Gillie brought back the good times with his mere presence. Perhaps it was a wake-up call to some as to what the club should be about. For if anyone epitomised the Spurs way it was the self-effacing, immensely friendly and impossibly skilled chap from the east coast of Scotland. As Snow Patrol's lead singer Gary Lightbody sang in the aforementioned pop classic, 'I need your grace to remind me to find my own.'

In the meantime, seeds were also sown to entice Gilzean back to the Lane in 2010, thanks to Steve Perryman. Gilzean had been nominated for Scotland's greatest-ever team across the generations after earning his spot in the Scottish FA Hall of Fame. And he agreed to be interviewed for a television programme about it in Bristol. Gillie, typically unstarrily, arrived on a public transport bus from his Weston-super-Mare home.

In the meantime, Steve Perryman was being interviewed about Gilzean at the same venue.

Perryman said, 'Who wants to take credit for getting Gillie back to White Hart Lane? It was sort of a bit me, a bit of Pat and a bit probably of someone else.

'I got asked to go to Bristol to do an interview about Gillie. So I said, "Yes, of course. You fix up a date." Wasn't a million miles from me [he lives in Devon]. It was in a particular hotel. They'd obviously booked a room. I said, "Are you talking to Gillie?" They said, "Yeh, he's doing a couple of hours before you." I said, "Would you ask him whether he'd mind if I got there a bit early to make sure I see him?" So the answer came straight back, "Gillie said he'd love to see you."

'And what do you do when you haven't seen someone for such a long time? When you have so much respect, hopefully for each other, certainly me to him?

'Gillie looked great. You hear certain things about people when you are not seeing them. You hear stories. Gillie looked a million dollars. He walked towards me with that same Gillie swagger I remembered. He always had a walk about him, whether he was walking across the car park or the pitch at the end of the game. It was lovely. He must have said it five times, "Stevie, you look like your da'. I can't believe you look like your da." Obviously referring to my Dad. Just lovely. Gillie had retained all his class that I always knew about. And more.

'It was a great meeting. I'm so pleased. I suggested to Gillie that the old players would do handstands just to see you. Talk to you.

'All our careers were over but you spin off each other, with stories, remembering things some had forgotten but others remember.

'I think I put him in touch with Pat who then involved him at Tottenham and stuff. Tottenham were very much open to a 'new face' being involved with the sponsors' lounges and all that. Gillie was perfect for it.

'He wasn't flustered. He had a good memory, could recall the stories. Gillie always said to me he could write a book about Dave Mackay. Just on the stories he told me about Dave Mackay, of course he could. For a lot of people, the older generation, Dave Mackay would have been their favourite player.

'I actually didn't spend that much time with him because I was not on the Spurs bandwagon, on "the firm" because I was working and helping at Exeter City [where he was director of football]. So when they were all meeting up at games I was often somewhere else. But I did go once or twice a season and of course one of the main reasons for going there was to meet Ossie [Ardiles], Pat and, of course, Gillie.

'Ossie was always sending me pictures of Gillie in a particular lounge because he knew how much I respected and loved this man. I always made Ossie aware of Gillie and the part he played in my upbringing as a Tottenham player so he could pass it on to those who were there. Gillie deserved to be known by great players and great people.'

Gilzean confirmed in his first major newspaper interview in 40 years rather more than just 'reports of his demise' were 'greatly exaggerated' amid those suggestions he was a 'down-and-out in the

West Country'. It established that the King of White Hart Lane would return from exile.

He said, 'I have not been back for years, I am going to go back. It is sentimental for me. It's some place, very special for me. I don't know why [I am adored].

'I was always treated well by Dundee and Spurs fans – but the Spurs fans were very special.'

Gilzean added how posted autograph requests were 'always from Spurs fans, it's amazing how many still remember me.'

There you had it. The heartfelt statement was unequivocal.

So how long had it been since Gilzean had seen his last Spurs first-team match live? That wasn't so unequivocal.

To quote Pattullo's piece: 'Asked for the last occasion he can remember watching Spurs in the flesh, he mentions something about "an FA Cup Final". He doesn't mean the club's last appearance in it either, or, indeed, even the second or third most recent. We are talking 1981 and the first game against Manchester City rather than the replay, Ricky Villa's mazy winning goal et al. He has been a slightly more regular attender of Dundee matches.'

Four months later Ron Scott quoted Gilzean in the *Sunday Post* thus: 'I saw Dundee earlier this season, but I'm not sure the last time I saw Spurs play. I think it was the 1982 League Cup Final, which we lost to Liverpool at Wembley after extra time [which would tally with Ian's memory].'

There was also talk of him attending a Bill Nicholson testimonial match against West Ham in 1983. And, of course, he popped along to watch Ian play on occasion.

We all know what it is like to be put on the spot and produce instant recall, but, whatever, it was a decade or three. A long, long time.

* * *

Gilzean was properly reintroduced to his Spurs fans at the Lane for the first time in over 30 years on Sunday, 25 November 2012 when his old team defeated West Ham 3-1 with Jermain Defoe, two, and Gareth Bale scoring and 2019 Champions League finalists Hugo Lloris and Jan Vertonghen in the home line-up.

It came about through a phone call from his eldest son Kevin's partner Justine inquiring about tickets, remembered Spurs commercial manager Mike Rollo.

Rollo, who had come up with the pioneering move to get former legends to entertain fans in the hospitality lounges, was unsure whether Gilzean would be there. And even when he was, there was no guarantee the King of White Hart Lane would want to be presented to his people.

Rollo, though, was able to get the thumbs-up from the man himself, and stadium announcer Paul Coyte interviewed grandad Gilzean, who kept a reassuring arm around his son Kevin's son.

The stadium remained all but full, with spectators foregoing interval refreshment after news had got round the place via Twitter with Coyte posting: 'A true legend here today, just hope I can entice him on to the pitch at HT #kingofwhitehartlane'. And there were word-of-mouth whispers as to the specific nature of the alternative to a cup of tea and a quick beer. When Gillie appeared the fans went 'crazy' singing, 'Born is the King of White Hart Lane'.

It was, to coin a phrase from footballer-turned-Hollywood actor Vinnie Jones, 'emotional'. Emotional for everyone involved.

Rollo, who completed his 36th and final campaign in the 2018/19 season, said, 'In the 1990s I launched a lounge called Legends in the old East Stand at White Hart Lane, invited back former players as our guests for a pre-match meal and to watch the game. We got fans paying to be members so they could meet their heroes. It was seen as a pioneering move and it grew from there. The first I think was Martin Chivers. Then the likes of Pat Jennings, Martin Peters and Alan Mullery. Slowly but surely we ended up with 24 by the late 90s into the 2000s.

'I used to say to Pat Jennings and Martin Peters, "How can we get hold of Alan Gilzean?" They said, "He's a like a recluse, there's no way of getting hold of him." I even went through Ian Gilzean who had been a player at the club and I'd got to know during my time. But again I drew a blank. Nothing against Ian but it seemed his father did not want to attend.

'It came to pass we got a call from a member of Alan's family. She mentioned Alan and my ears pricked up. He wanted to bring his grandson to a match at White Hart Lane and she was going to accompany them.

'Fantastic news! At one stage, I believe it was going to be just the family member and her son. I got in touch with Pat Jennings who was of great assistance. He persuaded Gillie to attend. "You must come," he said to him. All the time Gillie was showing great humility, saying, "Oh, no one will remember me there anyway." But Pat said, "You'll be in for a surprise."

'The day came and we were prepared for him. He was very reluctant to do anything other than be there just for his grandson. But lots of the former players like Cliff Jones, Martin Chivers, Alan Mullery and, of course, Pat made a big fuss of him. Yet he just wanted to stay where he was.

'The thing that changed things was when I asked him, "Why not take your grandson out on to the pitch at half-time." He agreed. But I knew in my head we would have to introduce him. So I said whether he minded if the stadium announcer interviewed him. He said, "Well, okay."

'You can imagine when he went out the whole stadium erupted, I think he was taken aback by the welcome he received.

'Although he was obviously just looking for his grandson to get the feeling of being on the pitch like his grandad had been, I think it very much dawned on Alan then that "they remember me!" It was amazing.

'So as a result we said, "You're more than welcome any time." He was quite a shy man and modest. Had to be careful because we didn't want to lose him so we did it slowly but surely. He came along to a few more matches. And we invited him to be inducted into the hall of fame with Mike England, something we'd started in 2004 with Bill Nicholson and the Double team being inducted.

'It all spawned from there and he became one of our regular hosts and went to quite a number of games.

'Alan knew I was a great Spurs fan and I'm so proud to think that Alan and I became like we did in the latter days of his life.

'I once told him the story from back in 1973 before he helped Spurs beat Norwich in the League Cup Final. I was on advertising sales for the *London Evening News* paper and wanted the Tottenham

Motor Company, a VW dealership, to put a big advert in the paper in the build-up to the final. I asked them whether they would pay a Spurs player if I could get one to promote their cars. They said yes. Martin Chivers couldn't do it but recommended Alan who agreed for £50 and a bottle of whisky.

'That advert was part of my portfolio when I applied for the Spurs job. And I told Alan how he had helped me get the job. He laughed.'

Coyte, who was to write the line 'the original King of White Hart Lane' when introducing Gilzean at the Lane's closing ceremony in May 2017, confessed he was a 'Spurs fan first, a Spurs employee second' while holding the microphone to the lips of the copper-bottomed legend standing in front of him.

Coyte said, 'We had a pre-match meeting as we always do. Mike I think mentioned Gillie was coming. There'd been talk for a long time about Gillie. Martin Chivers would say, "We just don't see him. I haven't seen him since the day he left."

'But when I discovered he'd be at the game I said, "You've got to be kidding me?! We have to do something. This is huge. The fans would go crazy for it. This is enormous."

'I'd only ever seen him on Youtube and videos of *The Big Match* TV programme, so when he arrived I couldn't see it was him.

'He started walking towards me to do a quick interview in the Oak Room where we did the presentations before the match. A waitress with a tray of drinks stepped in front of him and he threw his shoulder and he got round her. His balance was unbelievable. That's when I thought "that's him".

'When he came out at half-time and I introduced him it was one of the biggest thrills I've ever experienced.

'The whole thing was out of this world. Incredible. Amazing. I can't remember what I asked him exactly. I didn't prepare. It was the excitement of the whole thing. All the questions were from the heart.

'The questions were along the lines of: Why now? The occasion? What does it mean to you? Does it all feel the same? Why did you stay away?" On that last question he said he just didn't want a part of it and that he was just happy to be back. That was pretty much all he had to say about that. It was a lovely interview. It seemed to be all over in a second! His love of the club came over. It always did subsequently. And what added to it was his grandson, a Spurs supporter, being there.

'It felt special, a proper homecoming. Crowd went crazy. He was the man of legend we'd heard stories about but had never met. It felt as if he fitted in like he'd not been away. With the players, doing the interviews. It was ridiculous.

'It was obvious that he'd followed Spurs all the time even though he hadn't been back all this time. It was nearly 40 years since he'd left [as a player].

'I did the whole thing more as a Spurs fans than Spurs employee. Alan and the other players treated me as one of them when they spoke together. Chewing the fat with football talk. One of the funniest things was how lovely Alan was with my little son Joe. Joe was quite young and he sat next to Alan as he spoke using the word "fucking" a few times. Joe raised an eyebrow to me because Alan had sworn but I just looked back at Joe thinking, "It's Alan, we can let him get away with it." He was such a lovely, regular guy. Incredibly humble.

'He was just as lovely when we did the hall of fame. His love of the club, as I've said, always came over.'

Logan Holmes on Hotspurs HQ website posted, 'It was great to see Gilzean looking so well and willing to return to Tottenham and White Hart Lane. A few years ago concerns were raised on the internet about Alan Gilzean's health and whereabouts with rumours which thankfully proved to be unfounded.'

Gillie added building bricks to his comeback with a further interval pitchside natter with Coyte on 9 February 2013 when two Gareth Bale goals defeated Newcastle United, the team against whom the Scot had made his last competitive appearance – a goalscoring one – for Spurs.

Gilzean came further back into the fold through more efforts by Perryman, who thought it a good idea to act as the link in the chain to get the G-Men back in harness. Greaves revealed three years earlier that he had not seen Gillie 'for the best part of 40 years'. Greaves was providing the entertainment with his stand-up routine at a Sporting Club dinner at the Farmhouse Hotel on the Channel Island of Guernsey on 29 May 2013. Perryman thought it might be an opportunity to reunite one of the greatest goalscoring partnerships in Spurs's history.

He said, 'I was responsible for putting these two together [Gilzean and Greaves] again. I don't think they'd met for something like 30 years or more and Jimmy was doing a talk on Guernsey at a hotel of a friend of mine, Dave Nussbaumer – a Spurs supporter. And within a conversation of me going over there, well, it came about. I was more than happy to see Jimmy. I was seeing him quite regularly. Dave asked me, "You've been in touch with Gillie, haven't you?" I said, "Yes Dave, I have." So he said, "Do you think Gillie would come to Guernsey?" I said, "He would love it and Guernsey is very accessible from Exeter Airport." So I phoned up Gillie and he was up for it.

'We met at the airport and flew to Guernsey and Gillie and Greavsie met. I took a picture of the moment. So easy now on your phone. Should have taken a video. These two great people, two great players, meeting and showing their love and respect for each other. It was just amazing.

'We spent a lovely evening together and me and Gillie went back the next day to Exeter and Jimmy went off to where he lives Essex way.

'You can only do that sort of thing by talking to people. I don't believe people pass messages on. Why wouldn't you do that as good as you can do?'

Surprised they left it so long? Perryman said, 'Absolutely they were friends but I don't think Gillie saw anyone. If he had have done they'd have let him know how much people were missing him.'

Hotel owner David Nussbaumer said, 'It was a very emotional reunion. Jimmy had no idea it was going to happen. I'd booked Jimmy to come over and do a dinner at the Farmhouse and Steve – a wonderful man – said they'd found Alan. So I said to Steve, "Bung him a grand and get him over." It would be a fantastic night for all the Spurs fans in Guernsey. Two legends who loved playing together.

'We didn't tell each other what was going on. We picked them up separately. They came on separate flights. But we arrived at the venue at the same time. And literally one got out of the car and the other got out of the car ten yards away. It was like a double take. They couldn't believe it. Both of them were in tears hugging each other for a good couple of minutes outside. And we had the most wonderful evening afterwards. It all went upwards for Alan after that. I felt really good about it.

'Jimmy did his stand-up, then rather than put any pressure on Alan we got him up to do a Q&A with Jimmy. It was just wonderful.

'Alan was very quiet. Couldn't quite get over what all the fuss was about. Just a humble man. A lovely man.

'Did he say why he'd spent so much time away from the game? No it really wasn't for us to put him on the spot. Quietly I think he just disappeared and wanted a quiet life. But I don't know. From that moment onwards he was certainly back in the fold. Just sad we'd lost him for so long.'

Nussbaumer revealed he got to see Gilzean play through Spurs push-and-run legend Len Duquemin, a Guernsey native and a regular summer guest.

The hotelier, who has staged nights involving Spurs favourites Ossie Ardiles, Ricky Villa and Graham Roberts, said, 'I got into the Spurs dressing room thanks to Len and met Steve and watched the G-Men live.'

Barry Williams, the night's host and an after-dinner speaker, said, 'I've worked many times over the years with Jimmy and we occasionally discussed Alan Gilzean, and Jimmy was totally mystified as to his whereabouts. On this particular night, Alan Gilzean was stood there to welcome us!

'It stopped Jimmy in his tracks and then with his characteristic voice came a drawn out, "He-llo mate", as they hugged. On parting the emotion was huge and very visible. Everybody felt part of the warmth that these two great men shared.

'I was privileged to be there.'

'Should all acquaintance be forgot?', asks 'Auld Lang Syne', the 18th-century Scottish language poem written by bard Robbie Burns and reckoned one which 'symbolises reunion' according to the Burns scholar Thomas Keith. The old team-mates clearly would have answered the rhetorical question with a firm 'absolutely not'. Happy to remember the good old days.

It was reflected as the emotion and banter flowed between the two pals despite their decades apart. Gilzean said, 'We hugged. He said, "Where have you been?" I said, "Keeping away from you!" He used to say to me, "Were you born with so little hair?" I'd say to him, "I had hair when I came to Tottenham, but then I had to do all your heading for you!" He did all my running, I did all his heading!

'You never know what's round the corner [in reference to Greaves being confined to a wheelchair]. The question I get occasionally at these fans' nights is: I played with Denis Law and I played with Jimmy Greaves, who was the best player? In my opinion it's Greavsie. That's a shame because Denis is a Scot, and a good friend. Someone up there must like me – I played up front with Denis, Greavsie, Martin Chivers, and Alan Cousin at Dundee.'

25

'Golden Sunset'

THAT SPURS wanted to induct Alan Gilzean into their hall of fame had been part of Pat Jennings's sweet talk to lure his pal and former team-mate back to the Lane.

And it came to pass towards the end of a year which firmly placed him back in the bosom of a club which always held a torch for the Scot since he added culture to an era which became known for cloggers ahead of class.

Again, though, his aversion to being the centre of attention took a grip, just like it did when he invited Bobby Wishart to the Scottish Hall of Fame shindig for moral support four years previously.

And, when he heard Mike England was going to be similarly recognised, he wanted to deflect the glare of full focus on him by sharing the occasion with his former team-mate at White Hart Lane on Monday, 2 December 2013.

England said, 'Alan and I got calls from Tottenham. They wanted to put us in the club's hall of fame.

'Gillie had told them he would do the hall of fame if I did it. I had and still have great respect for Gillie and we agreed the best way to do it was for us to do it together. It was a fantastic night. Everything was done very nicely.

'I sat with Alan and his family. One of his sons was a goalkeeper or centre-half. Didn't realise how big he was! There were a lot of Scottish people from Dundee representing the club. Lots of directors and players. Very nice.'

Jennings, appropriately, and Alan Mullery, inducted in 2004 and 2005, conducted the ceremony in the Bill Nicholson Suite at White Hart Lane in front of other former players, including Graham Roberts, Paul Miller, John Pratt and Mark Falco and guests from Dundee. They presented Gilzean and England with their awards and, joined by John Pratt, recalled anecdotes involving them.

Gillie was also presented with the first bottle of Gilzean Whisky by Dark Blues chief executive Scot Gardiner. It was one of 169 bottles labelled 'Celebrating Gillie's Goals' to commemorate the number the forward had scored for the Dee (the 169th was received on behalf of Spurs by Andy O'Sullivan, head of the club's hospitality team).

Eight days later, Gilzean was on stage in front of 350 packed into Dingwalls, an otherwise live music and comedy venue in Camden Lock, Chalk Farm, in north London.

Organisers of *The Spurs Show* were understandably excited with their coup as the King of White Hart Lane spoke directly into the eyes of a big group of 'his people' in intimate surroundings for the first time in decades and those listening to the podcast on the internet around the globe. They billed it, 'Gillie? There he is. We finally found him! And he's brought Big Pat with him.'

And they sought further 'hits' by promoting the recording of it thus, 'The Spurs Show proudly present a Pat Jennings and Alan Gilzean Special at a packed out Dingwalls Club in front of 350 diehard listeners. A wonderful night of Spurs memories in the company of Lilywhite heroes.'

Gilzean sat alongside Jennings with actor/comedian Phil Cornwell and producer Mike Leigh hosting and asking questions of the Tottenham legends with the late John White's son Rob in the building. Gillie was witty, insightful and erudite as he gave full answers and further proof that his memory was fully intact relating to his Spurs career, Jimmy Greaves, Bill Nicholson, his supposed self-imposed exile and more (direct quotes used in other parts of this book).

Leigh said, 'It was Gillie's first public appearance as far as I'm aware since his 'return' ... We'd been trying for a while to track him down. No one had heard about him for years. There was a running joke, "Where's Gillie?"

'I think it was Paul Coyte who said the only person who had spoken to Gillie over the years is Pat Jennings so if he does resurface it'll be through Pat. We'd caught Pat to be on and got lucky as Gillie was in town seeing family. We didn't know what to expect but it was incredible how pin-sharp he was. How much he remembered. Hopefully the night reignited something because he started doing a few other things. Probably out of all our guests that was the most satisfying. He was genuinely taken aback by the reception he got – Dingwalls was heaving – which showed his humility. There was no ego.'

Gillie attended the Edinburgh funeral of another proud Scot who had spent most of his life in England, Dave Mackay, on 24 March 2015, captivating, as we have read, a five-star admirer in Sir Alex Ferguson, who was desperate to be introduced to him.

Alan, comparing Mackay to Duncan Edwards, who could have rivalled Pelé as the world's best ever if he had lived beyond tender years, said at the service, 'I really had to be here today.

'I was about 16 or 17, Hearts played St Johnstone in the League Cup. It was the era of Conn, Bauld and Wardhaugh. I was a Hibs supporter rather than a Hearts supporter but I went to watch.

'They beat St Johnstone about 5-0 or something. Even when they were four up, Mackay was still driving them on. It was the same when he was at Tottenham, driving you on. Any shirkers, he let you know. He wouldn't tolerate it.'

Gillie was interviewed for the last time pitchside at the Lane by Paul Coyte during a victory over Swansea, Cliff Jones's first club, on 28 February 2016. Harry Kane and Son Heung-min scored goals for a Spurs team which included other modern heroes in Dele Alli, Hugo Lloris and Toby Alderweireld. And a host of former Spurs stars were on duty as part of the match hospitality rota. But Coyte was well aware of his interviewee's place in the club's history, telling him, 'You sir, are a legend.'

Gilzean ended another exile in a White Hart Lane lounge after Spurs were defeated by Southampton on 8 May 2016 when he was reunited with former Highlands Park team-mates

Barry Bridges, the former Chelsea and England striker, and Martin Cohen. A getting-back-together sorted by ex-Spurs defender Phil Beal, a former team-mate of Cohen at LA and, of course, Gillie.

Cohen said, 'I hadn't seen him for 40 years. Barry came down from Norwich. It was fantastic seeing Gillie, thanks to Phil. It was an afternoon game and we spoke to each other afterwards until someone said, "Excuse me guys, you have to go now because we are closing the lounge." It was about 7.45! That's the last time I saw him – and he was looking good.'

Coyte's estimation of where Gilzean stood in the pantheon of Spurs greats was underlined when he introduced him to the crowd after the Lilywhites had played their 2,533rd and final competitive match at White Hart Lane – a win over Jose Mourinho's Manchester United – on Sunday, 14 May 2017.

More than 40 players from Tottenham's past walked to the centre of the hallowed turf – each with a build-up from Coyte – during a moving finale to the ground which had served the club for 118 years. All received rapturous welcomes. But it was Gilzean, along with Glenn Hoddle, who received the most rapturous before Mother Nature stole the show by producing a fully arced rainbow signposting the way to dreams coming true to the romantic. It reflected the esteem in which the original King of White Hart Lane and his only successor were held.

There was a similar reverence from the Spurs announcer when he nattered to Gilzean on pitchside during a five-goal win against Stoke City on 9 December 2017 at Wembley Stadium during Tottenham's two-year rental of the national stadium while the Lane's billion-pound replacement was constructed.

A few months earlier Gilzean had paid his last respects to Alan Cousin in the company of Bobby Wishart and the following year had that touching meeting with Doug Cowie and made a return to his home town to catch up first-hand rather than through the good offices of pal Bob Hynd, not knowing, of course, the end of his life was to come all too soon.

* * *

Despite his re-emergence into the public gaze, he remained in Weston-super-Mare through his final years. It seemed he had no wish to spend his dotage anywhere else. Not even Scotland. From the outside it seemed spending his final years in his own country would appeal for such a patriotic individual. The one who took a whack at Bob Wilson as he believed the Arsenal goalkeeper did not have the credentials to represent Caledonia. One who was distinctly unimpressed when his youngest son Ian was selected to wear the red lion, although born in England.

But a clue as to the town's attraction for him comes when you study its climate. It is, along with the rest of south-west England, temperate with milder temperatures than the rest of the country.

He led a low-key life in the north Somerset coastal town 18 miles south west of Bristol, known for its tourist trade, being the birthplace of writer-actor-comedian John Cleese, author and politician Jeffrey Archer and Deep Purple guitarist Ritchie Blackmore. And home to a young Bob Hope, the British-born comic actor who found fame in the United States, and engineer Isambard Kingdom Brunel (although it seems the fact Alan Gilzean also lived in the town did not warrant his name being added to Wikipedia's list of notables from the resort).

Even though his profile was re-raised on moving back into football circles, he maintained a typically modest, restrained way of going about his daily routines. No wish to draw attention to himself.

Ian Gilzean said, 'He liked his own company. Quite happy and comfortable in himself. That takes quite a bit of doing. But if you are you can do what you like then.

'Dad, though, knew a few people as he used to work down that neck of the woods. Had a few mates down there. He used to frequent the golf club and things like that. Think he had stopped playing but used to go up there with people.'

Ian mentioned a neighbour the family were in email contact with.

Architect pal Bob Hynd said, 'I looked up The Quantocks where he lived on Google Earth. Fairly modern block of flats. Unusual design. He was friendly with one guy in his block. An elderly single guy. The two of them would probably have got along fine.'

In the meantime, Gilzean had got himself back on the Tottenham payroll, joining the matchday hospitality team which included Pat Jennings, Phil Beal, Cliff Jones, Alan Mullery, Ossie Ardiles, Martin Chivers, Graham Roberts, Clive and Paul Allen, Micky Hazard, Tony Galvin, David Howells, Ray Clemence, Steve Hodge and John Pratt.

He was rather pleased with what he was earning too. His close friend Bob Hynd said, 'He was asked to host a table of 20 people and it would have earned him more than when he was a superstar player at the club.'

Gilzean earned his corn, arriving around three and a half hours before kick-off and wandering through the lounges and boxes meeting and greeting.

Some days he and Martin Chivers revived their on-field partnership by pairing up. Gillie's easy manner and elephantine memory made him a natural for the fans occupying the hospitality areas, each with jaws dropped and eyes wide and popped at the sight of the dynamic duo.

He said, 'I'd been 30 years away. I said okay I will come back and see if I like it or not – and I liked it. At first I wasn't sure if I would like to do it.

'I gave it a try last season until the end of the season. You meet a lot of old faces, old friends. I gave it a try and I enjoyed it. I amazed myself actually. And especially now, with the team doing so well. I am glad I came back.'

There was no hint of jealousy with others of his ilk – who were forced to take jobs outside the game on retirement from playing to make ends meet – hitching their wagon to the money gravy train earlier in an era, which now sees players earning six-figure wages each week. No concern about sliding out of view for such a long time.

Gilzean said, 'I don't think I could have done it all these years. Chivers has done it for 20 years! Terry Venables recommended him.

'Phil Beal was the second one. And it's just built and built. The amount of staff that's going about with Tottenham blazers on at games, it is unbelievable.'

Phil Beal was of the opinion there was a tinge of regret about not keeping in touch. Beal said, 'When I used to talk to him I think deep down he regretted it because he missed all the banter. All the things when the players get together and reminisce about the old times. Things that happened on and off the field.'

An odd thing to do to stay away? Beal said, 'Yes. When you think we had all played together in the same team for years and all of a sudden, after all those years, he just drifted along and did his own thing.'

Even for a 'suck it and see' commitment, though, there were logistics to be considered, given he had to make a round trip of close to 300 miles to perform his duties.

Initially, he sorted it out for himself. Phil Beal, his fellow host, legend, former team-mate, said, 'Gillie used to go on the National Express bus. He told me, "I'd go to Victoria Coach Station [central London], get the Tube out to near Cockfosters and stay at my eldest son's home. After games Martin Chivers gave me a lift to Oakwood." And he got either the bus or train next morning to Weston-super-Mare.'

Chivers said, 'Gillie didn't drive then and I used to drop him off at his son's at Oakwood because it was on my way home. It wasn't so much Phil's way. We talked about the game first of all but then inevitably got on to past games and past experiences and it was just wonderful to recollect all that. It was a big part of our lives and he was always a character, a wonderful character. We had plenty to talk about.

'Same old Gillie? No he wasn't. Very much more subdued. Quieter. More methodical. He was obviously slowing up. He was in his mid-70s when he joined us [in hospitality]. He had all his senses but obviously just that little bit slower, which we all get when we get into our 70s.

'Once he had been with us for a few months it was as if he had never been away. He liked it and agreed to take it on and we thought it was wonderful for him to be able to work for the club again.'

One day, Phil Beal volunteered to be Gillie's chauffeur. Beal, who shared League Cup (twice) and UEFA Cup glory with Gilzean at Spurs, said, 'He would only do the Saturday and Sunday matches when he did the hospitality. Never midweek. He would say, "They finish too late for me."

'At first, as I've said, he would stay over with his son Kevin, but he always wanted to get back home. I didn't live too far from Weston-super-Mare but didn't put two and two together at that stage.

'One day I said to him, "How far away am I from you, Gillie?" We worked it out that it would only be about 20 minutes out of my way to take him to Tottenham and back [Beal lived in Wellington, Devon, south of Weston]. So I said to him, "I'll tell you what Gillie, I'll pick you up, if you like." He said, "Yes, that would be great." I added, "I'll take you home too." He asked, "Are you sure?" I said, "Sure, it'd be no bother." I took over as his chauffeur from then on.

'He was so pleased. He told me, "That's brilliant, thanks very much." He was so thankful. I said, "It's all right, don't keep on!"'

It seemed he did. Insistently. Beal said, 'He always tried to give me petrol money. I said, "Gillie, it is okay." He said, "Take it." I said "No." He said, "Yes! If I had to go up by train or coach it would cost me a lot more. So take this money." I said, "Gillie, I don't want it." He used to put the money in a sidepocket or somewhere else in the car. I never used to see him do it. I'd be cleaning the car and I'd find this money. When I next saw him I'd said, "I found this money, you've got to take it back." He said, "Don't worry about it." We had so many arguments over it! I used to find this money all over the place in the car. He put it in a different spot all the time. He knew if he gave it to me I wouldn't take it.'

Even when it came to stopping off en route, Gilzean always deferred to Beal. Beal said, 'I'd ask him, "Gillie, do you want to stop?" He said, "It's up to you, if you want to stop, stop; if you don't, don't stop."'

They got on like a house on fire. Beal said, 'We would do a lot of talking there and back, about the game we were actually going to see on the way there and how the game went on the way back.

'He could be a bit shy but we got on great. After missing him for 30 years we'd also chat about the old times. The games we played in together. Things he remembered and I didn't. I asked him whether he had friends in Weston-super-Mare. He'd tell me, "I've got a couple of people."

'With someone else in the car the journeys went past so quickly. Before you know it we're at our destination.

'When we arrived at White Hart Lane the supporters couldn't get enough of him. They loved him. They were in awe of Alan Gilzean. Gillie would do anything for anybody. Get his photos taken with supporters, sign autographs. It was part of our job anyway but he would never refuse anybody, turn anybody down. He was as nice as pie. The supporters idolised him. All of them. They'd ask, "Is that Gillie over there? I'd like to meet him." It was always Gillie they wanted to meet.'

The car share, in common with Peter Kay's TV sitcom of that name (although the vehicle was a soft-top C Class black Mercedes as opposed to a Fiat 500L), had its share of laughs as each swapped their stories and discussed fuel payment. It also had a mystery element, befitting the passenger's former image of a recluse.

Beal said, 'I used to say, "Where should I pick you up Gillie?" He'd say, "Pick me up at Weston-super-Mare station." So I said, "All right, Gillie." I used to drop him at the station. He only lived round the corner. But I never went to his flat.

'It was strange about his flat. Me and Steve Perryman were talking. He never wanted anyone to come round his flat. That makes me think it was like he was keeping everything to himself.

'When he left Tottenham and not getting in contact with anybody, I suppose he didn't want anyone to look at his own private life. [That's] why he wanted to be picked up and dropped off at the station.

'I miss him as I drive there and back on my own. I look over at the passenger seat and think Gillie used to sit in that. It'd be just the two of us. God, I spent more time with Gillie than anyone else at Spurs. But I'm grateful he got back in touch so all of us had those last few precious years with him.'

Ian Gilzean said, 'Dad was quite happy about Phil giving him a lift.'

Gilzean said in 2017, 'He [Beal] picks me up and drops me off on the way back. On Sunday he will collect me at 9am and drop me off at 11.30pm to midnight. He does well. We leave Weston and are at White Hart Lane two and a quarter hours later.'

Close football and family friend Bobby Wishart, who remained in touch with Gilzean at all times from when they first met in the early 1960s, said, 'He loved getting back to White Hart Lane. Loved the involvement. It was great that we were able to push him into having a kind of golden sunset in his career.'

26

'We Didn't Realise It'd Be So Quick'

ALAN GILZEAN watched a crazy game unfold in front of him from the hospitality area of Wembley Stadium. It seemed every time either side attacked there was a goal as Tottenham Hotspur took on Leicester City in the final match of the 2017/18 season on Sunday, 13 May 2018.

To quote the immortal line penned by actor Keith Allen of Fat Les for his parody song 'Vindaloo' prior to Glenn Hoddle's England competing in the 1998 World Cup finals, Spurs managed to 'score one more than you', sealing a 5-4 victory and third spot in the Premier League against Jamie Vardy's 2016 champions.

The King of White Hart Lane and Dens Park and his fellow hosts and guests were relieved and delighted after being royally entertained.

Looking well and in great spirits, according to first-hand witnesses as he left with Phil Beal for the drive down to the West Country, he wished his hospitality team a fond farewell and looked forward to seeing them all again as they reconvened for the opening home fixture of the following campaign three months hence, at the new 62,062-capacity, near billion-pound stadium which had risen from the ashes of the Lane.

Exciting times for him and the rest of the Spurs family to look forward to.

But it proved to be the last time he saw Spurs. Less than two months later he was dead. Sadly, tragically, shockingly struck down by a brain tumour on the morning of Sunday, 8 July 2018 .

The next time the 'king's people' in lilywhite gathered for a game his image was up on the giant screens at the national stadium. Spurs were hosting for the first time in the 2018/19 season, construction delays holding up the official opening of the Tottenham Hotspur Stadium until the following April, when Spurs defeated Crystal Palace in the first competitive game at the beyond-state-of-the-art venue.

Fulham provided the opposition this day, Saturday, 18 August 2018. Gilzean's head-to-waist monochrome picture in a Tottenham shirt beamed out of the monitors at each end of the pitch, high above fans, players and officials commemorating him with a warm pre-match minute's applause. And Spurs went out and did the decent thing by securing a 3-1 victory that could be dedicated to the legend eulogised by announcer Paul Coyte in the build-up to the collective clapping of hands. Harry Kane even scored his first competitive Spurs goal in August to mark the occasion.

The 'king's people' in dark blue, as we have read, had already gathered to commemorate their famous son a month earlier – on Sunday, 22 July – when Dundee kicked off their Dens Park season against Dunfermline in a Scottish League Cup group match. A cup campaign that ended at home to Ayr United in the second round on the day Wembley remembered a player whose dreams of playing at the renowned stadium came true.

Ian Gilzean said, 'I got in touch with the Tottenham Tribute Trust when Dad first got ill. We didn't know what was going to happen. Just to have someone there who would reply to an email and then spoke to you was good. The Trust do great work. They helped Bobby Smith, who was in the Spurs Double team. Bobby had his injuries and got buttons compared with what they get today.

'Also spoke to Paul Allen, who was on the playing staff when I was at Spurs. He was involved with the Professional Footballers' Association. We discussed whether we needed anything. The PFA do great work too. Just to have people there for you was good.

'We didn't know the extent of what he had at the beginning. We thought Dad might just need a bit of respite for a few months until he was back on his feet. It was three or four weeks in before we knew what we were looking at.'

How did you cope? He said, 'Until you are in that position, you can't plan for anything like that. He had still been living independently. On his own. Still doing the games. It wasn't until just after the Leicester game that we had an inkling something wasn't right. One day he was as good as gold, brand new. Looking after himself. Doing his own washing, cooking, tidying up, not needing any help whatsoever. And the next day the tumour started to get a bit bigger and affect different parts of his brain.

'You've got to deal with it in the moment on a day-to-day basis, ain't you? It ain't going away. One of those things. Tried to tap into any help we could get or need. But at the end of it we didn't need any of that because it took him quick.'

Ian Gilzean kindly, patiently and stoically gave me the details as he went through the sequence of events in which his dad and a football great was lost to us all over a mere few weeks.

Gillie contacted his grandson Cameron, Ian's son, asking for 'grannie's phone number'. Ian Gilzean said, 'Cameron gave him my mother-in-law Barbara's number. He was obviously looking for my Mum's number.'

Ian rang his dad in Weston-super-Mare from his Carnoustie home and contacted elder brother Kevin in London. He said, 'Dad was just coming out with stuff that didn't make sense. So I thought "Hold on a minute, I'll call you back here." [I] Spoke to Kev and asked him, "When was the last time you spoke to Dad?" I used to speak to him every Sunday. Maybe in the week as well. Kev would speak to him on different nights.

'Anyway, Kev spoke to him and he rang me back and said, "No, this ain't right." I think it was a Saturday and I was due to go to Portugal golfing for four days with friends early on Monday morning. I thought, "I'm going to have to drive to Weston to see what's going on."

Kevin and his partner Justine arranged with the NHS to send a doctor to Gilzean's Weston-super-Mare home the same day. Ian said, 'Dad weren't for letting the doctor in so Kev had to get hold of one of his neighbours who we knew to let the doctor in!

'The first thought was that it was a urine infection because that can send you a bit funny [a symptom of delirium]. The doctor gave him tablets.'

Ian's brother went down to Weston to see their dad on the Sunday. Ian said, 'I think the doctor called when Kev was there. Kev felt Dad didn't seem too bad, that these tablets should kick in.

'Think Kev said to Dad, "Right, come up to London with us. Stay with me for a week. We can keep an eye on you."

'He wouldn't have any of it! His attitude was that he was independent, living on his own, didn't need any help.

'I spoke to Kev when he got back to London. He said, "Dad's on these tablets and we should see an improvement in a couple days." So I said, "Right, I'll go on my holidays if everything's going to be all right in a couple of days."

Ian flew off on the Monday morning as arranged and rang Kevin after landing in Portugal to check on their dad's condition. He said, 'Kevin told me, "I've got to go and pick him up. It is not great. He is still confused and disorientated. I asked him, 'Have you taken your tablets this morning?' He was like, 'Tablets, yeh. I've taken two. I could have had four tablets. Have I taken any?'" So Kev said to him, "Right I'm coming to get you."

'At least it was more manageable back at Kev's home? Yes. But he was getting up at one o'clock thinking it was a different time of day and getting his kit ready, packing his bag and saying, "Drop me at the train station."

Ian returned from his trip with friends and came down to his brother's family home in London to help sort things out. He said, 'I got there on the Sunday. He'd been given more tablets the day before I arrived. We had him back to a doctor I think on the Wednesday. That's when they said, "This ain't blooming right. This is not how it should be panning out." The urine infection had gone so he should have improved massively.'

Gilzean was checked into Chase Farm Hospital in Enfield. Ian said, 'This is where the practice we had been to on the Wednesday were brilliant. Luckily, the doctor there was also in the hospital at Chase Farm, which had an old people's assessment unit. They got him in and checked his heart. It was doing all sorts. They thought he had high blood pressure. He was on tablets for it but they were making it worse. They took him off them and did a little brain scan and they could see something there.'

Gillie was admitted to Barnet Hospital. He underwent a 'proper brain scan' and, after a week of expert consultants studying it, the brain tumour was diagnosed.

Ian said, 'Chase Farm said they wanted to transfer Dad to Barnet Hospital, like now! We need to look at this [the "something there"] straight away. Dad said, "We can think about that." I'm sitting there saying, "Like, really!" I said, "If we go out of here today, you ain't going to get better. We'll be back in three or four days' time with the same thing and you would have wasted that doctor's time. All these doctors' time. So you have to go." That's when the penny dropped. He said, "Yeh, okay then."

'So we went to Barnet and then they started. Did a proper brain scan and everything like that. But we were told we would have to wait a week for the results after the scan was studied by leading consultants in London. So it panned out over six weeks from start to finish, I think.'

Ian found dealing with his dad over the issue had elements of a role reversal in their relationship, finding himself acting more the father than the son. He said, 'I'm walking into the hospital and asking, "Had your dinner today?" He'd say, "I've had two dinners." I replied, "No you've not." He said, "Yes I'm telling you." He was adamant he was right. He could be stubborn at the best of times. But he's telling you that and you know he hasn't had two dinners. Then he's saying, "That little Scottish doctor was about again changing my tablets." I said, "You're making this up."

'I think I walked in once, asked him something and he's come out with the "answer", I just looked at Kevin and said, "I'm going for a walk!" I just took myself off for 20 minutes. Back outside. Bit of fresh air and left him to Kev before I came back in.

'I think you got to that point where, if he was going to say that sort of thing, you couldn't argue because he was SO adamant he was right. Even though me, the doctors and nurses knew it was not right, he was still adamant in himself.

'So there did come a point where you did take it with a pinch of salt and changed the subject. Wasn't worth arguing about. You were arguing against a brick wall. You weren't going to win. You've just got to let it go. Get into something else.'

Gillie's sons decided to find their dad a place where he could have care around the clock. And he was able to spend the final weeks of his life at the Greenhill Care Home in Waggon Road in Barnet, which Ian described as a 'nice place'.

A 'magnificent' converted country house of 67 rooms 'tastefully refurbished, extended and equipped to provide outstanding levels of care to the elderly' set in seven acres of 'beautiful mature grounds' including 'beautifully manicured' gardens with views of parkland and fields. It even provided an oak-panelled dining room.

Ian said, 'The hospital wasn't the best place for him. He was in a bed and they couldn't do anything for him there. He needed 24-hour care. I had spent two weeks down in London, came back for a couple of days and went back for a week and we – or rather Kev – got him into Greenhill, which was a nice place. Went back to bring down my daughter and then my son who wanted to see him.

'My life might sound like a holiday but it had been planned to go away with my wife. I said to Kev, "Right, I'll go on holiday because it is all sorted. I can't do anything else now we've got him into this place. When I get back I'll come back down for a bit to see how he is. Then see how it goes."

'You were on holiday but never had Dad out of your mind. I spoke to Kev every day. Or got a message to him. "How is he today?" Some days he'd better. Some not so great. He stopped eating a lot because of the steroids he was on. The tablets he was on made his memory a little better, but he didn't want to eat. It was a catch-22. What do you do?

'It was a Sunday morning and we were flying home. Kev rang me. Dad had died. We didn't realise it'd be so quick. He'd only been at Greenhill for two to two and a half weeks.

'Think his quality of life was good, though, up until the last couple of weeks, last ten days even. When I was down we'd have a little walk in the grounds. A little sit in the sun. Chatting away.

'You can get people who can be in a bad way for months and months. I think that's even worse.

'I don't know whether we were lucky or not. Would he have preferred to go quickly in that situation? Yes. I miss him.'

There were countless messages of condolences to Gilzean's family all as important as the other when the news of his passing broke. One came in the form of a letter to Ian Gilzean from Barry Graham, the founder of Glasgow Spurs, which is understood to be the only Tottenham supporters club in Scotland, a fact which no doubt would have tickled Gillie's fancy judging by what people have said to me for this book.

> Dear Ian,
> I just wanted to drop you a line to pass on my condolences at the passing of your dad and to express – on behalf of Glasgow Spurs Supporters Club – how much he meant to us as our Honorary President. As the former chairman of Glasgow Spurs, it was a pleasure for me to get to know him. Not only was he a true Spurs legend, but a lovely, friendly, engaging bloke. We couldn't have asked for anyone better to fill the role and he will be sorely missed by our members.
>
> I don't know if your dad told you how he and we came into contact; but if not, here goes: after forming Glasgow Spurs in 2012 we were looking for a prominent Scottish ex-Spur to become our Honorary President. We thought your dad would be ideal for the role and asked a friend who was attending a Spurs Show Live event, at which Gillie was the main guest, to approach him on our behalf. A few days later, I had the thrill of answering my mobile phone to find the great man on the other end – and he kindly agreed to our request.
>
> Although not a formal role, Gillie took it seriously. As well as keeping in regular contact with me by phone – to chew the fat over how Spurs were doing and to ask how the club and our members were – he twice flew up to Glasgow

to join us in the pub where we meet to watch televised Tottenham matches.

On both occasions he did a fascinating Q&A session, recalling what it was like playing for the great Bill Nicholson and alongside Jimmy Greaves, Martin Chivers and co. The pub was mobbed on both occasions and our members loved listening to his anecdotes. Your poor dad then kindly posed for countless individual photos and signed scores of old Spurs programmes and memorabilia. He did so not just with patience but with enthusiasm. He could not have been more accommodating. On both occasions, he then watched the televised match with us, cheering on Spurs as vociferously as anyone in the room.

On a personal level, as his point of contact for Glasgow Spurs, I loved chatting to Gillie about both the fortunes of the team and his experiences as a matchday host and Spurs Legend. I sensed he got a real buzz from being back in contact with some of his former team-mates and enjoyed travelling up to White Hart Lane from Weston-super-Mare.

It's just such a shame that he won't be alongside Cliff Jones, Alan Mullery et al. when the new stadium opens next month.

I had intended to attend Gillie's funeral but, sadly, was out of the country at the time. However, I can assure you there was great sadness expressed from members on our Facebook page at the news of his passing. We will also be making a donation to the Tottenham Tribute Trust in recognition of, and thanks for, his contribution to Glasgow Spurs.

I can only imagine the sorrow you and your family are experiencing at the moment but I trust you are taking comfort from the wonderful tributes paid to your dad from his Dundee, Spurs and Scotland peers and the wider football community.

As I had the pleasure of discovering, not only was he a wonderful player, he was an absolute gentleman too.

Best wishes and deepest sympathies,

Barry Graham.

Colleagues and also friends were devastated.

Beal said, 'I dropped Gillie off as usual after the Leicester game. His brain was brilliant. When I drove him he would say, "I remember when we played so-and-so and so-and-so. And that so-and-so and so-and-so played centre-half. Things I couldn't remember. He was spot on when he spoke to all the players who played with him. He'd remember everything.

'But on the Friday after the match he phoned me up and didn't quite make sense. A couple of days later I phoned him to ask how he was. This went on for a week. I tracked down his sons. They spoke to me and said they were taking their dad to London. He went into hospital, did some tests and found out he had a brain tumour. And a fortnight later he passed away. It was so quick.

'Gillie was the sort of fellow who always told me when we were talking that he would never want any help if he had any problems with him.'

Steve Perryman found out about Gilzean's passing from Phil Beal. Perryman said, 'Philip and Alan had got quite close with Philip driving him to and from Tottenham. Philip was more in touch with Alan than anyone. He told me Gillie, out of the blue, started making phone calls to him saying things like "what time tomorrow?" Philip would go, "Gillie what are you talking about?"

'Gillie would say to him, "You must remember two days ago we spoke to so-and-so who has invited us up there tomorrow." Gillie was talking normal but was not correct. It happened a couple of times. Philip told one of Gillie's sons – who are both lovely boys – and it all came to light he was struggling. Gillie was not an idiot but was having to cope with this thing he didn't know about inside his head. It started off the process and very soon he was gone. And of course you go into the operation of showing your respects and going to the funeral, which we did.'

Jennings said, 'I got the news he was in hospital and had a tumour. And I spoke to him. It was unbelievable how quickly he went after he was working with the rest of us on that last match of the season.'

Martin Chivers said, 'Phil Beal phoned me up and said that Alan had been phoning him up late at night. I think it was around four or five weeks later he went because the tumour was inoperable. That was it.

'I think for Gillie at 79 years of age and living by himself down there [in Weston-super-Mare] – and I'm not being cruel – he had a good death, he went quickly. He certainly wasn't the sort of person who would have wanted to go slowly. Our family thought, "That's a good way to go if you are going to go." Gillie wasn't going to be a patient for the rest of his life. He wouldn't have wanted that. I'll remember Gillie as he was.'

Jimmy Robertson said, 'Alan's passing was quite a shock. I saw him at White Hart Lane's last match. He was telling me he had had trouble with his gall bladder. That it wasn't a problem. It was in hand. Was to be done some time in the summer. I thought he looked well. We sat together. Obviously there was a whole presentation thing going on. We were having lunch and got chatting. Talking to him I know he was delighted to be back at Tottenham.'

Gilzean had spread his commitment to Spurs by attending non-matchday events and in the wake of the Leicester game was at an evening with Phil Beal and Martin Chivers.

Spurs stadium announcer Paul Coyte was the host. Coyte said, 'It was a two-hour long Q&A. Alan was completely on the money, on the button. Brilliant. Full of stories about Dave Mackay and others. That's why it was such a surprise when Phil told me Alan had phoned up a bit confused and everyone was a bit worried.

'It almost seemed to all of us like a blessing in disguise that it happened quite quickly because Alan didn't seem like the sort of character who wanted to stick around with something like that. So sad.'

Mike Rollo, the Spurs commercial manager and director of corporate hospitality, said, 'We were all backstage after the Leicester game. It was a big moment as were planning to move into the new stadium for the start of the following season. I can remember swapping pleasantries with Alan who was saying, "See you next season." He was really quite perky. You would never have thought there was anything wrong at all.'

We go all the way back to Coupar Angus for two postscripts.

Bob Hynd, a native of the town, revealed how he had set up delivery of the *Blairgowrie Advertiser* to his close friend's bedside during what proved to be his final weeks.

Hynd said, 'The local paper which covered Coupar Angus and other towns and villages in the area. Keeping up with news from his home town would have given him something to do. He'd have been able to read up the bowling club, his old school, the WI. Even pet dogs that had gone missing! Sadly, he died before even receiving the first copy.'

For Ron Ross – called Ronnie by Gillie – there was a tragic coincidence in the way his old team-mate and schoolfriend passed away three months short of what would have been his 80th birthday.

Ross said, 'My son Derek sadly died of a brain tumour a couple of years ago. Like Gillie, he went quickly too. He was a high flier in public relations and played rugby for Scotland. Only 47. Sad, but Florence, the French girl he married, is like the daughter we never had and we have two grandchildren.'

Rest in peace, Derek. Rest in peace, Gillie.

27

'Gillie Would Be Outstanding Today'

THE LAST thing Tottenham Hotspur manager Mauricio Pochettino's white and navy blue 'army' witnessed in the 2018/19 season was the club's first Champions League Final for the European Cup; either inside Atletico Madrid's spiffing, modern Wanda Metropolitano home, on enormous monitors at the new home of the Spurs, pre-stadium naming rights, or on smaller screens in pubs and front room 'barracks'.

It replaced the 1963 European Cup Winners' Cup Final as the biggest game in the club's history. Even the Glory, Glory Boys that won the Double were unable to get beyond the semi-finals 57 years previously when Europe's premier club competition was about just champions rather than, in England's case, the top four.

Perhaps that remembrance day for Alan Gilzean at the start of the home campaign against Fulham provided a spark which lit the fuse to the run unique in Spurs history (although Liverpool denied the Lilywhites the lifting of the big-eared trophy).

After all, he helped guide Tottenham to continental glory in 1972 with that UEFA Cup triumph over Wolverhampton Wanderers, the second leg of the final providing the cult hero's own favourite recollection of the Lane.

Certainly Harry Kane, Spurs modern-day talisman who captained England into the 2018 World Cup semi-finals the day before Gillie passed, would almost certainly not argue against it.

Kane is 'hugely respectful of Alan's legacy'.

And the feeling was mutual, Gilzean naming the number nine as a successor to the royal moniker prior to the Lane's demolition, although appreciating the need to tweak it with the move into the Tottenham Hotspur Stadium.

Gilzean said to Alan Pattullo in *The Scotsman* on 14 May 2017 on the day of the final match at the Lane in characteristically coy terms, 'The King of White Hart Lane – oh heck! Harry Kane will get a new name when the stadium is finished. I was the king, then Hoddle was the king, and then Harry. Oh I was the original I suppose, but then I am the oldest! You have to be 60-odd to remember me.'

And he hoped Kane and co would inherit the good vibes he felt at the old place when entering the new kingdom when he added, 'I just hope we can keep the atmosphere in the new ground. It is just unique. Jürgen Klinsmann was back recently and he told me that, for atmosphere, it's one of the greatest grounds he's played at. It's really something special.'

Spurs chairman Daniel Levy – showered with praise by people who would have once covered him in something rather less pleasant for overseeing the £1bn home move without the help of a Phil and Kirstie – had an appreciation of just what the Scot's service has given the club.

He said, 'Alan played a huge part in the history of our club. He is rightly remembered as one of the finest players to have worn a Spurs shirt and the success that he and his team-mates enjoyed in many ways laid the foundations of Tottenham Hotspur today.'

Gilzean is in exclusive company with Glenn Hoddle, his immediate successor to the Lane throne.

With Gillie throwing folk hero Kane's name into the mix, no other players wore the crown bestowed by the Lilywhite faithful during Spurs's 118-year stay at the old place.

Steve Perryman underlined the stature of the first two players with the potential to be addressed 'his majesty' when Hoddle suffered a heart attack in a television studio three months after Gilzean died.

Perryman said, 'When Glenn got ill, I sent him a text and said, "We've lost one King of White Hart Lane this year, we can't lose another." Gillie and Glenn were the two Kings of White Hart Lane in my 19 years at Tottenham and I don't think the crowd could have given them a greater honour.

'I'd have liked Glenn to have played with Gillie. Glenn would have put it on a sixpence for Gillie to head or volley in. Tottenham supporters always like a bit of class like those two.'

Hoddle recovered and returned to studio work as a pundit to witness the last steps of Spurs's run to Madrid, steps underplayed if they were to be described as merely 'dramatic'. More like out-of-control roller-coaster rides which played havoc with the well-being of any Spurs follower, let alone such a lauded one laid so low. Against Manchester City and Ajax, the 'club of kings' were at the jaws of an exit. The video assistant referee – a newly introduced system to judge tight decisions – came down in Tottenham's favour as Raheem Sterling's quarter-final 'winner' for Pep Guardiola's City billionaires was ruled offside. And a third goal from Lucas Moura in the sixth minute of injury-time at the Johan Cruyff Stadium in Amsterdam ensured the final date with Liverpool on 1 June 2019.

Gilzean's close friend Bob Hynd reflected, 'I'm sure Gillie and I would have enjoyed long phone conversations about all those games the following day.' And the fact that Gilzean kept in touch with the modern day further strengthened a legacy revitalised with his return to his former kingdoms. Also the fact he has drawn comparisons with a more modern Spurs favourite, Dimitar Berbatov.

Berbatov, the dark-haired, languid striker with a slicked-back Dracula-style hairdo, sucked the life out of Chelsea as Spurs sealed the 2008 League Cup, the club's last major final appearance prior to Madrid 2019.

He was a goalscoring hero – netting in the most casual of styles from the penalty spot at the new Wembley which was to become Spurs's home for almost two seasons until the return to London N17.

It was the highlight of a two-year spell at Spurs, during which the striker became a Lane idol. The Bulgarian also scored the match-winner against Sheffield United on his first Tottenham outing.

And cemented his place in the hearts of his Lilywhite admirers with four goals in a 6-4 win over Reading; joining a rare group of Spurs players – including Jimmy Greaves – to achieve such a haul in one match.

He became such a sought-after player that Manchester United manager Sir Alex Ferguson persuaded his club to flash the cash – £30m – to sign him, although he did not include the big-money signing as he masterminded a League Cup Final win over Spurs, which denied the north Londoners a successful defence.

Maybe Fergie, too, was drawn to Berbatov because he reminded him of Gilzean. Perhaps, fancifully, he was trying to gain some sort of indirect belated revenge for suffering from the eye for goal possessed by the ex-Perth clerk on the day Gillie sealed Dundee their 1962 Scottish title by beating his St Johnstone side.

Gillie and Berbatov were both forwards with a touch of unorthodoxy about them, wooing the Lane-ites with their brooding dark looks, delicacy on the ball and calm demeanour. Several football experts believed the parallel between Gilzean and Berbatov to be legitimate.

Cliff Jones has seen it. Jones, a Gilzean team-mate, regularly watched Berbatov while working as a matchday host at the old, beloved but razed stadium. He said, 'Gillie and Dimitar were both stylish, graceful. Could score and create goals. Were good in the air and on the ground and had class. All qualities of the perfect Spurs player. But I would put Gillie in front of Berbatov because of his "Scottishness", a tough grittiness. He could look after himself.'

David Lacey wrote in *The Guardian* on 7 November 2008, 'Older Spurs fans might have seen in Berbatov's ability to fool defenders by loitering in apparently harmless positions a glimpse of Alan Gilzean. When Berbatov first appeared at White Hart Lane some Tottenham fans thought he looked a bit slow when in fact he is simply unhurried. The brain is quick and so, when necessary, are the feet.'

David Pleat, who managed Ian Gilzean at Spurs, said to Alan Pattullo on 27 February 2009, 'It is quite an obvious comparison to me. Gilzean had a beautiful touch, the ball appeared glued to his feet at times. But he also had this gift for hanging in the air and deflecting balls to colleagues. He had this slightly languid style in an era when Spurs were the artists.'

John Motson, the respected broadcaster with the sheepskin-coat-wearing image, reckoned that, 'In the absence of Gilzean, Berbatov is the next best thing.' Hunter Davies, who wrote *The Glory Game* about Gillie and his mates in the 1971/72 season, said in the *New Statesman* published on 26 March 2007, 'Twice in the past week, two of the greatest brains in British football, John Motson and David Pleat, have made the same observation – that Dimitar Berbatov, the new taste thrill of White Hart Lane, reminds them of Alan Gilzean. Each hesitated slightly after their aperçu, realising that most listeners might not know who they were talking about.

'I have a totally clear memory of Gillie bought from Dundee in 1964, for £70,000, a Spurs star for ten seasons, scorer of 93 goals, but I hadn't seen the comparison – and still don't. Both elegant, artistic strikers, but Gillie was slimmer with a baldy head.

'His most distinctive skill was in the air, he could flick the ball on from corners and take free kicks so subtly that you half believed he hadn't touched it, yet he had changed its direction enough to land it in the corner of the net. He was adored by the fans, the first to my knowledge to be hailed in their chants as the King of White Hart Lane.'

Bobby Wishart said, 'Berbatov is good in the air, but not as good as Gillie.'

If you want to know the place Alan Gilzean stands in the history of Tottenham Hotspur there is one opinion which would count above all others in most who know and care about the club. That of one Bill Nicholson.

Bill Nick, by general consensus, is the club's greatest and most successful manager.

He put together the best team to have represented Spurs. A team which has been put forward as among the best ever seen in club football across the globe. You know, the one which won the

Double. And with a few tweaks took on Europe to become the first from Britain to win a major continental tournament. Rebuilt it to almost claim, with Gilzean's help, another Double and did the same a third time to guide Spurs to three trophies in successive years.

Hundreds of players, many world class, played for him. And hundreds more have followed. Yet when he came to selecting a 16-strong squad from all that talent, Alan Gilzean figured in it.

Nicholson wrote in his autobiography *Glory Glory* in 1984, 'It is not easy to overlook the many qualities of Alan Gilzean.'

Gillie, who helped Bill win four of the seven trophies lifted at White Hart Lane over his 16 years in charge, was one of three Scottish internationals included, with Dave Mackay and John White the others, to play a major role for Bill Nick's Tottenham teams. G-Men partner Jimmy Greaves was included too.

The rest of the squad? Well here goes: Pat Jennings, Ted Ditchburn, Alf Ramsey, Mike England, Maurice Norman, Cyril Knowles, Ron Burgess, Danny Blanchflower, Ossie Ardiles, Bobby Smith, Cliff Jones and Martin Peters.

Pat Jennings compared the teams he played in with Gillie to the Glory, Glory Boys of the early 1960s and the one of today, led by Mauricio Pochettino into the new home on the same site – given a handful of yards – as White Hart Lane.

He said, 'Were they among the greatest the club have had? We won a lot, but it is now maybe a bit harder to win. Yet having said that, we were always being compared with the 1960/61 team and that was the level we were always trying to get to. And NEVER quite made it.

'Over the years – from 1964 for me and Gillie – all you got was, "Can we do the Double again?" The closest we got to it was 1967 when we won the FA Cup and finished runners-up with Forest but Manchester United won the title by four points that year.

'We went on into the 1970s with success in the UEFA Cup and League Cup. But, as I said, never really got back to where we were in the early 1960s.

'I think the club decided "we're not getting involved" when people began to spend big money on players and all of sudden they ended in up in the Second Division three years after Gillie left.

'But it is mind-blowing when you look at the facilities now and see how massive the club is at the minute. The facilities are just incredible. The new stadium is a different world.

'Everything is in place now for us in the years ahead to really take off. Have no bother in getting players here. We have the background but, at the end of the day it is what you have on the field. It'd be fantastic to be a Spurs player now.'

Jimmy Robertson felt Gilzean was the 'perfect template' of a Spurs player.

He said, 'Spurs have always produced players that you would pay to see and Gillie was one. World class? Not a guy to promote himself, not fiery, but a top player. Very good in the air and the ground. Did step-overs before everyone else did. He knew he was good. Probably appreciated more by other players than the public. Marvellous times and great memories playing with him.

'The modern Spurs team is a marvellous one. They are a breath of fresh air in the way they play. It has produced a few folk heroes like Harry Kane and a manager in Mauricio Pochettino who has a great image. A lot of people I know say that if they could watch any team it would be Spurs. Gillie would slot in very well. Slot in with a lot of teams nowadays.'

Gilzean's funeral in Dundee displayed the depth of reverence still accorded him in the Tayside city.

Cameron Kerr, the Dee vice-captain picked out for special mention as Paddy Barclay eulogised Gilzean at the service, reckoned Gilzean has left a 'massive legacy' which gives 'hope in the future for the club' enough to bring back the good times.

Kerr, whose side suffered relegation from the Scottish Premier in 2018/19, said, 'What would we give to have Alan Gilzean in the team now? Yeh, exactly. What a player, eh? Way before my time but I've heard he was incredible. Dundee are so lucky to have had a person of that ability and stature associated with the club.

'I've seen videos of him. The goals he scored at Muirton that day we won the title. The ones he scored against Cologne in the European Cup. And you look at all his records too. Got 169 goals in 190 games. It is just amazing. If anyone now did that in a Dundee shirt it would be classed as … well, he wouldn't be at Dundee for a start. He'd get a big move. Like Alan did in his time to Tottenham. Obviously he went on to become a cult hero there as well.

'As a player he was similar in the air to Cristiano Ronaldo, without exaggeration. What impressed me most about his game? His heading ability was ridiculous, his timing and the fact he was able to hang in the air. On the ground he had that instinct to be in the right position.

'I'd probably say he left a legacy alongside Bobby Cox and Bob Shankly, who have had stands named after them at Dens. That shows the level he is rated at. The lounge he has in his name at Dens doesn't do him any justice in my eyes.

'People might laugh at the suggestion but the new stadium being planned could be named after Alan. No one could say why it shouldn't be because he is such a legend at the club. So highly regarded.

'I feel he leaves a specialness for Dundee. Makes Dundee mean something. Gives the fans something to live off. Gives the fans who never got to see him hope. He leaves a massive legacy in terms of providing hope in the future for the club. He's an inspiration.

'Talking about myself as a Dundee fan. I grew up in the era of Claudio Caniggia and Fabian Cabellero, but before I went to the games I was engrossed in the history of the club. I became more full on than my dad [Alastair] as a supporter. Obsessed. I saved programmes and had a season ticket right up until I didn't need one anymore.

'I read the centenary history *Up Wi' The Bonnets* by Norrie Price, on winning the league, European Cup and League Cup runs, learned about the players inside out. One name that sticks out is Alan Gilzean. He even wrote the foreword to the book.

'With Dundee, there's been a lot of bad times and uncertainty and that is what makes the good times – with Alan so central to so many of them – so special. You can just draw on those good times. A lot of people would say you are living in the past but history is what makes the club. Many fans today just live in the present and forget the past.

'It was a global achievement; to do so well in Europe. Put Dundee in a similar bracket to the likes of Barcelona [not forgetting

Ajax, Liverpool and even Spurs, judged on who made the semi-finals of the Champions League in 2018/19] of today.

'When some people look at Scottish football they view it as Celtic, Rangers and also-rans. But Dundee showed, with Alan, they were far from a provincial team as they got one match from the European Cup Final and proved themselves one of the best clubs in the world.'

Kerr viewed the winning goal for Scotland against England in 1964, which turned Gilzean into an instant national hero, as another example of the size of the legacy Gilzean has left at Dens Park. He said, 'That achievement goes straight back to the history of Dundee. He scored for Scotland that day as a Dundee player in front of an enormous 133,000 crowd. Incredible. That remains such big thing. Special. Something else he gave the club. To make us swell our chests with pride.'

Kerr also recognised Gilzean's impact at Spurs. He said, 'The number of Tottenham players who came to the funeral showed what he still means to Spurs too. He was a cult hero there too.

'I watched the closing ceremony at White Hart Lane on the television. All the stars coming out and the announcer giving each of them a wee spiel. Then I heard what I felt was the biggest compliment of the lot, "Here is the King of White Hart Lane." What a reception Gillie got. He had been away for a long time from White Hart Lane until his final few years. Good he was able to come back and experience what people really felt about him.

'I heard he visited Tottenham's training ground but what a feeling it would have been for him to be able to have gone into the new Spurs stadium after what he achieved with the club. Spurs fans totally loved him like we did. Spurs have done a proper job with the stadium from this outsider's point of view.

'I look back at it now and think how lucky were Dundee and Tottenham to have had Alan Gilzean playing for our team.'

Gillie remained a motivating factor for youth product Kerr as Dundee planned to bounce back from Scottish Premier League relegation in 2018/19 with a new manager, James McPake, who saw the defender as a figurehead in a policy of promoting academy graduates.

Kerr said, 'I want to give something back to the football club for the rest of my life because of what it means to me through its history, the ups and downs and what the likes of those held in such regard, like Alan Gilzean, have done for it.

'Modern football isn't like it used to be during Alan's time. It is not as much about the community as it used to be. I know it sounds ridiculous because I'm only in the first half of my 20s but I want to bring it back to what it was. A family day. Time away from work.'

John Nelms, Dundee managing director, said, 'Mr. Gilzean 'Gillie', without doubt, is one of the greatest players, if not the greatest, to ever grace a Dundee jersey. He is also remembered as an absolute gentleman. When I first came to Dens Park in 2013 one of the first places I walked through was the Alan Gilzean Lounge. I didn't have the full knowledge of Gillie and his history with the club, but quickly learned about him as a person, a player and, of course, his 169 goals.

'I was fortunate enough to meet him on quite a few occasions in the five years before his death, one being at his induction into the Tottenham Hotspur Hall of Fame. Amongst all of the fanfare, he seemed more interested in asking me questions about Dundee. I could see just how much he loved the club and the game at each of our subsequent meetings. He was sharp and insightful.

'When he passed in 2018, it was devastating for everyone connected with the club.

'In the club's 125-year history no one has come close to achieving what Alan Gilzean and his team-mates did while at Dens Park. It is doubtful anyone ever will.'

Richard Gough, who captained Spurs in the 1980s after playing for Dundee United, said, 'Gillie has left a fantastic legacy. That Dundee team are always very well remembered. Obviously Alan was a tremendous player for them.'

Craig Brown, a Scotland World Cup manager and Gillie's Dundee team-mate, reckoned the forward might have persuaded Pelé to consider him worthy of playing for Brazil.

Brown said, 'Was Alan world class? He was very good. I had to do a talk about Denis Law getting the freedom of Aberdeen. And

Alex Ferguson said to me, "Here's a line for you. I spoke to Pelé and in the conversation he said that the only British player who could have played for Brazil was Denis Law."

'Pelé didn't include Gilzean. Maybe I should have said to Alex, "Pelé hasn't seen Alan Gilzean." Gillie would be outstanding today. Majestic.

'It would have been lovely to have seen Gillie on the World Cup or Euro finals stage.'

Brown, who guided his country to the 1996 Euro and 1998 World Cup finals, said, 'Would Gillie have got into my Scottish squads? Oh yes. Most definitely. Absolutely he would. When you think of him and the likes of Law and Jim Baxter in his day. These guys were of superior quality. When I started [as Scottish coach to then national manager Alex] Ferguson's strikers were Charlie Nicholas, Graeme Sharp and Mo Johnston. They were good players. Charlie and Graeme were good players in the 1986 World Cup squad in Mexico when Alex was put in charge after the death of Jock Stein. Gilzean, with the best will in the world, was better than them. That's a value judgement.

'When I got the job my strikers included the likes of Ally McCoist, and Gillie was AT LEAST the equal of them. I also had Gordon Durie – who played at Tottenham – as one of my Scotland strikers.

'When I think of it now, there's a real dearth. Gillie could have played for Scotland now on one leg with the calibre on the go now!'

A return of 22 full caps seems scant reward for a player of Gilzean's ability.

Brown did not believe Gilzean's move into English football affected the number he won. He said, 'He was very highly regarded but there were fewer internationals in those days. Less or no substitutes. I don't think going to England was detrimental to his cap collection [with the suggestion that the international selectors preferred Scottish players to play their club football in Scotland]. In some respects there's a bit more credit when you are plying your trade with a big English club as opposed to Dundee.'

Denis Law hinted the figure was limited by playing his club football in England. He said, 'I think it would be because he went south. That'd definitely be part of it. The Anglo Scots were not looked on that well in the early days, although it got better as the years went on. Scotland preferred to pick players who were playing in their own country.'

He added with a smile, 'I was lucky [he got 55 caps and netted 30 goals, sharing the Scotland goals-scored record with Kenny Dalglish]. I was nearer Scotland [in Manchester] while Gillie lived in London. Expenses were a bit less!'

The late Johan Cruyff, one of the world's all-time great players, was a member of the Alan Gilzean fan club.

Cruyff was a prime mover in the Total Football movement, putting what he learned at Ajax under former Spurs defender Vic Buckingham and with the 1970s Dutch national team into practice at Barcelona, where he helped turn the Catalonians into a global force, mentoring Pep Guardiola along the way.

He took part in a benefit match for Ajax stalwart Sjaak Swart, who made close to 600 appearances, in Amsterdam on 8 August 1973. The Dutch side, inspired by Cruyff and winger Swart, had just lifted three European Cups on the bounce and secured a 4-1 win.

Cruyff, quoted in *In Search of Alan Gilzean*, said, 'Gilzean impressed me with his heading ability. He won nearly every ball in the air; he is just great with his head.'

Gilzean himself believed a lot of how a player is remembered is down to the fans.

He said, 'You are only what the people want you to be and they could make or break you. The Tottenham crowd are fickle and they will either take to you or they don't, and happily they took to me. They loved me and I will always be grateful for that.

'Curiously, they hated Terry Venables, they used to boo him and if he took a corner and put it into the side-netting they would cheer sarcastically.

'When I went there I was fortunate to strike up a good partnership with Jimmy Greaves in a very good side and happily I became one of their idols. I can't put my finger on it and say why but naturally I'm very pleased it happened that way.

'The Dundee thing was a part of my life I am very proud of. I am probably now a dual supporter. Dundee and Tottenham, but obviously I am closer to Tottenham and I was longer there, ten years compared to five at Dens Park so obviously the calling for Tottenham is greater … I will always be close to them but Dundee will always have a fond place in my heart.'

Gilzean, like Andy Murray in tennis, was a revered sportsman with a 'quiet, let's get on with it' attitude who emerged from a small Scottish town to make his mark on the biggest stages.

So how should he be commemorated beyond a small lounge at Dens Park?

There had been talk of a statue being put up in Coupar Angus for its famous son. But it was evident Gillie did not think much of the idea. Ian Gilzean said, 'They were on about that while he was still alive. Just a waste of time. The sort of thing he'd have said would have been, "What's this bloody stupid thing? You are always going to get someone who is going to piss up against it, draw on it, put a cone on its head."'

Ron Ross suggested it might be a 'good idea' to name a Coupar Angus street after his old team-mate and school pal. He said, 'There's not many boys with his kind of background rise to being world famous like Alan in the eyes of those of a certain vintage. Much loved by Dundee and Spurs fans. He was a decent, laid-back guy.'

Perhaps Cammy Kerr's suggestion might be the best physical legacy which could be left – the Alan Gilzean Stadium in Dundee. Well, football already has stadia named after players, like Johan Cruyff (Holland), Diego Maradona (Argentina), Ferenc Puskás (Hungary), Gheorghe Hagi (Romania), Santiago Bernabéu Yeste (Spain), Giuseppe Meazza (Italy), Ali Daei (Iran) and Georgi Asparuhov (Bulgaria).

Oh, and while everyone's at it, how about Spurs following suit instead of christening Tottenham Hotspur Stadium after a naming-rights sponsor with a few bob to help the club to pay off the cost of building it? Yeh, like that is going to happen? They could do worse.

28

The King's Club Historians

ALAN GILZEAN deserves the accolade of being rated one of the best footballers to have played for each of his clubs, according to two people who should know.

And the historians of both Tottenham Hotspur and Dundee, who both met the icon, have paid tribute to one of the game's true greats.

John Fennelly of Spurs and Kenny Ross of the Dee differ in their spelling of Gilzean's nickname; a north-south divide – the 'y' used at the end of the former's interpretation while the latter elected for 'ie', which is the family's preferred option and the reason it is used throughout this authorised biography apart from this chapter. But albeit 'Gilly' or 'Gillie' the fondness and appreciation for the Scottish forward dubbed the King of White Hart Lane and Dens Park shines through.

JOHN FENNELLY: Pat Jennings. Long kick upfield. Alan Gilzean flick. Jimmy Greaves/Martin Chivers goes through to score. It's a refrain that Spurs fans of a particular vintage can still visualise. Just close your eyes, think of White Hart Lane and it vividly flows back.

Add in Brian Moore's commentary on Sunday afternoon's ritual *Big Match* viewing and you've got it all.

For me I had seen it pan out that way so often from my view at the front of the Shelf. It always seemed to be a sunny day and the backdrop of the lower tier on the West side would glimmer in the afterglow as the light bounced off Gilly's bald pate before the massed ranks of the Park Lane End erupted as the ball hit the net.

Strange but that's the direction of flow that I always see in my mind's eye. Big Pat in front of the Paxton as we attacked south. Never left to right.

The fact that two different players are mentioned as benefitting from Gilzean's legendary aerial dexterity is so relevant. Greaves and Chivers. Such different players. One about subtlety; the other power. But Gilly could adapt. And he made two England internationals even better.

Yes, Alan too was a goalscorer but, in these days of perpetual stats, his name would top any 'assists' list. Never selfish; always the team player. A man of so many talents and the master of them all.

I first saw him at the Lane in the 1960s. I wasn't instantly impressed as to a schoolboy he wasn't Carnaby cool. He looked like one of my uncles and I sought to relate to one of the younger players with hair, like Neil Johnson, Joe Kinnear, Jimmy Pearce and, of course, my subsequent fellow suede head, Steve Perryman.

But with each game, while other either shone, flickered or faded, Gilly stayed constant. The fulcrum. A man of exquisite touch who was always unflustered. He surprised me with his bravery because he didn't cut that image and stunned me with his ferocity at times! He would not be cowed. Never intimidated. Opponents would concur.

He was like a walking wall that team-mates bounced the ball off. It was as if they had moved a slender part of the lower ballcourt wall behind the West Stand on to the pitch. One-twos, three-fours; the momentum would build with Gilly the catalyst.

I loved him as a player and, when it all ended, it happened so quickly. We were all there for his testimonial when, like Greaves, Gilly said a goalscoring farewell. But Greaves, deserving at it was, had twice as many people at his game. I can't help feeling that we let him down that night.

Did Gilly play again at his beloved Lane? I don't think so. But he remained massive in my memory and when I returned to Tottenham as the club's press officer in 1987 I began meeting many of my old heroes from that era but could not track down the main man.

Pat Jennings, Greavesey, Alan Mullery, Phil Beal, Chiv, Terry Venables, John Pratt, Perryman, Martin Peters, Ralph Coates … I caught up with them all regularly. Mike England took a few years – and then I met him in Edinburgh. But of Gilly there was no sign.

I worked with his son Ian and would regularly ask him about his dad. He would prevaricate, say he hadn't seen him for ages, not sure where he was and similar as he sought to end the conversation as quickly as possible. A Scottish journalist had tracked him down north of the border, but it was all so vague. He was gone. Yet not forgotten. Although I could not write the traditional 'Where are they now' type of programme piece with the great man, he could regularly crop up in other interviews.

One example was actor Kenneth Branagh, a Spurs fan sharing with me many heroes from that era. But although our interview flicked over many a great name, there was one that so resonated above the crowd: Alan Gilzean. Kenneth was on the phone from LA and I was in Tesco with my usual timing! But his intense affection for Gilly matched any of his onstage heroes. Maybe even eclipsed them all.

As Kenneth told *Hotspur* magazine in February 2010, 'Ah yes, Gilly. Such an icon to those of us old enough to remember the Scot with the spider's web touch that was so delicate, yet so deadly. Even cricket's famous TV 'snickometer' would be unable to detect a Gilly flick yet the result was simply stunning in its beauty.

'Gilzean at his best was fantastic. He seemed to have a magical touch; he could almost blow on the ball with his head and ease it just an inch away from a defender but perfectly into the path of a team-mate. The nature of it was nothing short of incredible, the control he could exert with the merest of touches.

'So, if asked about my memories of that time, I don't think of any one game in particular. I think of Gilzean receiving the ball with his back to goal or arriving at the far post to glance one in.'

Then it happened. I was at the Lane for a Hoddle reception, chatting to Big Pat who mentioned that he had met up with Gilly again. And, as if choreographed, suddenly the great man was with us. He looked just the same as ever and so charming that he even pretended that he knew who I was! And so patient. We had a great chat about the old days and, although he gave the appearance of being happy to do so, he must have endured the same so often! Suddenly a routine evening had become a bit special – for me anyway!

Sadly, I would not meet him again. I stopped working at games at around about the same time that he returned. But I did call him once more for an interview and was astounded at his memory.

The game was our first foray into the League Cup in 1966 when we lost our inaugural match in the competition – by the only goal at West Ham. And Gilly was sent off! There we were 50 years later, and he could describe every moment with uncanny precision. And he was also still annoyed at the perceived injustice of it all with some lively language to describe some of those involved!

Yet, as with our first meeting, it was all delivered with the dry humour and self-deprivation that made him such easy company. Still, I cherish those brief moments. They say, 'never meet your heroes.' As he did so often in his life, Gilly proved them wrong.

I was devastated when I was told that he was terminally ill yet not surprised that he refused radical treatment. He would leave us as he clearly always lived: on his own terms. And my respect for him soared; that's if it could ever be any higher.

KENNY ROSS: Alan Gilzean is an icon of Dundee Football Club; an enduring legend and arguably the greatest player to pull on a Dark Blue shirt.

'Gillie' as he was affectionately known to the Dundee support, was a member of the famous Dundee side to become Champions of Scotland in 1962, scoring twice at Muirton Park on the day the Dee clinched the title and followed that up the next year with nine goals on the run to the European Champions Cup semi-final which included a hat-trick against Cologne and Sporting Club of Portugal and the winner in the semi-final second-leg against AC Milan.

The next season Gillie scored a club record 52 goals in one season as the Dark Blues reached the Scottish Cup Final and in total netted 169 goals in 190 appearances, making him the highest goalscorer in the club's history.

The only player who could claim the mantle of the greatest-ever Dee might be world-record transfer signing Billy Steel from a decade earlier, but he didn't win the Scottish League title, score 17 hat-tricks for the club or score the winning goal for Scotland against England while as a Dundee player.

Both Gilzean and Steel have lounges named after them at Dens Park and both were inducted into Dundee's inaugural Hall of Fame with Legend Awards in 2009, but Gillie remains an abiding hero even today. Kids used to pretend to be Gillie in the city's 'backies' in the early 60s and there were tears when he left for Tottenham Hotspur in 1964.

In the 90s there was a fanzine that emerged entitled *Eh Mind O'Gillie* which remains as a social media blog today and in 2003 he was voted as the club's most valuable player from the championship-winning side.

When Dundee went into administration in 2003 Gillie signed some DFC retro shirts to raise some much needed funds and there was a clamour to get one of these limited edition prize possessions. When he spoke at the club's dinner at the Caird Hall to celebrate the 50th anniversary of that league title triumph, he was given a standing ovation as he took to the stage and when he spoke there was a hush that made the hairs stand on the back of the neck as he graciously held the 700 Dees in attendance in the figurative palm of his hand.

But why is Alan Gilzean held in such high esteem in the Dark Blue half of the City of Discovery? Goalscorers always grab the headlines and he was a goalscoring great but he was much more that. He had a tremendous shot and a great finishing prowess, plus a heading ability for which he became famed. He was able to spring high above the opposition and enjoyed a fantastic partnership up front with Alan Cousin, with whom he terrorised defenders both at home and abroad.

But Gillie was also a bringer of hope and a builder of dreams for the Dundee support and quickly became the answer to the Dee's goalscoring problems that would shoot them right to the top and would record and still hold five club goalscoring records. His name sums up and is synonymous with the glory days for those who weren't born to see Gillie play for the Dee as well as for those who were lucky enough to witness his footballing genius.

Post-war Dundee had always been a vibrant city and by the time Gillie made his debut in 1959 it was changing out of all recognition. Modernisation had begun to change the landscape, not only in the city centre but also in the north in the shape of the new housing schemes known as 'avenues of hope' and Gillie and his team-mates were part of this 'new' Dundee as the 'Swinging Sixties' began to hit town.

When the new Dundee FC stadium is built at Camperdown, alongside these old 'avenues of hope', there will no doubt be a part of it named in honour of Alan Gilzean. That's what he means to Dundee Football Club and his Dark Blue legacy will be complete.

A true Dundee legend in every sense of the word, we may never see his goalscoring like again. All hail Gillie – The King of Dens Park!

Gilzean (front row, centre) in Scotland team, circa 1968

Gilzean and Spurs celebrate lifting the League Cup for the first time after beating Aston Villa in 1971

Graeme Souness,
supported by Gilzean
when they were together
at Spurs

Gilzean (second left) enjoys the moment after Spurs win the UEFA Cup for the first time by sealing victory over two legs against Wolverhampton Wanderers at White Hart Lane in 1972. Captain Alan Mullery holds the trophy

*Gilzean with Irene and
sons Ian (left) and Kevin*

*Gilzean (second right) and 'room-
mate' Steve Perryman (left of Martin
Peters holding trophy and right of
manager Bill Nicholson) join team-
mates after 1973 League Cup Final
victory against Norwich City*

Gilzean's testimonial programme cover

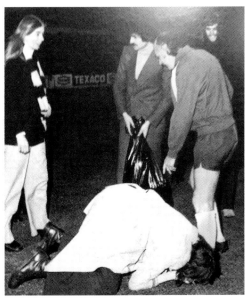

Gilzean fan kisses his boots at Gillie's testimonial in 1974. Tottenham Herald reporter Harry Harris is next to him

The Tottenham Weekly Herald *report Gillie's last game for Spurs while on tour in Mauritius in 1974*

Gilzean (back row, third left) with Highlands Park in South Africa in 1974

Gilzean reunited with former Highlands Park team-mates Barry Bridges (second left) and Martin Cohen (right). Far left is Spurs legend Phil Beal who arranged the get-together and became Gillie's 'chauffeur' on trips from and to the west country to work in matchday hospitality for Spurs

Gilzean managing Stevenage Athletic is pictured by the Stevenage Comet

Pat Jennings, who helped bring Gilzean back to Spurs after decades away, points to the 'faint' signature of his former team-mate when Gillie visited the new Spurs training ground in July 2017

Gillie and Greaves reunited. Picture by former team-mate Steve Perryman

Gilzean (back row, third left), with manager Mauricio Pochettino immediately to his left, joins other former Spurs stars, including Greaves (front row), and more current staff at the training ground in 2017

Gilzean back at White Hart Lane and being interviewed pitchside by Paul Coyte

Ian Gilzean (left), Alan's son and former Tottenham and Dundee player, with author Mike Donovan

The King of White Hart Lane with his 'people' at the stadium's closing ceremony following victory over Manchester United in May 2017

Hand-written letter by Gilzean to Spurs fan Karen Mitchell and her Dundee-supporting husband Jim

2 STUART CRESCENT
COUPAR ANGUS
PERTH PH13 9EB

15 MARCH '92

...r Mitchell,

...n receipt of your very interesting ...my son - Ian, forwarded it, ...present address.

...were born in Edmonton — a true supporter, I spent 10 very happy ...laying for Spurs and remember ...the Cheshunt training ground, ...ately it has now become a housing ...and Spurs now train at Mill Hill.

...have a home in the South at ...near St Stephens church, no doubt ...ow the area well. But am ...n Scotland looking after my ...who is in his 90th year.

...you done mind if I address your ...d in the second half of the letter

...r Mitchell,
...wife informs me that you are a ...g Dark Blues fan, and collect ...from former players, re-calling ...favourite games for the club,

my favourite game for the club, was the final game in the Championship winning season v St Johnstone at Muirton Park, Perty. Finally because it was the first major medal in my football career and also as it was the first time Dundee had won the League Championship, it also gave the club its first taste of European Competition — yes the early sixties was very exciting times at Dens Park and hopefully — happy times will soon be back.

During my spell in football — I signed for Dundee in January '56 and finished at Tottenham in 1974. I was very fortunate to play for two such good clubs, who always emphasised to play attractive football and were very successful doing so.

Finally I would like to wish you both lots of happiness in the future and success for Dundee and Spurs.

Kindest regards
Alan Gilzean

Gilzean with Karen Mitchell

Gilzean memorial programme: Dundee v Dunfermline (July 2018)

The programme for Gilzean's memorial service

A minute's applause from Spurs players and fans before the first home game of the 2018/2019 season against Fulham at Wembley

A letter of condolence from FIFA president Gianni Infantino to the Scottish FA on the passing of Gilzean

29

The King's Scribes

THE CONTEMPORARY writers loved Alan Gilzean, the King of White Hart Lane and Dens Park, describing him in either florid, amusing, affectionate or jaw-droppingly impressed tones. Or combining most or all of those attitudes in their prose. The artist amid artisans. Always.

IVAN PONTING (*Tottenham Hotspur Player by Player*): The difference between Alan Gilzean and the majority of his peers was the gulf between a Van Gogh and a competent, even excellent painting by a lesser artist. A cursory glance at the canvases by anyone but a true connoisseur might offer the impression that there was little to choose between them; closer examination, of course, would reveal the subtlety of colour, composition and texture that lifted the Dutch master into a class of his own. So it was with the King of White Hart Lane, who provided the Tottenham fans with everything they demand of their idols – sheer quality invested with character and style.

Pale, balding and frequently besuited, the intelligent Scot fitted the popular image of stockbroker or accountant rather than that of star centre-forward. Indeed, one irreverent team-mate reckoned that, even in his 20s, Alan looked the league's oldest player, while others spoke of an ungainly figure with one shoulder higher than the other. But dress him in a football kit, give him a ball and suddenly the butterfly emerged from the chrysalis.

TOMMY GALLACHER (*Dundee Courier*): An example of the great esteem with which he is remembered in Dundee as a player of exceptional ability was provided … when he returned to the city to play for a Dundee select in a benefit game for Dennis Gillespie, a long-serving player with city rivals Dundee United. A crowd of 11,000, one of the biggest gates of the season, turned up at Tannadice for the game and there is no doubt that the player the crowd wanted to see most was Alan Gilzean.

Chants of Gillie rang around Tannadice Street in increasing volume before the game and during it, and you could sense the expectancy among the crowd every time he touched the ball. The Spurs favourite did not let the fans down. The old touches were there. The clever flicks with the head. The concealed pass, and the ability to always be in the right place at the right time were still very much in evidence nine years later; and how those nostalgic fans lapped it up. You see, they remember[ed] Gilzean as a star well before the London crowds were able to appreciate it. They had seen him pop in over 50 goals in a season and score regularly week after week. They saw him play for Dundee when they won their first-ever league championship. They remember him scoring four goals against Rangers, at Ibrox, as great an individual performance as ever seen in the famous Glasgow ground.

They recall him scoring nine goals including two hat-tricks against Cologne and Sporting Lisbon in Dundee, their first venture in the European Cup. Despite his association with Spurs, Alan Gilzean will always be linked with Dundee as one of the greatest players ever to represent the club … The goals, the honours, the acclaim, all amassed in 17 years as a senior player have not changed Alan Gilzean one little bit. He was always a good player and a good bloke.

JACK McLEAN (*Scottish Daily Mail*): Strangely I suppose I have met very few footballers socially. This is probably because although I may have been impressed by players on the pitch, it is hard to be impressed by most of them off it. An exception was former Dundee player Alan Gilzean, whom I knew when he was the darling of the White Hart Lane crowds. I used to have the occasional drink with him, especially when he was upsetting the Spurs management for refusing to wear the club's rather tacky blazer [Gilly (sic) sported Saville Row suits] and wouldn't share rooms with team-mates. 'Most of my team-mates sit up all night reading *Commando* comics,' he once told me. 'It is like being in third year at school.' If you think Alan was being disdainful about his fellow players you should [have] heard him on footie management. But Gilly [sic] did not distain his public. He was the most approachable of stars.

FRANK McGHEE (*Daily Mirror*): This man [Gilzean] is one of those rare ones with a style all his own, completely original and different, not the product of some stereotyped coaching system. The way he moves, runs, shoots and heads are all the product of a talent as natural to him as breathing. He reminds me of no other player I've ever seen and I doubt whether I will be lucky enough to see another who reminds me of him.

HARRY HARRIS (*Tottenham Herald*): How to miss a story right under your nose! I was giving out the prizes of autographed footballs to the winners of the *Weekly Herald*'s competition prior to Alan Gilzean's testimonial night at the Lane. I was so nervous standing out there in front of the big crowd on a cold night that I completely missed a fan running on to the pitch to kiss the feet of the balding striker with the deft heading ability. Didn't ... know anything about what happened until I saw it (a photograph) in the *London Evening News* the next day.

KEN JONES (*Sunday Mirror*): There is more grey than black in what is left of his hair, but the skill is still special, delicate and subtle but no less murderous for that. The man is good value and not only because of definitive and exciting headwork, although that part of his game will always be memorable. What really appeals is the quality of instinctive football intelligence which is apparent in most of the things which Gillie has always attempted on behalf of Spurs.

If anything his popularity has grown, multiplying at the back end of a career which has been curious only because Alan Gilzean has not always looked as good as we know he is. He doesn't think deeply about football. It happens to be something he does well and that is enough for him. It's certainly enough for his admirers ... The good days are still plentiful. Those who don't know him well may be disturbed by what seems to be an aloof, almost distant, attitude. Gillie, of course, isn't that way at all. He knows his way around and is good company. Above all he can play football better than most. We should be grateful for that.

REG DRURY (*News of the World*): He [Gilzean] was an instant success when he played his first game for Spurs, a 2-2 home draw with Everton in 1964, and retained his popularity with the White Hart Lane crowd right until his final appearance ... In fact, quite remarkably, his value to the team increased as he reached the veteran stage. Perhaps the greatest tribute to Gillie is that in his time at Tottenham he earned a place in the elite company of the most skilful players ever to represent the club – even though he arrived after the glory, glory days of the Double team.

JEFF POWELL (*Daily Mail*): Gillie kept alive the hope that skill, flair and subtlety could again prevail over the rule of the stud. It would have been easy for the deft flicks of Gilzean's head and the exquisite timing of his runs, passes and goalscoring shots to flourish in the Tottenham Double team ... He kept faith with his own talent through a negative age ... and through it all remained a genuinely nice man. Football is in his debt.

NORMAN GILLER (*Daily Express*): Alan was not only one of my favourite footballers, but also one of my favourite people. You had to serve an apprenticeship with Gilly [sic] before you won his confidence. He was always a guarded, private man who never sought the publicity spotlight. His next boast would have been his first.

When he allegedly went missing after his retirement, I questioned him about what were rumoured as his 'lost' years. He gave me a long, silent stare and then said, 'Well I always knew where I was.'

Gillie was an extraordinarily gifted forward who could thread a ball through the eye of a needle. He specialised in flick headers, and was an intelligent positional player who often popped up in unmarked places that caught defenders napping.

BRIAN GLANVILLE (*Sunday Times*): The young fans have always loved him: 'Gilzean, Gilzean' they sing, 'Born is the King of White Hart Lane'. His fellow players swear by him. When … I wrote an appreciative profile of him for the *Sunday Times*, the warmth with which his fellow Spurs players spoke about him was remarkable. 'If it wasn't for Alan,' said Martin Peters to Martin Chivers. 'We two Martins wouldn't get the goals we do.'

What Alan Gilzean has, in super-abundance, is natural ability … Gillie is that not-so-rare phenomenon, the anti-athlete whose longevity and stamina put to shame those who look physically so much better endowed. Tall, dark, saturnine, prematurely bald, he was never a player who immediately caught the eye. Even at his best, he was inclined to do well by stealth, rather than explosion. Despite his great technical skill, there was none of the galvanic twists and turns of a Cruyff, the gymnastic marvels of a Pele. Nevertheless, his effectiveness round and near the goal was always formidable, and his sense of the game, his sharp awareness of what was going on around him, allowed him to make other people play as well.

What the young fans sensed in Gilzean, I think, was his essential decency and modesty; though of course these would have gone for nothing were it not for his immense ability. There was never anything flashy or pretentious about him, on or off the field. While other London players were conspicuously enjoying the good life, in the supposedly 'good' garish places, Gilzean was having a better time than they because he was his own man, doing what he wanted rather than what passing fashion dictated … Perhaps it was appropriate that my first meeting with Gilzean, soon after he had come down to London from Dundee, was in that gateway to the provinces, the Great Northern Hotel; the sort of place that might have been invented by Tom Webster, a place where white waistcoats and gold watch chains, the 'uniform' of the pre-war director, still seemed to haunt the corridors.

I liked him then, I like him now; was beguiled at once by his honesty, his objectivity. He knows his own value, of course; knows that such things as his outstanding skill in the air are things with which you are born, rather than things which you can learn. The hectic life of modern football and the capital have flowed around and over him, leaving him untouched, uncorrupted.

I think of ... Davies's book [*The Glory Game*]. Of Gilzean being brutally kicked from behind by a Dynamo Bucharest player in Rumania [sic], getting up, and calmly playing on. Of Gilzean saying he had no particular ambition or intention for when he had finished playing. Like a Scottish Micawber, he was waiting for something to turn up ... Too many players, alas, have tried too hectically to make things happen, and thus been drawn into the grasp of those who've fleeced them. Gillie, rolling along from day to day in life as he has rolled shrewdly along from moment to moment on the field, is unlikely to ever let that happen.

He was not always as cool as he was that cold afternoon in Bucharest; was capable of retaliation in his earlier days. But he has learned that this is futile, particularly for a player like himself, who prevails through talent, rather than force. Of the many goals I have seen him score, the one which sticks most in the mind is perhaps the one he got against Red Star in the UEFA Cup at Tottenham, himself beginning the move, if I remember right, and certainly concluding it with an immediate stab, as he ran to meet the low, left-wing cross. How simple it looked; but then that has always been Gillie's gift; to make the difficult look easy.'

FRANK GILFEATHER (Sky Sports and freelancer writer): I saw Gillie play a lot and I interviewed him when he was at Tottenham. He was so graceful. Unbelievably great in the air. I don't think people fully appreciated just how good he was until he went to Tottenham. Spurs were a huge, great team and he fitted in so easily. Proved a huge success. I think a lot of the Dundee fans were reawakened to his abilities after he left. It was like, 'Well, we had that player. What a player he is. We nurtured him.' That's just a feeling I get. They loved him even more when they saw what he did.

I have a theory about all great sportsman like that. When they go into the big league, without being brash or arrogant about it, they think to themselves, 'Why can't I do this?' It is an inner-confidence, a belief. A steely thing in the brain. Gilzean was quiet, softly spoken, understated, just got on with it – not a nature you might expect of a top footballer – and probably took the view, 'This is the best living I'm ever going to make so I'll work hard to make sure it works for me. I'm going to be up alongside some of these great players. I might be a guy from Coupar Angus but players come from small places. John White did. No reason I can't.'

I was an amateur boxer and helped Scotland beat England twice at the Royal Albert Hall. First time, I had a cloud over me, worried about the fight in front of 7,000. My coach said, 'Our opponent has two arms and legs the same as you.' I don't think Gilzean would have worried about that sort of thing. As it happened, I was a featherweight but another boxer was edging me out as I was moving up to lightweight – Ken Buchanan – who became a world champion.

I remember seeing Alan in Dundee's first European Cup game against Cologne. I was 16 and a trainee reporter and away on a job in Edinburgh. I told my boss, 'I'm going to have to go to Dundee tonight.' He said 'You can't do that.' I said, 'Listen I'll be back in the morning to finish this job.' He asked, 'Why are you going?' I told him, 'Dundee are playing Cologne – I've a ticket.' It was packed under the floodlights. I thought, 'This is the real deal.' I was back in time for work the next day.

I remember my boxing trainer Jim Munro – who never missed a Dundee game – went to AC Milan for the first leg of the semi-final and he met the future Pope who was archbishop at the cathedral in the Italian city at the time, and he gave him a tour round the cathedral.

My father-in-law was a big Dundee fan and, although my family were Celtic supporters, he told me, 'If you are going to marry my daughter you are going to have to be a Dundee supporter.'

Gilzean was hugely admired by Tottenham fans. I was doing a television programme once. Interviewed John Duncan at White Hart Lane and when the people found out I was from Dundee all they wanted to talk about was Gilzean. They loved him. He was brilliant there.

Denis Law is a good friend of mine. When he was a kid his mother and father used to tie a ball of wool on a clothes pulley in the kitchen and pull it up. That's how he developed his great leap. I understand Gilzean did something similar.

Alan and Denis were also exceptionally brave. Never pulled out of anything. How many goals did Gilzean score with his head low enough to put him in danger of having his skull kicked in. He was also a penalty-box, even six-yard forward and, if you put the ball over, like Denis, you'd expect him to get to the ball in that crowded area.

Another thing was that Gilzean and his Dundee team were able to produce fantastic football on awful, churned up pitches. Like public park pitches!

30

The King's People

KAREN MITCHELL: I have been a Spurs supporter along with my dad for as long as I can remember. My first clear memory is of the open-top bus celebrations after the 1967 cup win over Chelsea, cheering them on from Edmonton High Street. I can't remember seeing Alan, although he had played in the match and was there on the Sunday.

My family moved from Edmonton to Cheshunt in 1971. I was eight years old and already had my first Spurs strip, which I would wear with pride. The exciting thing for me about the move was that Spurs's training ground wasn't far from where I lived. My friends and I would regularly go there and watch the team train. There was no such thing as security, you just turned up, sat on the grass banking, and watched your idols work up a sweat!

My favourite time was pre-season, as you could be there nearly all day. The players would train in the morning, go and have their lunch, in what I remember as a basic one-level all-purpose building, then they'd come out again for the afternoon session. There would also be the odd low-key friendly to watch (I remember them playing Norwich one afternoon). We would sit about, chase after mishit balls, and patiently wait to get autographs.

The thing I remember about Alan was that he looked so much older than most of the team. He was already 'steely grey, and had a bald patch', whereas Steve Perryman and Martin Chivers, Joe Kinnear etc. all had longish hair. Only Ralph Coates could match him with his comb-over! They would all come out after training finished dressed in flared trousers and flash shirts, whereas I seem to remember Alan dressed more formally.

Some of the players were more outgoing and approachable. Alan seemed more reserved, quiet, it took a bit more nerve to speak to him, as he could seem somewhat gruff to us kids. In hindsight, I think it was his Scottish accent, and his reserved nature. However, he would always sign whatever you put before him.

When I moved to Dundee in 1975, I was aware that Alan had played for Dundee FC. (At that time I didn't know that he wasn't the only Dee to make his way to White Hart Lane.) I was also aware that Dundee played in dark blue, and white, so they were obviously going to be the team for me. Also, our next-door neighbour was Bobby Robinson, a current member of the team, who, like Alan, was another gentleman.

I married Jim in 1983, a life-long Dee, and together we support the team through thick and thin. We have attended many functions, player of the year, legend nights etc., and because of this I had the opportunity of meeting Alan on a few occasions. It has been an honour to sit and speak to him about those years back in the early 1970s. He really does deserve the legendary status, and high regard he is remembered by at both clubs.

NORRIE PRICE (*Up Wi' The Bonnets* author): I was 11 years old at the beginning of Dundee FC's championship-winning season of 1961/62, and 14 when Gillie departed for Spurs in December 1964. It was a hugely successful spell for the club and the scoring exploits of Alan Gilzean were a key factor. For kids of my age, Gillie was simply our own *Boy's Own* hero so, as you could imagine, it was a great thrill when 30 years later he agreed to be interviewed and wrote the foreword to my Dundee FC History, *Up Wi' The Bonnets*, after I'd got his contact details from Jim Hendry who'd written the excellent *Dundee Greats*.

In the early 60s we used to play small-sided games in the adjacent Dawson Park where we'd pretend to be the stars of top sides like Tottenham Hotspur or our own high-flying Dundee FC. For Spurs it would be Jimmy Greaves, Bobby Smith or Cliff Jones;

for Dundee, Andy Penman, Alan Cousin or, most popular of all, Alan Gilzean.

Frustratingly, I never saw Dundee as they went on to take the title though I read and heard plenty. Douglas Scott, one of the 'bigger boys' who lived in nearby Caenlochan Road, was a regular attender and he used to regale me with stirring tales from Dens Park and Alan Gilzean in particular.

It was September 1962 before I saw my first match against Aberdeen soon after Dundee's incredible 8-1 European Cup victory over Cologne. This was a 12th-birthday treat from my grandfather and my uncle but it was going badly until Gillie leapt high to head a last-gasp equaliser in a 2-2 draw.

In my first away game against Hibs a year later, Gillie again took centre stage. Outside Dundee Tay Bridge railway station myself and schoolfriend Billy Dryden spotted Alan Gilzean and Alex Hamilton, who along with the rest of the Dundee FC party were travelling on the same train to Edinburgh.

We had them pose for a photo taken with my Brownie 127 camera and our day was complete when Gillie scored all four goals – the third an audacious piece of skill – in a 4-0 Easter Road rout! Moving on to a bouncing though ball, Gillie chose neither to shoot or dribble past Ronnie Simpson, instead flicking the ball up, then turning to hook the ball back across his shoulder and over the advancing keeper! When I think about it, I don't recall many Gillie tap-ins. Watching from the Provie Road terracings on a sunny afternoon following Ian Ure's transfer to Arsenal, we saw the full range of the Gilzean scoring repertoire in a 3-2 win over Third Lanark. The first was a thumping 25-yarder, the second a classic flashing header and for the third he burst through to win a one-on-one with the keeper for the decisive goal.

Style, Gilzean was far more than a goalscorer. Bags of skill. In a break in play against Dunfermline, whereas another striker Bobby Waddell just sat on the ball, Gilzean displayed his keepy-up skills, left foot, right foot, thighs, ball stuck on top of head, then rolled slowly down his back between his shoulder blades.

In contrast to his laid-back off-field demeanour, on field Gillie was a predator with an absolute hunger to get amongst the goals. I once read that 'Gilzean padded the penalty box with great intent', an apt description for a big man who, such a powerful runner, was light on his feet and moved in so quickly for the kill in the area.

He was regarded as 'Gillie the King' long before he acquired the mantle of King of White Hart Lane, the 'Gilzean, Gilzean' chants often booming around Dens Park notably when he got his 40th to beat Alec Stott's Dundee record for a season and later when he smashed the 50-goal barrier. On visits to my grandparents in Arbroath I found Gilzean was a hero there too.

Another pal, Alan Yule, was with his father as he described Dundee's demolition of Cologne, 'We were there on the Provie Road, Dad, weren't we?' to which his father laughingly replied, 'Gillie gave the Germans hell!' And such was his hero-worship that when his new dog learned to knock the ball into the air with his nose if it bounced while we played 'heidies' in the back-yard, he was lovingly christened 'Gillie'.

I'd twice previously come across Gillie and Hammy at the Dundee swimming baths. And in the summer of 1964 there they were again, this time in Arbroath heading towards the now long-gone Arbroath Swimming Pool – perhaps to watch the Miss Arbroath contest – and Alan and myself were able to get their autographs and bask in the glow of stardom.

At Dave Forbes's Dundee FC 'All Stars' dinner at the Invercarse Hotel in 2016, I asked Gillie whether he felt swimming had given him the flexibility to leap so high but he simply laughed modestly, saying, 'Any exercise is good exercise.'

Gilzean was also a top man at international level and I believe ought to have won many more caps than he did. He will always be most famous for his winning header against England in 1964 but I also recall a memorable incident when he and Denis Law headed the ball back and forth to each other in almost a personal game of head tennis during the World Cup qualifier against Poland – which Scotland eventually lost 2-1 – before 105,000 at Hampden in October 1965.

Thereafter, it was always a pleasure to watch him on TV for Scotland – who he never let down – or Spurs. Dundee's loss was Tottenham's gain. Having moved to Aberdeen, I was on hand to once again see my hero in October 1973, when Tottenham Hotspur visited Pittodrie in a UEFA Cup tie. Then in his twilight years as a player, how would Gillie at 5ft 11in [sic] fare against the towering physicality of the Dons centre-half Willie Young. Repeatedly it appeared that Young would win the long, high ball, only for Gilzean to rise with perfect timing to head-flick on with his balding head. For the 'young pretender' it was a footballing lesson from the master as Spurs went on to a 5-2 aggregate win.

At a dinner in Dundee's Angus Hotel in 1992 to celebrate the 30th anniversary of Dundee's title win, guest speaker Jim Leishman's adjectival vocabulary appeared to be limited to fu***ing this, f***ing that and when I looked across the room there was Gillie amongst his old team-mates, first frowning, then scowling as the 'performance' continued.

His funeral was a who's who of Dundee legends including his remaining Dundee team-mates, representatives of the club and the current squad, Archie Knox, Jocky Scott, Gordon Wallace as well as the smartly dressed Tottenham contingent. It was a sad, sad day but for me and good friend Peter Shepherd [it provided] a great thrill – to shake hands with one Spurs legend in particular, Cliff Jones. I'd much admired him as part of that great Spurs team that reached the European Cup semi-final in 1962 – and talked to him about a picture of the Stan Matthews testimonial featuring Jones, Greaves and Gilzean.

Archie Knox reverently told me of his own fond memories of Gillie and how he'd been there that famous day when Dundee – his team, too – had defeated Rangers 5-1 at Ibrox. The whole occasion and the reception afterwards at Dens Park was handled extremely well. [Managing director] John Nelms, Bob Hynd and co and the club staff can take great credit for that.

Gillie not so great with the penalties. Following a miss/failure in a finely poised League Cup quarter-final against Rangers at Dens in 1960, Andy Penman very successfully assumed spot-kick duties. Failing illustrated in Penman's absence at Easter Road, Gillie had failed to convert for his hat-trick, only to net after Simpson's save.

NICK EDWARDS (Spurs Supporters' Trust): If I was asked to choose just one word to sum up Alan Gilzean it would be finesse. My first memories of watching Spurs live in the late 60s are etched with images of this tough but graceful Scot partnering Jimmy Greaves, Cliff Jones and Martin Chivers. Four players gifted in such different ways, who together formed such a potent strike force.

Gillie played in the first match I attended against Southampton in April 1968 and, although he was the only one of the quartet who did not score in the 6-1 win, I recall him playing a key part in the fluid attacking football on show that day, which helped hook me on this lifelong passion. He subsequently remained a lynchpin during my formative years as a fan into the early 70s.

In those days, as I entered my teens, I used to stand at the front of the Park Lane and so I was effectively looking up at the action from close quarters. That vantage point allowed you to smell the hallowed turf and see the sweat glistening on our heroes' brows. Looking back now, when our players, even the veterans, all seem so young to me, it's amusing and ironic to recall how old Gillie looked with his balding pate and thin hair slicked back at the sides.

Oh but how skilfully he used that shiny scalp with the precision of a scalpel! He was able to direct the ball seemingly at will in any direction he chose. One unforgettable trick was to flick a long throw from Chivers into the path of an onrushing team-mate, who would as often as not plant the ball firmly in the net.

Gilzean was no slouch on the deck either, with his ability to shimmy past bewildered defenders, turn on the ball, lay off passes with both feet and, of course, score plenty of goals himself with shots that could be as ferocious or subtle as the circumstances required.

He was a true master of his trade and it is no accident that he earned the nickname 'King of White Hart Lane' in the chant dedicated to him, which any Spurs fan of that era joined in with gusto.

GEORGE NORRIE: Gillie was a good friend of our family. Sometimes on a Saturday after the game he used to come for his tea at my gran's house in Broughty Ferry. He was good friends with my uncle George Sievwright. After their tea they used to go to The Chalet [an entertainment venue] in Broughty Ferry [close to Dundee]. Also, I think they were in the army together along with big Ron Yeats. Sure we have a photo of them in the army football team. George played for Dundee United.

ADE SHAW (a musician who has played bass guitar for Hawkwind, Arthur 'Fire' Brown and The Bevis Frond and followed Spurs since the 1950s): I always thought Berbatov reminded me a little of Gilzean. They both had a wonderful touch, although Gillie was more effective with his head, probably the best header of a ball I've seen at Spurs. Wonderfully deft and superb at finding his strike partner with head or foot. He didn't look like an athlete, being round-shouldered and wiry but was far stronger than his appearance would indicate and was as hard as nails. He made a wonderful foil for Jimmy Greaves.

STEWART RAMSEY: I consider myself to be very fortunate in seeing Alan Gilzean play for Dundee Football Club. As for my memories, they are plentiful; however, one stands out from others. On a late autumn evening in 1963, Sporting Lisbon visited Dens Park on European Cup duty. The game itself is a little fuzzy these days but [there was] a magic moment when Gillie got the ball on the halfway line. He set off on what I consider to be one of his best Dundee goals, leaving their defence in tatters and quick as a flash the ball hits the back of the net. There are many goals I still remember. His last one against St Johnstone as well. However, the Sporting Lisbon one will always be my favourite.

JAN OGINSKI (who attended *The Spurs Show* event at Dingwalls, north London, in 2013): Alan Gilzean. Football genius. Did have the good fortune to watch him play for Dundee all those years ago. What memories. Greavsie and Gillie. They don't make them like that anymore. What is incredible, in today's context, is how modest and 'real' they [Gilzean was with Pat Jennings] are unlike our contemporaries.

BOB COOK: Met the great man at the 40th anniversary of the [Dundee] league winners. I was born 11 November 1961. The day Gillie scored four at Ibrox on the way to the title. He also knew that I was wearing Forbes tartan that night as it was also his family tartan.

JOHN DAVIES: Alan Gilzean was a superb player and fantastic with the head. However, he was also good with the boot as I can testify. I remember being hit on the head by a shot of his that went just wide [Spurs v Middlesbrough] in the FA Cup in 1965/66. The person behind me tried to pull me out of the way of the shot but just succeeded in getting me in direct contact with the oncoming ball. Alan Gilzean. Remarkable player and one of my all-time greats.

STEVE MARTIN: I had the pleasure of knowing Alan over many years in my capacity as director of the club [Dundee]. Every year we brought out new club ties he would come into the boardroom and say to me, 'Nice one, Steve,' and basically gave me that look of, 'Can I have it?' He did get them of course but we used to laugh about it a lot. Great man. Great family. Sadly missed.

DAVE HARLEY: Wonderful player – unique in his heading style – how we [Spurs] could have done with him on quite a few occasions since he left the club.

ALLY DONALDSON (former Dark Blues team-mate of Gilzean's): A Gillie memory. Dundee Football Club were in London to play Millwall and we were taken to watch Spurs v Portsmouth in the FA Cup. Spurs get a free kick just over the halfway line. Mike England launched the ball into the penalty box and Gillie headed the ball into the top left-hand corner of the net from the penalty spot. Genius.

ANDREAS KOUMI (Memory Lane film-maker and Tottenham community worker): I know he preceded Hoddle as the eponymous King of White Hart Lane in the fans' song, which is testimony to his legendary status and quality.

BILL GIBB: My best memory of Gillie was against Cologne in the European Cup as he soared above their players to head home. I can still see their faces as they had never encountered anything like Gillie in full flight.

ZULKIFLY OSMAN (Malaysia Spurs): Alan Gilzean together with Martin Chivers made up one of the best twin-strike partnerships during the late 1960s and early 1970s. He was a regular Scottish international. A very humble footballer. One of the most underrated British footballers.

'BILL CAMPBELL'S GHOST': A few years back I went to RBS for a mortgage in Edinburgh and the young lad in the bank was Bobby Wishart's nephew. We had been chatting football whilst form-filling and I had mentioned I was a Dee. I knew Bobby from living a couple of streets from me, so that came into the chat too. I mentioned that Gillie was my Dad's hero and I had been brought up on tales of his excellence. I had to return to the bank a few days later to complete some other formalities but the lad asked me to meet him at my local branch rather than HQ in town, so that was very convenient for me. When I turned up he had Bobby Wishart there to say hello and ... Gillie! Gillie was staying at Bobby's on a trip north. What a great surprise. Unfortunately there were no camera phones then so it's all in my memory bank.

ADRIAN AKERS (world-ranked real tennis ace who has played Prince Edward, and Spurs supporter): My memory of Alan Gilzean ... taking over from Bobby Smith – the archetypal big barging bullying centre-forward. He initially seemed like a poor substitute ... balding, middle-aged (or so he seemed to me as a teenager) but so good with both feet and even more so with his head. Sadly, I never saw him in the flesh as I didn't go to White Hart Lane until the 1980s when Glenn Hoddle was in his prime.

RONNIE ANDERSON: As a ball boy at the Dens from 1960 to 1964, have had the pleasure as a young lad to have met all the great players of that era. So have too many to single out one, unfortunately, except the possible time, if my memory serves me, when he [Gilzean] was sent off at Dens Park near the end of the game for walloping the left-back of AC Milan who had been kicking hell out of Gordon Smith the whole game.

BARRY DAVIES (Broadcaster and Spurs supporter since the 1940s): I remember Alan Gilzean well, especially the subtlety of his heading.

STEVE CLARK: I was sitting in The Phoenix bar the Sunday after Gillie's funeral. A young couple sat next to us and we overheard this conversation:

> Him: Alan Gilzean is dead
> Her: Wha' he?
> Him: He used to pay for Coupar Angus Juniors.
> Her: Never heard o um.
> Bizarre.

TONY HARRIS: As majestic a footballer that there has been. Up there with Denis Law in terms of somebody who could hang in the air and gracefully head the ball. Jimmy Greaves has publicly said – and who can disagree – that he was the best striker he ever played with. I suppose one tribute would be that some 40 years and thousands of footballers later anyone who ever watched him play for whichever side of the fence they sat will remember him. He really was in a special class.

JOE JEFFERY: I remember the goal Gillie scored to make his record-breaking tally. He beat a couple of Partick defenders, rounded the keeper and blasted the ball into the net from all of two feet. Would probably get booked for that these days. Happy memories.

'BORN IS THE KING OF WHITE HART LANE': I was privileged enough to have seen the magnificent Gillie play live and on TV in the early 1970s and on DVDs of our cup finals and league matches of the era. The partnerships he had with Greaves and subsequently Chivers were an absolute joy to behold and there can't have ever been many better headers of a ball in football. We used to sing 'Gilzean, Gilzean … born is the King of White Hart Lane' and he earned and deserved that accolade. The song was subsequently given to Hoddle. Good company. Gillie largely kept to himself in recent years but was thankfully brought back into the Spurs family a few seasons back to do corporate and hospitality work for the club. He was treated and thought of like a king and older fans loved his on-pitch half-time interviews. A great Scot in a long list of great Scots to play for Tottenham.

'GBLUE': In my opinion, the best player who played in dark blue, well worth his legend status.

ALAN SWAIN (Spurs historian and supporter since the early 1950s): I have very fond memories of Alan Gilzean and I believe I was at the match when he made his Spurs debut against Everton back in 1964. I don't think I have ever seen such a finer header of the ball as Alan Gilzean. Very rarely did you see him make a bullet header as he was more renowned for his deft flicks and glances often resulting in a goal or flicked into the path of an onrunning Jimmy Greaves or Cliff Jones.

Cliff Jones was also a fine header of the ball but for such a small man it was his jackknife style of header and his ability to outjump players much taller than him that always impressed me. As for Jimmy Greaves, any kind of header was a rarity as he often acknowledged himself. When it came to bullet headers then Bobby Smith was your man, not only did he take the ball but very often the opposing player as well. What great memories! The closest player in a Spurs shirt who I have seen that matched Alan Gilzean was Dimitar Berbatov. They both had that languid style and a deceptive pace. Both players were renowned for their ability to flick or glance the ball using their head as well as contributing a good number of goals each season.

Back in January 1965, Spurs had narrowly avoided defeat by Torquay United when playing an away game in the FA Cup. As

I recall, Torquay had a young forward named Robin Stubbs who had caused Spurs all sorts of trouble and the match was nicely set up for the replay at White Hart Lane.

I attended the replay with my Dad and we were standing in the old enclosure in front of the West Stand. It was a cold January evening under the lights of White Hart Lane but on this night we witnessed the birth of the G-Men as both Gilzean and Greaves were mesmerising. I know that Torquay were lower league opposition but between Gilzean and Greaves they tore Torquay apart. This was the beginnings of a wonderful partnership that stood Tottenham in good stead for many years.

Alan Gilzean was never a physical player but able to look after himself and perhaps a stereotypical model professional throughout his playing career.

His Scottish roots came to the fore in 1967 when, along with Dave Mackay and Jimmy Robertson, they sang 'I Belong to Glasgow' on the Spurs commemorative record for the FA Cup Final that I still have in my possession.

'TRAVELLING DEE': Probably not of much interest to many DFC supporters but it is indelible in my mind, in one of my first visits to the 'dancing' who should appear next to us but Gillie and Penman. Naturally we started talking to them, then from underneath their coats appeared two bottles of Iron Bru which they claimed was half scotch. They wouldn't share with us as they thought we were too young. But it didn't matter my heroes were actually normal.

TERRY RANSOME: He [Gilzean] really was my boyhood hero along with Jimmy Greaves and John White. Never seen a better header of the ball and his little deft touches. Modern footballers should watch videos of this legend. We will never see his like again.

'BUDGEM': RIP the King; 169 memories of a true great! Met him, his son Ian and grandson a couple of years back and what a lovely man. A bit embarrassed by the adulation people gave him. Had time for everyone.

'JAH WOMBLE': As a kid I was lucky enough to see Alan Gilzean play more than once. He managed to be both elegant and pretty damned hard on occasion. He was a cracking centre-forward either way, creating killer partnerships with both Jimmy Greaves and Martin Chivers, the latter of which was in full swing when I first supported the team.

'BLUE DRAGON': A legend from my youth. Only one Gillie. What a real superstar.

'DFCMAN': I count myself fortunate to have been a teenager in the 1960s and to have many of his memorable goals home and away for Dundee etched in my memory.

'ISLAYDARKBLUE': Was fortunate enough to see Alan Gilzean play for Dundee including the 10-2 win against Queen of the South where Gillie scored seven goals.

'HIP PRIEST': RIP Gillie. You were some guy.

'AMOR DE COSMOS' (QPR and Hitchin Town fan): There are few pure strikers from that era whose play could be termed elegant but he was one – and probably the best of them.

'TEE REX' (Exeter City fan): One of the biggest names of my childhood. *The Big Match* (London Weekend) was my first TV window onto football. Spurs of the early 1970s featured a lot. Only 22 caps for Scotland and just too old for their World Cup [finals]. Unlucky.

'ADAMS HOUSE CAT' (Notts County fan): Saw him play a couple of times for Spurs. A fine player and seemed a modest man.

Appendix

QI (Quite Interesting)

WHAT'S IN A NAME?

* The name Gilzean is of Scottish and Gaelic origin meaning 'servant of St John', according to George Fraser Black (1866–1948) in his *Surnames of Scotland*.

   Black wrote: 'Gillean, Gilleon, Gillian, Gilzean, Gellion (in Inverness): These names are said to be all connected with Clan Maclean, from Gaelic Gilll' Eoin, "servant of (S.) John", once a personal name. Through the imaginary Gillean of the Mackenzie pedigree "a Geraldine descent was provided also for the Macleans."

   'Gaelic Gill'Eoin, "servant of (S.) John." The z is pronounced y. James Gilzean in Trows, 1696. and four more of the name are recorded in Moray (Moray). Gillzean 1695, Gilzeane 1633. See Gillean and Maclean.'

* According to the Forbears.io website, Gilzean is the 694,952nd most common surname in the world. And that 'approximately' 422 people bear the surname. It is most prevalent in the United States and the highest density of its use is in Jamaica.

* One of the occupations listed by Ancestry.com website for the Gilzean family in 1881 was 'General Clerk', not a million miles from the nature of Alan Gilzean's first job on leaving school.

   Ancestry.com state: 'In 1881, Annuitant (someone who receives an annuity), Farm Servant and Farmers Widow were the top-three reported jobs worked by Gilzean. The most common

Gilzean occupation in the UK was Annuitant. 7% per cent of Gilzean's were Annuitants. A less common occupation for the Gilzean family was General Clerk To Solicitor.'

* The Gilzean family name was in Scotland, the rest of the UK and USA between 1841 and 1920 according to Ancestry.com census records. Most were found in Scotland in figures totted up every ten years from 1841–1901. The genealogy company – based in Utah where Gillie's brother Eric was based when interviewed for the book – revealed that there are 1,000 census, 271 immigration and 105 military records available for the last name Gilzean.

* 'Notable people' with the surname Gilzean have been listed by Wikipedia, an online encyclopaedia, with Alan John top of their list, which also includes youngest son Ian and a 'fictional supervillain'.

It states: 'Alan Gilzean, former professional footballer; Andrew Gilzean, Labour Party politician; Butch Gilzean, fictional supervillain in the DC comics universe, better known as Solomon Grundy; Hugh Gilzean-Reid, Scottish journalist and politician; Ian Gilzean, former professional footballer.'

'A MUD BATH'

Tottenham Hotspur: Do you have any standout memories of your time behind the scenes at White Hart Lane?

Alan Gilzean: I have some great memories of my time at the club. However, if there was one not so good, it would be that in the winter months the White Hart Lane pitch was a mud bath. Older supporters will recall that in those days, unlike our marvellous bowling green-like pitch today, we had to play in such conditions. What I would give to have played on today's surface!

TH: Give us one of your memories which took place behind the scenes on a matchday at White Hart Lane.

AG: I recall arriving at White Hart Lane on a matchday just two hours before the kick-off of another FA Cup tie versus Burnley and being called into a meeting with Bill Nicholson. Bill informed me that Dave Mackay had taken ill and could not play, so he was playing Frank Saul at centre-forward and moving me to fill in for Dave. I thought to myself that was one hell of a job to try and fill the great Dave Mackay's boots. Fortunately for me, all turned out fine as we played really well as a team that day and we won.

TH: What is your abiding memory of your playing days at White Hart Lane?

AG: There are many reasons why I will always remember the Lane. I recall the fantastic atmosphere when I arrived at the stadium. In those days the Lane held 57,000 fans and the noise generated gave wonderful encouragement to the team, especially the fans on the Shelf – who had an individual song for each player. Wonderful memories that will live with me forever.

BITS AND PIECES

Gillie, with all the players and management in 1972, revealed fascinating facts and opinions as *The Glory Game* author Hunter Davies compiled lists for various appendices in a book rated a 'British football classic'.

A couple of warm-up stats like at 12st 7lb, Gilzean was the fourth-heaviest member of the playing staff behind Martin Chivers (13st 9lb), Mike England (13st 3lb) and Alan Mullery (12st 10lb). And with 22 caps he was the fifth most internationally decorated in the squad tucked in behind Martin Peters (55), Mullery (39), Pat Jennings (38) and England (35). That, as a bookkeeper at Coates, he was not the only player to have had a previous job, with Cyril Knowles a coal miner, defender Peter Collins an apprentice sheet metal worker and Terry Naylor a Smithfield meat market porter.

He views skill as the important quality a successful footballer needs. He said, 'Without skill you haven't got a chance. You could pick the best runner, the strongest athlete, but you couldn't turn him into a footballer unless he has the basic skill. I don't rate coaching very high. Any grade of manager or coach will give you that. That's what they're there for. I look upon training as getting fit to use the skills I've got naturally.'

He has a pre-match ritual. He said, 'I always have oils rubbed into my legs before a match. It's probably old age creeping up. But I haven't any superstitions. I never think about such things.'

He preferred playing football as a 15-year-old. He said, 'Football's meant to be enjoyed and I still enjoy it, but I probably enjoyed it more at 15. The finer points disappeared when England won the World Cup in 1966. Now the object is not to get beat at all costs.'

He read the *Daily* and *Sunday Express* and commented, 'There's nothing between them', when confirming his Tory politics.

His future? He said, 'I fancy going to South Africa for a year or so, play with some club and get a bit of sun. After that, I don't know. I never plan. I never worry. I've got no business interests at all. I admire wee Joe [Kinnear] with his property [business], but I couldn't do it. Today, I'm playing for Tottenham. Tomorrow, we'll have to wait and see.'

Statistics

DUNDEE

Honours

Scottish League Champions: 1961/62

European Cup semi-final: 1962/63

Scottish Cup runners-up: 1963/64

Scotland full caps: 5

Scottish League caps: 3

Scotland Under-23 caps: 3

Dundee Player of the Year: 1964

Dundee Hall of Fame (Legends Award): 2009

Dundee name a lounge after Gilzean: 2012

Club records

Top Overall Scorer: 169 goals in 190 competitive games

Top Scorer In One Season: 52 goals in 1963/64

Top European Scorer: 9 goals

Top Scorer In One Game: 7 goals against Queen of the South in 1962
(record shared with Bert Juliussen)

Top Hat-Trick Scorer: 17

Appearances and goals

League: 134 matches, 113 goals

Cup: 15 matches, 15 goals

League Cup: 24 matches, 26 goals

Europe: 8 matches, 9 goals
TOTAL: 190 matches, 169 goals

1961/62 – Scottish League championship
Appearances and goals
29 matches, 24 goals

League season
August
23rd: Falkirk 3-1 (Smith, Cousin, Wishart) a 7,000

September
9th: Dundee United 4-1 (Penman, Smith, Briggs og, Robertson) h 20,000
16th: Aberdeen 1-3 (Gilzean) a 12,000
23rd: Heart of Midlothian 2-0 (Gilzean 2) h 12,000
30th: Third Lanark 3-1 (Gilzean 2, Cousin) a 9,500

October
7th: Kilmarnock 5-3 (Watson og, Penman 3, Gilzean) h 14,000
14th: Motherwell 4-2 (Penman, pen, Cousin, Smith, Gilzean) a 15,000
21st: Dunfermline 2-1 (Cousin 2) a 10,000
28th: Partick Thistle 3-2 (Cousin 2, Penman, pen) h 16,000

November
4th: Celtic 2-1 (Wishart, Gilzean) h 24,500
11th: Rangers 5-1 (Gilzean 4, Penman) a 38,000
18th: Raith Rovers 5-4 (Gilzean 2, Wishart, Seith, Smith) h 15,000
25th: Hibernian 3-1 (Gilzean, Penman, Smith) a 16,000

December
2nd: Stirling Albion 2-2 (Robertson, Cousin) h 11,500
16th: Airdrieonians 5-1 (Wishart, Smith, Cousin, Robertson 2) h 11,500
23rd: St Mirren 1-1 (Wishart) a 11,000

January
6th: Falkirk 2-1 (Gilzean 2) h 15,000
13th: Heart of Midlothian 2-0 (Cousin, Gilzean) a 25,000
17th: Aberdeen 2-1 (Cousin, Penman, pen) h 16,000
20th: Third Lanark 2-1 (Penman, pen, Robertson) h 17,500
24th: St Johnstone 2-1 (Gilzean, Penman) h 16,000

February
3rd: Kilmarnock 1-1 (Cousin) a 14,000
10th: Motherwell 1-3 (Robertson) h 19,000
24th: Partick Thistle 0-3 a 15,000

March
3rd: Celtic 1-2 (Wishart) a 39,000
7th: Dunfermline 1-2 (Seith) h 17,500
14th: Rangers 0-0 h 35,000
17th: Raith Rovers 3-2 (Cousin, Penman 2) a 5,000
24th: Hibernian 1-0 (Waddell) h 12,000
31st: Stirling Albion 3-2 (Cousin, Smith, Gilzean) a 4,500

April
7th: Airdrieonians 2-1 (Penman 2, 1 pen) a 7,000
9th: Dundee United 2-1 (Gilzean 2) a 20,000
25th: St Mirren 2-0 (Cousin, Penman) h 20,000
28th: St Johnstone 3-0 (Gilzean 2, Penman) a 26,500
Gilzean also scored three in the League Cup

August
19th: Third Lanark 2-3 (Smith, Gilzean) a 12,000
26th: Airdrieonians 5-0 (Cousin, Smith, Penman, Gilzean 2) a 4,500
Total appearances: 35 matches 27 goals (top scorer)
* Dundee used 15 players through the league season: Pat Liney, Alex Hamilton, Bobby Cox, Bobby Seith, Ian Ure, Bobby Wishart, Gordon Smith, Andy Penman, Alan Cousin, Alan Gilzean, Hugh Robertson, Craig Brown (9 appearances), Bobby Waddell (4), George McGeachie

(3), Alex Stuart (2). Manager: Bob Shankly. Assistant: Sammy Kean. Physio: Lawrie Smith.

1962/63
Appearances and goals
League: 27 matches 24 goals

League Cup: 3 matches, 2 goals

Scottish Cup: 5 matches, 6 goals

European Cup: 8 matches, 9 goals

Total: 43 matches, 41 goals

European Cup run
5 September: Preliminary round, first leg: Cologne 8-1 (Hemmersbach og, Wishart, Robertson, Gilzean 3, Smith, Penman) h 25,000

Dundee: Slater, Hamilton, Cox, Seith, Ure, Wishart, Smith, Penman, Cousin, Gilzean, Robertson

Cologne (West Germany): Ewert, Regh, Sturm, Hemmersbach, Weilden, Benthaus, Thielen, Schäfer, Müllar, Habig, Harnig

26 September: Second leg, Cologne 0-4 a 40,000

Cologne: Schumacher, Schnellinger, Benthaus, Pott, Wilden, Regh, Habig, Hornig, Müller, Schäfer, Thielen

Dundee: Slater, Hamilton, Cox, Seith, Ure, Wishart, Smith, Penman, Cousin, Gilzean , Robertson

(Dundee win 8-5 on aggregate)

24 October: First round, first leg, Sporting Club of Portugal (Lisbon) 0-1 a 50,000

Sporting: Carvalho, Hilário, Carlos, Lucio, Morais, de Silva, Jülio, Domingos, Mascarenhas, Peridés, Sarmento

Dundee: Slater, Hamilton, Cox, Seith, Ure, Wishart, Smith, Penman, Cousin, Gilzean, Houston

31 October: Second leg, Sporting Club of Portugal 4-1 (Gilzean 3, Cousin) h 32,000

Dundee: Slater, Hamilton, Cox, Seith, Ure, Wishart, Smith, Penman, Cousin, Gilzean, Robertson

Sporting: Carvalho, Lino , Hilário, Carlos, Lucio, Jülio, Figuerido, Osvaldo, Mascarenhas, Domingos, Morias
(Dundee won 4-2 on aggregate)

6 March: Quarter-final, first leg, RSC Anderlecht 4-1 (Gilzean 2, Cousin, Smith) a 64,703
Anderlec: Fazekas, Cornelis, Heylans, Hanon, Jurion, Lippens, Verbiest, Janssens, Puis, Stockman, Van Himst
Dundee: Slater, Hamilton, Cox (c), Seith, Ure, Wishart, Smith, Penman, Cousin, Gilzean, Robertson

13 March: Second leg 2-1 (Cousin, Smith) h 40,000
Dundee: Slater, Hamilton, Cox (c), Seith, Ure, Wishart, Smith, Penman, Cousin, Gilzean, Robertson
Anderlecht: Trappeniers, Heylens, Cornelis, Hanon, Verbiest, Lippens (c), Janssens, Jurion, Stockman, Van Himst, Puis
(Dundee won 6-2 on aggregate)

24 April: Semi-final, first leg, AC Milan 1-5 (Cousin) a 78,000
AC Milan: Ghezzi, David, Trebbi, Benítez, Maldini (c), Trapattoni, Mora, Sani, Altafini, Rivera, Barison
Dundee (Scotland): Slater, Hamilton, Stuart, Seith (c), Ure, Wishart, Smith, Penman, Cousin, Gilzean, Houston

1 May: Second leg, AC Milan 1-0 (Gilzean) h 38,000
Dundee: Slater, Hamilton, Stuart, Seith (c), Ure, Wishart, Smith, Penman, Cousin, Gilzean, Houston
AC Milan: Ghezzi, David, Trebbi, Benítez, Maldini (c), Trapattoni, Mora, Pivatelli, Altafini, Rivera, Barison
(Dundee lost 5-2 on aggregate. Milan beat Benfica 2-1 in the final at Wembley on 22 May)

League:
1 December: Queen of the South 10-2 (Gilzean 7, Penman, Houston, Ryden) h 12,000.
1963/64
Appearances and goals
League: 30 matches 33 goals.

League Cup: 7 matches, 8 goals
Scottish Cup: 7 matches, 9 goals
Summer Cup: 4 matches, 2 goals
Total: 48 matches, 52 goals

Scottish Cup run
January
11th: First round, Forres Mechanics 6-3 (Waddell, Gilzean, Penman, pen, Stuart, Cousin, Cameron) a 5,681
25th: Second round, Brechin City 9-2 (Penman 2, 1 pen, Waddell, Cousin 2, Gilzean 3, Cameron) a 8,022

February
15th: Third round, Forfar Athletic 6-1 (Waddell 2, Gilzean 2, Cousin, Cameron) h 17,574

March
7th: Quarter-final, Motherwell 1-1 (Cameron) h 30,443
11th: Quarter-final, 4-2 (Cameron 2, Gilzean, Waddell) a 26,280
28th: Semi-final, 4-0 (Gilzean 2, Penman, McFadzean og) Ibrox 32,664

April
25th: Final, Rangers 1-3 (Cameron) Hampden Park 120,982

1964/65
Appearances and goals
7 matches, 5 goals (all league), including hat-trick in 4-4 home draw with St Johnstone and double in 2-0 Dens win over St Mirren.
* Gilzean also scored 18 in friendlies, Forfarshire Cup, Dewar Shield and Anglo-French Cup matches

Gillie's Dundee goals
(as compiled by club historian Kenny Ross)
Goal 1: Gillie's historic first goal for Dundee came at Dens Park on 27 February 1960 when he scored a well-placed header in a 3-1 League win over St Mirren in front of a crowd of 11,000.

Goal 2: Gillie's second Dark Blues goal was in a 6-3 home win over Hibernian on 26 March 1960 when he thundered home the opener after just 90 seconds.

Goal 3: 2 April 1960 Gillie scored his first Dundee goal away from home in a 3-3 draw with Airdrieonians at Broomfield.

Goal 4: 16 April 1960 Gillie scores Dundee's first in a 2-0 home win over Celtic in front of 16,000 fans.

Goals 5–7: Gillie's first hat-trick for Dundee came in the last home game of the campaign in a 4-1 win over Stirling Albion on 23 April 1960.

Goal 8: 30 April 1960 Gillie scored Dundee's first in a 2-2 draw with Third Lanark at Cathkin Park in the last game of the 1959/60 season, giving him eight goals in ten games in his first season.

Goals 9–11: Gillie's first League Cup goals for the club are a hat-trick against Raith Rovers in a sectional tie at Dens on the first day of the 1960/61 season on 13 August in which Dundee win 5-0.

Goal 12: Gillie's first away League Cup goal for The Dee comes on 17 Aug 1960 later at Somerset Park when he scores the first in a 2-1 win over Ayr United.

Goal 13–14: On 20 August 1960, it's six goals in eight days for Gillie as he scores a brace in a 4-1 win over Aberdeen at Pittodrie in the League Cup.

Goals 15–17: It's Gillie's second League Cup hat-trick of the season and his second against Raith Rovers when he scores all three goals in the victory at Starks Park on 27 August 1960.

Goal 18: Dundee record their second 3-0 League Cup win in four days later on 31 August 1960 against Ayr United at Dens with Gillie getting the second.

Goals 19–21: Dundee finish their League Cup sectional ties with a 6-0 win over Aberdeen at Dens on 3 September 1960 . Gillie scores his third hat-trick of the season to make it 13 goals in 6 games to help The Dee qualify for the quarter-final top of their group.

Goals 22–24: A second hat-trick in consecutive weeks against The Dons at Dens on 10 September 1960, sees Dundee open their home League campaign with a 3-3 draw.

Goal 25: Gillie scores his first goal in four games when he notches The Dee's second in a 4-1 home win over Clyde on 24 September 1960.

Goal 26: Gillie's first goal in five against Dunfermline at East End Park on 29 October 1960 isn't enough to prevent the Dark Blues from going down 4-2 in Fife – the first time Dundee have lost when Gilzean scores.

Goals 27–29: Gillie's second League hat-trick of the season on 19 November 1960 helps the Dark Blues win 4-2 at Somerset Park against Ayr United.

Goals 30–31: A 1960 Christmas Eve double from Gillie earns Dundee a 2-2 draw with Hearts at Dens as well as his 30th and 31st Dark Blues goals in just 34 games.

Goal 32: Gillie first foots Aberdeen at the new year with a goal at Pittodrie on 2 January 1961 but The Dee lose 2-1 to The Dons in front of 23,000.

Goal 33: Gillie's first goal in a Tayside derby earns Dundee a point at Muirton Park against St Johnstone on 21 January 1961.

Goals 34–35: Two goals from Gillie help Dundee defeat League leaders Rangers 4-2 at Dens Park on 8 February 1961 in front of 22,000.

Goal 36: A Gillie goal against title-chasing Kilmarnock at Rugby Park on 18 February 1961 isn't enough to prevent Dundee losing 2-1.

Goal 37: Gillie nets the third in a 4-1 home win over Dunfermline at Dens on 4 March 4 1961 in front of a crowd of 11,000.

Goals 38–39: Gillie surpasses 30 goals for the season with a double in a 6-1 home win over Ayr United on 25 March 1961.

Goal 40: Gillie scores Dundee's fourth in a 4-2 win over Airdrieonians at Broomfield on 12 April 1961. It's his 32nd goal of the season which sees him finish as Dundee's top goalscorer for the first time.

Goal 41: Gillie's first goal in the championship campaign comes when he scores Dundee's second in a 3-2 defeat to Third Lanark at Caithkin Park in a League Cup sectional tie on 19 August 1961.

Goals 42–43: A Gillie brace helps complete a League Cup double over Airdrieonians with a 5-0 win at Broomfield on 26 August 1961.

Goal 44: Gilzean's first League goal in the championship campaign comes at Pittodrie on 16 September 1961 when Dundee were already 3-0 down to Aberdeen but the 3-1 defeat is Dundee's last for 19 games.

Goals 45–46: Gillie's first championship goals at Dens come as a brace in a 2-0 win over Hearts on 23 September 1961. The first is a tap-in after Andy Penman had intercepted a short pass and squared to Dundee's number ten and the second comes from his head after a Hugh Robertson cross.

Goals 47–48: Dundee gain revenge for the League Cup defeat at Caithkin with a 3-1 win away to Third Lanark in the League on 30 September 1961, with Gillie scoring two goals from Bobby Seith crosses.

Goal 49: Dundee go top of the league for the first time with a dazzling 5-3 home win over Kilmarnock on 7 October 1961, with Gillie putting Dundee 3-2 ahead nine minutes after the interval.

Goal 50: Gillie's 50th Dark Blues goal is Dundee's fourth in an impressive 4-2 win over Motherwell at Fir Park on 14 October 1961 – a match which Bob Shankly described as 'our finest all-round display of the season.'

Goal 51: Gillie scores the winner in a crucial 2-1 win over Celtic at Dens on 4 November 1961 when he nods home an Alan Cousin head-flick in front of a crowd of 24,500.

Goals 52–55: In an incredible afternoon, Gillie notches four second-half goals as Dundee defeat Rangers 5-1 in the fog at Ibrox on 11 November 1961. Just 30 seconds after the restart, Gilzean finished off a three-man move by heading Dundee in front before adding a second a minute later. He completed his hat-trick on 73 minutes and thundered home a fourth three minutes from time.

Goals 56–57: Two headed goals from Gillie put Dundee 2-1 ahead against Raith Rovers on 18 November 1961 but Raith storm back to lead 4-2 with 27 minutes left. Late goals from Wishart, Seith and Smith ensure the points stay at Dens after an incredible fightback.

Goal 58: A Gillie goal on the stroke of half-time helps Dundee secure a 3-1 win over Hibernian at Easter Road on 25 November 1961 – their first win in the Scottish capital for three years.

Goals 59–60: Gilzean returns to the side against Falkirk on 6 January 1962 after missing the last two games with a broken jaw. Wearing sandshoes to combat the frozen Dens pitch, Gillie scores twice with shots from the edge of the box to win 2-1.

Goal 61: Gordon Smith had been in a car crash on the way to Tynecastle but insists on playing and sets up both goals for Cousin and Gilzean in the 2-0 win over Hearts on 13 January 1962.

Goal 62: Gillie opens the scoring with an 18-yard strike in a 2-1 home win over St Johnstone on 24 January 1962 which sees The Dee go 20 games undefeated in all games including league, Dewar Shield and a friendly (an 8-1 win over Swedish Champions Elfsborg in November in which Gillie scored the first).

Goal 63: Gillie's return to the side on 31 March 1962 after missing the last three through injury coincides with Dundee's return to the top of the League after he scores the winner with a header in a 3-2 win over Stirling Albion at Annfield.

Goals 64–65: Gillie scores his first goals in a Dundee derby on Easter Monday 1962 with a double over Dundee United in front of a capacity crowd at Tannadice. Gillie equalises right on half-time with a header before a thunderbolt 25-yard strike, with four minutes left, gives Dundee a priceless 2-1 win.

Goals 66–67: Muirton Park, 28 April 1962, Dundee win the Scottish League Championship after a 3-0 win over St Johnstone. Gillie opens the scoring midway through the first half when he heads home a Gordon Smith cross and doubles the lead with an expert finish from a long pass from Alex Hamilton just before the hour mark. Not only is Gillie a champion of Scotland, he is also Scotland's top marksman with 24 league goals and 27 in all competitions.

Goals 68–69: Dundee head to the USA at the end of the season to play in the prestigious New York Tourney and in the third game Gillie nets a brace in a 3-3 draw against Hajduk Split of Yugoslavia on 30 May 1962.

Goal 70: Gillie is on the scoresheet as Dundee record their first victory in the New York Tourney with a 3-2 win over Guadalajara of Mexico on 3 June 1962.

Goal 71: Gillie scores against FC America of Brazil as Dundee finish the New York Tourney on 16 June 1962 with a 3-2 defeat to finish fifth in their section.

Goals 72–73: Gillie opens the 1962/63 season with a brace on 11 August but it's in a 3-2 defeat to Dundee United at Tannadice in a sectional League Cup tie.

Goals 74–76: Gillie's first goals in Europe came as a headed hat-trick in an amazing 8-1 European Cup preliminary round, first-leg win over Cologne at Dens on 5 September 1962 in front of 25,000 fans.

Goal 77: 8 September 1962 Gillie heads home an Andy Penman cross in the 90th minute to earn a 2-2 draw with Aberdeen at Dens.

Goal 78: Gilzean heads home another Penman cross on 6 October 1962, this time the winner against Falkirk at Dens.

Goal 79: Dundee score with a six-man move which starts with Bobby Cox in his own box and is finished by Gillie close in to defeat Kilmarnock 1-0 at Dens on 20 October 1962.

Goals 80–82: It's a Happy Halloween 1962 for Gillie as he scores his second European hat-trick of the season in a fantastic 4-1 win over Sporting Lisbon in front of 32,000 at Dens.

Goal 83: 3 November 1962 later Gillie heads home a Gordon Smith cross to secure a 2-1 win over Airdrieonians at home.

Goals 84–85: Two late goals from Gillie at Cathkin Park on 24 November 1962 aren't enough as Dundee went down 4-3 to the Third Lanark.

Goals 86–92: On 1 December 1962 Gillie scores a sensational seven against Queen of the South at Dens to equal a club record for most goals in a game now jointly held with Bert Juliussen who scored seven against Dunfermline in 1947.

Goal 93: Gillie scores against a gale-force wind which aids both Motherwell goals in a 2-2 draw at Dens on 15 December 1962.

Goals 94–96: Gillie scores his first League hat-trick of the season in a 4-2 win in Kirkcaldy on 22 December 1962 and his opener is an early Christmas present from the Raith keeper who drops the ball at his feet to tap in.

Goals 97–98: On 5 January 1963 Gillie opens the scoring and then restores Dundee's lead after a one-two with Alan Cousin at Shawfield, but Clyde hit back to win 3-2.

Goal 99: On 12 January 12 1963 Gillie wears rubber boots to combat the conditions and scores his first-ever Scottish Cup goal in a 5-1 win against Highland League side Inverness Caledonian at Telford Street.

Goals 100–101: Gillie scores his 100th goal for Dundee as he helps the Dark Blues ease through to the next round of the Scottish Cup with a brace in an 8-0 win against Montrose at Dens on 5 February 1963.

Goals 102–103: Gillie scores twice in the opening 18 minutes to help Dundee on their way to a fantastic 4-1 win against Anderlecht in front of 60,000 at the Heysel Stadium in the European Cup quarter-final, first leg on 6 March 1963.

Goal 104: Gillie gets some rough treatment from the Hibs defenders in the Scottish Cup third round at Dens on 18 March 1963 but gets the best possible revenge with the only goal of the game when he heads home an Andy Penman cross.

Goal 105: A Gillie goal on the hour is scant consolation in a 4-1 defeat to Celtic in front of 42,000 at Parkhead on 23 March 1963.

Goals 106–107: Gillie scores a brace at Ibrox in a Scottish Cup quarter-final replay with Rangers in front of 82,000 on 3 April 1963 but Rangers still win 3-2. He equalises for Dundee on 34 minutes by heading home a Bobby Wishart free kick and then a minute after the break gives Dundee the lead when he smashes home from 18 yards.

Goal 108: Gillie nets a scorcher from 25 yards two minutes before half-time as The Dee defeat St Mirren 5-1 at Dens on 13 April 1963.

Goal 109: 20 April 1963, Gillie heads home a Gordon Smith cross on 47 minutes to make it 1-1 at Fir Park but Motherwell get a last-minute winner to keep the points in Lanarkshire.

Goal 110: On 27 April 1963, Dundee draw 1-1 with already relegated Raith at Dens after a long ball from Ure is nodded on by Cousin and smashed home by Gillie.

Goal 111: Dundee defeat AC Milan 1-0 in the European Cup semi-final, second leg at Dens in front of 38,000 on 1 May 1963. Gillie heads home a perfect cross from Gordon Smith six yards out to score his 40th goal of the season and his ninth in Europe – a club record.

Goal 112: Gillie finishes the season as Dundee's top scorer with 41 goals after he opens the scoring in a 2-0 win over Falkirk at Brockville on 18 May 1963. It's a bizarre goal as the ball bounces off Cousin's knee before Gillie hits the ball into the air by accident and as The Bairns keeper leaves it, it drops under the bar and into the net.

Goal 113: Gillie starts the 1963/64 season in goalscoring form by netting the winner away at Third Lanark on 10 August in a League Cup sectional tie.

Goal 114: 17 August 1963, Gillie nets in a 4-1 League Cup sectional win against Dunfermline at Dens.

Goals 115–117: Gillie's first hat-trick of the season sees Dundee maintain their 100 per cent League Cup record with a 3-2 win over Third Lanark at Dens on 23 August 1963 in front of 16,500.

Goals 118–119: Dundee win their League Cup section with a 4-3 victory away to Dunfermline on 31 August 1963 with Gillie netting a brace alongside Kenny Cameron.

Goals 120–121: A brace from Gillie on 7 September 1963 helps Dundee earn their first League victory of the season with a 4-2 win over Aberdeen at Pittodrie.

Goal 122: In front of 25,000 at Dens on 11 September 1963, Dundee draw 3-3 with Hibs in the League Cup quarter-final, with Gillie getting Dundee's first.

Goal 123: In the first derby of the season at Dens, Gillie is on the scoresheet in a 1-1 draw with Dundee United in front of 22,000 on 14 September 1963.

Goal 124: Dundee record their third win of the season over Third Lanark on 21 September 1963, with Gillie netting the winner in a 2-1 victory at Cathkin Park.

Goal 125: Gillie scores 13 goals in 13 games with the opener against East Stirlingshire in a 3-1 win at Dens on 28 September 1963.

Goals 126–127: A Gillie double helps Dundee record a comfortable 5-0 win over Queen of the South at Palmerston a 5 October 1963.

Goals 128–131: Gillie scores all four goals in a superb 4-0 win away to Hibernian on 19 October 1963. His first goal is a touch of brilliance when he runs on to a through ball and instead of shooting, hooks it over his own head before calmly turning to loft it over the keeper's outstretched arms.

Goal 132: Dundee beat Dunfermline for the third time of the season on 26 October 1963 thanks to a 2-1 win at Dens, with Gillie notching the winner.

Goals 133–134: Gillie celebrates his full international debut in midweek with a brace against Airdrieonians in a 4-0 win at Dens on 9 November 1963 and scores his first and only penalty in a Dark Blues shirt.

Goal 135: Gillie nets the first in a 6-1 win over St Johnstone at Muirton on 16 November 1963 in front of a crowd of 12,000.

Goal 136: Gillie opens the scoring away from home for the second week in a row in a 3-1 win over Hearts at Tynecastle on 23 November 1963.

Goal 137: Gillie helps Dundee stay third and keep in touch with leaders Rangers and Kilmarnock by scoring in a 1-1 draw with second-placed Killie at Rugby Park on 7 December 1963.

Goal 138: Gillie scores Dundee's second in a 4-3 win over Falkirk at Dens four days before Christmas 1963.

Goal 139: Aberdeen are the Dens Park first-foots on 1 January 1964 and leave with a 4-1 win, Gillie getting Dundee's consolation.

Goal 140: Gillie scores his second new year goal within 24 hours in a 2-1 derby defeat at Tannadice on 2 January 1964.

Goals 141–142: Dundee get back to winning ways two days later with a 6-0 win over Third Lanark at Dens, with Gillie contributing a double.

Goal 143: Dundee start their 'Road to Hampden' and Gillie gets Dundee's second as the Dark Blues hit six for the second week in a row in a 6-3 Scottish Cup win away at Highland League Forres Mechanics on 11 January 1964.

Goal 144: On 18 January 1964 Gillie finished the scoring at Firs Park in a 5-1 win over East Stirlingshire.

Goals 145–147: Dundee have a 1964 Burns Night to remember after beating Brechin 9-2 at Glebe Park in the Scottish Cup, with Gillie netting his first Scottish Cup hat-trick.

Goals 148–150: It's a hat-trick in successive weeks for Gillie as Dundee defeat Queen of the South 6-2 at Dens on 1 February 1964 and he sets a new club record of scoring in seven consecutive games with his 150th goal for the club.

Goals 151–152: Gillie nets a brace as Dundee defeat Forfar Athletic 6-1 at Dens in the Scottish Cup on 15 February 1964 with his second goal, his 40th of the season, one more than Alec Stott's record of 39 in season 1948/49.

Goals 153–155: Gillie scores his fifth hat-trick of the season and gets his 150th goal for Dundee as they defeat St Mirren 9-2 in the League at Dens on 29 February 1964 to make it an incredible 54 goals in ten games.

Goal 156: Gillie's goal for Dundee at Fir Park on 11 March 1964 helps them defeat Motherwell 4-2 in the Scottish Cup quarter-final replay.

Goals 157–158: Gillie nets a brace as Dundee book their place in the Scottish Cup Final. He opens the scoring from close range in the Scottish Cup semi-final against Kilmarnock at Ibrox on 28 March 1964 and adds another two minutes from time.

Goal 159: Gillie scores a consolation goal at Celtic Park for the second season in a row as The Dee go down 2-1 in Glasgow in front of a midweek crowd of just 7,000 on 1 April 1964.

Goal 160: Dundee defeat Kilmarnock for the second Saturday in a row, this time in the League at Dens on 4 April 1964. Gillie scores the winner in a 2-1 victory a week before scoring the winner for Scotland against England at Hampden.

Goals 161–162: Dundee sign off the week before the 1964 Scottish Cup Final with a 5-2 home win over Partick on 18 April. Gillie nets a brace with his second being his 50th goal of the season.

Goal 163: Gillie scores in his first goal in the inaugural Summer Cup on 16 May 1964 with the consolation in a 3-1 defeat at Aberdeen.

Goal 164: Gillie completes the season with his 52nd goal in a 5-1 Summer Cup win over St Johnstone at Dens on 20 May 1964. He finishes as the country's top goalscorer with an incredible 55 goals for club and country and his 52 Dundee goals is the club record for most goals in a season.

Goals 165–166: In only his second game of the season, Gillie nets a brace in Paisley to defeat St Mirren 2-0 on Halloween 1964.

Goals 167–169: Gillie signs off his Dundee career in typical fashion with a brilliant headed hat-trick – a club record 17th treble – in a 4-4 draw with St Johnstone at Dens on 5 December 1964.

* To add to his 169 goals in 190 senior competitive appearances, Gillie also scored a further 19 goals for Dundee in the Forfarshire Cup (6), Dewar Shield (5), Anglo-French Friendship Cup (2) and friendlies (6) to take his number of goals in a Dark Blues shirt to 188.

TOTTENHAM HOTSPUR

Honours
FA Cup: 1966/67
League Cup: 1970/71
UEFA Cup: 1971/72
League Cup: 1972/73
Football Writers' Association Footballer of the Year (third): 1973
Scotland full caps: 17
Spurs Hall of Fame induction: 2013

Appearances and goals
First Division: 343 matches, 93 goals
FA Cup: 40 matches, 21 goals
League Cup: 28 matches, 6 goals
Europe: 28 matches, 13 goals
Total: 439 matches, 133 goals

1964/65
Appearances and goals
First Division: 20 matches, 11 goals
FA Cup: 4 matches, 5 goals
Total: 24 matches, 16 goals
* Spurs sixth in the league and reach the FA Cup fifth round

1965/66
Appearances and goals
First Division: 40 matches, 12 goals
FA Cup: 3 matches, 3 goals
Total: 43 matches, 15 goals
* Spurs eighth in the league and reach the FA Cup fifth round

1966/67
Appearances and goals
First Division: 40 matches, 17 goals
FA Cup: 8 matches, 4 goals
Football League Cup: 1 match, 0 goals

Total: 49 matches, 21 goals
* Spurs third in the league, FA Cup winners

FA Cup run
28 January: Third round, Millwall 0-0 a 41,260
1 February: Third-round replay, Millwall 1-0 (Gilzean) h 58,189
18 February: Fourth round, Portsmouth 3-1 (Greaves, Gilzean 2) h 57,190
11 March: Fifth round, Bristol City 2-0 (Greaves 2, 1 pen) h 54,610
8 April: Sixth round, Birmingham City 0-0 a 51,500
12 April: Sixth-round replay, Birmingham City 6-0 (Greaves 2, Gilzean, Venables 2, Saul) h 52,304
29 April: Semi-final, Nottingham Forest 2-1 (Greaves, Saul) Hillsborough 55,000
20 May: Final, Chelsea 2-1 (Robertson, Saul) Wembley 100,000

1967/68
Appearances and goals
First Division: 32 matches, 8 goals
FA Cup: 5 matches, 0 goals
European Cup Winners' Cup: 4 matches, 2 goals
FA Charity Shield: 1 match, 0 goals
Total: 42 matches, 10 goals
* Spurs seventh in the league, FA Cup fifth round, European Cup Winners' Cup second round and shared FA Charity Shield with Manchester United after a 3-3 draw at Old Trafford.

1968/69
Appearances and goals
First Division: 37 matches, 7 goals
FA Cup: 4 matches, 0 goals
Football League Cup: 6 matches, 0 goals
Total: 47 matches, 7 goals
* Spurs sixth in the league, FA Cup sixth round and Football League Cup semi-final

1969/70
Appearances and goals
First Division: 34 matches, 10 goals
FA Cup: 4 matches, 0 goals
Football League Cup: 0 matches, 0 goals
Total: 38 matches, 10 goals
* Spurs 11th in the league, FA Cup fourth round and Football League Cup first round

1970/71
Appearances and goals
First Division: 38 matches, 9 goals
FA Cup: 3 matches, 4 goals
Football League Cup: 7 matches, 4 goals
Texaco Cup: 4 matches, 0 goals
Total: 52 matches, 17 goals
* Spurs third in the league, FA Cup sixth round and Football League Cup winners

League Cup run
9 September: Second round, Swansea City 3-0 (Perryman, Peters, Morgan) h 15,848
7 October: Third round, Sheffield United 2-1 (Chivers, Pearce) h 23,559
28 October: Fourth round, West Bromwich Albion 5-0 (Gilzean 2, Peters 3) h 31,598
18 November: Fifth round, Coventry 4-1 (Gilzean, Chivers 3) h 31,864
16 December: Semi-final, first leg, Bristol City 1-1 (Gilzean) a 30,201
23 December: Semi-final, second leg, Bristol City 2-0 aet (Chivers, Pearce) h 29, 982
27 February: Final, Aston Villa 2-0 (Chivers 2) Wembley 100,000

1971/72
Appearances and goals
First Division: 38 matches, 11 goals

FA Cup: 5 matches, 4 goals
Football League Cup: 4 matches, 0 goals
UEFA Cup: 11 matches, 6 goals
Anglo Italian League Cup Winners' Cup: 2 matches, 1 goal
* Spurs sixth in the league, FA Cup sixth round, Football League
Cup semi-final and UEFA Cup winners

UEFA Cup run
14 September: First round, first leg, Keflavik 6-1 (Mullery 2,
Coates, Gilzean 3) a 18,000
Spurs: Jennings, Kinnear, Knowles, Mullery (Souness), England,
Beal, Coates (Pearce), Perryman, Chivers, Peters, Gilzean

28 September: First round, second leg, Keflavik 9-0 (Knowles,
Coates, Perryman, Chivers 3, Holder, Gilzean 2) h 23,818
Spurs: Jennings, Evans, Knowles, Mullery (Pearce), England,
Beal, Coates, Perryman, Chivers, Peters (Holder), Gilzean

20 October: Second round, first leg, Nantes 0-0 a 20,033
Spurs: Jennings, Kinnear, Knowles, Mullery, England, Beal,
Neighbour, Perryman, Chivers, Peters, Gilzean (Morgan)

2 November: Second round, second leg, Nantes 1-0 (Peters) h
32,630
Spurs: Jennings, Evans, Knowles, Pratt, England, Beal,
Neighbour, Perryman, Chivers, Peters, Gilzean (Pearce)

8 December: Third round, first leg, Rapid Bucharest 3-0 (Chivers
2, Peters) h 30,702
Spurs: Jennings, Evans, Knowles, Coates (Pearce), England, Beal,
Gilzean, Perryman, Chivers, Peters, Neighbour

15 December: Third round, second leg, Rapid Bucharest 2-0
(Chivers, Pearce) a 12,000
Spurs: Jennings, Evans, Knowles, Coates, Collins, Beal, Pratt,
Perryman (Naylor), Chivers, Peters, Gilzean (Pearce)

7 March: Fourth round, first leg, Unizale Textile Arad 2-0 (England, Morgan) a 20,000
Spurs: Jennings, Evans, Knowles, Pratt, England, Beal, Gilzean (Collins), Perryman, Chivers, Peters, Morgan

21 March: Fourth round, second leg, Unizale Textile Arad 1-1 (Gilzean) h 30, 253
Spurs: Jennings, Evans, Knowles, Coates, England, Naylor, Gilzean, Perryman, Pratt, Peters, Morgan

5 April: Semi-final, first leg, AC Milan 2-1 (Perryman 2) h 42,064.
Spurs: Jennings, Kinnear, Knowles, Coates (Neighbour), England, Naylor, Gilzean, Perryman, Chivers, Peters, Mullery

19 April: Semi-final, second leg, AC Milan 1-1 (Mullery) a 68,482
Spurs: Jennings, Evans, Knowles, Mullery, England, Beal, Coates, Perryman, Chivers, Peters, Pratt (Naylor)

3 May: Final, first leg, Wolverhampton Wanderers 2-1 (Chivers 2) a 38,362
Spurs: Jennings, Evans, Knowles, Mullery, England, Beal, Gilzean, Perryman, Chivers, Peters, Coates (Pratt)

17 May: Final, second leg, Wolverhampton Wanderers 1-1 (Mullery) h 54,303
Spurs: Jennings, Evans, Knowles, Mullery, England, Beal, Gilzean, Perryman, Chivers, Peters, Coates

1972/73
Appearances and goals
First Division: 35 matches, 5 goals
FA Cup: 3 matches, 1 goal
Football League Cup: 8 matches, 2 goals
UEFA Cup: 9 matches, 3 goals
Total: 55 matches, 11 goals

* Spurs eighth in the league, FA Cup fourth round, Football League Cup winners and UEFA Cup semi-final

League Cup run
6 September: Second round, Huddersfield Town 2-1 (Gilzean, Chivers) h 21,422
3 October: Third round, Middlesbrough 1-1 (Pearce) a 23, 822
11 October: Third-round replay, Middlesbrough 0-0 h 19,256
30 October: Third-round, second replay, Middlesbrough 2-1 (Gilzean, Peters) h 19,287
1 November: Fourth round, Millwall 2-0 (Perryman, Peters) h 28,904
4 December: Fifth round, Liverpool 1-1 (Peters) a 48,677
6 December: Fifth-round replay, Liverpool 3-1 (Pratt, Chivers 2) h 34,565
20 December: Semi-final, first leg, Wolverhampton Wanderers 2-1 (Pratt, Peters) a 28,327
30 December: Semi-final, second leg, Wolverhampton Wanderers 2-2 (Chivers, Peters) h 1,653
3 March: Final, Norwich City 1-0 (Coates) Wembley 100,000

1973/74
Appearances and goals
First Division: 21 matches, 3 goals
FA Cup: 1 match, 0 goals
Football League Cup: 1 match, 0 goals
UEFA Cup: 4 matches, 2 goals
* Spurs 11th in the league, FA Cup third round, Football League Cup fourth round and UEFA Cup final

HIGHLANDS PARK
1974: South African National Football League Cup Final (lost 2-0 to Arcadia Shepherds)

STEVENAGE ATHLETIC
1 March 1976: Ray Dingwall Benefit: Stevenage All Stars v Cambridge United 2 -2 (scored)

As manager:
1975/76: Southern League Division One North 22nd (bottom)

SCOTLAND
Honours
Inducted in the Scottish FA Hall of Fame in 2009

Appearances and goals
22 full caps, 12 goals between 1963–71

Cap by cap

1: 7 November 1963: Friendly: Norway 6-1 (Denis Law 3, Dave Mackay 2, Per Kristoffersen og) h (Hampden Park, Glasgow) 35,416

2: 20 November 1963: Home International Championship 2-1 (John White, Denis Law) h 56,067

3: 11 April 1964: Home International Championship 1-0 (Alan Gilzean) h 133,245

4: 12 May 1964: Friendly West Germany 2-2 (Alan Gilzean 2) a (Hanover) 65,000

5: 25 November 1964: Home International Championship Northern Ireland 3-2 (Davie Wilson 2, Alan Gilzean) h 48,752

6: 8 May 1965: Friendly Spain 0-0 h 60,146

7: 2 October 1965: Home International Championship Northern Ireland 2-3 (Alan Gilzean 2) a (Windsor Park, Belfast) 50,000

8: 13 October 1965: World Cup Qualifier Poland 1-2 (Billy McNeill) h 107,580

9: 9 November 1965: World Cup Qualifier Italy 1-0 (John Greig) h 100,393

10: 24 November 1965: Home International Championship Wales 4-1 (Bobby Murdoch 2, Willie Henderson, John Greig) h 49,888

11: 22 November 1967: Home International Championship and European Championship Qualifier Wales 3-2 (Alan Gilzean 2, Ronnie McKinnon) h 57,472

12: 6 November 1968: World Cup Qualifier Austria 2-1 (Denis Law, Billy Bremner) h 80,856

13: 11 December 1968: World Cup Qualifier Cyprus 5-0 (Alan Gilzean 2, Bobby Murdoch, Colin Stein 2) a (Nicosia) 5,895

14: 16 April 1969: World Cup Qualifier West Germany 1-1 (Bobby Murdoch) h 97,628

15: 3 May 1969: Home International Championship Wales 5-3 (Billy McNeill, Colin Stein, Alan Gilzean, Billy Bremner, Tom McLean) a (Wrexham) 18,765

16: 10 May 1969 Home International Championship England 1-4 (Stein) a 89,902 (Scotland runners-up to England overall)

17: 17 May 1969: World Cup Qualifier Cyprus 8-0 (Eddie Gray, Billy McNeill, Colin Stein 4, Willie Henderson, Tommy Gemmell) h 39,095

18: 22 October 1969: World Cup Qualifier West Germany 2-3 (Jimmy Johnstone, Alan Gilzean) a (Hamburg) 70,448

19: 5 November 1969: World Cup Qualifier Austria 0-2 a (Vienna) 10,091 (Scotland fail to qualify for the finals)

20: 18 April 1970: Home International Championship Northern Ireland 1-0 (John O'Hare) a (Belfast) 31,000

21: 25 April 1970: Home International Championship England 0-0 h 137,438

22: 21 April 1971: European Cup Qualifier Portugal 0-2 a (Lisbon) 35,463

Acknowledgements

THERE ARE so many who helped turn this labour of love into, I hope, a fitting memoir of a copper-bottomed football legend.

I feel mean about singling out individuals because everyone I have dealt with has been nothing but helpful, smoothed the bumps.

But a trio of individuals have opened crucial pathways in my bid to get a handle on Alan Gilzean the person as well as Alan Gilzean the icon.

First off, his youngest son Ian. The fact he backed the project gave it instant credibility. Gave me access to a host of people who knew, loved and admired his dad. Provided information from the horse's mouth. And he supplied the foreword.

Secondly, there is Bob Hynd. A Dundee director and leading architect in the city but most importantly he was a close friend of the subject of this biography and someone who hailed from his home town, Coupar Angus. Bob has gone above and beyond the call to assist, showing me much kindness, thoughtfulness and time along the way. He introduced me to so many people from his late pal's life and helped at every stage. I will always be grateful for all he has done.

Thirdly, there is John Fennelly, the club historian at Spurs. He could not have been more supportive, helping me contact Alan's old team-mates and supplying opinion and information.

All three have cast their eye over the manuscript, along with Dundee club historian Kenny Ross and Kevin Brennan, a mentor and Gilzean fan. These are people I trust. And again I thank them.

Kenny Ross has also supplied me with essential material and comment. Lloyd Briscoe and Pete Stanford, club historians at Stevenage and Aldershot, were similarly helpful.

Dave Forbes, another Gillie pal and a former Dundee director, opened up his black book to provide contacts, and gave me invaluable insights and general support. Thanks Dave.

My gratitude goes to all of Gillie's old team-mates who gave me their insights and time.

They include, alphabetically: Phil Beal, Craig Brown, Martin Chivers, Martin Cohen, Doug Cowie, Mike England, Jimmy Greaves (through Terry Baker and previous interviews), Pat Jennings, Cliff Jones, Denis Law, Pat Liney, Steve Perryman, Jimmy Robertson, Ian Ure and Bobby Wishart.

I appreciate the trouble of the Spurs press office in their efforts to obtain comments on Gilzean from Harry Kane and Daniel Levy.

I am grateful for the views of other Gilzean associates such as: Norman Bannerman, Patrick Barclay, Paul Coyte, Ally Donaldson, John Duncan, Frank Gilfeather, Norman Giller, Richard Gough, Brad Kaftel, Cameron Kerr, Mike Leigh, Steve Mahoney, James Morgan, David Nussbaumer, Norrie Price, Mike Rollo, Jack Scott, Lawrie Smith, Rob White and Barry Williams. And for previously published comments by Reg Drury, Tommy Gallacher, Ken Jones, Frank McGhee, Jack McLean, Giller, again, Brian Glanville, Harry Harris, Ivan Ponting and Jeff Powell.

Thanks to Jim Thomson for opening the Coupar Angus Heritage Association headquarters for the benefit of the project. And Helen Ferdinand, a teacher at Alan's old school.

A special thank you to Eric Gilzean who furnished me with vital details to help me colour in his brother's early life in Coupar Angus and more.

I am grateful to Alan Pattullo, the fine journalist with *The Scotsman*, for his inspirational and empathetic interviews with Alan Gilzean which provided crucial sources of reference. As did Hunter Davies's *The Glory Game*. Appreciate it, Mr Davies.

Thank you to contributing fans, including Bob Cook, John Davies, Nick Edwards (Spurs' Supporters' Trust), Barry Graham (Glasgow Spurs), Andrea Koumi, Steve Martin, Karen Mitchell,

George Norrie, Jan Oginski, Zulkifly Osman (Malaysia Spurs) and Stewart Ramsey.

Appreciation to the ever-helpful and friendly staff at the Bruce Grove Museum (Deborah and team), Alan Swain (Spurs historian), Erin Farley, historian and librarian with Dundee Leisure and Culture at the Dundee Central library, and Paul, Jane, Duncan, Michelle, Graham, Ivan *et al* at Pitch Publishing.

My family and friends have also provided encouragement and inspiration, so thank you Matthew, Benny, Sean, Christine and Mum, Kate, Keith, Mims, Mark, Dave and Sue, Tony, Adrian and Aaron, Nick and Jan, Debbie, Jon and Sadie, Kev and Pauline, Mac and Caroline, Ray and Jackie, Marc and Louise, Terry and Linda, and Tony and Sue. So have the Loughton five-a-siders, the Bexhillians and unnamed but unforgotten helpers. Above all I owe the most thanks to my wife Rosemary who has provided the support which has allowed me to focus on the project.

Mike Donovan

Quotation Credits

Quotes from sources beyond interviews undertaken by the author:

CHAPTER 1: Alan Gilzean, 'I was just a guy whose dreams came true …' (*The Scotsman*, Alan Pattullo, 14 January 2012).

CHAPTER 2: AG, 'I remember an old man there …' (TS, AP, 14 May 2017).

CHAPTER 3: AG, 'A lot of my uncles on my mother's side …' (TS, AP, 14 January 2012). Ray Hepburn, 'On the equivalent of the head of a pin' (*The Courier*, Dundee).

CHAPTER 4: AG, 'They were much too good for us …' (*Sporting Post*, July 1964); AG, 'I signed provisional forms for Dundee under Willie Thornton …' (TS, AP, 14 January 2012); AG, 'I was with Coupar Angus Juveniles …' and 'I saw Billy Steel play and he was fantastic …' (*Dundee Greats*, Jim Hendry); Sgt Beck, 'Basic training brought out the best and the worst in us …' (Forcesreunited.org.uk); 'The man is a mountain, go into the dressing room and take a walk around him …' and 'Turning point …' (Bill Shankly on Ron Yeats's Wikipedia page); AG, 'He was always the golden boy …' and 'an absolute travesty …' (TS, AP, 28 February 2017); AG, 'I was practically an "old soldier"…' (*The Scottish Football Book*, Hugh Taylor); Jack Rollin, 'Possibly because it was late on in the season …' (Aldershot v Chester City Programme, 25 April 2009). AG, 'I signed [for Dundee] in 1956 but was called up for National Service the following year …' (*Sunday Post*, Ron Scott, 22 April 2012); AG, 'During my last six months of so in the army …' (DG).

CHAPTER 5: AG, 'Unfortunately, in my debut for the first-team …' (DG); AG, 'Shankly gave me my big chance …' (Dee TV, 20 April 2017, first broadcast 20 July 2018); AG, 'Obviously I had played not too badly …' and , 'I was one of a number of young players …' (DG); AG, 'Shankly was an honest man …' (*Up Wi' The Bonnets*, Norrie Price); AG, 'Give Willie Thornton his due …' (DTV); Craig Brown, 'I, too, was the butt of one of his famous quips …' (*Backpass magazine*, 2018); AG, 'Hammy used to room up with Urey ...' (DTV); Hugh Taylor, 'The real reason Scotland's international prestige has slumped ...' (*Scottish Football Book No.7*, 1961) AG, 'When I was a youngster ...' (SFB7).

CHAPTER 6: AG, 'I felt I still had a year or two left ...', Bert Henderson, 'Cowie was the best player I ever played with' and Sammy Kean, 'McGeachie was a tricky little player' (UWTB); AG, 'I always remember when Gordon came to Dundee (DTV); AG, 'Recalling that, Gordon was a member of the Hibs attack ...' (SP); AG, 'Well, Dundee were really playing so well ...' (DTV); AG, 'It was obviously going to be a hard test ...' (DG); AG, 'I finished with four of our five ...' (SP); Bobby Seith, 'It was a key moment in the title-winning year ...', Bob Shankly, 'Number one match ...' and 'Dundee's terrific fight and last gasp winner ...' (Dundee Football Club); AG, 'We just pounded them ...' (DTV); AG, 'That derby win was a huge step ...' (UWTB); AG, 'Yeh, that's right ...' and 'I think we just needed one point ...' (DTV); AG, 'I was told I jumped for joy ... (*Evening Telegraph*, Dundee); AG, 'My state of mind that day ...' (DG); AG, 'It was a wonderful, wonderful feeling ...' (DTV); AG, 'The scenes at the final whistle ...' and 'I was one of a number of young players coming through ...' (ETD); AG, 'I was a local lad ...' (DG); AG, 'Unlike today it was quite common ...' (SuP, RS, 22 April 2012); Bobby Cox, 'We knew we had some great players ...' (DG); Ian Ure, 'I have never been too happy to lose £10 ...' (UWTB); Sir Alex Ferguson, 'Dundee at that time were a team without a conspicuous weakness ...' (*Managing My Life*, Sir Alex Ferguson).

CHAPTER 7: AG, 'These European nights were very special ...' (*UWTB*); AG, 'There is no doubt Pat was very unlucky to be discarded ...' (DG); IU, 'The American thing was a real eye-opener, but it served us well for the European Cup ...' and Bob Shankly, 'I am delighted the boys rose to the occasion ...' (Alan Gilzean Official Memorial Programme, Dundee v Dunfermline Athletic, 22 July 2018); AG, 'That was the first indication we had that ahead of us a frightening football experience' (SP); 'Revenge mission ...' (German Media); AG, 'Stir up trouble ...', 'I'm continually recalling something else that happened – and seeing red' , 'When we started to talk about a training session' and 'I felt this hardy lad ...' (SP); Zlato Cajkovski, 'If say, the Dundee goalkeeper was injured.' (GM); AG, AG, 'It was a horror film ...', 'The officials ignored it ...' and 'She'd gone to the game. "You dirty dogs", she kept shouting ...' (SP); Gordon Smith, 'The dirtiest in my 22 years of football ...' (UPWTB); AG, 'What a contrast to Cologne ...' (SP); AG, 'The forwards took a lot of credit but defensively we were outstanding ...' (DG); AG, 'Anderlecht were a delightful team ...', 'Well, how we lost 5-1 is an old story. We didn't play ...' and 'Well we beat them ...' (SP); AG, 'Mind you, they had goalkeeper George Farm carried off that day ...' (DG); AG, '(Farm) dived at my feet to save ...' (SP).

CHAPTER 8: AG, 'Gordon was one of the first guys apart from the Italians who always watched their diet , 'Bobby was very similar to Doug Cowie', 'Yeh. When you think of the clubs he had,' and 'They were different types of player (DTV); Bobby Seith, 'Alan was an exceptional striker' (ETD).

CHAPTER 9: AG, 'I had a good chance ...' and 'It was a very, very wet day ...' (DG); Gordon Banks, 'This was my first match at Hampden' (England Football Online, Norman Giller); AG, 'I was John White's roommate with Scotland ...' (*The Spurs Show*, Dingwalls, 9 December 2013). AG, 'He [White] would tell me what he was earning ... (DG). AG, 'I was impressed with the whole set-up both on and off the pitch' (Tottenham Hotspur Football Club); AG, 'At the next home game the Tottenham fans had these banners up, "We want Gilzean!"' (TS, AP, 14 May 2017); AG, 'Eventually you would come to the conclusion that you would have to move ...' (DG). Bill Nicholson, 'I watched many strikers leading up to Christmas 1964 before deciding on Alan Gilzean ...' (*Bill Nicholson Football's Perfectionist*, Brian Scovell); AG, 'Well, first of all I asked for a transfer from Dundee ...' (TSS).

CHAPTER 10: Cyril Knowles, 'I couldn't settle on that side of the pitch.' (*Tottenham Hotspur Football Book*, Dennis Signy); BN, 'Before every match he used to soak his boots in hot water ...' (BNFP); Jimmy Greaves, 'We had an almost telepathic understanding right from the very first game ...' (*Greavsie*, Jimmy Greaves); Alan Mullery, 'We did a lot of running ...' (*Glory, Glory Lane*, Mike Donovan).

CHAPTER 11: AM, 'It was tough to start with ...' and 'There were things you had to do to achieve greatness at Spurs ...' (GGL); AG, 'My most memorable match has to be a FA Cup home tie versus Burnley ...' (THFC); Julie Welch, 'Tossing his head ...', 'old-fashioned ...' and 'almost unworldly ...' (*The Biography of Tottenham Hotspur*, Julie Welch); BN, 'He was an unorthodox player ...' (FP). Miljan Miljanic, 'If ever there is a football university ...' (Alan Gilzean Testimonial Programme, Spurs v Red Star Belgrade, 27 November 1974); AM, 'Gillie was not tall but was fantastic in the air ...' (GGL); Ivan Ponting, 'So gently did Alan caress a football ...' (*Tottenham Hotspur Player By Player*, IP). AG, 'When you line up with the guy ...' (TSS); AG, 'Well I didn't see too much of Greavsie off the pitch ...' (THFC); Jimmy Greaves, 'I was to form a great partnership with Alan Gilzean ...' (*Greavsie*, Jimmy Greaves) and 'As soon as we started playing I felt he had the ability ...' (*Natural*, David Tossell, Pitch, 2018); AM, 'He was something special ...' (THFC) and 'To buy those now you'd be talking about the price of a Cristiano Ronaldo for Alan and the price of a Lionel Messi for Greavsie ...' (GGL).

CHAPTER 12: Terry Venables, 'The fans may have been heckling me ...' (TBOTH); AG, 'I remember it well – for all the wrong reasons ...'

(THFC); BN, 'Gillie was reported to the FA ...' (BNFP); AG, 'The Cup final, that was special ...' (TSS); AG, 'What was Davey like ...' (THFC); AG, 'Yes [when asked if he was nervous]. Everybody's nervous (TSS); AG, 'I remember before the game ...' (THFC); AG, 'It wasn't niggly' (TSS); IP, 'Ungainly figure with one shoulder higher than the other ...' (THPBP); BN, 'When I heard that [he'd abandoned the sweeper system], I told my players, "He's done us a favour"...' (BNFP); Ron Harris, 'I thought we were unlucky to be a goal down by half-time ...' (*Sunday Express*). Julie Welch, 'As the Spurs players gathered in the centre-circle before the kick off, two fans ran on the pitch with a cockerel ...' (TBOTH); AG, 'Forest ...' (TSS).

CHAPTER 13: Desmond Hackett, 'Alan Gilzean, who was becoming a problem player, is now thriving ...' (*Daily Express*); Geoffrey Green, 'All that spoilt it [a Spurs victory] was the incessant whistle of the Bulgarian referee ...' (*The Times*); BN, 'The match was a disgrace ...' (John Oakley, *London Evening News*); Brian James, 'Riot ...' (*Daily Mail*); The Glory Glory Nights, 'Unconscious on the turf ...' (Colin Gibson and Harry Harris); AM, 'Kicked me full in the mouth ...' and 'I retaliated. I punched him ...' (TGGN); BJ, 'The teams fought with fist and foot ...' (DM); AG, 'What happened was, Mullery and a guy called Guy clashed ...' and 'An enjoyable match ...' (TSS); AM, 'It took another three years to build a side without Mackay as captain ...' (*Alan Mullery The Autobiography*); James Morgan, '[Gilzean] pulled him [Souness] aside and told him the two Scots had to stick together ...' (*In Search of Alan Gilzean*, JM). Graeme Souness, 'Gillie is a marvellous player ...' (*Tottenham Hotspur Football Book No.6*); AG, 'There was no mistaking his ability [Souness] ...' (BNFP); Souness, 'There are times when I think I should have stuck it out at White Hart Lane.' (ISOAG).

CHAPTER 14: Bob Wilson, 'It was like sitting on the edge of a volcano. (*Behind The Network*, BW); AG, 'I remember whacking him ...' (TS, AP, 2016); AG, 'I remember one of my first games against Arsenal ...' (THFC); AG, 'I don't think I ever played in a classic north London derby ...' (AP, *The Scotsman*, 2016); AG, 'As Davey finished, Stevie was the heir to the Dave Mackay throne ...' (THFC); Martin Chivers, 'I'd always been a timid player' (*The Biography of Tottenham Hotspur*, Julie Welch); AG, 'I went more towards the right wing with Martin ...' (TSS); AG, 'Martin Chivers was a very important player for Tottenham ...' (THFC); BN, 'A bloke is measured by what he wins.' (*And The Spurs Go Marching On*, Phil Soar); AG, 'My biggest regret at that level was not getting to the World Cup finals ...' (DG).

CHAPTER 15: AG, 'Ask anyone at Spurs to name the most disappointing matches of 1972 ...' (*Tottenham Hotspur Year Book* No.6, Edited by Peter Smith); GS, 'I had already played in Iceland ...' (THYB6); Geoffrey

Green, 'Jennings – a lonely figure at the other end...' (TT); Hunter Davies, '[Bill Nicholson] was on his feet ...' (The Glory Game,1972); GG, 'The Romanians threw every at them...'(TT); Norman Giller, 'Hacked and kicked about like rag dolls ...' (*Daily Express*); Peter Batt, '(*The Sun*) most shameful exhibition of thuggery ...' (*The Sun*); Jeff Powell, '(One of the most) savage matches in European football history ...' (DM). AG, 'I was beginning to wonder if one would ever go in ...' (DE, NG). AG, 'My outstanding memory ...' (THFC, John Fennelly).

CHAPTER 16: HD, 'That's your brother then, Cyril?' (TGG); David Leggat, 'He went to a lot of supporters' events ...' (ISOAG); AG, 'We used to have some nights in here ...' (TS, AP, 5 March 2016); AG, 'I got a reputation ...' (TSS); HD, 'On the train home ... (TGG, 1972) and 'I suppose a superficial reader ...' (TGG, 2001); AG, 'Some players weren't happy about it ...' (*The Spurs Show*); AG, 'I've never had a bloody budgerigar ...' (TS, AP, 5 March 2016); BN, 'Most of them took a lager. I know Alan Gilzean was a drinker. He liked Bacardi and Coke ...' (*Glory, Glory*, BN); AG, 'Greavsie would never go to the Tottenham pubs ...' (THFC, John Fennelly); JG, 'I don't think I was ever happier than when playing with Gillie.' (G); Ricky Prosser, 'We were great, great friends. He never acted like a star ...' and David Leggat, 'Jimmy Burton, who was Dave Mackay's partner ...' (ISOAG).

CHAPTER 17: Brian Moore, 'It was a big match ...' (ITV); AG, 'I wanted to beat Villa more than Norwich ...' (THFC, JF); Ray Clemence, 'Spurs had a bigger reputation in Europe than ourselves.' (TGGN); AG, 'Defensively it was much the same ...' (TSS); DL, 'Gillie was very kind to me ...' (INOAG); AG, 'Once you get past 30, people start writing you off ...' (*Shoot* magazine, 13 January, 1973); BN, 'It was the most disappointing season since my first as manager.' (*And The Spurs Go Marching On*); AG, 'I don't want to make any decisions until the end of the season ...' (*Tottenham Herald*); BN, 'We shall be letting him go and I should imagine ...' (TH); Charles F. Cox, 'God made Mauritius first and then Heaven ...' (*Spurs 1974–75 handbook*); Harry Harris, '[A] final tribute to a great player and friend ...' (TH).

CHAPTER 18: AG, 'Football breaks your heart when you've got to leave it.' (TSS); AG, 'Bill was a very fair man ...' (THFC, JF); AG, 'Eddie played in that great push-and-run Tottenham team ...' (THFC); AG, 'Pat was a quiet guy ...', 'Knowlesy was a very good player...', 'Martin was wonderful ...', 'Very good. They were fantastic to me ...' and 'For me Tottenham have always been a big club ...' (THFC, JF); AM, 'All of them ...' (GGL); BN, 'He has been a great player for us ...' (*The Tottenham Hotspur Football Book No.8*); BN, 'I liked Gillie ...' (GG).

CHAPTER 19: AG, 'My team, Highlands Park, reached the final ...' and BN, 'Don't kick up fuss because I'm returning ...' (TH); Miro Radojcic,

'Apostle of Total Football.' (AGTP); Reg Drury, '[Gilzean] retained his popularity with the White Hart Lane crowd ...' (*News of the World*); Frank McGhee, 'Take a good, long lingering look at Gillie in action ...' (*Daily Mirror*); Ken Jones, 'There is no need to apologise for including Alan Gilzean among my favourite footballers ...' (*Sunday Mirror*); Jeff Powell, 'Alan Gilzean brought grace and touch ...' (*Daily Mail*); Brian Glanville, 'It is not often that you get a Players' Player who is also, and emphatically, a Fans' Favourite ...' (The *Sunday Times*); Tommy Gallacher, 'When Alan Gilzean phoned me ...' (*The Courier*, Dundee); Frank Hampton, 'We can all remember ...' (AGTP); AG, 'I just can't wait ...' (TH); Mandy Stanton, 'I think Alan Gilzean is one of the greatest footballers of his time ...', Paul Murphy, 'He was never selfish with the ball ...' and Terry Hill, 'The classic, magical performances ...' (TH).

CHAPTER 20: AG, 'I'm looking forward to the new season.' (TH); AG, 'I am in no hurry to decide where my future lies ...' (TCD, Tommy Gallacher); Bill Coldwell, 'When I came here three years ago I promised promotion ...' (*Stevenage Comet*); Jimmy Burton, 'These [Highlands Park contract complexities] are not insurmountable problems ...' (SC); AG, 'I was at Tottenham for ten years ...', 'In my time I always admired Denis Law ...', 'Dave Mackay is an old buddy ...' and 'I don't think it's fair.' (SC); Jim Briscoe, 'Jimmy Burton knew everyone ...' (JB Memoirs), Ernie Ward, 'Alan has got down to the task ... (*Stevenage Comet*), Jim Briscoe, 'Effective immediately ...' (JBM).

CHAPTER 21: *Glasgow Evening Times*, 'Now he's manager of the Blue Dart ...' (1980); AG, 'I wouldn't have a pub now ...' (GET); 'Formertrucker', 'I do remember Leggett Freightways of Chingford ...' (TrucknetUK); 'Mushroomman', 'Well there ya go ...' (TUK, 2016).

CHAPTER 22: AG, 'This reporter had me saying ...' (TS, AP, 2012) and Ian Gilzean, 'I think he just needed ...' (TS, AP, 27 February 2009); AG, 'I have never been a recluse ...' (TS, AP, 2012); AG, 'I lost interest in football ... (TS, AP 5 March 2016); AG, 'I went down with my work, and I liked it ...' and 'Someone wrote that on a Tottenham website ...' (TS, AP,2012).

CHAPTER 23: Dundee Hall Of Fame programme, 'There have been some great forwards in Dundee's history but ...' (3 April 2009); Scottish Hall of Fame programme, 'Going to Tottenham Hotspur was the best move ever for me ...' (15 November, 2009); AG, 'I wouldn't miss this gathering for anything ...' and 'Dundee's still the first result I look for, closely followed by Spurs ...' (*Sunday Post*, RS, 22 April 2012); AG, 'It's a shame the whole lot of us can't be present ...' (TS, AP, 28 April 2012); AG, 'Shankly was a real hard taskmaster ...' (SP, RS, 22 April 2012); AG, 'Pat was the reason I came back ...' (TSS).

CHAPTER 24: AG, 'He [Simpson] came over to me …' and 'I have not been back for years.' (TS, AP, 2012); Alan Pattullo, 'Asked for the last occasion he can remember watching Spurs in the flesh …' (TS, AP, 2012); AG, 'I saw Dundee earlier this season, but I'm not sure the last time I saw Spurs play …' (SP, RS, 2012); Logan Holmes, 'It was great to see Gilzean looking so well …' (Hotspur HQ, 2013); AG, 'We hugged …' (TS, AP, 5 March 2016).

CHAPTER 25: AG, 'I really had to be here today …' (TS, AP, 25 March 2015); AG, 'I'd been 30 years away …' and 'I don't think I could have done it all these years …' (TS, AP, 5 March 2016); AG, 'He [Beal] picks me up and drops me off …' (TS, AP, 14 May 2017).

CHAPTER 26: Barry Graham, 'I just wanted to drop you a line to pass on my condolences …' (Glasgow Spurs, 2018).

CHAPTER 27: AG, 'The King of White Hart Lane – oh heck …' (TS, AP, 14 May 2017); AG, 'You are only what the people want you to be.' (DG).

CHAPTER 29: IP, 'The difference between Alan Gilzean and the majority of his peers …' (THPBP); Tommy Gallacher, 'An example of the great esteem …' (AGTP); Jack McLean, 'Strangely, I suppose, I have met very few footballers socially …' (*Scottish Daily Mail*); Frank McGhee, 'This man [Gilzean] is one of those rare ones …'(AGTP); Harry Harris, 'How to miss a story right under your nose ...' (TH); Ken Jones, 'There is more grey than black in what is left of his hair …', Reg Drury, 'He [Gilzean] was an instant success …', Jeff Powell, 'Gillie kept alive the hope that skill …', Norman Giller, 'Alan was not only one of my favourite footballers, but also one of my favourite people …' and Brian Glanville, 'The young fans have always loved him …' (AGTP).

CHAPTER 30: Social media: Jan Oginski, 'Alan Gilzean. Football genius …'; Bill Campbell's Ghost, 'A few years back I went to RBS …'; Born Is The King Of White Hart Lane, 'I was privileged enough …'; Gblue, 'In my opinion, the best …'; Travelling Dee, 'Probably not …'; Terry Ransome, 'He [Gilzean] really was my boyhood hero…'; Budgem, 'RIP the King. 169 memories of a true great! Met him, his son Ian and grandson a couple years back and what a lovely man …'; Jah Womble, 'As a kid I was lucky enough to see Alan Gilzean play …', Blue Dragon, 'A legend from my youth …'; DFC Man, 'I count myself fortunate..', Islaydarkblue, 'Was fortunate enough …'; Hippriest, 'RIP Gillie …'; Amor de Cosmos (QPR and Hitchin Town fan), 'There are few pure strikers from that era …'; Tee Rex (Exeter City fan), 'One of the biggest names of my childhood …'; Adams House Cat (Notts County fan), Saw him play a couple of times …'

Picture Credits

Alamy, Coupar Angus Heritage Association, Mike Donovan, Dave Forbes, Harry Harris, Highlands Park Football Club, Bob Hynd, Getty Images, PA Images, Steve Perryman, The *Stevenage Comet*, DC Thomson, Jim Thomson.

* We have made every effort to list all text and image credits. Let us know if you are due one and we will try to put it right in future editions.

Abbreviations: AG: Alan Gilzean; AGOMP: Alan Gilzean Official Memorial Programme; AGTP: Alan Gilzean Testimonial Programme; AP: Alan Pattullo; AM: Alan Mullery; BN: Bill Nicholson; BNFP, BS: Bill Nicholson Football's Perfectionist, Brian Scovell ; DE: *Daily Express*; DL: David Leggat; DG, JH: Dundee Greats, Jim Hendry; DM: *Daily Mail*; DTV: Dee TV; ETD: Evening Telegraph, Dundee; GET: *Glasgow Evening Times*; GG: Geoffrey Green; GGL, MD: *Glory, Glory Lane*, Mike Donovan; GM: German Media; GS: Graeme Souness; HD: Hunter Davies; HH: Harry Harris; DFC: Dundee Football Club; IP: Ivan Ponting; IU: Ian Ure; JG: JM: Jimmy Greaves; James Morgan; JF: John Fennelly; JBM: Jim Briscoe Memoirs; SP: *Sporting Post*; SC: *Stevenage Comet*; SFB7: *Scottish Football Book No.7*, Hugh Taylor; SuP, RS: *Sunday Post*, Ron Scott; TBOTH, JW: *The Biography of Tottenham Hotspur* , Julie Welch; TCD: *The Courier*; TGGG: *The Glory Glory Game*; TGGN: *The Glory, Glory Nights*, Colin Gibson and Harry Harris; THPBP: *Tottenham Hotspur Player By Player*; THFB, DS: *Tottenham Hotspur Football Book*, Dennis Signy;); THFB8: *The Tottenham Hotspur Football Book No.8*; THFC: Tottenham Hotspur Football Club; TS, AP: *The Scotsman*, Alan Pattullo; TSS: *The Spurs Show* (Dingwalls, Camden, north London, 9 December 2013); TT: *The Times*; TUK: TrucknetUK; UWTB, NP: *Up Wi' The Bonnets*, Norrie Price.

Bibliography

Books: *Alan Mullery The Autobiography* (Alan Mullery, Headline, 2006); *And The Spurs Go Marching On*, Phil Soar, Hamlyn, 1982); *Behind the Network* (Bob Wilson, Hodder & Stoughton, 2004); *Bill Nicholson Football's Perfectionist* (Brian Scovell, John Blake. 2011); *Deadly Dimitar* (Chris Davies, John Blake, 2009); *Dundee Champions of Scotland* (Kenny Ross, Desert Island, 2003); *Dundee Greats* (Jim Hendry, Sportsprint, 1991); *Dundee Legends* (Kenny Ross, Yore, 2010); *Dundee's Hampden Heroes* (Kenny Ross, Kenny Ross, 2012); *Dundee FC On This Day* (Kenny Ross, Pitch, 2017); *Glory, Glory* (Bill Nicholson, Macmillan, 1985); *Glory, Glory Lane* (Mike Donovan, Pitch, 2017); *Greavsie* (Jimmy Greaves, Time Warner, 2003); *In Search of Alan Gilzean* (James Morgan, BackPage, 2011); *London's Cup Final 1967* (Ralph L Finn, Robert Hale, 1967); *Managing My Life* (Sir Alex Ferguson and Hugh McIlvanney, Hodder and Stoughton, 1999); *Memoirs: Jim Briscoe* (Stevenage, 2008); *Natural, The Jimmy Greaves Story* (David Tossell, Pitch, 2019); *Spurs Greatest Games* (Mike Donovan, Pitch, 2012); *Surnames of Scotland* (George Fraser Black); *Spurs' Unsung Hero* (Terry Dyson with Mike Donovan, Pitch, 2015); *The Biography of Tottenham Hotspur* (Julie Welch, Vision Sports, 2015); *The Glory, Glory Game* (Hunter Davies, Mainstream, 1972 and 2005); *The Glory, Glory Nights* (Colin Gibson and Harry Harris, Cockerel, 1986); *The Scottish Football Book No.7* (Hugh Taylor, Stanley Paul, 1961); *The Spurs Alphabet: A Complete Who's Who of Tottenham Hotspur FC In Memory of Andy Porter* (Bob Goodwin, Robwin, 2017); *The Tottenham Hotspur Football Book* (Dennis Signy, Stanley Paul, 1967); *The Tottenham Hotspur Football Book No.6* (Edited by Peter Smith, Stanley Paul, 1972); *The Tottenham Hotspur Football Book No.7* (Edited by Peter Smith, Stanley Paul, 1973); *The Tottenham Hotspur Football Book No. 8* (Edited by Peter Smith, Stanley Paul, 1974); *Tottenham Greats* (Harry Harris, John Donald, 1990); *Tottenham Hotspur A History From 1907* (Historic Newspapers, MGN, 2011); *Tottenham Hotspur 1974–75* *handbook* (1974); *Tottenham Player By Player* (Ivan Ponting, Guinness, 1993); *Tottenham Hotspur: The Complete Record* (Bob Goodwin, Breedon, 2011); *Up Wi' The Bonnets*, foreword by Alan Gilzean (Norrie Price, Norrie Price, 1993).

Newspapers: *The Scotsman, The Courier* (Dundee), *Sporting Post* (Dundee), *Sunday Post* (Dundee), *Evening Telegraph* (Dundee), *Evening Times* (Glasgow), *Scottish Daily Mail, Tottenham Weekly Herald, London Evening News, Stevenage Comet, Daily Express, Daily Mail, Daily Mirror, The Sun, The Times, News of the World, Sunday Mirror,* the *Sunday Times.*

Magazines: *Backpass, Shoot.*

Programmes (various): Dundee (including Alan Gilzean memorial edition), Tottenham Hotspur (including Alan Gilzean testimonial), Aldershot, Hall of Fame (Dundee FC and Scottish FA).

Online: Dee TV (Dundee FC), ITV (Brian Moore's commentary for 1973 League Cup final). **Podcast:** *The Spurs Show*, Dingwalls, north London on 9 December 2013. **Reputable websites (various):** Including Tottenham Hotspur FC official, Dundee FC official, Stevenage FC official, Aldershot FC official, Highlands Park FC official, Scottish FA, TrucknetUK.

Index

Also available at all good book stores

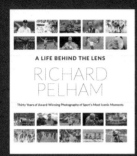

9781785315466

9781785313929

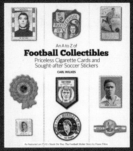

9781785315602

9781785314384

9781785315237

9781785315015

9781785315046

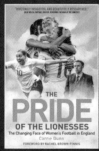

9781785315411

9781785315060

9781785315312

9781785315381